MAY 2 1 1990

D1276263

Since 1970 the Red Brigades, one of the world's leading terrorist groups, have killed and "knee-capped" in the name of justice for the oppressed in Itlay. The group's most spectacular exploit – the 1978 kidnapping and assassination of Aldo Moro, Italy's leading political figure – rocked the country and stunned the world. Many others before and since Moro have met a similar fate. And, as the group approaches the twentieth anniversary of its founding, the terrorists continue to kill. This book tells this dramatic story. It describes who the young terrorists were and what they believed in and examines the forces that gave them and their many imitators birth. It explains the group's structure, methods and inter-national connections and recounts the major operations of the *brigatisti*, with emphasis on the Moro affair. And it evaluates the government's anti-terrorist efforts and considers the lessons to be drawn from the experience that Italians justifiably refer to as "the years of lead".

The book is provided with a foreword by Richard N. Gardner, who was United States Ambassador to Italy from 1977 to 1981.

RED BRIGADES

Red Brigades

The Story of Italian Terrorism

Robert C. Meade, Jr.

Foreword by Richard N. Gardner

St. Martin's Press   New York

© Robert C. Meade, Jr., 1990
Foreword © Richard N. Gardner, 1990

All rights reserved. For information, write:
Scholarly and Reference Division,
St. Martin's Press, Inc., 175 Fifth Avenue,
New York, N.Y. 10010

First published in the United States of America in 1990

Printed in Great Britain

ISBN 0–312–03593–4

Library of Congress Cataloging-in-Publication Data
Meade, Robert C., 1949–
The Red Brigades: the story of Italian terrorism/Robert C.
Meade, Jr.
p. cm.
Bibliography: P.
Includes index.
ISBN 0–312–03593–4
1. Brigate rosse—History.   2. Terrorism—Italy—History.
I. Title.
HV6433.I8M4 1990
364.1'0945—dc20   89–34719
                                                              CIP

For my parents and Mary Jo

'Intolerance contradicts the reason for being of the democratic state. Violence is the precise antithesis of it. Intolerance and violence, the reasoning of partisanship as against the objectivity of the law, appear as grave signs of a crisis of the State that must be overcome and overcome rapidly. Intolerance is inconceivable when all is dialogue in our society. Violence is inadmissable and absurd when what is involved is not struggling against the exercise of arbitrary power, but contesting the difficult creation of the free consciences of all the citizens, the order that has been created by liberty and that is open to all the evolutions that liberty, without any limit, makes possible.' — **Aldo Moro** (1976)

'This disorganized and discordant Italy is, however, infinitely more rich and alive than the more or less well ordered Italy of the past. But this is only a small consolation. Because also in growing and from growing one can die.' — **Aldo Moro** (1974)

Contents

Foreword

It is unfortunate but true that Italy does not receive outside its borders the attention its achievements in the years since 1945 ought to have won for it. I do not speak here so much of official attention; the foreign ministries and embassies of Italy's allies have been, and continue to be, very active in the official interchange that is diplomacy. I refer, rather, to a cultural fact, to the disparity between Italy's importance and its recent accomplishments, on the one hand, and, on the other, the attitudes toward it as a political, social and economic force in the contemporary period that are noticeable among the press and the public of Italy's allies.

In the United States, for instance, the political, social and economic realities of Italian life are consistently accorded far less coverage from the media than are those of Italy's neighbors. This situation matters. One would not wish to push the analogy too far, but it is fair to say that relations between nations resemble those between individuals. It is enough to sustain a solid acquaintanceship that an individual deal with another with politeness, respect and the observance of formal proprieties. But true friendship demands more – interest in, concern for, sympathy for the difficulties of the other's life, appreciation for the other's successes, a desire continuously to seek ways to improve and deepen the relationship. More can and should be done among the public and press of Italy's friends than has been done to learn about and understand the story of Italy's life as a nation over recent decades.

The story that has thus gone incompletely reported and understood is, viewed as a whole, one of truly stunning success. At the end of World War II, Italy was a country in defeat and in ruins, with a doubtful political future, still largely agricultural and suffering considerable poverty and deprivation. Today Italy is one of the economic powers of the world and one of its leading democracies, and its people are, on the whole, prosperous and comfortable. This success, however, has not been achieved smoothly or without cost. There have been many ups and downs and many grave and persistent problems. The worst time of all for Italy was the period commonly known as 'the years of lead'. It is also important for

Italy's friends to understand its problems and none more so than this most serious one. In his book about this period and one of its protagonists, Robert Meade helps to fill this gap. This well-researched and well-written book provides an interesting and dramatic portrait of a truly terrible time, when an advanced Western society, afflicted by an array of economic, political and social problems, was besieged by groups of radicals determined to overturn that society through the use of systematic violence. This is a study of what can be seen as a great historical incongruity or irony — the extremist activity of anti-democratic, revolutionary zealots violently laboring to destroy a democratic state.

This story is important, too, and worth being told for another reason. It is no revelation to say that our era has been a time of terrorism. In many places around the globe, on so many tragic occasions, airplanes have been highjacked and sabotaged, statesmen kidnapped and assassinated, ordinary citizens held hostage and murdered. The threat is so serious and has so often been realized that it has become part of the general public consciousness. As Robert Meade points out, the Red Brigades have been one of the most significant terrorist groups. They and some other groups like them for many years subjected the Italian people to a reign of terror, committing thousands of acts of brutality in order to establish what these radicals apparently believed would be a society free of injustice and exploitation. The differences between the means employed and the ends purportedly sought could not have been greater. Thus, as an instance of terrorism in practice, and of the effort to control and defeat terrorism, the history of the Red Brigades here recounted is one that ought to receive the serious attention of a public rightly alarmed about the terrorist menace.

When I arrived in Rome in 1977 to begin what would prove to be four busy years as the United States Ambassador to Italy, the situation in which the country found itself was very grave. The crisis was, as Robert Meade explains, a multifaceted one, a combination of economic, political, social and public security difficulties that had been some time in the making. Economically, Italy suffered in the 1970s from, among other things, serious inflation, low growth, capital shortages necessitating heavy borrowing abroad, and unemployment, especially for young people. On the political front, the arrangements that had sustained center–left governments for some years appeared to many no longer to function and the governmental coalitions of the first half of the 1970s were widely perceived to be less stable and effective than the seriousness of the circumstances required.

Then, in 1975 and 1976, the Communist Party registered unprecedented successes at the polls, and it appeared possible that the Communists were on the verge of becoming the first party of Italy. For many of Italy's friends, the advance of the Communists created unprecedented worry about the political and economic future of the country, while the prospect of Communist participation in an Italian cabinet raised concern about the consequences for the Western alliance. Inside Italy, there was social unrest throughout the decade among factory workers, among the employed and unemployed of the urban centers and among young people in the schools, universities and working-class districts of Rome and other cities and even of the provinces. The unrest had been percolating and erupting for many years and, in 1977, there occurred another eruption, this time a quite serious one. As Robert Meade makes plain, the discontent was not simply a severe form of labor–management discord or an exaggerated form of the normal desire of young people to rebel. The source of great anxiety for the authorities and for Italy's friends was that, among workers and young people, extreme left-wing philosophies seemed to be driving the unrest and there was much enthusiasm for the goal of revolution. More particularly, a serious public security problem had developed by 1977. Mass demonstrations occurred, followed often by serious violence practiced by advocates of revolution. There were confrontations between the far left and the far right. Secret organizations on the far right engaged in terrorism against average citizens selected at random, as in the bombing of trains. And a growing number of left-wing terrorist groups practiced systematic violence on behalf of the revolution. The most active, most characteristic of these groups, the leaders in this national turmoil, were the Red Brigades.

From a dramatic perspective the great Italian crisis reached its apogee in the spring of 1978, with the kidnapping of Aldo Moro by the Red Brigades, and his subsequent ordeal. This event was intensively covered by all the newspapers and weekly magazines of the world. It was, however, probably never fully appreciated outside Italy just how momentous and shocking this event was for the Italian people and the Italian political system. In part, this was so because neither the Red Brigades nor the troubled situation in the country was fully understood. Nor were the identity of Aldo Moro and the significance of the part he had played in Italian public life for decades fully appreciated abroad. Robert Meade illuminates these matters. The reader becomes aware of the origins of these terrorists, the nature of their ideas, their tactics and strategy, the actions that had already considerably battered the country and that prepared the way for the great crime of 1978, as well as what followed it.

The author also presents an interesting analysis of the factors that produced the discontent of the young and the most malignant offshoot thereof, the Red Brigades, and places the activities of the group and the others like it in the context of the time. We learn why it was the Red Brigades chose Aldo Moro for their victim, a selection due to more than the defects in the protection that surrounded him. We see the human tragedy of Aldo Moro as his fate unfolds. And we see the failure of the plan of the Red Brigades. They continued to wreak havoc upon Italy for years after 1978 and continued to kill even after the other aspects of the great Italian crisis had faded. But their plan for the subversion of the institutions of the country had clearly failed.

It was not so long ago that a diplomat going abroad was expected to know something of the country to which he was posted, ideally to speak the language and to be willing to work hard to promote better relations between his country and that to which he was assigned. Now, unfortunately, an additional requirement has become routine for the diplomat from many countries – he must be prepared to live with the constant danger of kidnapping or assassination. At a subconscious level, one never entirely becomes accustomed to this situation, to the idea of being hated not for anything one has done or has failed to do, but because of what one represents. As we see from this book, however, the hatred felt by the Red Brigades and like groups for other people because of the positions these others held in society was very broad. To put it another way, their definition of who was 'culpable' was very loose and expansive. Fascists, supporters of the Italian Social Movement and purportedly reactionary capitalists were 'the enemy'; but so were progressive politicians and magistrates; so were journalists who merely reported what was taking place; so were policemen, security guards and low-ranking employees in the prison system; so were middle-level political figures; so were enlightened businessmen; so were professors, even inside the hallowed halls of universities. The actions of the Red Brigades were not a campaign against a tyrant and his armies nor a battle to repel an armed invader. The Red Brigades were seeking to bring down a democratic state. That they believed in and acted upon a definition of 'culpability' that was so distorted and reflected so small a sense of reality is one mark of the bankruptcy of their ideas.

Robert Meade enlightens the reader about both the successes and failures of the Italian authorities in their efforts to apprehend the Red Brigades and the other terrorists and he discusses and analyses 'the emergency', drawing some conclusions about the wisest means a state should adopt in order to suppress terrorism. I think Robert Meade is correct in noting the positive side of the record, that is, Italy's success in managing to bring the Red Brigades and the others to justice and to survive the great crisis without falling into the traps of severe repression into which other nations have toppled, often at great cost to the welfare and liberties of their people.

During the height of the crisis, many experienced observers seriously feared that Italy was about to collapse. But they failed to take account of the basic good sense and democratic commitment of the average Italian. For years, scholars and journalists had been remarking upon what was variously called the indifference, bitterness, cynicism, alienation or disaffection of the Italian citizen toward his government, the consequence of a complex history. It was widely feared that, while a minority would continue to join or support the Red Brigades, the majority would stand aside as the system came apart under the onslaught of repeated attacks of the kind of which Aldo Moro was a victim. But that did not happen. The pessimism about the strength of the system proved unwarranted. From their past experience with fascism and from this new experience with political violence, the Italian people understood the value of a democratic system. Ultimately, the history of the Red Brigades is about the triumph of the democratic ideal over violence and intolerance.

New York RICHARD N. GARDNER

Acknowledgements

George Orwell, who knew what he was talking about, said that writing a book is 'a horrible, exhausting struggle, like a long bout of some painful illness'. It is only lately that I have come to a full appreciation of the accuracy of this observation. Writing a book, at least a book of non-fiction, though a solitary endeavour for the most part, is also, in some important respects, a co-operative one. Thus it is that one who comes to the end of his task, who survives his illness, feels the obligation to acknowledge the help of those who saw him through it. I do this now very willingly, though following what is, for good reason, the custom, noting that I have tried hard to avoid errors of fact or judgement, but that, should any such shortcomings remain, they are, alas, my responsibility alone.

Dr Henry Viscardi, Paul S. Eriksson and William Connolly lent me a hand at an early stage, as did Walter Black and Michael E. Hoffman at a later one. Mary T. King was supportive, as always. In Italy Franca Rame offered me contacts and the benefit of her experience. Dott. Tozzi of the Corte d'assise d'appello in Rome helped me gain access to some important documents. Pier Luigi Vigna, Sostituto Procuratore della Repubblica, Avvocato Tommaso Mancini and Professor Giuseppe Mammarella spared me some of their valuable time. Avvocato Antonino Filastò went far out of his way to introduce me to some of the offenders he has helped, to answer my questions and to provide me with a view of things from his perspective, all this without concerning himself in the least about the approach I intended to take to the subject. Dott. Arturo Parisi of the highly respected Istituto di studi e ricerche Carlo Cattaneo of Bologna generously allowed me to study, at my convenience, the collection of resolutions and other documents produced by the terrorists, and documents issued in legal proceedings against them that the Istituto has laboriously collected, and the able scholar, Donatella della Porta, kindly paved my way to the Institute. The Biblioteca Nazionale in Florence and the New York Public Library were of immense help. To all of these my thanks.

Professor Richard N. Gardner of Columbia University, former Ambassador to Italy, and Professor Joseph LaPalombara of Yale University took time from busy schedules and took the trouble to read a portion of the manuscript and to give me encouragement. These kindnesses came at an important moment and were of great help to me.

I am deeply grateful to those who gave me their friendship during my time in Italy and who were interested in what I was doing: Bill and Melissa Eichner, Amadeo Pinto, Eleanor DeForest, Donato Falcicchio and Marlaine Cacouault. Mary Ann Pinto, Nathan Levi and Roberto and Jan Martini were extraordinarily generous and unsparing with their time, their friendship, their hospitality and their encouragement. A special debt is owed to Roberto, who shared with me his interest in, and knowledge of, Italian politics, who never tired of discussing things with me, and whose justifiable love for, and pride in, things Italian were contagious. All these friends made my time in Italy one of the great joys of my life.

Finally, another category, one as to which words of gratitude are too frail to suffice: I thank Dr Dennis Meade, for his helpful prodding, his interest, and his faith, with regard to this project and other matters, and for his diligence as a correspondent over a very long time. I thank my parents, who have always stood by me. Above all, I thank Mary Jo Meade, whose patience was, and still is, boundless, and whose belief in me sustained me throughout and helped me over the hard patches. *Senza di lei, non avrei fatto niente.*

ROBERT C. MEADE, JR.

Preface

In the north of Italy late in 1976, a young man named Walter Alasia misplaced his eyeglasses, thereby setting in motion a series of events that would end in murder and disaster. Although he had taken the precaution of going to another town, he had given the eyedoctor his real name. Later, Walter left his glasses behind in the hideout in Pavia. When the police raided the place, they found the usual pile of guns and documents – and the eyeglasses. The police traced the eyeglasses to the doctor and, through him, to Walter. The police then placed a tap on the phone in the apartment in Sesto San Giovanni, just outside Milan, where Walter lived with his parents and his brother, Oscar. In this way, the police discovered that it had been Walter who had led the recent attack on a Christian Democratic political center in Milan. Armed with pistols, Walter and a girl had tied and gagged the office workers, rifled the cabinets and taken documents and money. With a can of spray paint, Walter had written on the walls slogans denouncing the Christian Democratic Party. And then Walter, who from an early age had shown talent at drawing, had painted on the walls a terrifying symbol. The five-pointed star. The insignia of the Red Brigades.

Of Walter's other life, of pistols, robberies and sequesters of the enemies of the people, his parents and his brother knew nothing. Walter had lately become sullen and taciturn, but they attributed this change to personal frustration. And although, as they also knew, Walter had for some time been deeply interested in politics of a radical variety, there was nothing peculiar about that, in those years in that part of the country.

Walter's was a working-class family. Guido and Ada Alasia were Communist Party members. As a boy, Walter was cheerful, unreserved, incessantly talking and singing. He and a group of friends played soccer and all the normal childhood games in the courtyard outside the family apartment and in the open fields nearby.

Things began to sour for Walter when he was failed at school. He then transferred to a technical school across the road from his home in Sesto. The schools and factories in Sesto and in the whole industrial zone of the country were in turmoil. In 1970, the students had occupied the local school for over a week, until they had been cleared out by the police. From that point on, the school, like so many others, had become the setting for a routine of student protests and police interventions, until, in the end, all pretense at serious instruction and study had ceased. Many, including Walter, were drawn into the agitation. He took to hanging about the State University of Milan, a mecca for young people unhappy with the educational system and other social institutions. He came into contact with radical groups led by university students, who argued over how best to achieve profound social change in Italy. In school and in Milan, he 'practised politics', taking part in countless protests. Sometimes he would bring friends home and they would pass time making banners for the next demonstration. In April 1973, but 17 years old, Walter participated in a skirmish between students and a group of neo-fascists in the streets of Milan. For Walter, it was an exhilarating, perhaps decisive experience. The students charged the advancing neo-fascists and the latter took to their heels. Walter excitedly reported to his parents that the people watching from their windows had applauded the students' victory. He gravitated farther and farther to the left.

Hoping to find work in one of the rebellious large factories around Milan, Walter gave up school. But he could not get a position and was forced to settle for a job as a machinist in a small plant. He also began to attend night sessions at his old school, largely in order to try to raise the political consciousness of the night students, many of whom were workers loyal to the Communist Party. Walter and his friends had little success there, but during the day sessions, the pot was boiling nicely. When, late in 1973, bars were installed on the ground floor windows of the school building, the students claimed that the authorities had turned the place into a prison. Hence a demonstration, during which three students, wearing ski masks and using drills and hammers, succeeded in cutting through the 'prison' bars before the police arrived. The three, one of whom was Walter, escaped. Forty-one other students were charged with destruction of public property, which provoked yet another student occupation of the poor, beleaguered school.

Walter loathed his job, the authoritarianism of the bosses and the lack of ardour for the working-class cause among the workers there. He came home one day and announced that he had resigned his post. Once more he tried to find a job in a large plant; once more he failed. Finally he found temporary work, but he quit this too. His parents were upset.

Walter hung about the house, listening to records and doing some reading, principally of revolutionary texts. He owned a few works by Lenin and decorated his room with posters of Lenin, Che and Stalin. He had abandoned his old neighborhood friends and confided little in his parents or brother. A revolutionary ideal had now become master of him. For a time, he was an active militant in *Lotta Continua* ('Continuous Struggle'), the chief of the many grouplets then prospering on the left of the Communists. But a schism occurred within *Lotta Continua* when some members attacked the leadership for being unwilling to go beyond revolutionary rhetoric. The priority, said the dissidents, was to arm the proletariate and begin the struggle *now*. Walter was one of the dissidents.

Walter worked for the postal service for a few months and then quit. He again spent much of his time at home. For companionship, he went to a coffee shop in Sesto frequented by a small group of heretics from *Lotta Continua*. Together, they talked and dreamed of revolution. The others from *Lotta Continua* he saw no more. He kept his distance too from his brother, Oscar, a bourgeois who worked in a bank and had a girlfriend. Sometimes Walter would get into arguments with his parents and shut himself in his room. Then, without warning, his habits changed. He tidied up his room and his clothes and set up a neat, private corner for his books and papers. When Walter's father, an amateur photographer, tried to take his picture, Walter became angry and destroyed all but a handful of the pictures and negatives of him that Guido had made over the years. Walter began to go out and occasionally did not return at night. His mother had no idea where he went or what he was doing. She and his brother thought he had found a girl. And then, one day, Walter went out and got himself a pair of glasses.

After a month of telephone interceptions, the police decided it was time to bring Walter in. Very early on the morning of 15 December 1976, ten policemen took up places outside while five others approached the door of the Alasia apartment and rang the bell. 'Police. Open up!' one of them yelled. Guido Alasia, in his pyjamas, searched for the key and finally opened the door. His wife was standing in the corridor in her nightgown. They were confused and frightened. Ada heard movement in the room where her two sons were sleeping. The police entered and two of them headed toward the boy's room. Suddenly, Guido and Ada saw Walter at the door to his room. His arm was extended. He opened fire with a pistol. The two policemen were hit and fell to the floor. Ada noticed that there were no signs of agitation on Walter's face; it was as though he had been prepared for this moment, as though what he had just done was an act of every day. Oscar, in the room with his brother, saw Walter pull out the pistol and fire. Walter reloaded the pistol. Oscar too was struck by the strange calm on Walter's face. 'Walter, what have you done?' shouted Oscar. Walter did not respond. He put the revolver in his belt, went to the window and jumped to the ground.

In the apartment, there was noise, movement, shouting. Then Oscar heard shooting outside. He looked out the window. Walter was lying on the ground. Oscar was pulled away from the window. He went to the living-room, where his father was lying on a couch, looking very ill. There was shouting and confusion. Chaos. Policemen everywhere. Ada was crying. When Ada asked after Walter, the police told her not to worry. A *maresciallo* gave Oscar some stunning news – his brother was a member of the Red Brigades. The police took Oscar to his room and began to search. They found Red Brigades' documents among Walter's neat pile of papers and a gun hidden in a bag. Oscar learned then that the two policemen had been mortally wounded. And his brother? How badly had he been hit? The *maresciallo* told Oscar that there was nothing to be done. Walter lay dead on the pavement, his legs bent and his face turned upward, in the courtyard where, not so long before, he had kicked around a soccer ball with his friends from the neighborhood. He was 20 years old.

The 1970's and early 1980's were the darkest period in Italian post-war history. This was a time of ideological excess, of virtually the apotheosis of the idea of revolutionary violence. Someone called them the *anni di piombo*, the 'years of lead', and the name stuck, for good reason. Beginning in 1969 and continuing for over a decade, against a backdrop of general instability and widespread discontent, terrorism of the right and the left took the lives of 415 people and wounded 1181. There were assassinations, kidnappings, shootings in broad daylight, bombings, gun battles with police, beatings with chains and metal clubs, the sacking of political party offices – more than 14 580 acts of political violence. Many hundreds of thousands took part in the general unrest over the years, while a small army of terrorists did battle with the state:

in 1987 there were over 3000 revolutionaries against whom the
state was pursuing criminal charges for terrorist activity. In the
worst years, judges, prosecutors, policemen, politicians, businessmen, journalists and others were methodically hunted down: if
they were lucky, they spent some time in a people's prison or got a
bullet in the knees; the less fortunate, like Aldo Moro, the nation's
most important political leader, were assassinated. The category of
'the enemies of the people' was an expansive one and, as a result,
thousands in such seemingly non-political professions as business
and journalism had to watch their backs and their movements
outside their homes. The prominent bought bullet-proof cars and
took lessons in defensive driving, while the leading political
figures travelled with armed escorts. Ordinary life in the great
cities took on a nightmarish quality and the reading of the morning
newspaper became an ordeal. The pillars of the system of criminal
justice swayed and, at some points, cracked from the tremors of
terrorism and the countermeasures of the government. The political violence was the most serious by a wide margin – in the number
of terrorists involved, in the extent of support for them among
some sectors of society, and in the virulence of their attack – of any
such violence in any of the advanced industrial societies (with the
exception of Northern Ireland and Spain, which are special cases of
nationalism in excess). So great was the turmoil that many citizens
wondered whether what seemed a fragile Republic could survive,
and those with long memories worried that a corpse from an even
more dreadful past might spring up, reanimated, from the grave.

At the center of all this turbulence was the five-pointed star. The
Brigate Rosse. The Red Brigades. They spread their roots most
widely, endured the longest – 18 years and still counting – had the
greatest influence on events, and spilled the most blood. For all
their ferocity, though, they were not mad. They were not reasonable about their cause, failed to test its postulates and were blind to
the facts of Italian life and the truth about working-class Utopias,
not to mention blind to humanitarian considerations – but they
were not mad. Rather, they pursued, with intensity and passion,
the goal of a Marxist-Leninist revolution, believed in the possibility
of a socialist Utopia in Italy and had no hesitancy about accepting
the elementary Marxist-Leninist notion that that Utopia could be
reached only through revolutionary violence.

Behind these ideas and the newspaper accounts of the revolutionary *praxis* of the Red Brigades lay thousands of stories of

ordinary people: the victims, the dead and the hobbled, and their
families, destroyed or devastated by enemies who regarded human
beings as no more than symbols. And there were the families of the
protagonists; they too were victims. Like the Alasia family. Guido
Alasia believed that his son had been led to violate the law not by a
vicious nature, but by a fatal interaction of personal defects –
ignorance, impatience, credulousness and self-deception – and of
the peculiar conditions of the country in the years in which Walter
had come of age. In this there may be some consolation for the
Alasia family. But it can hardly suffice to soften materially the
recollection of that dreadful morning in December 1976. Nor can
such thoughts relieve the sorrow provoked by the realization that
Walter, in destroying himself and ruining his own family, took the
lives of two human beings and wrecked two other families as well.
And there cannot be compensation for the Alasias in the knowledge that Walter was considered by those who shared his aims to
have died the death of a revolutionary martyr, and that the Red
Brigades paid him the tribute of baptizing one of their groups with
his name, the 'Walter Alasia Column' of Milan, which carried
forward the practice of revolutionary violence for years after
Walter's death in the courtyard outside the family apartment in
Sesto San Giovanni.

This is the story of the Red Brigades. It is a book about what
happened during the 'years of lead' and about why it happened. It
is a book about who the terrorists were, where they came from and
what they believed in. It is an account of the state's efforts to
respond to the threat, its successes but also its errors and mis-
judgements. Ultimately, perhaps, this is a cautionary tale. At the
moment there is more apathy than radicalism in democratic
societies. But pendulums swing. And when next the pendulum
swings, it will be useful to recall the Italian experience and to
remember what can follow from the infatuation of students and an
intellectual élite with the apocalyptic promises of revolutionary
ideology.

The Italian penal code does not define terrorism and scholars
and observers in Italy and outside it have had trouble arriving at an
accurate, useful and clear definition of the term. This book does not
purport to have resolved this problem. It proceeds, however, upon
the belief that the term terrorism is a meaningful one in the Italian
context. There was much more or less low-level political violence
in Italy in those years, but there was also something that was

recognized by everyone as different. There was terrorism: the use of violence, often of a very grave type (such as bombs in public places), by clandestine right-wing groups intent upon sowing terror among the public, destroying the democratic system and creating an authoritarian state; and the systematic use of violence, often of a very grave type (such as assassinations and 'knee-cappings'), by clandestine left-wing groups, such as the Red Brigades, who were intent upon attacking 'capitalist enemies', undermining the democracy and the public's faith in it, inciting the proletariat to revolt, destroying the democracy in a civil war and installing a 'people's state'. The leaders of the Red Brigades have never appreciated the universal designation of them as terrorists and of their enterprises as terrorism. In their own minds, the *brigatisti* were and are fighters for revolutionary justice. But, as will become clear during the course of this book, the designation is appropriate and reflects that common-sense humanity that the *brigatisti* lost sight of, thereby dooming their dreams for a socialist Utopia.

Abbreviations

AK-47	An extremely powerful automatic assault rifle made in the Soviet Union and used by the Red Brigades on occasion. The most notorious weapon used by the *brigatisti* was the Skorpion, a small and easily concealable but deadly machine pistol made in Czechoslovakia. The concealability of the Skorpion made it preferable to the AK-47, while its rapid firing capacity made it preferable to an ordinary pistol.
BR	The *Brigate Rosse*, the Red Brigades.
CESIS	The Executive Committee for Information and Security Services, a committee in the office of the prime minister and presided over by him that co-ordinates and supervises the work of the secret services, SISMI and SISDE. CESIS was established by the reform legislation of late 1977, as were these two services.
CGIL	The General Italian Labor Confederation. The CGIL is the most powerful union in Italy. Together with the CISL and the UIL, it makes up an alliance that is by far the leading spokesman for Italian workers. Though the CGIL was originally formed as a multiparty union, for decades the majority of the CGIL has been, and is, Communist and the minority has been, and is, Socialist. Domination by the left led to a split in the CGIL shortly after World War II and to the foundation of the CISL and the UIL.
CIA	The United States Central Intelligence Agency, the *bête noire* of many on the Italian left and, according to some of these, the engineer behind right- and left-wing terrorism in Italy.
CISL	The Italian Confederation of Workers' Trade Unions, the second-ranking union in Italy, traditionally affiliated with the DC.
DC	The Christian Democratic Party, since the founding of the Republic the leading political party in Italy

and the source of most cabinet ministers and, until recent years, all prime ministers. A frequent DC prime minister and cabinet minister, and at different times the secretary and the president of the party, was Aldo Moro.

ETA The terrorist group demanding independence for the Basque provinces in Spain.

FGCI The Italian Communist Youth Federation, the young people's arm of the Italian Communist Party. Once a key force in the Italian communist political world and a training ground for party leaders, including party secretaries Enrico Berlinguer and Achille Occhetto, the Federation has fallen on lean times in recent years. Some terrorists were once members of the Federation.

FUCI The Italian Catholic University Federation, an organization of Italian Catholic university students that was once led by Aldo Moro and, after him, Giulio Andreotti, frequent DC cabinet minister and prime minister.

GAP Groups of Partisan Action, a left-wing revolutionary group founded and led by the millionaire publisher Giangiacomo Feltrinelli. The group's name was borrowed from that of a partisan group that had been active in the Second World War.

IRA The Irish Republican Army.

KGB The Soviet secret police and espionage organization.

LC 'Lotta Continua' ('Continuous Struggle'), a left-wing revolutionary organization that grew up out of the student and labor agitation of the late 1960s in Italy. LC advocated an overthrow of the state through violence and the establishment of socialism in Italy, but did not itself practice clandestine violence of the type employed by the BR. Many terrorists, however, at one stage in their lives were members of LC.

MPC The Metropolitan Political Collective, a forerunner of the Red Brigades founded in 1969 by Renato Curcio, Margherita Cagol and others and headquartered in Milan. The MPC advocated revolutionary struggle centred on the metropolis.

MRPO   The Proletarian Offensive Movement of Resistance, a concept of the Red Brigades described and elaborated upon by them in strategic resolutions and other documents. This Movement was thought by the *brigatisti* to arise out of, and embrace, all the most active, most subversive elements present on the peculiar, unruly political scene beginning in 1977.

MSI   The Italian Social Movement, the neo-Fascist political party.

NAP   Armed Proletarian Nuclei, the third most prominent left-wing Italian terrorist group. The group was far less skillful, and thus was more short-lived than the BR.

NAR   Armed Revolutionary Nuclei. Despite the ring of the name, this was a leading right-wing terrorist group. The principal agent of rightist violence in the later period of terrorism in Italy, the group used newly learned left-wing tactics in an extreme right-wing cause. In addition, NAR and like groups gave voice in right-wing language to some dissatisfactions with the state of Italian society – the alienation, the anonymity, the social and economic problems of youth – that were also agitating the left.

NATO   The North Atlantic Treaty Organization, one of the leading forces for evil in the eyes of the *brigatisti* and other left-wing terrorists, a controlling element in the capitalist, multinational imperialism that outraged the BR and a target of BR attention and action in the BR's final period as a great national menace.

P2   Propaganda 2, a masonic lodge led by one Licio Gelli, Venerable Master. The members of the lodge included an extraordinary number of high-level military officers, secret service officials, businessmen, politicians, journalists, and so on. Gelli's past, the identity of the membership, the political loyalties of many members and other factors have led investigators and prosecutors to conclude that the

P2 was pursuing a subversive reactionary, conspiratorial strategy.

P38 A pistol used by some leftist extremists. A sign made with the hand in imitation of this gun became a common feature of demonstrations by the far-left movement of 1977 and a symbol of the movement's aspirations.

PCI The Italian Communist Party, since shortly after the Second World War the second most powerful political party in Italy.

PL 'Prima Linea' ('Front Line'), the second most important left-wing terrorist group in Italy. In competition with the BR for membership and in disaccord with the BR over points of revolutionary doctrine and aspects of revolutionary practice, the group spilled much blood and caused much suffering.

PLO The Palestine Liberation Organization.

PSI The Italian Socialist Party, since shortly after the Second World War the third-ranking political party in Italy. The PSI has often collaborated with the DC in forming governments, but the PSI's socialism, even watered down from that of the immediate post-war period, has made it an uncomfortable ally for the more conservative DC.

RAF The Red Army Faction, originally the Baader–Meinhof gang, the leading West German terrorist group and sometime friend of the BR.

SID Defense Information Service, the military secret service, successor to the SIFAR.

SIFAR Armed Forces Information Service, the military secret service.

SISDE The Democratic Information and Security Service, the internal security service created by the 1977 reform that abolished the SID.

SISMI The Military Information and Security Service, the military secret service in charge of espionage and counter-espionage. Created by the 1977 reform that abolished the SID.

SIM The Imperialist State of the Multinationals, a basic

concept of the BR, much-discussed in BR documents. According to the BR, capitalist imperialism dominated the globe, in particular, the imperialism of the United States and Germany exercised through the multinationals, NATO and other instruments. The Italian political system, like every other system, had to conform to the dictates of this imperialism. The Italian state had therefore been undertaking to fulfil its role in the international imperialist scheme, crushing the proletariat, oppressing the poor, exploiting the workers' labor and robbing them of their health for the sake of profit, stifling all hopes for change and engaging in counter-revolutionary activity, especially police attacks on the demonstrations of the proletariat and criminal assaults against the most advanced of the proletariat. The Italian state had begun to transform itself into the SIM, with the DC at all critical points of control. The State's effort in a time of economic crisis was to restructure, the better to be able to carry out its role as the SIM.

UIL   Italian Union of Labour, the third-ranking union in the country, primarily allied to the Socialists and the Republicans.

1

Il Sessantotto

TRENT: OF SOCIOLOGY AND REVOLUTION

In the early 1960s the Christian Democrats were luxuriating in a warm sea of encouraging statistics. Finally, after centuries of frustrated hopes, Italians had witnessed the disappearance, within an astonishingly brief time, of the underdeveloped Italy. Not only had the devastation of the war's end been overcome, but the 'economic miracle' of the 1950s and early 1960s had transformed an agricultural economy into a predominantly industrial one, and, in the process, had revolutionized life for millions of ordinary people. In a self-congratulatory mood, the Christian Democrats concluded that a class of technocrats should be created to manage the new prosperity, and thus some Christian Democrats brought about the establishment of an Institute of Sociology in Trent, a conservative Christian Democratic stronghold in northern Italy. But one objection – that the proposed instruction might degenerate into raw politicization – proved prophetic, if understated. In the turbulent late 1960s the institute became a training ground for an unwanted kind of leader. It was there, and in a collective of disaffected young Communists at Reggio Emilia, that much of the first generation of the Red Brigades began their political careers. It was in Trent that the two most influential of the founding *brigatisti*, Renato Curcio and Margherita Cagol, took their first steps on the road to the revolution.

The institute was a natural tinderbox in the second half of the 1960s.[1] With its founding, sociology had been recognized, for the first time in the stodgy Italian system of higher education, as a subject worthy of serious study. As a result, magnet-like, Trent attracted from around the country students who were fascinated by this novelty and preoccupied with the uncertain health of Italian society. The first sparks glimmered in late 1965, shortly after the institute's opening, when the Student Movement (as it was to be called) occupied the school to protest at what the students viewed as parliament's attempt to scuttle the degree in sociology. School occupations were then uncommon and this one was a mild affair, as well as, it turned out, a successful one. Encouraged by this outcome the students in the fall of 1966 again briefly, and again successfully, occupied the institute, this time in a contest over their right to influence the shaping of the curriculum. A significant harbinger of things to come was the galloping radicalization of the students' ideas: the sociologist, they said, could not be politically neutral. In March 1967 the students organized a week of demonstrations, vigils and rallies throughout the city of Trent in support of the 'national liberation struggle' in Vietnam. The headmaster called in the police for the first time and thereafter things would no longer be what they had once been. Students were photographed and carried out onto the sidewalk, amidst revolutionary songs and slogans and shouts of 'Johnson Executioner!' A sit-in followed and the headmaster shut the school until a kind of calm returned.

At the start of the academic year 1967–8 the opening of the institute was blocked by a strike of the students. With the participation of some instructors, the Student Movement opened a 'counter-university', which offered 'counter-courses' on the current phase of capitalist development, the Chinese Revolution and Mao-think. This venture grew out of an initiative for a so-called 'negative university', of which the future leader of the Red Brigades, Renato Curcio, was a leading advocate. The state of Curcio's thinking and the swiftly-changing mood at Trent are reflected in the manifesto prepared by exponents of the 'negative university'.[2] The student who wants to enrich himself intellectually, the manifesto declared, has no place in the university, which is the instrument of a dominant class; instead, he becomes a mercenary, paid off with a degree and honors to be exchanged on the labor market for money. The objective of the enlightened, the manifesto asserted, must be a 'radical overturning of the system of mature capitalism through new forms of class struggle'. It need hardly be said that this sort of thing was little understood and even less appreciated by the local people of Trent.

By early 1968 the discord had intensified, with the students' anger spreading beyond academic concerns to what was now being seen as the central evil – the oppression of capitalist society.[3] The official organs of student government had collapsed and been displaced by the hallowed general assembly, which, under the banner of 'student power', declared an occupation of the school that lasted for several months. The occupation was marked, on the students' side, by political seminars and commissions, disruptions of Lenten services in the cathedral, 'counter-services' and 'counter-sermons', and by protests by scandalized residents of Trent, who threw rocks and rotten fruit at the school and shouted at the students to go back where they had come from. An institute occupied by the students, protected by the army and beseiged by an outraged crowd of *Trentini* was very far from the kind of institution the Christian Democratic founders had had in mind, but so it had become.

The events at Trent were not isolated phenomena. Rather, Trent was an experimental stage for a drama that soon engulfed the entire Italian university system. The revolt of Italian students in late 1967–8 was so vast and profound that it co-opted the date *'il sessantotto'* ("68"), which, 20 years later, is still universally used as a short-hand reference to the ideas, attitudes and events of that unruly season.

In the fall of 1967, the Catholic University of Milan was occupied by the students. Then it was the turn of a faculty at the University of Turin. Then one in Genoa. By the end of December 1967 the unrest – demonstrations, occupations, general assemblies, political seminars and collectives – was spreading across the country. The traditional student representative groups were everywhere ignored; lessons were disrupted or barred altogether; the police were frequently called in; there were battles in the streets and students were injured and arrested. The occupations, some of which continued for months, brought virtually the whole university machine to a halt.[4]

The evolution in student thinking at Trent was typical of the storm that gathered on all the campuses. The students began with relatively limited, often justified demands: for example, for improved educational facilities, reform of the programs of study and changes in the prerogatives of professors. Within a remarkably short time, however, such criticism turned into 'global contestation', first of the university and its aims and then, with the help of Marxist analysis, of society itself. For some students, Marxism was merely a fashionable language with which to express a confused utopianism, but for large numbers of students, many more than in other countries, the rhetoric was taken with the utmost serious-

ness. The remedy for the inequities and malfunctions of society,
these students came to believe, was not social-democratic reform,
but one thing only: revolution.

The leading force in the agitation on the campuses was the
Student Movement. Milan was the fortress of the Movement and
the State University of Milan its nerve center. The students
virtually took over the university. They engaged in endless
theorization about the revolution; continually blocked up the
streets in the heart of Milan with their marches; fought with police
and right-wing extremists; and attacked bourgeois opinion, throwing rotten eggs and fruit at the high-toned crowd attending the
opening night at La Scala.[5]

The disorders were long-lasting and the reverberations thereof
even more enduring. Peace was long in returning to Trent. In July
1970 the authorities finally achieved a Pyrrhic victory – the institute
was closed. By the time this decision was taken, however, Renato
Curcio and Margherita Cagol had already migrated to Milan and
started to put into practice the revolutionary theory that had first
begun to take shape at Trent and that was to end in the creation of
the *Brigate Rosse*.

DREAMING OF THE HAPPY ISLAND

Renato Curcio's family background was inauspicious.[6] He was
born in 1941 at Monterotondo, near Rome, the product of a brief
affair between Yolanda Curcio and Renato Zampa, a prosperous,
philandering married man. The young Renato was taken by his
mother to a town in Piedmont, where she went to work. The boy
became close to Yolanda's brother, Armando, a member of the
Resistance who was later killed by the Fascists. Years after, Renato
asserted that his uncle Armando had always occupied a special
place in his heart and he sounded a theme that appears frequently
in the development of left-wing terrorism in Italy – the theme of
the Resistance. The Resistance was a critical event for Italy, a
struggle for liberty conducted by ordinary people that helped
considerably to wash away the stain of fascism. Curcio and his
fellows sought to appropriate the moral content of the partisan
struggle, thinking of themselves not as terrorists, but as the 'new
Resistance'. In 1974 Curcio wrote to his mother:

There come to my mind memories from long ago. Uncle Armando, who carried me piggyback on his shoulders. His clear eyes, always smiling, which looked far ahead towards a society of free and equal men. And I loved him like a father. And I have picked up the rifle that only death at the hands of the Nazi-Fascist assassins had ripped from him.[7]

Curcio also picked up his uncle's name: in false documents employed by him in his terrorist career, Curcio used the battle-name 'Armando'.[8] To suit the spurious parallel between his cause and that of his uncle, he had recast his memories. At the time of his uncle's death Curcio had been five months short of his fourth birthday. How much could he recall of his uncle, of his clear eyes and generous vision of a better society?

While Yolanda worked, Renato was left in the charge of a local family. For years, Zampa, an arrogant and selfish man, paid no visits to his son. Renato grew up among the Waldensians, a tiny religious minority to which Yolanda belonged. But, this strong, perhaps domineering woman insisted later that her son was unaffected by this tie to a minority, and if he had become a rebel, that had been due to other factors. Religion was not imposed on the boy; he made a choice and he chose Catholicism. Thereafter, he was a practicing Catholic and, his mother believed, he got married in a Catholic church, not just to please his wife-to-be, but because he, like she, was a believer.

After elementary school Renato was sent to stay with family friends and to continue his schooling. After an indifferent beginning, he became a good student. For a time, he stayed with his mother in the hotel in Milan where she was employed and he was put to work operating the lift. Then he went off to a school to study chemistry and his mother moved to be near him. He and she, Yolanda said, were great friends. Occasionally Renato saw his father. Their relationship, she thought, was 'correct, perhaps even affectionate',[9] but she was surely deluding herself. After the death of his wife, Zampa offered to give Renato his name, but the boy refused, though his mother insisted lamely that this had not been due to any marked resentment towards his father. Zampa found him a closed, introverted boy with whom it was difficult to communicate, and the boy's refusal to accept his name ended their relationship. Zampa saw neither the boy nor Yolanda thereafter.[10]

In 1962 Renato obtained his diploma and took up a teaching post at his school. Yolanda was very pleased, nurturing hopes that he would marry and give her grandchildren. He began, however, to talk about going to university. He told her he wanted to follow his ideals, which she did not understand. He tried for a scholarship to the institute at Trent and won it, but told her nothing of this, in order, she felt afterwards, not to displease her. One Friday he told her he was going to Genoa to visit some friends. Leaving his keys behind he went to Trent, from where he wrote to her explaining what he had done and asking her forgiveness. What had caused her son to flee without a word, Yolanda could not say. Her hopes dashed by this, the greatest sorrow of her life, she saw an advertisement in the paper, wrote away for a job and left Italy for England, where she remained. It was 1964.

After a while they began corresponding. Occasionally he would write to her about his studies and his political ideas. After he had met his future wife Yolanda received more letters, sometimes from both of them, sometimes from her alone. On several occasions after Renato's marriage a visit to England was raised as a possibility, but something having to do with politics always prevented it.

Renato Curcio's personal history provides a wealth of material for psychological interpretation. As the illegitimate son of an uncaring man, he may have felt a sense of victimization and a deep resentment, emotions that translated themselves into a need to strike out at authority. Deprived of affection, he may have sought, through an abstract, idealized solidarity with others whom the world had mistreated – the proletariat – the affection due the revolutionary liberator. He may have over-compensated for the sufferings of his childhood by becoming unyieldingly convinced of his moral superiority. These are speculations and psychology is a minefield, but there is no doubt that he did come to believe himself the lonely, persecuted possessor of higher truth, as is clear from his own words in a 1974 letter to his mother:

Years have passed since the day I left to encounter life and left you to face life alone. I have worked, I have studied, I have fought. Now I am in jail and what I have done in these last years is at the center of a furious polemic. I feel the hate of my enemies and the love of my friends. And I also, oh God, and I also love. You taught me loyalty, to not have fear of the new and of sacrifice, to fight against resignation. And I have kept these banners high. In that, I am your son and for this schooling I am grateful to you without limit.

Looking for my road, I have found exploitation, injustice, oppression. And people who practiced these. And people who were suffering these. I was among these last. And these last were the larger part. I have thus understood that my story was their story, that my future was their future ... My enemies are the enemies of humanity and of intelligence. Anyone who, upon the material and intellectual misery of people, has built and builds his cursed fortune. That is the hand that has closed the door of my cell.[11]

For Yolanda Curcio, however, the roots of Renato's deviation could not be found in the abnormality of his youth. Many children, she said, had not had the attention Renato had. 'My son never suffered ... I never let him lack for anything'.[12]

At the institute Curcio immersed himself in study. Marx, Lenin and Mao were to him a spiritual revelation, disclosing the bases of injustice in the world and justifying the anger he felt. He joined the student agitation, but not as a rabble-rouser. Theory was his chief interest and it would remain so all his career. He launched the idea of the 'negative university'. In the fall of 1967 he and others became involved in publishing *Political Work*, a journal 'whose origins are connected to ... the proletarian cultural revolution guided by the thought of Mao-Tse-tung, the invincible struggle of the Vietnamese people and the contemporary degeneration of the [Italian Communist Party] ...'.[13] The preference for Chinese and Third World versions of the revolutionary struggle over that of the Italian Communist Party (the PCI) was fundamental to the spread of student protest and to the eventual development of the left terrorists in Italy. In theory, the PCI was the most important exponent of Marxist-Leninism on the scene. To Curcio and others like him, however, the PCI could not be entrusted with the noble task of making a revolution because the party was revisionist. Revisionism was the principal enemy of Marxist-Leninism, not merely a tactical error of some revolutionary leaders, but a counter-revolutionary strategy of the bourgeoisie. Still, Curcio was not convinced in the fall of 1967 that the time was ripe to begin the 'armed struggle' in Italy. On the contrary, the 'adventurism' of certain 'filo-Castroite formulations' only served, he believed, to breathe life into the cause of revisionism. Anyone who thinks that the revolution can be reduced to the idea of guerrilla war, wrote *Political Work*, is an emotional bourgeois, not a true revolutionary.[14]

By the fall of 1968 Renato Curio had become disillusioned. The world-wide movement toward revolution had lost some of its impetus. The ever-so-promising French May had ended very badly, and in Italy the revolutionary cause had weakened noticeably. Too many students, in Curcio's view, were merely playing at revolution. A renewed and deepened but realistic commitment to a socialist revolution must be made. Starting from the university and the school, the revolutionaries, Curcio wrote, must undertake the 'long march through the institutions':

> This is not a revolutionary moment, but a pre-revolutionary one, and hence it is not a moment in which it is the problem of the taking of power that immediately presents itself but the organization of political work. Thus, it is necessary to say that it is adventurism to make people, the masses, suppose or believe that the taking of power and the realization of an egalitarian society is a facile and rapid piece of business; it is necessary, instead, to underscore continually that it will be difficult and long. What we have ahead is not the Cuban example but the Chinese example; that is, the organization of the happy island is not possible with two years of struggle, but is possible through 40 years of resistance.[15]

Margherita Cagol's background, it is interesting to note, was quite unlike Curcio's.[16] Born in 1945, she came from a small town near Trent. The family was stable, quiet, conservative, religious, close-knit, and its economic circumstances were comfortable. Margherita's sister, Milena, could recall no trauma, oppression or absence of affection in Margherita's youth that might have determined the course her life was to take.

Though not a gloomy girl, Margherita took seriously everything she did, hobbies included. She was a perfectionist and was reserved and modest about her accomplishments. The strongest characteristic of her personality was a need to give to others. She regularly paid visits to the old and sick in hospitals, for instance; it was her way of being religious. She was, her sister said, consciously searching for answers to the great problems of life.

After graduating from school in the summer of 1964 with an

excellent set of grades, Margherita faced the question of university. It was a decisive moment in her life. Living near Trent, she naturally thought of the institute. She preferred sociology to the dry subjects of economy and commerce to which her type of diploma would otherwise have restricted her, and no doubt, too, she was attracted by the progressive image of the modern institute of advanced studies. Trent it was, a choice made by her alone. She had the ill luck to arrive at the institute in a very hot season, a reality for which she was splendidly unprepared. The Cagol family had never occupied itself with politics, and Margherita had never pursued the subject on her own. Provincial, politically naïve, intense, longing for great truths by which to live her life, she was exceptionally vulnerable to the forces that were disrupting the university and that would, in short order, disrupt the whole nation. In time, with her customary quiet conviction, she threw herself into the movement.

And at Trent she met Renato Curcio, an introverted, studious, somewhat melancholy young man. Margherita's mother thought her daughter became involved with him because of her generous nature. Milena Cagol attributed her sister's interest in Curcio to intellectual affinity. Curcio had a gift for words, and Margherita was impressed by his intellectual rigor and righteous anger. She and he shared certain traits: a deep seriousness about life, an acute moral sense, fierce determination and an unwillingness to compromise. Margherita was small, but only seemed fragile. 'If Margherita started down a path', her sister said, 'she was convinced it was the right one and would go down it to the end. Once having chosen, she had no more doubts. It was the others who erred'.[17] The future co-founder of the Red Brigades, Alberto Franceschini, who knew Margherita well, saw the same certitude in her. She was, he said, 'full of the wish to live, to do: if she decided to reach an objective, whatever it might have been, no obstacle would stop her'. She wanted 'to do everything and right away'.[18]

During the unrest at Trent, Margherita and Curcio came to believe that the problems of Italian society were the direct result of economic arrangements. Being disposed to do things in a thorough-going way, she and he found the solution in a commitment to left-wing ideology, and for them the lodestar became the (perceived) needs of the oppressed, the working class. It was the old story of susceptible personalities who, anxious to do good, desperate for moral and intellectual certitudes in a troubled and

confused time, swallowed uncritically the false advertisements of
Marxist-Leninism, to which they then grappled themselves with
hoops of steel.

After the intellectual affinity that first brought them together, a
deep emotional bond developed between Margherita and Curcio.
Her sister said:

> Renato was very important for Margherita. He was her only
> man. She loved him profoundly and he loved her with equal
> intensity. However, it is not possible to say that it was only
> Renato who changed Margherita, not even politically. When
> they met, neither of the two had a precise political orientation.
> They matured together. Many now say, she went along behind
> him, followed his ideas. It is not true. Margherita was an
> intelligent girl, perfectly aware of what she did ... It was a
> choice.[19]

Even after Margherita had begun her journey towards radicalism, she remained to her family the 'sweet, affectionate and normal
Margherita' she had always been. She and Curcio came to stay
with Milena and her family, ate big meals and passed the time in
idle conversation. Curcio was accepted in the family just as the
husbands of Margherita's two sisters had been. Margherita and
Renato made no effort to justify their political ideas in the family,
where politics was a matter of no importance.

For Margherita, however, in the pressure cooker of Trent, radical
politics had become the central concern of her life. She toiled away
on the journal *Political Work* while Renato traveled to study the
exploitation of the working class elsewhere. Late in 1968 Margherita wrote to Yolanda Curcio that she and Renato faced a decisive
choice – whether or not to join a revolutionary party.[20] This was
the Communist Party of Italy (Marxist-Leninist), a miniscule group
of pro-Chinese and anti-democratic intellectuals. Curcio, Margherita and the editors of *Political Work* joined the party, but the
moment was ineptly chosen, for the party was even then on the
edge of collapse as a result of internal bickering. In December the
party split up.

By the summer of 1969 Curcio and Margherita had reached the
point of a truly decisive choice. *Political Work* was dead, and the
adventure with the Communist Party (Marxist-Leninist) had been
a fiasco. Renato and Margherita were looking for a new organiza-

tion and new methods by which to promote the revolution. They decided to move to Milan and to carry out there their rapidly maturing revolutionary program. This time the decision was not a false start; in Milan they would find what they were seeking, and, unimaginable though it would have seemed at the time, the country would be shaken by the consequences for years thereafter. But before leaving Trent Margherita took her degree. Then the two of them got married. When the oral examination on Margherita's thesis was over, she saluted the professors with a closed fist.[21]

FROM THE COMMUNIST HEARTLAND

The other main component of the early *Brigate Rosse* came from Reggio Emilia in the region of Emilia-Romagna.[22] Whereas Trent is a Christian Democratic zone, in Reggio Emilia the overwhelming presence is that of the PCI. Since the rise of the socialist movement in the late nineteenth century, Reggio has always been devoted to the socialist cause, and, in particular, to the Communist Party version thereof after the PCI's founding in 1921. During the Second World War the partisan struggle was very bitter in and around Reggio, and the future *brigatisti* grew up steeped in the traditions and myths that came out of that experience. The Resistance was not merely a military struggle in Reggio; it was to have been the first step on the road to a socialist society. This dream died very slowly. After the war the PCI took over the city and that whole area of the country (the 'red belt', – the regions of Emilia-Romagna, Tuscany and Umbria), which it has controlled ever since. If you are not connected to the PCI, you are on the margins of public life; if you are a member, on the other hand, you can be suffocated by the embrace of the earth-mother, the party.

Alberto Franceschini was the organizer and the dominant personality among the rebellious *Reggiani*. His background suggested more clearly than Renato Curcio's the course his life would take. Franceschini was born in 1947 into a decidedly Communist family. His father, Carlo, had spent time in prison for anti-Fascist activity, had been a partisan and had worked for the General Italian Labor Confederation (the CGIL), the main labor union, which was dominated by the PCI, and for the party itself. If Carlo was not exactly a Stalinist, he ably impersonated the role. After Alberto's terrorist career had come to an end, Carlo continued to defend his son because of the purity of his intentions. This kind of thinking was not unique to Carlo. In Yolanda Curcio's mind, too, her son was not a criminal because he was an idealist who had never acted for money.

Alberto Franceschini attended university in Bologna, the capital city of the Communist domain. He never completed his studies, however, for along the way he lost all interest in obtaining a bourgeois degree. At an early age he became involved in political activity in the Italian Communist Youth Federation (the FGCI), the national youth organization of the PCI. The 'myth of Che', as Alberto put it, overtook him and others in 1967. He frequented a group of left-wing Catholic activists and the FGCI. Said Alberto:

> There were 50 of us friends ... We dressed like Guevarists ... We also had a flag, of red silk with at the top the signatures of the Vietnamese delegation that came to Reggio for May Day of '68. It accompanied us everywhere, in demonstrations and during trips in the mountains. Once a fascist stole it, but his terrorized friends returned it to us with apologies. And Saturday nights, to pass the time, we diverted ourselves by going to the bars to beat up those few right-wingers that there were in the city.[23]

Alberto had concluded by 1968 that Italian democracy ('these pseudo-democratic institutions')[24] was worthless. He believed that the PCI should be energetically promoting the cause of the protesting students, the cause of revolution that the party professed to believe in. The PCI, he concluded, was being weak and dishonest. He put it this way:

> The peaceful road to socialism truly existed, they [the PCI leaders] said. It was only necessary to accept the rules of the game and one day we would have won because we were the stronger and more determined. But if I had accepted this logic, I would have betrayed my grandfather and his ideals, together with my wish to live in a different world ... Many of my comrades at the Youth Federation thought as I did: we did not listen to those in the Party who advised us to remain calm because the moment for weapons had not yet arrived. It was necessary, they said, first to weaken the bourgeoisie with the parliamentary struggle and then to arm ourselves to conquer the victory. We considered these the speeches of well-camouflaged

opportunists or of ingenuous dreamers who had understood nothing of the path that the Party was pursuing.[25]

Alberto and his friends became increasingly isolated within the FGCI and finally, in 1969, a definite rupture took place. He and his friends formed the so-called 'Group of the Apartment'. Some former PCI types attended the group's meetings, some who were still loyal to the party but open to dialogue, and some dissenting Catholics, of whom there were a notable number in those feverish times.

In the circle of impatient young Communists around Franceschini were a number of *Reggiani* who were to play major, often very bloody roles in the drama of the *Brigate Rosse* and whose names are unfortunately all too well known to Italians. Although it became fashionable for a time for some observers to accuse the terrorists of being *figli di papà*, members of the upper classes at play in the fields of revolution, most of these *Reggiani*, like many of the *brigatisti* over the years, had modest family backgrounds. For example, Lauro Azzolini, Fabrizio Pelli, Tonino Paroli and Franco Bonisoli all had experience as workers. Prospero Gallinari, ultimately the most notorious, was the son of a small farmer who worked on the farm, then briefly in a factory in Milan and took part in many demonstrations.

The 'Group' quickly grew extreme. Franceschini and the others traveled to Milan and Turin and received visitors from there, and thus learned what collectives of workers and students were doing in the great cities, where, for someone interested in a working-class revolution, the action really was. Franceschini met and became close friends with Renato Curcio. Some members of the 'Group' abandoned it because of what they deemed its growing detachment from reality. But Franceschini and the others were determined to prove at all costs that they, not the PCI, were the keepers of the revolutionary flame.

So it was that the 'Group', too, eventually reached the point of decision – whether or not to leave inhospitable Reggio and take part in the establishment of an organization that would lead the working class to revolt. Many did leave, spurred on by a 'myth of the worker'. This myth, Franceschini said,

[w]as the patrimony of our past culture, and among everyone, we were the most working-class oriented. So much so that as

brigatisti we gave ourselves a salary, regulating ourselves according to what a worker on the Fiat line earned. When, after some
struggle, the workers of Turin obtained a wage increase, we too
increased our monthly pay. Nothing of what we did would have
been possible without the myth of the working class. And we
imagined a prospective of a world populated by workers.[26]

Franceschini was the first to depart, in the summer of 1970, when
he left for Milan, where he lived in a commune of office workers
from the corporation Sit-Siemens, which was also the home of
Mario Moretti, who, together with Franceschini, Curcio and Margherita Cagol, comprised the key founders of the *Brigate Rosse*. In
1971 Franceschini burned his boats, as he put it, by failing to
appear when called for military service.

In 1984 Franceschini, Franco Bonisoli and another *Reggiano*,
Roberto Ognibene, looked back. More than ten years before, they
recalled, they had left Reggio, considering themselves volunteers
in a war. They, and many others with them, had believed that the
time had come finally to bring about the dream that had inspired
their grandfathers and their fathers from Emilia, that land of
protest and passion.[27]

AT THE SEASHORE, 1969

In July 1969, Renato Curcio wrote to his mother to announce that
Margherita would shortly receive her degree and that they would
then be getting married and leaving Trent. The marriage ceremony
'will be a fast, fast thing without useless formalities. We are putting
aside any bourgeois tinsel and going . . .'. A postscript from Margherita, of a personal, bourgeois kind:

I am very content to be getting married . . . With Renato life will
be very unpredictable, but this makes me enthusiastic. You
know, in this period I have not had much time to think about it,
but now that I am writing to you, I feel myself taken by a
transport of life, of joy, of love.[28]

They got married in church, which seemed natural to everyone.
Margherita's sister said: 'Margherita . . . had an enormous need to
give, give, give. And Curcio, who had grown up without a true

family, had a need to receive. It was a very profound love . . . one of those that naturally end in marriage'.[29]

The couple went off for a honeymoon-vacation. Margherita sent Yolanda Curcio a postcard and some photos of Renato and herself on holiday.[30] This is a peculiar image, but revolutionaries too need to rest from their labors: thus, every August throughout their history, the Red Brigades would suspend the armed struggle and go away with everyone else. Renato and Margherita were making plans for their life in Milan: not the plans of typical newly-weds; their plans were for the revolution. She and he thought themselves farsighted and secure in their ideas, but, on the beach that summer, they did not foresee the tribulation that awaited them nor the suffering they would cause the country.

2

Progress and its Discontents

The disorder that began with *il sessantotto* was on a scale and of a resilience without equals in the industrialized world. Though everyone recalls the French '68, that revolt ended after only a few months, while the Italian student protest as a virtually universal phenomenon began to subside only by 1970. Moreover, the legacy of the student unrest in Italy was uniquely profound. For years afterwards, though there were a mass of non-activists, and a small minority of right-wing extremists, many thousands of Italian students continued to advocate extreme left-wing ideology and march through the streets and do battle with the police. In the first half of the 1970s demonstrations in Milan alone could, on occasion, enlist the participation of 30 000 or 50 000, and it was not unusual for these demonstrations to end in violence. A variety of radical political groups flourished among students, intellectuals and workers, groups that had sprung up during *il sessantotto* and that refused to abandon the cause of revolution. Among these groups and among many intellectuals, students and workers, the goal of a violent revolution against capitalism was accepted without qualm and had become something more than merely fashionable; it had become a passion. Accordingly, these groups practiced politics uncompromisingly and often violently. Again in contrast with other countries, the working class in large numbers joined in the dissent, beginning with a positive explosion in 1969, easily the worst breakdown in labor-management relations in the whole post-war period and one whose effects would be felt for many years to follow. And in 1977, another revolt of national dimensions burst out on the nation's campuses. In short, the seeds of left-wing ideology that had been planted in 1967–8 and that in other countries withered or were swept away, in Italy rooted and grew, and the result was a decade of widespread radicalism, of Marxist-Leninist rhetoric and practice in the streets and piazze. And the

16

1970s became also a period of terrorism in the narrow sense.

This radicalism was not a historical accident. The stimulants were many: the Vietnam war, the Frankfurt school of philosophers, the student movements in Germany, the United States and France, activism in the Third World, the Cultural Revolution in China, South American revolutionary movements, the 'myth of Che', the 'myth of the working class', and so on. These influences were felt as well in other countries that never were to know the devastating instability and violence that Italy endured in the 1970s and early 1980s. Thus, to understand the Italian case you must seek out additional explanations, the springs of revolutionary desire that were unique to the Italian condition, causes that are to be found in the deficiencies and injustices of Italian society, in the shortcomings of the political system, and in the long and potent revolutionary tradition in Italian political life.

In the mid-1960s the economic engine was sputtering. The rate of growth declined, employment grew very slowly, productivity was down, and, in contrast with the boom years, inflation began to afflict the economy. These were the signs of an incipient crisis.

Though the bloom was now fading from the economic miracle, no objective observer could deny that the country had been transformed. The reaction of the radicals of the late 1960s, however, was wilfully myopic, as well as contradictory. On the one hand they despised the success of the capitalist economy – the refrigerators, Fiats and TV sets that ordinary families were beginning to be able to afford. On the other hand the activists, many of whom were too young to have known the poverty of pre-war Italy or the desperation of the post-war years, took the new Italy for granted and gave scant thought to the means by which the miracle had been achieved. The radicals could not bring themselves to acknowledge that a capitalist economy had produced so vast an improvement in the lives of the people, but were fixed upon the things left undone, and, by contrast, upon the lovely perfections of the theoretical socialist state. That there was much undone, much social injustice, unfortunately could not be denied.

The benefits of the boom had not been distributed evenly among all segments of society and ancient differences between rich and poor had even grown worse. The North was advanced and industrialized. During the boom, millions of southerners had left the countryside for the cities but, even afterwards, the South remained poor, backward, and heavily dependent on agriculture, resembling the Third World more than, say, Denmark. In 1964 the gap between North and South was wider than it had been 100 years before.[1]

The boom created a large, urban, industrial working class. In the 1950s and 1960s there was a massive flight from the rural areas of the center, North and, above all, the South to the great cities of the North, as well as significant emigration. Between 1951 and 1971, the percentage of the labor force working in agriculture declined precipitously (from 43.9 to 18.8 per cent), as over four million persons left the South, mostly headed North.[2] In the cities these immigrants found an escape from the chains of a harsh agricultural life, which was no small thing after centuries of hardship; they did not, however, find the promised land. As dramatized, for instance, in Visconti's film *Rocco and His Brothers*, the country people paid a high price for this sudden urbanization: personal isolation and disorientation, subjection to an environment that was often hostile, conditions that strained the family. As elsewhere in the industrialized world, progress on the whole brought economic benefits and enhanced personal freedom, but many individuals were left in a state of bewilderment about their roles in the world and about social ties that no longer seemed to bind as once they had. Such general difficulties of adjustment were complicated by problems of a very concrete kind. The population of the major cities swelled out of control. Between 1951 and 1966 there was an increase of 5.5 million inhabitants in the larger urban areas. As agricultural land was swallowed up by development, a vast industrial sprawl grew in the triangle Milan-Genoa-Turin, and small businesses and factories sprouted in the fields of the North and center. The authorities in the central government in Rome and in the cities failed to make timely and adequate plans to deal with such great change. Little was done to provide decent housing, transportation, health care or other basic services for the urban immigrants. What housing there was tended to take the form of huge developments in the hinterlands of the great cities, bereft of roads, sewers and other elementary services, where anonymity prevailed and people long accustomed to open fields and living things were confined to concrete blocks and miles of asphalt. Had the mass urbanization happened more slowly, the wrenching side-effects might have been better managed. As it was, a significant part of the new working class in the new metropoli became embittered by the personal costs of the transition to an industrial way of life, believed itself to be exploited, and was simply hostile to the assembly line and the businessman who ran it.

This feeling of exploitation on the part of the immigrants coexisted with exaggerated optimism on the part of others. Although the economic base was, in fact, considerably more shaky than in other countries, it was supposed, by union leaders, for example, that the imbalances of the recent development could be corrected very quickly and painlessly by the application of sudden pressure in the right places. Fuelled by this naïve optimism, unrealistic demands were made upon government and the economy, demands for, for example, higher wages irrespective of productivity or government assumption of the costs of social insurance. The political leadership was incapable of resisting such demands. Politically, it did not pay to say no.[3] This peculiar juxtaposition of feelings of exploitation and of optimism contributed to the mass protest out of which came the terrorism of the late 1960s to the 1980s. No such upheavals occurred at other points in recent history when there were compelling reasons for overwhelming public discontent, during, for example, the far less prosperous, less promising years of Fascist domination, or in the aftermath of the Second World War. The feelings of optimism and feelings of exploitation and frustration interacted like an unstable mixture of volatile gases.

For many young people it was the poverty of the educational system that was most sharply felt. In the post-war period, especially in the decade prior to 1968, the student population expanded greatly and the university ceased to be the preserve of an élite, as the children of the middle and lower-middle classes enrolled in record and growing numbers. By 1968 the number of enrolled students – about half a million – was double that of ten years before, and ten times that of the 1920s. During the late 1960s and 1970s the student population grew by about 13 per cent a year, reaching the figure of a million.[4] This immense social as well as educational emancipation ought to have been a cause for rejoicing rather than, as it became, for worry and dismay. Despite considerable talk, however, the government, as in the case of urban policy, failed to prepare the system for change on this scale. The number of professors in 1968 was not significantly larger than the level of the 1920s, nor did the facilities come anywhere near to meeting the demand. On any given day, lectures might, or might not, be held, depending on whether or not a hall could be found. Students often would have to stand or sit on the floor during lectures for lack of space, or wait a day for a book, if the library were open. Although it clearly knew that it was only compounding the problems, the government in 1969 gave in to demands and approved a system of open admissions. The University of Rome, bloated in the 1970s by over 100 000 students, many times the number for which the school had been intended, became almost surrealistic, or, as one professor put it, a 'Kafka-like castle'.[5] Serious education and study in such conditions ceased to be possible. Many students stayed away, to study on their own – or to do other things. This was just as well; had all enrolled students tried to make use of the facilities, the system would have collapsed.

Furthermore, students who had flooded the university hoping to win the promised place in the middle class saw their dreams quickly crushed. If they found jobs at all, the jobs were apt to be well below the level for which their study had prepared them. Large numbers of students were cast on the sidelines, were *emarginati*. The university became a social ghetto for young people whom the economic system could not absorb, and with the growth of this intellectual proletariat, students began to feel a kinship with the traditional proletariat of Marxist analysis.

There were additional problems. By an old tradition professors enjoyed great power. The professors were 'barons' who gave their lectures (in a formal, non-Socratic style) and collected their pay and often made little attempt to establish contact with students. Many professors had other occupations and devoted only a handful of hours to the school. They were frequently unwilling to countenance any modernization, so that the academic program was often inflexible and out of date. Students felt themselves impotent in the face of a rigid, or, as they put it, authoritarian system, an attitude that degenerated easily into anger at society at large and the embracing of an anti-authoritarian utopianism. There were, moreover, economic disparities. As financial assistance was minimal, many poor students were forced to work rather than attend classes. It was not uncommon for a student to have contact with the school only when he paid his fees and took his examinations. These students often joined the *fuori corso*, those who failed to complete examinations within the normal time but who remained enrolled. In 1965–6 almost 40 per cent of the student population fell into this category. Ultimately, only about one out of four students ever triumphed over the obstacles and emerged from the chaos with a diploma in his hand.[6]

If the Christian Democratic Party (the DC) could claim some credit for having produced, or at least not having prevented, the economic boom, it also had to take responsibility for the social problems that had been left in its wake. The Italian state is, to a large degree, the creature of the Christian Democrats. Had DC government been strong and efficient, the social dislocations that accompanied the economic transformation might have been avoided, or, at least, mitigated. But strength and efficiency are just what government in Italy has lacked.

The weakness of Italian government is partly structural and historical. Constitutional arrangements established in the immediate post-war years ensured governmental instability and inefficiency, within what has proven to be overall a very stable democratic system. Parliament is selected by proportional representation and there are many voices that attract support from the voters. The best any party has ever done was in 1948, when the Christian Democrats received 48.5 per cent of the vote. The support for the DC has since declined to about one-third of the total; Communist support has grown and until recently was only slightly less; and the remaining votes are divided up among an array (always described by foreigners as 'bewildering') of other parties, of which the Socialists (the PSI) are first by a wide margin. From 1947 on (save for an interlude to be touched on later), the Communists have been pariahs on the national level (though not in various localities, Reggio Emilia, for instance). The system has been 'blocked', incapable of producing the change at the helm that is taken for granted in other democratic countries. The government of the country thus has depended for 40 years upon the DC, either alone or in coalition with members of other parties. No government has been possible without the DC, and yet DC incumbency often has been insufficient to ensure the stability of cabinets. The erosion in Christian Democratic popularity since 1948, and the allocation of support among many other parties has meant that the DC has had to look to the Socialists and several tiny parties in order to build coalitions, which, as alliances among political adversaries, have been fractious and fragile. (The chronic internecine warfare within the DC has not helped matters.) On the one hand, the *system* has been stable, with the DC always in charge, but *governments* have been anything but: governments have toppled like bowling pins; to date, the Republic has had 48 administrations. Clearly this is a system crying out for reform, but the memory of fascism, among other things, has prevented any modification of fundamentals.

Between 1947 and 1953 the country was governed by centrist coalitions, with an anti-Communist DC as the focal point. From 1953 on, however, the formula began to unravel in the face of political and electoral changes. The most enlightened DC leaders, like Aldo Moro, began to press for a major alteration in DC strategy. Since an accommodation with the neo-Fascist Italian Social Movement (the MSI) was impossible and the Communists were beyond the pale, the only direction in which the DC could look for political support to reinforce the government was to the left, to the Socialist Party, which, up till then, had been isolated in a fruitless alliance with the Communists.

After a series of half-steps forward, the PSI formally entered into a coalition in 1963, a government led by Prime Minister Aldo Moro. As this marked the first achievement of a share of national power by the socialist movement since its beginnings at the end of the last century (apart from the special coalitions immediately after the Second World War), the working class, farmers, progressives and intellectuals all had great expectations for a significant change in economic and social life, for a levelling of the differences that the boom was not removing on its own. Although these expectations were excessive, and although the record of the center-left governments of the 1960s and early 1970s has probably been unfairly belittled, on critical social and economic issues the center-left experience was a failure. The center-left proposed reforms and issued solemn promises to the four winds, but proved ineffective at carrying out those promises, perhaps most conspicuously in the cases of urban and educational policy. By the late 1960s, as unrest swept through the West, many in Italy had come to believe that reformism as practiced by the Socialist Party could never bring real change. Public discontent with the center-left experiment, and tensions and misgivings within the PSI itself, helped to produce during the troubled 1970s a series of especially weak coalition governments and to create a new obstacle to stability – the phenomenon, lasting from 1968 into the 1980s, of legislatures unable to survive for the full five years of their constitutionally-allotted life.

Another problem was the style of governing of the dominant DC, a style perhaps unique in the democratic world. Aware that there was no chance that the party could be booted from office because there was no practical alternative, the Christian Democrats were pleased to build what the critics called a 'regime', the grasp of which extended not just to the ministries, but to numerous governmental agencies and a vast state-capitalist sector. The results were inefficiency, waste and budgetary problems on a large scale. The DC pursued this practice partly out of a belief in governmental intervention and partly out of a lust for spoils. Votes were effectively purchased in return for official favors. The economic sectors that the government controlled or had an interest in were expanded greatly and the Christian Democrats tended to treat them as the party's private pasture. A characteristic propensity of the DC to flee difficult economic choices by throwing government money or shares of stock at social problems, or at foundering, inefficient companies, had produced, by the 1980s, a situation in which the government literally had its fingers in many pies: along with railroads, the postal service and the like, the government owned or subsidized enterprises producing cakes, muffins, pasta and items of similar strategic importance to the nation. And Christian Democrats have also often been caught up in obscure political or financial machinations, and yet have frequently escaped jail, because, people charged, the power of the 'regime' extended into the halls of justice as well. That these defects were not the fantasies of cynical reporters or dyspeptic opposition politicians was conceded in the 1980s, when the party secretary began a much-publicized campaign of renovation within Christian Democratic ranks. The secretary argued to the voters that the Christian Democrats had done more than any other party on the subject of internal reform. To which one response might have been that this was a questionable cause for pride, since the Christian Democrats had more need of reform than anyone else.

The accumulation of many serious social problems by the end of the 1960s called for a vigorous response on the part of the political system, which promised such a response but failed to deliver. To a great many students, intellectuals and members of the working class, nothing seemed to change except the identity of the Prime Minister, which changed all too often. The institutions of Italy were thus in a substantially weaker position than the French, German, or American, to ride out the storm of *il sessantotto* without major damage. This helps to explain the large-scale breakdown in civility in the years after 1967–8. It helps to explain why radicalism spread from the campuses to the factories, and why, years after the student unrest had come to a peaceful end in France and the United States, policemen and journalists were dying in the streets of Rome or Milan at the hands of young revolutionaries.

Those who were dissatisfied with the social and political situation in Italy in 1967–8 and thereafter did not have to search far to find inspiration for a very different vision. Political violence had not been uncommon in Italy's past. Italy has had a long tradition of banditry with political overtones. In the nineteenth century there had been the secret societies and the anarchists. Bakunin had spent time in Italy working on how to generate an anarchist uprising there, and Italy produced important anarchist theorists of its own, such as Malatesta. The anarchists also put their theories into practice, most spectacularly with the 1900 assassination of King Umberto I. The Fascists, of course, institutionalized violence. More important to the development of dissent in the late 1960s and 1970s, though, was the socialist heritage. In Italy, the notion of the replacement of capitalism through socialist revolution was no late, trendy innovation.[7]

Since the late nineteenth century the socialist question has never been far from the top of the political agenda in Italy. With early industrialization, an embryonic working class was born and the socialist idea spread, quickly and widely. The Socialists also gathered support among agricultural laborers, very important in the overwhelmingly agricultural country Italy then was. The movement suffered from a chronic illness not unique to Italy – fierce, often petty discord between unreconstructed revolutionaries and reformers, like Filippo Turati, who were willing to pursue social change through democratic means. Nevertheless, the power of the Socialists increased rapidly. They won control of thousands of local governments and, after 1919, were the largest group in parliament. Even fascism was linked to the socialist question, not only because fascism in its earliest stages contained some left-leaning ideas (Mussolini himself having been at one time a leading Socialist and the fire-breathing editor of the Socialist daily, *Avanti!*), but also because Mussolini achieved power by exploiting fear of the Socialist menace among industrialists, farmers, the church and other important forces in society. By 1914 the Socialists were indeed quite radical.

In 1914, during the so-called 'Red Week', a million or more people rioted in the streets, particularly in the region of Romagna. There was a general strike and widespread looting, a red flag flew over the city hall of socialist Bologna and Romagna declared itself an independent republic. 100 000 troops had to be sent to Romagna to restore order. In 1919–20, peasants seized land and, in September 1920, hundreds of factories in the North were occupied by workers who were agitating for the formation of committees of laborers that would participate in the running of the factories as a first step towards the eventual take-over of the means of production. It was a reflection of the political importance of socialism in this period that the violence of Fascist squads – the *squadristi* – was directed primarily at the Socialist Party, beginning with the burning of the offices of *Avanti!* in 1919. The Socialists were the principal, though, in the end, a surmountable, obstacle to Mussolini on his road to power. It was only after Mussolini had survived the storm that followed the Fascist murder of the Socialist deputy, Giacomo Matteotti, that the Fascist regime could be said to have consolidated its stranglehold over the country.

After the Second World War, the Socialists were the second largest party in the country. They remained leftist on policy matters and joined the Communists in a popular front that endured for years. Gradually, however, the Socialist Party evolved into a more democratic, less ideologically-rigid organization, until finally it joined with the Christian Democrats in the governments of the center-left.

Since the end of the Second World War the Communist Party has been the most important element in the socialist equation. Founded in 1921 by Socialists discontented with what they considered the lack of revolutionary resolve of the Socialist Party, the PCI was important to the defeat of the Fascists and the liberation of the country from the Nazis, which brought the party the trust and gratitude of a sizeable segment of public opinion. The PCI's political strength grew considerably. At the war's end the party had 400 000 card-carrying members. Within a few years it had surpassed the Socialists to become the second most powerful party, and by 1947 it had achieved dominance over the major union organization, the CGL. In the 1950s the PCI reached the impressive membership level of two million. During all these years, using its daily newspaper, its influence upon the CGIL, its clout in parliament and in certain local governments, its uniquely efficient organization, the PCI spread its message – the evil of capitalism and the need for a socialist revolution.

There is even something of a far-left, extra-parliamentary tradition in Italy. In July 1945, for example, some former partisans, upset at what they regarded as the government's leniency toward Fascists, summarily executed 53 Fascist prisoners. Early the following year partisans once again took to the hills, especially around Reggio Emilia, and established armed groups to attack Fascist and capitalist targets. In the late 1940s a group called the 'Red Flying Squad', which had been the name of a formation during the Resistance, busied itself issuing popular justice (from pillorying to killing) to ex-Fascists and capitalists.[8]

The foregoing illustrates the extent to which the idea of socialism has pervaded Italian politics for 100 years. Socialist theory has become profoundly intertwined in the fabric of political life. The students and workers of the late 1960s and 1970s had long been accustomed to the ideas that socialism and social progress were synonymous, and that a working-class Utopia could be and should be reached by means of a revolution against capitalism. Although most Italians were opposed to Marxism, a sizeable minority, of workers, students and intellectuals, were firm believers. To be a socialist was not considered scandalous or even remarkable, and Marxist-Leninism was not, as it was, for instance, in the United States, an intellectual ornament of cocktail-party radicals. It should have come as no surprise, therefore, that extra-parliamentarians in the late 1960s and 1970s, in a period of great public unease, uncertainty and social change, should have taken the ancient ideas of socialism to heart and should have raised in a new context the age-old conflict between social democracy and revolutionary socialism.

By the late 1960s the Socialist Party had cast its lot with the Christian Democrats, with disappointing results on the balance sheet of social reform. Existing political circumstances could, it seemed, produce only more Christian Democratic *malgoverno* or, at best, a government with a pale social-democratic tint. To those influenced by the socialist tradition, the only conceivable alternative offered by the system was the Communist Party. But the chances of the PCI ever coming to power remained slim. More important to the most impassioned on the left – Renato Curcio, Margherita Cagol, Alberto Franceschini and others like them – the Marxist-Leninism of the PCI had become a fraud.

The Communist Party has changed in the post-war years. The change has been slow, laborious, reluctant and ambiguous, but it has been change all the same.[9]

In the immediate aftermath of the war the position of the party on domestic issues, rhetoric aside, reflected a recognition that armed revolution was not practicable. Palmiro Togliatti, the long-time PCI secretary, who was nothing if not shrewd, realized that the party would have to collaborate with progressive non-Communists and avoid alienating the church and faithful Catholics. The PCI thus co-operated with Socialists and Christian Democrats in the development of a single labor confederation, the CGIL. The PCI was a member of cabinets from April 1944 to May 1947, and Togliatti himself served as Minister of Justice, and when the Communists (and Socialists) left the government it was quite against their will. The Communists were members of the so-called 'constitutional arc' of political groups that drafted and approved the Constitution of the new republic. The PCI voted to include the Lateran Accords of 1929 in the Constitution, even though the Accords had been one of Mussolini's more clever achievements and had granted the church a privileged position in Italian life. Togliatti conceived of the PCI as a party with strong roots in Italian society, and so membership was not restricted to believing Marxist-Leninists, despite Stalin's polite advice to the contrary.

While such compromising was going on, the PCI followed the Soviet line on international questions and praised Soviet society as a model of socialism and Stalin as a benevolent father figure. But on this front, too, change was not long in coming. Khrushchev's denunciation of Stalin at the 20th Congress of the Soviet Communist Party in 1956 rocked the PCI. Not long afterwards Togliatti asserted that blind imitation of the Soviet model was not obligatory and that the watchword was 'polycentrism'. The 'Italian path to socialism' was being charted. Thereafter, the PCI opposed re-establishment of a central organization of world Communism (the Comintern having been dissolved in 1943 and the Cominform in 1956). In the early 1960s the Italian Communists stated that, in the event of a PCI election victory, they would retain parliament and a multiparty system. In 1964, just before his death, Togliatti wrote a memorandum that insisted upon the autonomy of Communist parties around the world, the need to increase democratic freedoms and co-operation with non-Communists and the right to criticize socialist societies. In 1968 the PCI openly disapproved of the Soviet invasion of Czechoslovakia, something it had not dared to do in the case of the suppression of the Hungarian revolt of 1956. In the 1970s this process continued in highly visible form under the leadership of PCI secretary Enrico Berlinguer. It was Berlinguer who developed, for example, the PCI's theory of an 'historic compromise' with the Christian Democrats and the idea of 'eurocommunism'.

Some opportunism there surely was in the PCI's voyage away from Stalinism. Though advertised as a choice based upon principle, the PCI's evolution also happened to coincide very neatly with a course dictated by unvarnished considerations of politics and power. Moreover, the PCI's policy gave rise to an obvious 'duality', a professed loyalty to democratic values on the one hand, and, on the other, a refusal to jettison altogether an ideology that was simply irreconcilable with those values.[10] This duality was expressed in the advocacy of inherently contradictory notions, like the goal of a parliamentary, revolutionary path,[11] the clinging to principles – democratic centralism, for instance – that only a Marxist-Leninist theoretician could reconcile with faith in democracy. By the second half of the 1970s Italian non-Communist voters no longer regarded the Communist Party as a serious threat to democracy,[12] and, by way of a further barometrical reading, the level-headed secretary of the level-headed Republican Party, Giorgio LaMalfa, has more than once declared his conviction that the PCI has been fully converted to democratic ways. Perhaps these are instances of self-delusion, but what is important for present purposes is that, by the late 1960s, the PCI had changed, whether sincerely or not, from the days when it hoped to transform the country into a Bulgaria on the Mediterranean. The radicals of the late 1960s and 1970s took this change at face value. The PCI's failure to attack the bourgeois state boldly amounted to revisionism, to a betrayal of the working class.

In the aftermath of the PCI's reaction to the un-deification of Stalin, dissidents began to leave the party, some traveling to the right and others, those who took the party's propaganda and its proclaimed Marxism seriously, to the left. The left-wing dissidents created alternative organizations and found elsewhere an inspirational model of revolutionary rigor.

In 1961 the magazine *Red Notebooks* was begun by a group of former Socialists and Communists. Stridently anti-capitalist, *Red Notebooks* argued that the capitalists, recognizing their inability to repress the working-class struggle altogether, had managed to divert it into safe channels. Strikes, for instance, were deemed acceptable, so long as they were scheduled in advance. The suggestion for wildcat strikes that the 'masters' could not control was taken up by some workers in the fall of 1969. *Red Notebooks*, and like-minded journals that proliferated after it,[13] hoped to shape the course of events in the late 1960s and afterwards by emphasizing the working class and its problems, and by importing into Italy news about revolutionary ideas and developments from abroad, from the leading Third World centers of revolutionary activity and above all from China. China, with its condemnation of the Soviet Union and the PCI, with its Cultural Revolution and its Red Guards, was a powerful symbol of revolutionary seriousness for Italian radicals like Renato Curcio, occupying a position analogous to the one filled by the Soviet fatherland in the hearts of the Italian Communists of the 1920s, 1930s and 1940s. Accordingly, a number of little Maoist parties sprang up in Italy, such as the Italian Communist Party (Marxist-Leninist) to which Curcio and Margherita briefly belonged.[14]

Out of this intellectual ferment, and out of the turmoil of the late 1960s, emerged several extreme-left, extra-parliamentary groups that were to play leading roles in the agitation of the 1970s. These groups were impressed by Maoism but not in thrall to it and were more sophisticated than the Maoist parties. What most distinguished these groups from the Maoist parties and what accounted for their far greater success was their strong emphasis upon the leading role of the working class in the revolutionary process. Among these *gruppuscoli* were 'Workers' Avant-garde', the former dissident PCI members of 'Il Manifesto', and, most important, 'Lotta Continua' ('Continuous Struggle') and 'Workers' Power'. Founded in 1969, 'Lotta Continua', among whose leaders were two prominent contemporaries of Renato Curcio at Trent, believed in a violent socialist revolution. For 'Lotta Continua', the true driving force behind the revolution was to be, not the bureaucratic avant-garde of Marxist-Leninist tradition, but the working class itself. As one leader put it, 'our choice is ... that of being thoroughly and totally within the violent, brutal, and not very elegant logic of the struggle of the proletariat for its emancipation'.[15] To 'Lotta Continua' the unions and the PCI were anti-revolution and merely stifled the just opposition of the workers. The group concentrated its agitation and propaganda (through *Lotta Continua*, its journal) on the workers of the industrialized North. By 1972, 'Lotta Continua' had offices in 150 locations in north-central Italy and a security apparatus or 'service of order', which, however, did not always remain faithful to its name.

The general ideological fixations of 'Workers' Power' were somewhat similar. Its central notion was that of 'workers' autonomy', the independent activity of the working class (that is, independent of the PCI and the unions) as the main force in the process of revolution. Among the leaders of 'Workers' Power' were Professors Oreste Scalzone, Franco Piperno and Antonio Negri, all of whom subsequently participated in what investigators described as terrorist activity. Negri, a cultivated intellectual, became the leading domestic theoretician of terrorism.

Though not terrorist groups themselves, these *gruppuscoli*, especially 'Lotta Continua' and 'Workers' Power', played a critical role in creating the climate in which terrorism was to grow. These groups stoked the fires of rebellion, spread the revolutionary ideology and myths, and served as way-stations on the line to terrorism, and 'Lotta Continua' and 'Workers' Power' for a time lent rhetorical support to the activities of the *Brigate Rosse*. To these extra-parliamentarians, the PCI was a major enemy. For them and for the members of the *Brigate Rosse*, the contest with the PCI was not merely theoretical; it took concrete form in the factories of Milan and Turin, where these radicals sought to wean the workers away from the stultifying influence of the Communist Party.

There are many ironies to the story of the *Brigate Rosse*. One of these is that the two basic enemies of Curcio, Margherita Cagol, Franceschini and the rest – the corrupt Christian Democratic State and the revisionist Communists – coalesced in response to forces generated by the *Brigate Rosse* themselves. On 16 March 1978 the Red Brigades were to kidnap Aldo Moro, then President of the Christian Democrats and the principal architect of a policy of *détente* between the Communists and the DC. That same day, parliament, with the votes of the Communists, was to support a government of national solidarity. The two great rivals, the Christian Democrats and the Communists, were to co-operate with one another – to battle the *Brigate Rosse*.

3

A Little Private War of Our Own

THE HOT AUTUMN

The decades-long quiescence of the Italian labor movement came to a resounding and definitive end in 1969, in particular during the 'hot autumn', a term that did not refer to a meteorological anomaly.[1] National contracts were up for renewal that fall and the workers were determined for the first time to grab a major share of the benefits of economic progress. There was a marked ideological tenor to the discontent. The young and unskilled immigrants on the assembly lines, and the working class as a whole, had heard the siren call of the student revolt, and thus demands were made for wage increases as an 'independent variable', an equal wage increase for all, and the like. For these reasons this proved to be no ordinary labor-management dispute. To win their demands the union movement undertook strikes and agitation in the fall of 1969 on a scale and of a vehemence without parallel since the occupation of the factories in 1920. A record-breaking 303 million hours were lost in 1969, as more than 7.5 million workers struck.[2] For strikes there was no place like Italy.

An important innovation of the time was the formation within the generally angry working class of extreme, highly-politicized fringe groups of workers and extra-parliamentary radicals. At first, paralleling what had occurred within the student movement, these 'Cubs' (for 'unitary rank-and-file committee') and 'study groups' made relatively modest demands, but quickly became bitterly anti-capitalist and anti-union. For example, the Study Group (Sit-Siemens), out of which were to come a number of *brigatisti*, challenged the union establishment over the issue of salary increases, demanding 'a salary unconnected to productivity or a particular task [which] must be the first step ... toward the abolition of salaried labor.'[3] These 'autonomous groups' employed

31

unauthorized, spontaneous disruptive tactics in the factories – wildcat strikes, marches, the blocking of deliveries, sabotage and violence directed at management. The groups also promoted 'workers' autonomy' in the forms of general assemblies and councils of delegates elected directly by the workers. The incendiary effect of the rhetoric and actions of the 'Cubs' and 'study groups' contributed greatly to the radicalization of the mainstream labor movement, the leadership of which was forced to race furiously merely in order to keep pace with its membership. Thus, industry, capitalism and the entrepreneurial class were under unprecedentedly heavy fire in 1969 from the official labor opposition and from profoundly discontented and intransigent elements to the left of it.

The months of strikes and marches and disorder ended in victory for the workers, as first the state capitalist sector and then, pressed hard by the government, the private sector capitulated. New labor agreements were signed that granted the workers huge pay increases (21 per cent in industry as a whole in 1970 alone), improvements in the wage indicization system (the *scala mobile*), a reduction in the work-week and other benefits.[4] Unfortunately, this steep rise in labor costs occurred at an economically delicate moment of slower growth and rising prices. In addition, early in 1970, under the influence of the 'hot autumn', a 'workers statute' was enacted. The 'statute' protected the unions against management interference with their right to organize and conduct union activity, and, in this respect, was an historic, long-overdue advance. The legislation, however, also severely limited the ability of management to lay off workers or to monitor sick leave, thereby hindering the efficient deployment of labor and maintaining an official shield for absenteeism. Absenteeism subsequently reached absurd levels and productivity declined further.[5]

The 'hot autumn' also left a dismal psychological legacy. The signing of labor contracts did not placate the aroused feelings of the workers and 'permanent confrontation' overtook many a factory floor. For years afterward the factories were beleaguered by ideologically-motivated protests, absenteeism, and intimidation of management; production was halted on insignificant pretexts and by sabotage; businessmen and factory foremen were physically threatened and the threats were carried out with dismaying frequency. The continuing strife coincided with, and aggravated, a series of serious economic problems. In the 1980s labor leaders repented of their sins. But in 1969 and thereafter a sense of realism was difficult to sustain. Everyone was throwing rocks, rhetorical or real.[6]

Although the working class was now at the center of things, the students did not return to their books. Within the Student Movement the process of radicalization accelerated. The Movement preached a philosophy that it called 'Marxism-Leninism-Thoughts of Mao'. It urged the destruction of the bourgeois state and attacked the PCI for its revisionism. The Movement aimed to become a national organization and to ally itself with the working class in the class struggle. It failed to achieve these aims. Still, in the early 1970s it was an important player on the scene, especially in Milan, where it could mobilize large crowds of students and kept the city under a more or less constant barrage of demonstrations in the name of such slogans as, 'The bourgeois state will not change; it must be brought down'. The Movement in Milan had a directorate, a propaganda contingent and a security force. The security force, like those of 'Lotta Continua' and other new left groups, consisted of the toughest members of the group, who, in helmets or ski masks, using metal bars, chains and the like, provided 'democratic self-defense' against the police and engaged in what was known as 'militant anti-fascism', a euphemism for bashing the skulls of neo-Fascists. The security apparatuses degenerated into forces with a taste for gratuitous violence, the most absurd examples of which were skirmishes between the security forces of the Movement and those of new left groups.

The new left groups were directly involved in the labor agitation in the fall of 1969. The most important of these, 'Lotta Continua', was a product of this agitation. 'Lotta Continua', 'Workers' Power' and other groups were present at the factories and in the streets, urging the workers to seek not compromise but confrontation in pursuit of revolution. During the 'hot autumn' 'Lotta Continua' proposed a 'cultural revolution in Italian factories' that would turn upside down the traditional organization of labor. The 'masters' had power, 'Lotta Continua' argued, because the workers had accepted a situation that they had the force to change. The workers must lose their fear of the bosses; the bosses must become afraid of them! At Fiat's Mirafiori plant, workers in fact forced the bosses to walk a gauntlet and beat and spat on them, and similar incidents took place elsewhere. The emphasis upon the factory and 'workers' autonomy' of 'Lotta Continua', 'Workers' Power' and others attracted students, who abandoned the Student Movement because they deemed it no more than an insular talking shop.[7]

To the unrest of the working class, the students, and the extra-parliamentary groups, was added the violence of the far right, which made for a very explosive combination. For years prior to the late 1960s two different spirits had co-existed in the neo-Fascist movement: the quasi-respectable parliamentarianism of the Italian Social Movement, the political party that had arisen out of the ashes of fascism, and the lust for violence of right-wing extremists, such as the members of the terrorist groups 'New Order' and 'National Avant-garde'.[8] These different spirits reacted differently to the advance of the left in the late 1960s. While the MSI sought to reap political advantage from the situation, the extremists on the right began to apply some very undemocratic methods of response. The result was that the period of left-wing tumult and terrorism in the late 1960s to the early 1980s was also a period of right-wing violence and right-wing terrorism. These two extremisms battled each other and fed off each other. The one was bound up with the other in a dance of death.

There were two levels to the neo-Fascist violence. The first was violence in the streets, especially in Rome and Milan. The State University of Milan was repeatedly raided by neo-Fascists and the University of Rome was home to legions of right-wing extremists, and in both places left-wing students were assaulted frequently. There were attacks upon newspaper offices, Communist and Socialist headquarters, schools and left-wing clubs. Piazza San Babila in the heart of Milan was the hub of neo-Fascist activity there. If you looked as though you might be a 'red' it was unwise for you to go there unarmed or unescorted.

Against this backdrop right-wing extremists also committed crimes of a different order. Beginning late in 1969, far-right terrorist groups, like 'New Order', 'National Avant-garde' and 'Black Order', perpetrated devastating bombings in public places. The propensity of the new Fascists to use bombs against the public distinguished them from the terrorists of the far left. As a general rule, the left-wing terrorists did not use bombs and did not kill indiscriminately, concentrating on the wounding or execution of carefully selected, 'guilty' targets. What the far right desired was so much, so widely-diffused, and such serious social upheaval as would produce an authoritarian transformation of the national government, in which, it was expected, the 'silent majority', out of a longing for public order, would calmly acquiesce, as the leading political forces and much of the general public had acquiesced in the Duce's arrival in Rome in 1922. This plan was served by blood and bodies; whose blood and whose bodies were matters of secondary importance. The forces of the far right thus achieved a terrible primacy: between 1969 and 1980, the majority of those killed by terrorists in Italy were the victims of extreme right-wing groups.[9]

Another aspect to the activities of the far right in these years was intrigue involving the armed forces and the secret services. Fears about such plots were widespread on the extra-parliamentary left and among adherents of the parliamentary left and other political forces. These fears were exaggerated, but, unfortunately, not wholly paranoid. There was, for instance, the SIFAR affair. From 1956 to 1962, under General Giovanni DeLorenzo, the 'Servizio Informazioni Forze Armate' (SIFAR) ('Armed Forces Information Service'), as the military secret service was then called, collected, through surreptitious surveillance and other means, detailed dos-siers on the political inclinations, business activities, private affairs, and so on, of over 150 000 Members of Parliament, political party officials, union leaders and so on. In addition, in the summer of 1964, while the country was being run by a center-left government, General DeLorenzo, then head of the *carabinieri* but still influential in SIFAR, held a series of secret meetings with SIFAR officials and *carabinieri* officers to review certain secret plans that he had formulated. DeLorenzo later claimed that he and the others had merely been discussing precautionary measures against a possible future uprising from the left. It came out, however, that these measures included the arrest of named politicians, labor leaders and others, the occupation of police stations, radio and TV networks, and so on. As was to happen with inquiries into later, similar events, the obscurities surrounding this affair were never entirely cleared up. Nevertheless, it was plain that DeLorenzo had abused his powers (for which he was removed as chief of the army in 1967). Another incident of this kind was the aborted coup attempt led by the notorious 'Black Prince', Junio Valerio Borghese, in December 1970.[10]

Almost without exception, the awful bombings of these years went unpunished. The SIFAR and Borghese episodes and the impunity with which the far right went about its work suggested to the new left, and to many on the old left, that right-wing violence was being tolerated or even promoted by important people and that the bombings were, in a phrase given much currency at the time, 'massacres by the state'. The neo-Fascists, it was said, were in league with extreme elements in the secret services and the army who were upset at the leftward drift in the nation, and a 'strategy of tension' was being orchestrated behind the scenes by obscure conspirators, generals of the armed forces, or generals of industry, or nationally prominent political figures.[11]

In February 1969 a student died during a neo-Fascist assault on a division of the University of Rome occupied by the students. In Milan there were battles at the State University, and, on 25 April 1969, the anniversary of the liberation of Italy, bombs exploded in Milan at the trade exhibition and at the train station, wounding 19. On a single day in August eight bombs went off on trains around the country. In Pisa in October, demonstrators protesting against frequent neo-Fascist violence in the city clashed with the police. A student was killed and many were wounded. On 19 November a police agent was killed during a battle with demonstrators near the State University in Milan.

On 12 December three bombs exploded in Rome; 18 people were injured. Milan was less fortunate. On that day a bombing took place that profoundly shocked the whole country. The bomb went off during business hours in the National Bank of Agriculture in Piazza Fontana. The toll was horrifying: 17 dead and 88 wounded.

The bombing was manifestly the work of extreme neo-Fascists. The police, however, at the suggestion of the 'Servizio Informazioni Difesa' (SID) ('Defense Information Service'), the military secret service, successor of the SIFAR, arrested two anarchists, one of whom proceeded to make a fatal flight from a window in the stationhouse. It was charged that the bombing was a 'massacre by the state' and that the authorities were trying to discredit the left by casting the leftists in the role of pitiless assassins. Though it is difficult to evaluate such accusations, the following facts are disturbingly clear. Despite the accumulating evidence of neo-Fascist responsibility, the authorities refused to abandon the anarchist theory and for years prosecuted the surviving anarchist. Eventually several right-wing extremists were implicated in the case, including one Guido Giannettini. A tortuous, seemingly interminable legal process began. At one stage in the proceedings, Giannettini and the other right-wing radicals were convicted and sentenced to life in prison. When, however, the legal dust settled in January 1987, 17 years after the event, these defendants had all been found not guilty on the ground of insufficient proof. In all this time, the anarchist had remained trapped in the wheels of this case and was liberated by an acquittal only in 1987. The Piazza Fontana case has thus been a scandal.[12] The case, however, is still not over. In July 1986 two more right-wing extremists were indicted on charges of having planned and executed the bombing.[13]

Despite the inability to resolve the case, the legal system did produce evidence to demonstrate unsavory contacts between some sectors of the secret services and the neo-Fascist community. The aforementioned Giannettini, for instance, in addition to being a radical of the right, was an agent for the SID. And a general and a captain of the SID were found guilty (in sentences that stood up on appeal) of furnishing a false passport to a suspect in the case in an attempt to impede the investigation. As a result of such facts a shadow fell over the secret services that has never dissipated.

Their pleasant summer vacation over, Renato Curcio and Margherita Cagol moved to Milan and settled in amidst all this delicious disorder. They did not follow what later became a firm rule of the *Brigate Rosse* – when you take an apartment or a house, always use a false name. To support themselves Margherita took a job at a foundation and Curcio with one of the jewels of the publishing industry, Mondadori. Margherita's family may not have known in these months the full extent of her activities, but they had at least an inkling of what she was up to and where she was headed. In November 1969 Margherita sent her mother a very revealing letter:

I could tell you many things about my new life here in Milan, but none is more important than the maturation of my conscience . . .

For me, Milan is a great experience. This great city, which at first seemed to me luminous, full of attractions, increasingly seems to me a ferocious monster that devours all that is natural, human, essential in life. Milan is barbarity: it is the true face of the society in which we live. This is an observation that I now make every day, but I don't dislike living here because of this; rather, this produces in me a whole series of convictions that I was already reaching at Trent and the importance of which I only now know how to measure.

This society, which violates all of us every moment, taking

from us anything that might in some way emancipate us or make us feel truly what we are ... has extreme need of being transformed by a profound revolutionary process ...

[I]f we think that all this could easily be eliminated (remember when I said to you that, using to the maximum all the technological projects that have been studied and committing them to the productive process, it would be possible to maintain ten billion people at the level of the current medium American income), but this is not possible as long as political systems such as the current European and American ones exist.

However, many conditions exist today to transform this society and it would be criminal (towards humanity) not to exploit them. It is a duty to do everything possible to change this system, because this, I believe, is the profound sense of our life ...

I am very happy at having chosen Renato as the companion of my life because I am convinced that I would in any case have understood these things doing my work as a sociologist, and think a little what misadventures could have befallen me if I had chosen someone else who understood none of these things. Renato and I are planning a whole new way of life, aimed at the achievement of these objectives. This is the love that unites us and that opens us to society – to construct in a new and solid way a relationship that goes beyond us two to the service of the exploited and thus to the service of the people.

Dear mamma, you have contributed much to the building of this, my happiness; because you have always had great faith in Renato and in me. You have never questioned my choices but instead have always aided me in all ways possible and, I would like to say, sometimes also impossible. Your attitudes have always induced in me many reflections and considerations that have made me mature a great deal. Thus, when I have decided, I have decided with certainty and thus I have acted with certainty, without caring what others might say. In fact, I have not erred. And this I owe to you, not to others who have not aided me and indeed have hindered me, both on the ideological plane and on the sentimental plane.

Dear mamma, you know well that, in any case, I have nothing against anyone for now. However, I cannot abdicate my convictions, which I live day by day, and thus I don't like to maintain relationships with those who cannot or wish not to understand me. You understand me, no? Life is too important a thing to spend badly or throw away in useless chatter or squabbles. Each minute is important, above all here in Milan, where the city robs you of hours and hours that could be used in a thousand creative ways . . .

Ciao, mamma. Many large kisses from your revolutionary!

'Margherita'[14]

The first phase of Curcio and Margherita's revolutionary work involved the development of bonds with 'autonomous groups' in the factories of Milan, which were looking for allies to assist in transforming the raging spontaneous confrontation into a broad anti-capitalist struggle. In September 1969, therefore, the Cub (Pirelli), the IBM and Sit-Siemens Study Groups, Renato Curcio and his associates and others, formed the Metropolitan Political Collective (MPC), the group that was shortly to lead to the Red Brigades. The MPC set up its headquarters in Milan. Its symbol was a design of a hammer and sickle and a rifle.

In November 1969 the MPC held an important meeting. In a theoretical document produced at the meeting,[15] the group addressed the nature of the revolutionary undertaking. Although the MPC did not at this point embrace the armed struggle, it had no doubt that violence was justifiable. The group also assumed that the revolutionary struggle would be a long one, just as Curcio had thought at Trent. 'Revolutionary *process* and not revolutionary *moment*', the MPC wrote. And, true to its name, the MPC emphasized the metropolitan context of capitalist exploitation and therefore of the working-class struggle. The theories of urban guerrilla warfare of the South American revolutionaries had had an effect. Probably, too, the provincial origins of Curcio, Margherita Cagol and their allies in Reggio Emilia contributed to the revulsion for the metropolis of Milan that was embodied in theorizing of the MPC and in the letter that Margherita sent to her mother at approximately the same time. Milan and the new Italy it represented were, they all felt, barbarity.

The MPC's document is important for the light it sheds on a major question – how could the terrorists have convinced themselves that a revolution against the state was possible in Italy? The answer lies in the document's premise, a fundamental misinterpretation of recent events. The future *brigatisti* made an enormous and, in more senses than one, fateful mistake in concluding that support for the goal of revolution, revolutionary consciousness, had reached levels that would insure the inevitable demise of the bourgeois system. A revolutionary process, the MPC wrote, had begun in 1968 with a spontaneous movement of the masses. Of course this supposed 'movement of the masses' had largely been a movement of students, and, as Curcio himself had recognized at Trent, the 'masses' and the students are not the same thing. But the 'autonomous' activity of the workers in 1969 had decisively changed the complexion of the movement; now, as the sacred texts prescribed, the working class was on the march and a 'qualitative leap' of boundless importance for the revolution had been achieved.

The 'autonomous' struggles, however, must now be expanded to the whole of society. The working class, the MPC said, must organize in order to make a further leap, 'from spontaneous mass movement to organized revolutionary movement', in order to overthrow bourgeois power, above all in the cities. The cities are the heart of the system, but also its weak point, and it is here, 'in its heart, that the system must be hit. The city must become for the adversary, for the men who today exercise a power ever more hostile and foreign to the interest of the masses, untrustworthy terrain'.

Using the 'Cubs' and study groups as bases, the MPC tried to advance these notions within the factories, most notably at Sit-Siemens, Pirelli and Alfa Romeo, and to find recruits. From Sit-Siemens came a group of future *brigatisti*, including Mario Moretti, whose name will recur in the course of this account. And the MPC reached beyond Milan, drawing into its web Franceschini's 'Group of the Apartment' and others.

Over the next few months, the MPC changed its name (to 'Proletarian Left' and then to 'New Resistance'), as its members agitated among the workers and debated the wisdom of commencing the armed struggle. 'The years of autonomous struggles', they wrote, 'have not passed in vain. Today we know that one must not go unarmed to an encounter with the armed master'.[16] In the meantime they pursued less extreme tactics, joining with 'Lotta Continua' to promote housing occupations and like forms of social protest under that banner of realism, 'Let's grab the city!' As 'Proletarian Left' saw it, 'everything that exists in this society we have made with our labor'; it belongs 'to the people and not to that handful of scoundrels who exploit us from the heights of some administrative council or some parliament' and therefore 'we do not have to pay anyone for it'.[17]

In January 1971 'Proletarian Left' wrote that the moment had arrived 'to spread among the proletarian masses in struggle the principle, "one has no political power if one has no military power", to educate the revolutionary and proletarian left through partisan action to resistance, to the armed struggle'.[18] The Red Brigades were coming to life.

During 1970 Margherita Cagol remained in contact with her family by telephone and letter. In February 1971, however, Margherita and Curcio had a run-in with the police in connection with a housing occupation in Milan. Around the same time Margherita lost a child she had been expecting.[19] Perhaps, as Milena Cagol ruefully speculated, a child might have forced Margherita into a normal existence.[20]

After the rousting by the police, Curcio and Margherita took a new apartment using false names. Despite repeated requests, they did not give the address to their families. Margherita called or wrote home from time to time. She always tried to reassure her family that all was well and that they should not believe everything they read in the newspapers. These fleeting contacts became more and more rare, until in the end they ceased altogether. Throughout this period, though a rebel toward the rest of the world, Margherita remained toward them what she had always been, save that now she seemed more satisfied, for she had found the ideal that had previously eluded her. The gradual withdrawal from her family that this ideal forced upon her must, her sister was certain, have caused her great pain. There was, however, no hope of reclaiming Margherita by reasoned argument. She would say that she was in the right and that history would prove her so.[21]

THE REVOLUTION BEGINS: 1970–73

The grand revolutionary struggle started modestly enough. In the summer of 1970 leaflets were found in Milan in facilities belonging to Sit-Siemens. The leaflets contained discussions of problems within the company, insults directed against its officials, and a list of the names and addresses of officials and allegedly traitorous employees who, it was said, must be attacked. The leaflets were signed with the name of an unknown group – the *Brigate Rosse*

(BR).[22] The name had been chosen by Margherita, Curcio and Franceschini. Its purposes were to claim kinship with the Resistance and readily to convey the idea of the group's objective – the achievement of revolutionary communism. They also selected a symbol, which was to become sadly familiar and a source of fear for years to come – a five-pointed star enclosed in a circle. Here is Franceschini:

We had thought about a symbol of our own for some time. It had to be clear and simple, easily designable, including on walls. That it had to be a star was beyond discussion; it was the emblem of all the revolutionary armies: the Vietcong, the Tupamaros, Che Guevara, the Garibaldi Brigades. But we had to make it recognizable, to invent one of our own. For me and Renato it had become almost a vice to design stars on any available piece of paper; we discovered that the 100 lire coin, which any comrade would have in his pocket, furnished the circle to contain our star. We tried to design the star with the technique learned at school, that which teaches how to design one with five points without ever taking the pencil off the paper. However, we did not succeed in making it perfect: it was bent to the right or the left, one point was larger than another. But that could only be our star, and we decided upon the error that we all would have to commit: the highest point would be shorter, giving the sensation of a star projected upward, towards the future.[23]

In September 1970 came the first actions, an attempted fire-bombing of the automobile of the staff director of Sit-Siemens and a menacing note directed at another official of the company. A few months later the BR repeated this scenario at Pirelli. In accordance with what was to be the *modus operandi* for years to come, the BR distributed bulletins claiming responsibility and articulating the motives behind the acts. 'Comrades', they wrote, 'these years of proletarian struggle have finally matured a new fact and a flower has blossomed: the struggle, violent and organized, of the new partisans against power, its instruments and its servants'.[24] After fire-bombing three large trucks owned by Pirelli, the BR explained themselves thus:

Piazza Fontana [the December 1969 bombing at the Bank of

Agriculture], Pinelli [the anarchist mysteriously defenestrated], policemen who shoot, comrades in jail, Della Torre and many others laid off, ugly fascist squads protected by the police, judges-petty politicians-rulers, servants of the masters . . . These are the instruments of violence that the masters turn against the working class to suppress it always more. To ask us to struggle respecting the laws of the masters is like asking us to emasculate ourselves! But one thing is certain: *there is no turning back!* We shall continue with more advanced forms of struggle on the road already undertaken: *attack upon production*, much damage for the master, little expense for us.[25]

Still, the gasoline for fire-bombings and paper for all those communiqués cost hard, capitalist money, so the *brigatisti* took to 'expropriations', or, translated from the revolutionary argot, robberies of banks and other places, which, together with kidnappings for ransom, was to be their main source of financing over the years.

The BR continued the fire-bombings of automobiles throughout 1971. They were optimistic. The 'fascists' were being attacked and punished and the workers in the factories were looking on approvingly and offering the *brigatisti* names of prospective targets. Lenin, after all, had begun with a train ride. But the BR were not complacent:

We are only at the first stages of the 'Popular Trial of All Fascists'. We intend, however, immediately to issue a warning: for now, we are striking at and will continue to strike at 'things'; but when we move on to their disgusting persons, it will certainly not be simply to 'massage' their muscles and bones! They should get this into their heads. Their disgusting biographies are under our eyes and every day are brought up to date with great care. Their houses begin to be surrounded by revived partisan Brigades in many districts. Around them the knot is tightening and the *Brigate Rosse* today say: Nothing must be left unpunished! Nothing shall be left unpunished![26]

As would be true throughout their history, the *brigatisti* meant what they said.

In March 1972 an official at Sit-Siemens was kidnapped by the BR for an hour. There was undoubtedly rejoicing among some Sit-Siemens employees at this daring 'arrest'. To the general public, however, the event seemed inexplicable. The BR's communiqué[27] went to some lengths to try to explain the action, but these revolutionaries suffered from a grave weakness – an invincible incapacity for expressing themselves in the words and concepts of the normal man. Though they purported to be the representatives of the people acting for their liberation, they made not the slightest effort truly to communicate with the people, and this would be so throughout their history. This bulletin, like all later ones, was written in political jargon, and anyone who read it who was not a devotee of such prose would have been perplexed. The victim, it seemed, was 'a brutal snarling dog', one of those responsible for 'the war that the bourgeoisie has commenced on all fronts and on all aspects of the productive and social life of the masses'.

By this time, the Red Brigades had a 'column' in Milan and were building one in Turin as well. Turin had to be a site for the revolutionary struggle; revolutionaries could not ignore the city of Fiat, the premier capitalist institution in the country. The *brigatisti* thus worked hard at drumming up support among the workers and here too, in late 1972, fire-bombed the cars of the enemies of the working class.

The activities of the Red Brigades took place in a setting of continuing generalized instability in the streets and piazze and on the factory floors. Policemen, political militants and ordinary citizens were killed or wounded in many violent incidents, often involving neo-Fascists. A number of persons were shot dead by the police during demonstrations by 'Lotta Continua' and other groups of the extra-parliamentary left. Three *carabinieri* were blown to bits by a bomb planted by right-wing extremists, who apparently were aided by rogue elephants in the state administration.[28] At the conclusion of a ceremony in Milan, a right-wing extremist threw a hand grenade into the departing crowd, leaving the Minister of the Interior unscathed, but killing a young woman and three police officers and wounding 12 others. So it went into 1973.

Of the climate of this period, Renato Curcio now says:

What happened in Latin America exerted undoubted influence ... [T]o what we then called the 'movement' (a differentiated and fluctuating social reality, a collective state of effervescent and creative contestation) it did not seem at all excessive, at least in certain cases, to justify political homicide. Thus, for example, when Quintanilla, one of the assassins of Che Guevara, was killed in Germany, few were unhappy about it.

Speaking of slogans such as 'Calabresi, fascista, sei il primo della lista' ('Calabresi, fascist, you're the first on the list'), Curcio says: 'Not only were those slogans shouted out with rage in the marches, but there was not a journal of counter-information that did not accord them ample space'.[29] Calabresi, a commissario involved in the controversial Piazza Fontana investigation, was assassinated in 1972.

In Milan and Turin the *brigatisti* conducted routine operations – fire-bombing of automobiles, robberies, and so on – and other, bolder, more newsworthy undertakings. In the first half of 1973 the *brigatisti* kidnapped and interrogated for several hours a business-man from Alfa Romeo and an official of the country's right-wing union confederation. Before their escape the *brigatisti* took the union official to the gates of Fiat's Mirafiori plant and chained him to a lamppost, with a card full of anti-capitalist invective hung round his neck. It said something about the state of mind of the working class that the official was left chained there for 20 minutes and none of the workers changing shifts at the time came to his aid.

In the wake of the staggering blow of the Arab oil embargo in late 1973 (Italy imports almost all its requirements of oil), the BR struck again, kidnapping Ettore Amerio, staff director of Fiat's large auto group. The BR were certain they knew the mood of the workers and reflected their desires, and to judge by the comments of *Lotta Continua*, the *brigatisti* were right:

It is difficult to find among the workers pietistic comments with regard to the kidnap victim, about whom the notices of the company are at pains to advise that he suffers from heart troubles. It is discovered that all these functionaries of capital have heart problems; and yet, tranquilly, without heart attacks and without tears, they adopt retaliatory lay-offs, punitive transfers, threats to put tens of thousands of laborers out of work ... Now it is his turn, and there is no one who cries about it, except perhaps his colleagues in exploitation.[30]

The Red Brigades, taking another step forward in their in-creasingly serious revolutionary practice, did not release Amerio after a few hours. After days of interrogation, the kidnappers took

Amerio's photograph and sent copies of it to the Italian press agency, together with a communiqué.[31] This was the first employment of a procedure that was to become familiar: the distribution of a photograph of the victim while still in the hands of the BR, his face set against a flag bearing the five-pointed star and the words *Brigate Rosse*; and the bulletin, filled with political sloganeering and ransom demands. The technique of distribution also became familiar: a telephone call to the press advising where a bulletin could be found. In the document the BR claimed to have uncovered the Fascist, anti-worker face of Fiat and asserted that the problem created by Fiat's policies could be resolved only by an armed confrontation. With false humility the BR added:

> We do not think of resolving it ourselves, with a little private war of our own. On the contrary, our action is strongly united with all the components of the workers' movement that work towards the construction in the factories and the neighborhoods of real, popular, armed workers' power.

After eight days Amerio was released and a final communiqué followed. In this document the BR damned the 'historic compromise' between the Communists and the Christian Democrats that Enrico Berlinguer, the PCI secretary, had proposed a few months before, an idea that, to the BR, constituted the nadir of PCI revisionism. As Franceschini explains:

> In preparing the kidnapping of Amerio, we conceived of it, beyond its being our way of participating in the struggles over the [labor] contract, also as the first and a concrete step in our strategy of attack upon the historic compromise ... [A]ccording to us, the agreement between Communists and Christian Democrats that was delineating itself could not but provoke a division in the working class. It was the moment that we had been waiting for and of which we would have to make use to become a solid reference point for those who saw in the 'compromise' the definitive renunciation of the revolution, of the struggle for the taking of power. And the facts, at the beginning, showed we were right. The Amerio kidnapping was a success. The requests to meet us increased. The brigades in the factories became increasingly vital nuclei. There also came to us comrades who had always been Communists, members of the base of the PCI and the unions.[32]

In these early years, but even for years afterwards, the reaction of the political establishment to the activities of the Red Brigades was obtuse, self-deluding and disingenuous. There was a failure to take the BR seriously and to recognize who they really were and what they really wanted. For some time, the Christian Democrats argued that there were 'opposed extremisms', one of the right and one of the left. The DC's adversaries refused to accept this, though it happened to be true. Then in 1974 the DC Interior Minister sided with the DC's critics, saying that the Christian Democrats had brandished the slogan of the opposed extremisms in order to reinforce the DC's central position and suggesting that there was but one extremist reality – the neo-Fascist right, acting overtly or camouflaged as leftists.[33] This analysis was hard dogma inside the PCI. Considering itself the exclusive repository of left-wing truth and unable to accept that terrorists could be the ideological children of the left, the PCI maintained that the *brigatisti* were provocateurs acting to assist the right by discrediting the left. It became common practice to use quotation marks – the 'Red Brigades' – and qualifying words – the 'so-called' or 'self-styled' Red Brigades. In the wake of some revolutionary action by the BR, the PCI would trot out its tired old horse, as in this editorial from the party paper in 1974:

Once again, in a moment among the most delicate, the life of the country is profoundly disturbed by a criminal episode of pro-vocation. The analogies cannot escape notice. For years now the mechanism of the strategy of tension has functioned against Italian democracy. From the bombs on the trains and from the massacre of Milan onwards there has not been a significant moment of national life in which it has not been necessary to face some new provocative outrage . . .

Many words are not necessary to understand whom these criminal episodes serve and are intended to serve. Whoever the material executors might be, it is wholly evident that this strategy is desired by those who want to attack Italian demo-cracy . . .

That there are, by now, professionals of such undertakings is evident. That these self-described 'brigate rosse' appear to complete their evil business in the moments most indicated to favor the reactionary forces is just as evident.[34]

The widespread refusal to see the truth about the BR damaged the anti-terrorist effort and led to a state of unpreparedness that would prove costly. This mistake was particularly grave on the part of the PCI, because it was the most vigorous in the perpetuation of this myth and, more than anyone, was in a position to know better. The PCI and the CGIL were in closer touch than anyone else with the situation in the factories and the state of mind of the workers. They ought to have known, as 'Lotta Continua' did, that the BR were just what their communiqués depicted them to be. And, indeed, according to Alberto Franceschini, the PCI did know:

> The Communist Party . . . knew well who we were. It knew that the majority of us came from its ranks and that some of us, with our party cards in our wallets, still frequented the party's local offices.
>
> It was informed but did not collaborate with the police and *carabinieri*. It restricted itself to presenting a mysterious and turbid image of us in order to keep the people and the workers away from us. Probably it believed that the armed struggle, in an advanced capitalist country like ours, was madness, that it would never have any possibility of finding a mass following. It was enough to create a void around us and thus provoke our extinction from natural causes.[35]

The PCI must have thought that telling the truth would have damaged the party's image as infallible and beyond any criticism from the left, and the party was probably loath to condemn young people whose hearts had once been in the right place and who, in many cases, were former PCI or FGCI members. Eventually, in 1977, the PCI changed its tune, but the change was late and reluctant and the price paid for this was high.

SETBACKS

The success of the Red Brigades in 1970–3 was considerable. It was not, however, achieved without misadventures, which occurred in mid-1972 in bizarre circumstances.

On 15 March 1972 the mutilated body of the millionaire publisher and trendy leftist, Giangiacomo Feltrinelli, was found under a high-tension pylon near Milan. The far left claimed that Feltrinelli had been murdered as part of the 'strategy of tension'.[36] The truth was simpler – he had blown himself up while trying to dynamite the pylon in order to bring on the revolution.

Feltrinelli had been a strange person.[37] Heir to a large fortune, he had begun his political career, incongruously, as a millionaire member of the PCI. Later he had drifted into Castroism. During 1968–70, he had written a series of pamphlets predicting a *coup d'état* by the DC, the Central Intelligence Agency (CIA), the North Atlantic Treaty Organization (NATO) and other archons of reaction.[38] To forestall such disaster he had called for revolutionary resistance and had set up a paramilitary group, 'Groups of Partisan Action' (GAP), that had conducted a series of terrorist acts. Feltrinelli had established contacts with radical groups inside and outside Italy. He had been a friend of Ulrike Meinhof, founder of the leading German terrorist group, the Baader-Meinhof gang or 'Red Army Faction' (RAF), and had aided other German terrorists.[39] In 1971 a German terrorist committed an important political assassination in Hamburg using Feltrinelli's pistol.[40] According to Alberto Franceschini, the Italian publisher had had cordial relations with the Soviet security forces (KGB) and the Cuban secret services. Although dealings between the BR and Feltrinelli had been reasonably friendly, the BR had rejected Feltrinelli's proposal for an alliance. The BR had not agreed with Feltrinelli's excessive concern about a coup, nor with his strategy, which contemplated partisan-style attacks from bases in the mountains. More important, the BR had believed that he was isolated from the working class and that he understood very little of the new social reality that had emerged out of the upheavals of 1968–9.[41] Franceschini recalls:

Renato and I met with him once a week in the gardens of Sempione park. We had to pretend not to know that it was Feltrinelli; for us, he had to be only Osvaldo, a militant of GAP, and even though we had known him since the days of the movement at Trent, it was necessary to play the game. He did the talking. Seated on a bench, his legs stretched out, his hands in his pockets, looking at the sky as if he were seeking inspiration, he submerged us in speeches about revolutionary strategy, the structure of the proletarian army, the Soviet Union and its guiding role. We had given up trying to interrupt him to state our views. Although we listened patiently, his projects did not convince us. We did not want to build an army but an armed party in which the political dimension would be fundamental. Nor did we believe in the guiding function of the USSR and its allies: the revolution had to count only on its own forces. And his idea of blowing up high tension pylons in the mountains . . . seemed to us at the least extravagant. The attack had to be carried to the metropoli; the days of the partisan war to be fought in the mountains were over.

Agreements with Osvaldo-Feltrinelli were impossible. And also impossible, therefore, was accepting his financial aid: we preferred to act on our own; we were jealous of our autonomy.[42]

In the aftermath of Feltrinelli's death, the police crushed GAP. It was at this point that the police achieved their first notable successes in their contest with the Red Brigades, arresting a number of *brigatisti* and discovering several safe houses, which were filled with guns and documents, including Feltrinelli's original passport.

The strange figure of Marco Pisetta appeared on the scene. After arrest and interrogation, the *brigatista* Pisetta was released and fled abroad. In the fall a lengthy memorandum became public in which Pisetta revealed detailed information about the BR and other terrorists.[43] The memorandum also contained some accusations against prominent left-wing militants and it was vigorously attacked by the left.[44] In a later memorandum,[45] Pisetta disavowed the first memorandum, announcing that he had been pressured into writing it by agents of the Italian military secret service (SID), who had arranged for its publication in a right-wing journal. Later, the head of the Interior Ministry's Office of Confidential Affairs confirmed Pisetta's story.[46] Pisetta's memorandum contained a substantial amount of truth about the BR, but his credibility was undermined by the SID. Further discredit was brought down upon the already compromised secret services and support was provided for the exaggerated beliefs of those who attributed all of the violence in the country to the combined work of right-wing extremists and subversive elements in the government.

The discovery of the hideouts and arsenals and the arrests in mid-1972 were serious blows to the BR, which was then small and in uncertain health (though the *brigatisti* arrested then were released months later, usually because the relevant period of preventive detention had expired). The BR realized that they would now have to be more careful and they set to work to change their organization, by compartmentalization and other means, in order to reduce to a minimum the risk of such mishaps in future. Previously, clandestinity had been limited to those whom the police had been actively seeking and the BR had all been known by name in the factories where they had been trying to elicit support.[47] From mid-1972 on, however, clandestinity became a deadly serious matter.[48] The distinction between 'regulars', full-time militants who lived underground, and 'irregulars', who, to all appearances, lived normal lives in the world of legality, had its roots in the trying experiences of mid-1972.

Clandestinity, however, posed certain problems, the gravity of which the BR underestimated. Life underground, it was to turn out, was extremely hard and unpleasant: moments of great danger and fear, almost constant tension and long periods of isolation, loneliness and excruciating boredom in an unvarying, stultifying atmosphere. More important, life underground was disastrous for the BR's political strategy and relations with the proletariat. The fervor of their ideological faith led the BR to misinterpret the protests of students and workers and the rise of left-wing radical-ism in 1968–9 and the early 1970s as the great, historically pre-determined turning point. Life underground reinforced this error by cutting the *brigatisti* off from currents of opinion that might have challenged their preconceptions and brought them face to face with things as they were. And clandestinity isolated the *brigatisti* from the proletariat. For a time the *brigatisti* enjoyed the support of some workers who opposed the 'masters', and this support was a great incentive and inspiration to the BR. When the *brigatisti* later made a 'qualitative leap' in the conduct of the armed struggle, the knot of clandestinity tightened and the BR failed to notice that the proletariat was gradually deserting them as they traveled onward in an intoxicating spiral of brutality.

In mid-1972, however, the consequences of these problems lay in the future. At the moment, it was the authorities who were committing the errors. The authorities failed to press their advan-tage and the BR successfully reorganized and regrouped. For the forces of order, another such opportunity would not present itself for years. Within a few months of the near disaster of May 1972, the BR were once again hard at work, building their column in Turin, fostering unrest at Fiat and developing plans for the expansion of their campaign of kidnapping.

29996

OPERATION SUNFLOWER

After the successful conclusion of the Amerio kidnapping, the Red
Brigades decided to open the second phase in the group's history.
Their attention was turning away from the factory as the main
stage, and neo-Fascists and alleged 'Fascist' businessmen as the
exclusive targets. The BR were becoming increasingly preoccupied
with the political course in the country, the 'historic compromise',
the state and its representatives and the Christian Democrats. The
armed struggle, the *brigatisti* believed, would have to take on
national dimensions, to be more ruthless, more violent. Circumstances now required a direct attack upon the state.

Accordingly, on 18 April 1974 the *brigatisti* kidnapped Mario
Sossi, assistant prosecutor in Genoa, an ultra-conservative magistrate. The BR chose him because he was in their eyes 'a fanatic
persecutor of the working class, of the student movement . . . of the
organizations of the left in general and of the revolutionary left in
particular'.[49] The *brigatisti* also envisaged the action as a response
to what they, in a pamphlet released to the media,[50] described as
an institutional plot being carried out by counter-revolutionary
forces, namely, a constitutional reform of a neo-Gaullist character.
'Against neo-Gaullism', they chanted, 'carry the attack to the heart
of the State! Transform the crisis of the regime into the armed
struggle for communism'. There were in circulation proposals to
reform the political system, which, as noted earlier, in some
respects stood in need of reform. But the *brigatisti* were not truly
worried about whether or not such proposals might entail reversals as far as civil liberties were concerned; to them the whole
system was worthy only of being immediately discarded. As
publicly announced, the BR subjected Sossi to a 'trial' by a
revolutionary tribunal, which was conducted by Franceschini. As
the days passed, the *brigatisti* effectively orchestrated the kidnapping to assure maximum publicity. They issued communiqués,
photos of Sossi and letters written by Sossi pleading for help and
blaming his superiors for the 'crimes' of which he stood accused.
They managed to force the authorities into splitting over how best
to respond. And they issued threats on their captive's life.

The BR had, in one sense, chosen well in kidnapping Sossi when
they did. The nation was then in the middle of a campaign for a
referendum on the 1970 law allowing divorce for the first time, the
revocation of which was sought by the church, the Christian

Democrats and the MSI. The battle had more to do with, though, than this narrow question; at stake were a vision of the state, relations between church and state, the place of women in a traditionally male-dominated society, and the balance of political power among the DC, the Socialists, the PCI and other parties. In the end the vote went strongly against the church and the DC, but by kidnapping Sossi just then, the BR assured themselves the chance to create great dissension and public unease. On the other hand, the timing subjected the action to the usual conspiracy theories. The Communist daily, *L'Unità*, asserted that the kidnapping was the work of 'a band of provocateurs' and was part of a 'vast design tending to transform the campaign for the referendum on divorce into an occasion to feed the "strategy of tension"'.[51] The Communists were not alone in so thinking.[52] But they were wrong.

Eventually the BR demanded the release from prison of eight members of a revolutionary group in exchange for Sossi. Otherwise, the *brigatisti* warned, Sossi would be killed. The threat was not an idle one; as he told Sossi, Franceschini intended to perform the execution himself as a test of his ability to overcome personal humanitarian feelings out of devotion to the revolution.[53] The government refused to give in, but a court granted an application from Sossi's family to release the imprisoned revolutionaries. The government did not free the eight and took an appeal instead. The BR then liberated Sossi after 35 days of detention. They did so, they said, because they wished to deepen contradictions within the state and to prevent their victory from being robbed of its political significance. They had also achieved their goal of publicizing the neo-Gaullist plans and their own ideas. Killing Sossi would have diverted attention from these things and would have healed some of the contradictions inside the state.[54]

Sossi, then, was free. He was luckier than he knew. The days of the 'historic nucleus' of the BR were numbered. Their successors would prove a great deal more determined and cruel.

As this second phase in the BR's life began, anyone who took a glance at the statistics would have been very worried about the future. The last few years had been a social paroxysm, to which the BR had contributed, but which they had by no means determined. The violence had also arisen out of the activities of the Student Movement, 'Lotta Continua', 'Workers' Power' and other far-left groups, the far right, battles involving the left, the right and the police and so on. In the period 1969–74, 92 persons had died and 2792 had been wounded in over 2300 acts of political violence, and there had been over 1000 politically-motivated assaults on universities, police stations, public buildings, political party offices and other property. To make matters worse, most of this violence had been concentrated in the provinces of Milan, Turin and Rome.[55] And yet, serious though things were, the 'years of lead' had not even begun.

4

Getting to Know the General

PORTRAIT OF A *CARABINIERE*

It was at this point that Carlo Alberto Dalla Chiesa, *carabinieri* general and the chief antagonist of the terrorists, made his first appearance on the scene. Dalla Chiesa was born in Piedmont in 1920. The son of a *carabinieri* general, he joined the corps. He participated in the Resistance. After the war he took two degrees at the university, studying, as the ironies of fate dictated, with the young professor, Aldo Moro. Carlo Alberto, now a captain, was sent to Sicily to lead the *carabinieri* of Corleone, one of the main mafia strongholds in the province of Palermo. In the 1950s and 1960s, his career prospered and he held important jobs in many postings around the country. In 1966, a colonel, he was again transferred to Sicily, where he remained for seven years as commander of a legion. There was then a new mafia, involved in drugs and the pollution of legitimate commerce, and the challenges for the *carabinieri* were great. It reveals something of his attitudes that he made a particular effort to see to it that the activities of the *carabinieri* were publicized so that the common people of Sicily, where fear of the mafia and lack of confidence in the state are epidemic, would know that the state was present and was actively defending itself and its laws.[1]

Dalla Chiesa had the look of a bulldog and he was, as his occupation required, tough and resilient. He was accused from time to time during his struggles against the terrorists of being overbearing, but he was not a brutal man and could justify relentless determination and 'protagonism' as necessary to defeat the effective, secretive and ruthless *brigatisti*. His personality seemed at first glance a severe one, yet his collaborators and subordinates served with him enthusiastically because they recognized his seriousness of purpose, idealism and willingness to run risks personally. He was at the top of all the hit lists of the terrorists. Every day, for years, his life was in danger, and he was forced to spend long periods away from his family, in austere quarters in some barracks, his location unknown even to his wife, in clandestinity like his antagonists. When his wife died the *brigatisti* even studied the condolence notices in the hope of getting a lead on the general's location. After he had become famous he could have chosen an easier and safer way of life, but he never did, driven on by that sense of duty. Underneath the stern exterior, he was sensitive and emotional. He was intensely devoted to his family. He was criticized for the system of super-secure prisons for terrorists that he was instrumental in creating. He believed these jails were essential for reasons of security, but also that the terrorists placed in them, for all the difficulties they encountered, enjoyed better conditions than they would have found in some places, like Ucciardone of Palermo or Poggioreale of Naples, where he felt it was unjust even to imprison a dog. He was not above sending Christmas presents to reformed *brigatisti*, who were living in isolation and threatened with death, out of sympathy for their plight.[2]

In 1973 Dalla Chiesa was promoted to the rank of general and sent to Turin to take command of the first *carabinieri* brigade. In view of the extensive turmoil in the country, he must have known that his new job would be even tougher than the last.

CONCERNING MORE BOMBS AND ANOTHER GENERAL

The Fascists allowed very little time to pass after the Sossi affair before once again unpacking their bombs. In May 1974 anti-Fascist groups and the union federation of the CGIL, the Italian Confederation of Workers' Trade Unions (CISL) and the Italian Union of Labor (UIL) held a rally in Brescia to protest the neo-Fascist violence rampant in the province. As about 2500 people in Piazza della Loggia listened to a speaker denounce the violence, a bomb exploded in a garbage can in the square. Eight were killed and over 100 wounded.

There was little room for doubt about who was responsible for this, the second major massacre of recent years. To many on the left it was another 'massacre by the state', and when the President of the Republic and the Prime Minister attended the funeral, they were jeered at by the crowd. The outcome of the usual lengthy legal proceedings was once again grossly unsatisfactory, with the absolution for insufficiency of proof of all persons charged.[3]

A little over two months after the bombing, the train 'Italicus' was bombed in a tunnel near Bologna, with the loss of 12 lives and over 100 injured. The rail system has been a favorite target for right-wing bombers, especially that portion of track between Florence and Bologna. Yet again, legal proceedings were mired down for years in a morass and only in December 1986 were jail sentences handed out to anyone, two neo-Fascists from Tuscany.[4]

Evidence also began to pile up in public view of right-wing 'deviations' of the secret services. Though caution is advisable in this area, it can be said with confidence that some in the services exceeded their institutional roles, maintained contacts with right-wing extremists, and may have sought to exploit the violence of the far right for authoritarian ends.

In September 1974 the Minister of Defense, Giulio Andreotti, transmitted to the investigating magistrates a report of the SID, the military secret service, concerning the right-wing plots of earlier years. This report brought to light evidence that compromised the SID itself. The head of SID, General Vito Miceli, had had some very suspicious contacts with key figures in the Borghese plot, including Borghese himself. At about the same time evidence was adduced in the so-called *Rosa dei venti* case that suggested the existence of an organization outside the administration, a kind of SID parallel to the official one, that was linked to right-wing extremists. On a related front, Defense Minister Andreotti was assured in writing by the SID that, after an arrest warrant had been issued for Guido Giannettini, the right-wing extremist and SID informer implicated in the Piazza Fontana bombing, then abroad, the SID had had no further relationship with the informer, which was untrue. It was the SID that had had Giannettini flee abroad and it had aided him financially and was still doing so. For having transmitted this false information, General Miceli was removed from a new military post to which he had in the meantime been assigned. In October 1974 the former head of the SID was arrested on a charge of having been involved in the *Rosa dei venti* plot. Again, the judicial inquiries did not clarify this obscure business. Miceli declared his true colors by running for parliament on an MSI ticket. He won.[5]

DALLA CHIESA MAKES SOME MOVES

After the Sossi affair and the bombing at Piazza della Loggia, the
government took its first serious measures to respond to the
terrorist menace. A General Inspectorate for the Struggle against
Terrorism was established in the Interior Ministry. At the same
time, General Dalla Chiesa headed up a special anti-terrorist squad
of *carabinieri* operating out of his command in Turin.[6]

Apparently reacting to the bombing of Piazza della Loggia, a
group of *brigatisti* raided the office of the MSI in Padua in June
1974, as the BR had done numerous times before. But this time the
brigatisti did something they had never done before – they killed.
Two militants found by chance in the MSI office were murdered by
bullets in the neck. This obscure episode, a seemingly 'on the job
error', damaged the BR's reputation as revolutionary Robin
Hoods, but the BR were about to suffer more than a mere dent in
their public image.

Not long before these events Silvano Girotto had returned to
Italy. Girotto was an extraordinary character who would not be out
of place in a disposable summertime thriller. As a young man
Girotto had been, successively, a thief, a member of the French
Foreign Legion, a thief again and a prison inmate. In jail, he, like St
Augustine, had decided to change his life and had become
religious. Freed from prison, he had joined the Franciscan order
and in 1970 had been ordained a priest, taking the name of Father
Leo. Father Leo had worked among the poor in Italy and then had
gone to Bolivia and Chile. There, his faith and his concern for the
wretched of the earth had acquired political dimensions and,
departing from the example of St Augustine, he had ended up
preaching and practicing a theology that had embraced the use of
guns. Father Leo had left Chile when things had got out of hand.
On his return he had found that journalists had made him famous
as 'Friar Machine-gun', though the church had not appreciated his
unorthodox reading of the Gospel, de-frocking him in 1973.
Having an intuition that the BR might try to convert Friar Machine-
gun to their religion, General Dalla Chiesa had one of his men
approach Girotto to seek his help against the *brigatisti*. Girotto
claimed to regard the *brigatisti* as arrogant dilettantes who were
playing the Fascists' game and damaging the working-class
cause, and, according to Girotto, it was for this reason (and not, as

some alleged, for 30 pieces of silver) that he agreed to help the *carabinieri*.[7]

Through intermediaries Girotto put out a feeler to the BR. In July 1974 he went to the train station at Pinerolo near Turin to meet a contact, who turned out to be none other than Renato Curcio. Curcio showed an almost comical ineptitude in handling the application for admission of Friar Machine-gun. (Franceschini says that he and Margherita, each instinctively and independently of the other, tried to protect Curcio and keep him from having to face the small difficulties of their work, this out of pride in and respect for 'our theoretician'. But another, tacit motive for this treatment was that both regarded Curcio as ill-adapted to deal with the daily realities of the revolutionary life.)[8] Though Curcio was supposed to be a clandestine revolutionary and was now at the top of the most wanted list, he met this stranger, who obviously possessed the resourcefulness, if so disposed, to act convincingly the role of aspiring *brigatista* on behalf of, say, the nefarious SID. But the error was not Curcio's alone: Curcio and his friends now foolishly thought themselves almost invulnerable because they were on the side of the people; as Alberto Franceschini explains, 'we had a myth about ourselves and our organization that did not correspond to reality'.[9] And not only did Curcio himself show up, before long he was revealing to Girotto many of the secrets of his organization, while Dalla Chiesa's *carabinieri* surreptitiously snapped photographs.

On this occasion, and at a second meeting in August, Curcio described the BR's history and ideas and explained the group's structure in detail. Important actions were being planned for the autumn; the BR were aware of the valuable disruptive effect caused by long kidnappings of prominent people. (Curcio did not say so, but the *brigatisti* were planning to kidnap both a prominent businessman in Milan and no less than Giulio Andreotti, former Prime Minister and minister of everything and one of the most important Christian Democratic politicians since the founding of the Republic. Mario Moretti had undertaken an investigation of the prospective victim in Milan, while Franceschini had moved to Rome to do the same for Andreotti. Franceschini had found that Andreotti's security was poor and that he could be kidnapped without difficulty as he walked alone to daily mass in the early morning.)[10] On the military side, Curcio said, the BR were insufficiently trained. Curcio suggested to Girotto that he might be given the task of organizing a school to provide the *brigatisti* with the military training they lacked. Curcio said the police were inept and that the only danger the BR faced was that of infiltrations. In that regard, Curcio proposed to assign to Girotto the job of developing an anti-infiltration program for the BR.

At their first encounter Curcio advised Girotto that it would take some time to assemble the BR hierarchy to reach a decision on Girotto's application since the *brigatisti* were on vacation. A final appointment was fixed for 8 September at the station at Pinerolo, at which time Girotto would be given his assignment. It was decided by the *carabinieri* that they could not let Girotto go underground and be forced to participate in 'expropriations' or other crimes and that the opportunity to arrest Curcio simply could not be passed by. And so, on the appointed day, when Curcio appeared accompanied by Franceschini, the *carabinieri* captured them. Franceschini tried to flee, but the *carabinieri* were everywhere. Curcio sat in the car with a pistol near at hand, but he did nothing. A day or two later, photographs of the arrest appeared in the papers (because, Dalla Chiesa explained years afterward, the Interior Minister wanted some favorable publicity). There was Franceschini, struggling vainly in the grasp of the *carabinieri*, while Curcio sat at the wheel, looking over his shoulder at what was happening, as though he had accidentally come upon a strange scene that did not concern him.[11]

Other arrests of *brigatisti* were made around this time and other hideouts located. By this time a habitual weakness of the BR had become apparent – namely, an obsession with maintaining archives, despite the recognition reflected in their handbooks on revolutionary method that documentation should be reduced to a minimum. Perhaps it was reverence for a sacred cause that required such care for the historical record. Whatever the reason, the practice was an aid to the prosecutors. It also had become common to find in the BR's bases lists of prospective targets and data gathered about their work, their homes, their commuting arrangements and so on.

Among those arrested was Alfredo Buonavita, who had only just been chosen to fill one of the leadership spots left vacant by Curcio and Franceschini. Buonavita's background is interesting and does not coincide with stereotypes about the *brigatisti* as middle or upper-class intellectuals with ennui. Born in 1948, he went to work in a factory at 16. In 1971 he left his job in Taranto and went to Turin to find a new position in a factory, where he proceeded to conduct political work for the BR.[12] He had always had an acute sense of class and had been a militant in the PCI and the CGIL. But he had deserted them in 1969, the year of the 'hot autumn',

> because these historic organizations of the Workers' Movement did not offer . . . any prospect of power to the great struggles of the masses of those years. I left, and then opposed these organizations and aligned myself with the first nuclei of the emerging BR. In the BR I saw the only prospects for the working-class, which operated in several directions: the stable construction of armed groups of the masses; the function of stimulus to the proletarian struggle, to make it escape from the narrow areas of school, factory and neighborhood; a guarantee of revolutionary intervention against the Fascists in white shirts and/or black shirts and their bombs and their massacres and all the counterrevolutionary crimes in which the Fascists were involved. We intended to offer ourselves as initial nuclei for the formation of a revolutionary party, where the political and military would march together.[13]

A process of formalization and centralization of the BR's structure was taking place.[14] The fundamental unit of the group was the column, composed of regulars, who were paid a monthly salary. The irregulars were grouped in 'brigades', which reported to the column. By the fall of 1974 there were columns in Milan, Turin and the Veneto, and, not long afterwards, additional ones would be created in Rome and Genoa. Some time after this geographical structure had been in existence, the BR added a horizontal structure intended to provide a thematic centralization: a 'logistical front', which obtained weapons, bases, and so on; a 'front of the great factories' (or 'front of the masses'), the objective of which was to spread the BR's message directly among the workers; and, subsequently, a 'front for the struggle against the counter-revolution', conceived of as a means to carry the attack outside the factories to 'the heart of the state'. Later still, out of sheer necessity, a 'front of the prisons' was added. These structures were co-ordinated and directed on a daily basis by the Executive Committee, composed of a small group of the most influential *brigatisti*.

Around the fall of 1974 a Strategic Direction was created. The BR believed that the 'historic nucleus', the founding *brigatisti*, had achieved for the organization an 'indisputable role of avant-garde', but now that the organization, its influence and its responsibilities had grown, the historic nucleus was insufficient. The Strategic Direction was to represent all the energies and ideas that were developing in the columns, fronts and irregular forces. The supreme authority of the BR, a kind of revolutionary council, it would meet once or twice a year to discuss and formulate a single political line for the group, develop and enforce internal rules, control the budget and nominate the Executive Committee.

These organizational matters were not unimportant technicalities. Rather, they reflected the BR's efforts to resolve one of the great dilemmas of their mission, one of the great problems faced by all such groups: how to maintain the compartmentalization and secrecy needed to evade the police while remaining in touch with the masses. Reconciling efficiency and basic ideological principle would prove very vexing. The entire experience of the BR suggests that revolutionaries in advanced, democratic societies cannot help but be overmastered by this problem, that at the heart of the revolutionary project is a contradiction that, with good policework, will sooner or later prove fatal. The capture of most of the leading *brigatisti* and the discovery of important bases in 1974–5 provided a strong impulse towards rigid centralization. The BR fell under the control of a small, imperious leadership dominated by concern for efficiency and military security. The hierarchical structure took precedence over the horizontal one, the 'front of the masses' virtually ceased to exist and the link to the masses deteriorated as the BR spent less energy on political activity inside the factories and in the working-class districts and more on military operations. The militarization became the subject of extended quarrels between the jailed historic nucleus and the leaders on the outside and among different factions within the group's leadership.

THE FATE OF REVOLUTIONARIES

With the arrests and the loss of bases, the general situation was desperate. But for Margherita Cagol, these were more than professional setbacks; she had lost her husband.

In 1972 she had written to her parents about her hope for

a better society, where no one is exploited by anyone else, where the liberty of one is the limit and condition of the liberty of another, where everyone can express freely his opinions and ideas, where the riches of the earth and of industry are shared equally.[15]

A Communist society, in short, if unlike any that had yet existed. The loss of Renato had made this hope seem more distant than it had two years before, but still she did not doubt. In September 1974 she sent another letter to her parents:

Now it is up to me, and to the many comrades who want to fight against what is by now a rotten bourgeois power, to continue the struggle. Please don't think that I am irresponsible. Thanks to you, I grew up educated, intelligent and, above all, strong. And in this moment, I feel all this force in me. What I am doing is just and sacrosanct. History will show that I am right, as it did with the Resistance in '45.

But you will say, are these the means to use? Believe me, there are no others. This police state is maintained by force of arms and anyone who wants to fight it must fight on these terms. In recent days they shot and killed a boy, as if he were nothing. He had committed the error of wanting a house to live in with his family. This happened in Rome, where the quarters of the poor constructed with cardboard and rusty old tin clash with the sumptuous residences of EUR [a modern sector of the city]. This is not to mention unemployment and the conditions of life of the working classes in the great factories of the cities. Is this the result of the 'reconstruction', of so many years of work from '45 to today? Yes, it is this: waste, parasitism, boundless luxury, on the one side, and uncertainty, exploitation and misery on the other.

Dear parents, you have worked for a lifetime, you have known fascism and post-fascism and these things you know better than I. Today, in this phase of acute crisis, it is more than ever necessary to resist, in order that fascism under new, 'democratic' forms does not once again gain the upper hand.

My revolutionary choices, therefore, despite the arrest of Renato, remain unchanged. Love me the same, even if I know that for you it is very difficult to understand me. Have faith in my capacities and in my extensive experience. I know how to get by in any situation and no prospect disturbs or frightens me.[16]

Once out of Dalla Chiesa's hands, Curcio entered the bureaucratic labyrinth of the prison system. Someone decided to send him to jail in Casale Monferrato, near Turin, a small prison run, Dalla Chiesa said later, with a frightening inattention to security.[17] The prisoners were permitted to move about freely inside the jail. On 18 February 1975 a cryptic telegram was delivered to Curcio. 'A package will come for you', it said. Some hours later a young woman knocked on the door of the prison and asked to be admitted to deliver a parcel to an inmate. As it was visiting day and all seemed normal, the guard opened the door. Margherita Cagol pulled out a machine-gun. She entered the heart of the prison, a corridor containing the cells. 'Where's Renato?', she asked. Then she yelled, 'Renato, come out!' A voice responded, 'Here I am, I'm here'. The expectant Curcio walked out of his open cell and the BR commando squad escaped undisturbed. At the time his wife and friends came to call on him Curcio had been reading a manual on the fabrication of explosives, a book that he had found in, of all places, the prison library.[18]

For the most part the BR tried to lay low. They prepared the first of their 'Strategic Resolutions', elaborate, usually prolix statements of policy and political theory issued periodically by the Strategic Direction. In May 1975 they took the most notable action of these months, the wounding of a conservative DC member of the Milan city council. This was the first incident of its kind, the deliberate wounding in the knees, a tactic that was to be repeated so often as to give rise to a new verb – *gambizzare*, 'to knee-cap'.

In the Strategic Resolution (April 1975),[19] the BR launched what became a famous phrase. In current conditions of economic crisis the state, according to the BR's analysis, was becoming a tool of the great imperialist, multinational groups, the 'Imperialist State of the Multinationals', the renowned SIM. The DC wants, the *brigatisti* wrote, to reform the state along conservative lines (for example, a presidential republic) and to adopt repressive public-security measures in order to defeat the working class in a counter-revolutionary civil war. The PCI's notion of the 'historic compromise' would merely obstruct development of the class war. The tasks facing the BR were to conduct 'armed propaganda' for the revolutionary cause and to produce the greatest possible 'disarticulation' of the regime by an attack on 'the heart of the state'; in a later, more advanced phase of the class struggle, the armed avant-garde would organize the masses around the idea of the armed struggle and would wage civil war and smash the state.

Meanwhile the general violence continued in the nation's streets. The worst trouble occurred during the 'days of April' in 1975. A right-wing extremist shot and killed a young leftist in Milan, large-scale violence broke out, and it then grew worse and spread around the country when the police ran over and crushed one of the demonstrators. Sacking and looting went on for days.

Over the previous year and a half another important terrorist group had joined the action, the 'Armed Proletarian Nuclei', commonly known as 'NAP', the third most significant group on the terrorist left (after the BR and 'Front Line', which had not yet been born). NAP was a peculiar group. In contrast with the BR and 'Front Line', NAP came from the South, from Naples, and unlike its Northern brothers, NAP's ideology revolved around a single obsession – the prison system.

Between 1968 and 1971 students from left-wing groups spent time in prison, where they taught Marx and Lenin to the common prisoners and spread the notion that crime was merely a response by the exploited to the repressiveness of bourgeois society. A prison movement thus came to life, in which 'Lotta Continua' was particularly active. Dissidents were dissatisfied, however, with 'Lotta Continua's' failure to approve the immediate use of revolutionary violence to destroy the prisons. These dissidents joined with other radicals and politicized former common criminals to form NAP.

Beginning in July 1974, the *nappisti* conducted a variety of terrorist actions, with the oppression of the prison system as the central theme. Among other things, they set off bombs simultaneously in front of prisons in Rome, Naples and Milan, kidnapped a magistrate, shot and wounded another magistrate and three police officers, and killed a fourth agent. For a time, it seemed as if the group might become another *Brigate Rosse*, but NAP's season in the revolutionary sun was brief; the group went into an irrevocable decline in 1976, and what remained of their membership and resources was transferred to the *Brigate Rosse*. NAP failed in part because, as a result of their overwhelming emphasis upon destroying the prisons, they were unable ever to gather more than the most exiguous support among the working class. And the group failed because it was inept at the deadly business of terrorism, repeatedly bungling revolutionary actions and habitually leaving behind a trail of evidence for the police to follow. In pursuit of their ideas, this strange collection of middle-class students and former criminals sacrificed a number of their members, like the fellow who blew himself to shreds in a Naples apartment, or the converted proletarian gunned down in a failed bank robbery. The saddest story connected to the career of NAP, though, is surely that of the Mantini family of Florence, which lost a son and a daughter first to the delusions of NAP and then to the bullets of the police.[20]

On 4 June 1975, for the purpose of raising money, the BR kidnapped Vittorio Gancia, a well-to-do manufacturer of wine. One of the members of the commando got himself captured and promptly declared that he was a *brigatista*. General Dalla Chiesa thus knew that this was a political kidnapping and not one of the many like enterprises being conducted in those days by private entrepreneurs. The *carabinieri* began scouring about in the hills nearby in search of isolated houses or other locations where Gancia might be hidden. On the morning of 5 June a squad of four *carabinieri* went to inspect the Cascina Spiotta di Arzello, near Acqui Terme, not far from the scene of the kidnapping. This country house, it was discovered afterwards, had been purchased two years before by Margherita Cagol under a false name and had since been used as a BR safe house. One *carabiniere* waited by the squadcar as the other three approached the door of the house. The inhabitants, Margherita Cagol and at least one other *brigatista*, had left no one on guard and were taken by surprise. There are different versions about what happened next. According to the *carabinieri*, after the three officers had announced themselves and asked the inhabitants to come out, the *brigatisti* threw out hand grenades, and Margherita and a *brigatista* ran out firing machine-guns. The grenades immediately wounded the three *carabinieri*, one lightly, one severely, one mortally. The *brigatisti* tried to make a getaway in their cars, but the road was blocked by the squadcar. The fourth *carabiniere* returned the BR's fire and after a shootout the *brigatisti* yelled out that they were surrendering. Margherita and the other *brigatista* began to move towards the fourth officer when, suddenly, the *brigatista* launched a hand grenade. The fragments missed the officer and he returned the fire. The *brigatista* escaped into the woods in this confusion, but Margherita was hit twice. One bullet caught her in the left shoulder and the other passed through her neck. She lay on the ground, oozing blood, and before long was dead.

After the smoke had cleared reinforcements arrived. There were no more *brigatisti*, but the kidnap victim was there, unhurt.[21]

The next day Margherita's two sisters came down to Acqui in response to a call from the authorities and performed the dreadful task of identifying the body. The body lay on a slab in the morgue and her sisters noticed that she was wearing a watch that had belonged to her father, a wedding-ring and one of three identical rings that Elsa Cagol had given her three daughters many years before.[22] How greatly had things changed since then! How greatly had Margherita changed! The body was taken home and laid to rest in a religious ceremony performed by the family's parish priest.

Shortly after, the BR issued a communiqué[23] that must have been written by Curcio:

> Margherita Cagol, 'Mara', Communist leader and member of the Executive Committee of the Red Brigades, has fallen fighting. Her life and her death are an example that no fighter for liberty will ever be able to forget. Founder of our organization, 'Mara' has made an inestimable contribution of intelligence, of self-denial and of humanity to the birth and growth of workers' autonomy and of the armed struggle for Communism. Politico-military column commander, 'Mara' knew how to guide to victory some of the most important operations of the organization. For example, the liberation of one of our comrades from the jail at Casale Monferrato. We cannot permit ourselves to shed tears over our fallen, but we must learn from them the lesson of loyalty, coherence, courage and heroism! In the final analysis, it is war that decides the question of power: revolutionary class war. And this war has a price: a high price, certainly, but not so high as to make us prefer the slavery of salaried labor, the dictatorship of the bourgeoisie in its Fascist or social-democratic variants. It is not the vote that decides the question of power; it is not with a ballot that liberty is conquered. May all sincere revolutionaries honor the memory of 'Mara', meditating upon the political instruction that she knew how to give with her choice, her work, her life! May a thousand arms stretch out to pick up her rifle! We, as a last salute, say to her: 'Mara', a flower has bloomed, and the Red Brigades will continue to cultivate this flower of liberty until victory!

The death of Margherita was an enormous blow to Curcio, who

fell into a depression. His zest for battle seemed to have vanished,[24] but he would not abandon his group. How could he deny the work and effort of virtually his entire adult life, the cause he had passionately shared with Margherita? And how could he acknowledge that the death of Margherita had been a pointless waste? He preferred to shield himself and his memories of Margherita behind a solid wall of ideology.

In the months after Margherita's death the *carabinieri* made a series of important arrests and discovered more hideouts. And, in January 1976, after surveillance on a safe house in Milan, Dalla Chiesa's men captured a *brigatista* named Nadia Mantovani and recaptured Renato Curcio. Curcio was to continue to play a critical role in the story of the Red Brigades, the role of founder, inspirational figure, grand old man and, as ever, principal theoretician, but he was to play this role from inside jail, where he remains to this day. His career as a free and active revolutionary was over for good.

5

Slouching Towards Disaster

INSTABILITY AND CRIME: POLITICS AND ECONOMICS, 1968–76

In the parliamentary elections of 1968 the public expressed its displeasure with the center-left governments, dealing a severe blow to the Socialists, who lost a quarter of their support, while rewarding the opposition PCI, which came in at just under 27 per cent of the vote. Unfortunately for the hopes for social reform, the eight governments that followed through October 1974, most of them center-left cabinets, were riven by internal discord and proved to be even less stable and less effective than the coalitions led by Aldo Moro between 1963 and 1968. Eight governments in six years; the lack of an authoritative leader at the helm; the absence of a coalescent political idea; weakness and instability and drift – these could not have come at a worse time. The governments failed to halt the tide of right-wing and left-wing violence. In the areas of education and labor relations the governments followed a policy of appeasement. Action on the grand reforms was neither incisive nor efficacious. The economy sank virtually into a coma. The nation was in a full-scale emergency.

Economically the 1970s were a test of national fortitude. The 'hot autumn' ushered in a period of extravagant wage increases: for instance, an average annual increase in 1970–8 of over 22 per cent for blue-collar agricultural workers and of around 20 per cent for blue-collar laborers in industry and commerce. Employers were also obliged to pay a very high level of social insurance costs, in 1970 the highest in the Common Market.[1] As a result unit labor costs in industry rose an average of over 15 per cent per year in 1970–8, which was greater than the increase in virtually all of Italy's competitors.[2] Investment and competitiveness declined and a wage-price spiral developed (aggravated by the automatic wage indexing mechanism). The country was living beyond its means.

In addition, from the 'hot autumn' on, Italy attained, by a wide margin, an undesired primacy among the industrialized nations of the world for strikes. Whereas, for example, Germany and France in 1970–7 lost to strikes an annual average of 40 and 230 days respectively (per 1000 industrial workers), Italy lost the staggering figure of 1374. The incidence of absenteeism was more serious still.[3] Discipline in the workplace broke down. Factory foremen were often insulted, threatened and beaten up. The Red Brigades or other members of the avant-garde of the working class would burn their cars, rough them up, or shoot them in the knees.

Rising labor costs, expansionary fiscal and monetary policies and the oil crisis caused a severe inflation. Inflation was over 10 per cent in 1973 and almost 20 per cent in 1974, and, over the whole period 1970–8, was notably worse than in any other industrialized nation (save Britain, another sick man). The balance of payments was upset, the lira came under pressure and there was a flight of capital. Things were so bad by early 1974 that private lines of credit disappeared and the government had to borrow to prevent a general collapse in economic activity. In 1975 inflation dropped a bit but still exceeded 17 per cent and the economy went into recession, the first negative growth (-4 per cent) since the war, and the sharpest decline among the major economies.[4] Naturally, employment suffered. During the 1970s the category of the unemployed comprised many more first-job seekers than ever before.[5] A youthful and educated underclass with scant economic prospects was being created.

The ineffectiveness of government in the face of these difficulties drained public confidence. Among young people, the problems were burning fuses. For the likes of the *Brigate Rosse*, as their documents unequivocally reveal, the economic crisis and the inadequacy of the response of democratic government were construed, not as passing things, but as the long-awaited 'crisis of capitalism'.

In November 1974, as yet another government was put in place, a third epoch in the political life of the Republic seemed to be struggling to be born. Progressive Christian Democrats and Socialists, most importantly the influential DC leader Aldo Moro, suggested that, in order to confront the hydra-headed crisis and to obtain needed restraint from the workers, a strategy of openness to the PCI, of, in Moro's phrase, 'paying attention', should be pursued. The idea was not to bring the PCI into a cabinet, but merely no longer to ostracize it. Mere hints to this effect tended to produce from conservative Christian Democrats and members of some other forces a response bordering on the apoplectic, for which reason Moro and friends proceeded with great caution.

In recent years the PCI had been virtually begging for such attention. The PCI did not try to foment the chaos to advance the revolution, and it began to convince many non-Communists that the explanation for its behavior was not prudence, but that, in its heart, it no longer believed in the goal of revolution. In fall 1973, PCI secretary Enrico Berlinguer was drawing lessons from the coup in Chile against the government of Salvador Allende. Democratic-socialist renewal in Italy, Berlinguer wrote, would require the support of the great majority of the people. But, as the Chilean experience showed, that renewal could be prevented by the formation of an anti-socialist block of right and center forces; it was illusory to think that even if the left received 51 per cent of the votes and the seats in parliament, its survival was guaranteed. Berlinguer therefore rejected as a goal for the immediate future a government of the left as an alternative to the DC. Instead, the PCI should follow a policy of cooperation among Communists and socialists and the popular forces that voted for the DC. The PCI should push for a great 'historic compromise' with progressive forces in the DC.[6]

This new theory proved not to be a momentary fancy. Over the next few years, though the Communists continued to vote against the DC, they also made overtures of peace. The PCI announced its contentment with Italy's continuation as a member of NATO and took the lead in pressing the cause of 'eurocommunism', the basic tenet of which was the right of European Communist parties to decide their politics for themselves, a principle the roots of which, as we have seen, could be traced back to Togliatti. In 1975, the PCI and the Spanish Communist Party issued a joint declaration affirming that socialism was to be arrived at democratically and with respect for individual rights. A similar joint declaration was entered into with the French Communist Party.

The PCI, however, was still awash in contradictions. It is clear that Berlinguer had not changed his basic opinion of the DC, that this alliance was tactical and that the PCI still wanted ultimately to bring about some kind of dimly perceived but profound transformation of the economic and social structure. Even in his articles on the Chilean lesson, in which he was at pains to strike a pose of reasonableness, Berlinguer could not resist the allure of standard boilerplate about the 'spirit of aggression and conquest' of American imperialism, its 'tendency to oppress nations and to deprive them of their independence', and the contrasting heroism of Cuba and Vietnam.[7] Although the PCI did not question Italy's place in the block of nations led by the US and said that it did not wish to see Italy assume 'a position of hostility either toward the Soviet Union and the other Socialist countries or toward the United States',[8] something very like hostility was evident in Berlinguer's analysis. Nor was it possible for a non-Communist to be comfortable with the PCI's placing of the US on the same footing as the USSR.

The elections of 15 June 1975 (for regional, provincial and local office, but with national import) stunned everyone and shook up the balance of power.[9] In a country in which, because of the stability of voting patterns, a gain or loss of a percentage point of popular support is considered significant, the PCI increased its share of the vote by over 6 per cent, won over ten million votes and reached the highest percentage total in its history – a very healthy 33.4 per cent. The PSI also gained. The big loser was the DC, which dropped over 3 percentage points to 35.3 per cent, only just slightly ahead of the Communists and a regression to the level of 1946.[10] In practical terms, the numbers translated into a red tide. Left governments led by the Communists and Socialists were now in control in the regions of Piedmont, Liguria, Tuscany, Emilia-Romagna and Umbria, and in Naples, Rome, Milan, Turin, Genoa, Bologna and Florence. Left coalitions now governed over 2700 cities, containing over 50 per cent of the population of the country.[11]

For Berlinguer, the vote was a hugely encouraging confirmation of his leadership and, he supposed, of the 'historic compromise'. Forced by this rout to seek a better image, the DC chose as its new secretary the candidate of the left and of Aldo Moro, Benigno Zaccagnini, a man of impeccable moral qualities and progressive ideas. To Moro and the DC left, a policy of attention to the PCI was more necessary than ever before if something productive were to be done about the interminable crisis. The success of the PCI, however, and the seeming inexorability of its drive towards power, contemporaneous with what loomed as a Communist take-over in Portugal, alarmed many an Italian and interested observers outside the country, like Henry Kissinger, all of whom let it be known to Moro that a policy of *rapprochement* with the Communists would encounter strenuous opposition. Among traditional PCI supporters, young people who had voted for it and those drifting towards, but not yet committed to, one of the many extra-parliamentary groups, the PCI victory represented a historic opportunity finally to change something other than façades, to bring the power of the proletariat to bear for the first time.

SETTLING A SCORE

On a scorching day in June 1976, the Prosecutor General, Francesco Coco, left his office to make the brief drive to his home in the Salita Santa Brigida in Genoa. He was protected by a bodyguard and a driver, and an escort vehicle manned by *carabinieri*. Coco had made many enemies in his long career as a prosecutor and lately had been receiving death threats. A crucial election campaign was in progress, and there were those, like the Red Brigades, who favored the staging of their actions in coincidence with elections. Coco was, as a logical matter, an obvious potential target for the BR both because of his general 'anti-proletarian' attitudes and actions and, more specifically, because it had been he who had opposed the extorted court order to release Mario Sossi in 1974. Back then, when journalists had questioned whether his firmness was not facile since Sossi was in the BR's hands and he was not, he had responded that he did not travel in an armored car and that anyone who wanted to could kill him. He still did not travel in an armored car; he was merely being minimally cautious.

Coco and the guard alighted and started to climb the ascending staircase of the Salita Santa Brigida towards Coco's home, where his family and his lunch were waiting. The escort vehicle departed, while the driver awaited the return of the guard. Coco and the guard climbed slowly. The scene was deserted and waves of heat rolled up from the pavement. Then, in an instant, three individuals emerged from the wings of an underpass and, with guns equipped with silencers, including a Skorpion, a small, easily-hidden but deadly Czech-made automatic weapon, opened fire at the backs of the unsuspecting Coco and his guard. The guard was hit 19 times. Eleven shots caught Coco in the head and body and he fell to the ground and lay still, face down. The driver was sitting in Coco's car, oblivious to what had happened, when two persons ran up and shot him dead. Disastrous was his luck: he had been substituting for the day for the regular driver.[12]

The crime was shocking, especially in its ferocity. It seemed to have political overtones. The parliamentary elections that were to take place in 12 days, on 20 June 1976, would probably be the most significant since 1948, since they could well confirm or accelerate the left's remarkable advance of the year before. Who had an interest in disrupting the campaign? Leonardo Sciascia, the eminent writer, spoke for many when he said that the murders were not the responsibility of the left. Such crimes did not serve the left's interests. Rather, Sciascia asserted, 'the crime probably is part of the so-called "strategy of tension" that precedes every electoral period'.[13]

Sciascia was wrong. The murders had been the work of the BR, the first planned assassinations in their history. They had had no desire to disrupt the elections, which to them were merely an unusually favorable occasion for resonant publicity. The motive was the vengeance of the proletariat.[14]

With the death of Margherita Cagol the year before, the first death of a BR militant, and the arrests that followed it, the BR had been in terrible trouble; there had only been about 15 regulars left.[15] But the press had once again been mistaken about the BR when it had written that they were finished. At this point of life or death for the organization, Mario Moretti and one or two others had decided to face the alternatives – either acknowledge defeat or conduct this contest with the state as the war it was, as a war to be won. Moretti had chosen the second alternative and sealed more than his own fate. Why had he not given up? As far as purely personal considerations were concerned, he could not have had a normal life in Italy now and would have had to go abroad, which he had not wanted to do. More important, he had believed fervently, with his whole soul, in the ideas and objectives of the BR, and, whatever the group's problems at this moment, the situation in the country, he had still been convinced, was a potentially revolutionary one. Given all the turbulence, all the violence in the streets, all the excesses of the Fascists, given the extensive acceptance of the revolutionary idea among students and workers, the revolutionary process, already begun, could, he was sure, still be brought to victory by a properly-trained and properly-led avant-garde. So Moretti had begun to rebuild and to carry out a new strategy, one in which there was no place for gentleness.

The *brigatisti* had trained with unusual care for the Coco operation because they could not afford to fail. They had been short on
bullets and had had only one home-made machine-pistol and had
been forced to borrow the Czech Skorpion from radicals in Rome.
Originally planned for 5 June, the first anniversary of the death of
Margherita Cagol, the operation had been postponed several
times. One last day was chosen, 8 June. It was deathly hot and no
one was in the Salita to interfere with the revolutionary ritual.[16]

Just who was this Moretti, who, with this crime, seemed to have
resuscitated the BR? Even now, years later, surprisingly little is
known about him, or, at least, little that can account for the depth
of his revolutionary commitment, or explain how such a seemingly
modest character could, in a diabolic sense, have gone so far. Like
Curcio, Cagol, Franceschini and some other early *brigatisti*, Moretti
was no member of the urban underclass; he was a provincial, from
the Marche. Fatherless, he was raised in a youth home through the
support of a rich family. As a young man he frequented a Catholic
student group. After finishing high school he moved to Milan
where he took a job at Sit-Siemens. He signed up at the Catholic
University, but soon abandoned his studies, as well as his religion.
Sit-Siemens was a hotbed of revolutionary feeling and Moretti
became one of the most fervent advocates of revolution. For
several years he lived in a commune of radical Sit-Siemens workers, where there was constant talk of bringing down the system.
Moretti was but one of the members then. He married a girl from
the commune. She thought him 'a rebellious character', 'rational,
methodic, precise, with a great sense of duty'. Renato Curcio and
Margherita Cagol came to the commune to visit and to talk, and
Moretti became involved in the activities and the political discussions of the Metropolitan Political Collective and then of the BR, in
which from the first he was a leading figure. After the arrests of
May 1972 he went underground, abandoning his wife and young
son. He sent her no letters or money, paid no visits and has never
since seen his wife or his son, now a young man who does not
know who his father really is.[17] Moretti's whole life became the
Revolution. When the critical moment for the BR came in 1975–6,
Moretti took charge, rebuilt the organization, and became the key
leader in the group over the next, very bloody years.

The BR timed the Coco assassination both to exploit the atmosphere of the political campaign and to respond to the trial, which

had just begun in Turin, of 23 *brigatisti*, including Curcio, Franceschini, Alfredo Buonavita and Prospero Gallinari.[18] The charges
embraced a variety of specific crimes (robberies, kidnappings, and
so on), but the main accusation was that of the establishment of a
subversive group in the form of an 'armed band'. Turin was in a
state of siege, the zone around the courthouse looked like a
military camp, and the courtroom itself was jammed with security
forces.

The *brigatisti* had some legal arguments available to them. They
had decided, however, not to conduct a normal defense. One of
the myths about the *brigatisti* is that, although they proclaimed
themselves revolutionaries, once captured they promptly sought
refuge in every advantageous corner of the penal law and the code
of criminal procedure. What happened later was something different, but in legal proceedings over years the BR maintained a brand
of revolutionary integrity, insisting that the bourgeois state could
not put the revolution on trial and using every available means and
the dramatic occasion to put, according to their lights, the state on
trial instead. Their first step was to revoke the authorization given
to their attorneys to represent them. In the Italian system a
defendant had the right to choose his attorney but would be given,
in effect, a legal aid counsel if he lacked his own. Representation by
counsel was necessary to the validity of the proceedings; the state,
in other words, both offered and imposed counsel. The *brigatisti*
refused to accept court-appointed lawyers, thereby giving birth to
a nice question. It was not unreasonable to argue that the state had
no right to impose counsel upon a rational defendant who declined
representation. Still, this question was overwhelmed by the larger
issues that surrounded it, and the *brigatisti* themselves considered
it of no intrinsic importance. They wanted no bourgeois counsel to
appear for them, nor did they want to appear on their own behalf
in the normal sense. They wanted to be on their own, to speak
without inhibition or obstacle against the state and for the revolution.

As the lawyers discussed this and other matters, the BR put on a
display of the intransigence of revolutionaries in the temples of
bourgeois justice. They shouted; they threatened the lives of
defense counsel; they hurled imprecations; they disrupted the
court sessions whenever and however they could. The presiding
judge was remarkably indulgent and allowed the BR to have their
say. The sessions were frequently marked by the reading by the BR

of lengthy communiqués setting forth their ideas about the revolution and attacking the state and all its representatives. On the first day of the proceedings, for example, one *brigatista* read a statement[19] on behalf of all the defendants in which they proclaimed themselves 'militants of the Communist organization Red Brigades' and went so far as to assume responsibility for all past, present and even future undertakings of the organization, an admission that would have made very difficult the work of any defense counsel who might have been recruited. On the day after the killings in Genoa, Prospero Gallinari rose and began to read a document concerning the execution of the 'State hangman, Francesco Coco'.[20] At this point the judge had had enough and tried to interrupt. Gallinari proceeded. Chaos broke out in the courtroom: the *carabinieri* fought with the defendants, as Gallinari tried to read on above the din and the public shouted. Finally the courtroom was cleared. The document Gallinari had been reading contained familiar charges against the 'revisionist' PCI and others, but it also contained a new emphasis, worrisome in view of what had just happened: to kill Coco was not, it said, 'an "exemplary" reprisal. With this action a new phase in the class war opens that aims at disarticulating the apparatus of the State', the Imperialist State of the Multinationals, by attacking 'the men who personify it and direct its counter-revolutionary initiative'.

The problem of defense counsel for the BR blocked the case. Counsel resigned when the BR revoked their approval. The court then ruled that substitutes be appointed, but willing replacements could not be found. Some counsel declined the appointment out of a sincere belief in the right of a defendant to reject representation, others out of fear. The proceedings were therefore adjourned for what turned into a long time, until May of 1977, when violence and intimidation would again be brought to bear on the court by the BR. It seemed apparent in 1976, and would become undeniable in 1977, that the *brigatisti* were not content merely to use the trial as a megaphone for the cause; they wanted to obstruct the proceedings, at least to drag out the case as long as possible, at best, through threats announced and threats executed, to register a political victory for the revolution by making it impossible to bring the *brigatisti* to justice. The revolution would not be put on trial! The case became a test for the legal system and for the public as well, and from 1976 into 1978, it was a test that appeared to be going in favor of the *brigatisti*.

ELECTIONS AND THE RUN-UP TO A NEW REVOLT

Prior to the elections of June 1976 some observers had sensed in the offing a *sorpasso* – the PCI's surpassing the DC for the first time ever. Fear of the Communists had always been one of the arrows in the DC's quiver and no doubt it hit home this time out. The DC received 38.7 per cent of the vote, a gain of several points over the 1975 administrative elections. But there were, as Aldo Moro later observed, two victors in these elections. The Communists amassed 12.5 million votes, or 34.4 per cent of the total, an increase of more than two million votes (and one point) over the 1975 figures, and of more than seven points, by Italian standards a shift of monumental dimensions, over the percentage the PCI had achieved in the last parliamentary elections in 1972. This seven-point increase almost equalled the electoral progress of the PCI between 1946 and 1972. Although there had been no *sorpasso*, there was delight among the PCI leaders in Via delle Botteghe Oscure as the returns came in. The PCI was closer now to a real share in national political power than it had been in 30 years. From a non-partisan point of view, though, the results were disturbing. Because the Socialists and some of the DC's smaller allies lost votes, the results accentuated the bi-polarity of the system – DC on the one side, PCI on the other – and reduced the system's flexibility. The margins for forming a government with the DC but without the Communists became smaller. In short, at a moment of great economic and social difficulties for the country, in a situation that was, as the DC's perennial minister, Giulio Andreotti, put it, 'bordering on catastrophe',[21] the system had become more polarized and even less governable, if that were possible, than it had been before.[22]

Giulio Andreotti was designated to try to form a government. A center-left coalition, it quickly appeared, was not practicable. A one-party, DC minority government began to seem the only option available. The DC, however, knew that it would need broad support if it were to be able to do anything about economic problems and social disorder. At the same time, as the DC's progressives recognized, there was very strong opposition inside the party to any kind of arrangement by which the DC would contract for, or depend upon, the support of the Communist Party or accept a political program negotiated with the PCI. After extensive and difficult discussions, a resolution to the seeming stalemate was developed, a formula as fragile as it was complex: a

one-party, DC government that would survive a vote of confidence
with the votes of the DC and the abstentions of everyone else (save
the right and other marginal groups). And so, in August 1976, it
came to pass. The new political arrangements were, the worldly-
wise could not help but feel, a splendid step forward in the
baroque art of Italian government: an administration founded
upon abstention, or, as it was soon nicknamed, a 'government of
non-no confidence'.[23]

Behind the complex formula lay a dramatic reality: for the first
time in three decades, since long-ago 1947, the PCI was not in
opposition. It was not in the government either; it was in a kind of
limbo, but its position there was a change of the greatest importance. Berlinguer and the party leaders were determined to carry on
with ostentatious reasonableness, hoping to win a formal place in
the government and to establish, once and for all, the PCI's
credentials as a democratic force capable of governing, credentials
it would need when it came time, in the longer term, to lead a 'left
alternative' of Communists, Socialists and a smaller party or two.
Conservatives and some moderates, however, as Aldo Moro,
Zaccagnini and other DC leaders were aware, remained uncon-
vinced. These doubters would resist any further concession to the
Communist Party, which was, after all, the natural enemy of the
DC. The recalcitrants were fortified by the knowledge that, at least
until the commencement of the new presidential term, the United
States would strongly oppose all such compromises, as would the
leading governments of the Atlantic Alliance, a point that Chancel-
lor Schmidt had occasion to underscore in the summer of 1976.

At the other end of the spectrum the conduct of the PCI had as
loud an echo, but for the opposite reason. After two consecutive
election triumphs, which spawned hopes and indeed expectations
that the new power would be put to good use, the PCI was
following a policy light years away from a program of revolution.
For the time being at least, custom restrained the more radical
members of the PCI from breaking with the party of the working
class, of Gramsci and Togliatti, but the patience of the party base
was not inexhaustible. This was just one of many reasons why the
formula of the 'non-no confidence' would have to give.

On the extra-parliamentary left there were no barriers of loyalty
to contain the bitter disappointment. While some on the new left
had been sliding into violence before 1975-6, others had been
willing to give the electoral system a chance. Recognizing reality,

'Lotta Continua' (LC) had concluded that the hated revisionism indeed had roots among the workers. For a time LC had believed that the cause of an eventual revolution would be advanced if the PCI were to join the government, and it had therefore urged a vote for the PCI in the 1975 administrative elections. LC then reversed ground and returned to advocating independent organizations of the masses as the means to the revolution. In the 1976 elections, 'Lotta Continua' and other new left groups presented a unified list of candidates, hoping for a plebiscite in favor of policies to the left of the PCI to serve as a spur that would force the PCI to return to the faith. In the event, the ticket garnered fewer than 550 000 votes in the whole country, while the supposedly moribund DC made a comeback. At this point the LC leadership was being bombarded by criticism – from working-class supporters angry about the leaders' decreased concern with factory and working-class problems, and from youth, the new proletariat, who were upset with the group's political line. After a congress late in 1976 LC began to disintegrate for lack of a coherent political program. Many of its local offices thereafter remained open and they and the group's daily newspaper, *Lotta Continua*, continued to function as points of reference for very many radicals on the left, especially in 1977. As a political organization, however, 'Lotta Continua' was finished.[24]

The death throes of 'Lotta Continua' in 1976 coincided with a general crisis of the extra-parliamentary left, the various 'little parties' that had come out of '68, 'Il Manifesto', 'Workers' Avantgarde' and the like. The returns had shown that there was no room for a serious alternative to the left of the PCI on the spectrum of democratic politics in Italy.

To many young people the PCI was committing the ultimate betrayal of the proletariat and the revolution. Absorbed in directing its maneuvering towards power at the national level, the PCI squandered a great part of the (not very large) credit it had retained with young people or made enemies out of young people who had before been only indifferent or mildly opposed to it. If this is what comes of power to the left in the democratic system, many young people said to themselves by the end of 1976, then there was simply no hope. Thus, for a considerable number of young radicals, here, in late 1976-early 1977, between the failure of the new left groups and the betrayal of the PCI, ended the democratic illusion. As with the Grand Coalition in Germany in December 1966, the apparently emerging agreement between the DC and the

PCI cut off any outlet for a non-violent, far left opposition and pushed many frustrated radicals over the edge. In consequence, 1977 was to be a year of upheaval.[25]

6

The Movement of 1977

HISTORY KILLS US

The spark that ignited long-smouldering tensions was an unpopular plan of educational reform proposed by the Minister of Public Instruction. A great shout of protest rose from the universities against this allegedly reactionary plan and also against the alternative offered by the PCI. By the middle of February 1977 the whole of the vast university city in Rome was occupied by the students, and universities in Bologna, Florence, Urbino, Milan and other cities were occupied as well, and there were many student marches, among which the extra-parliamentary left was very active.

On 17 February there occurred one of those events that symbolize an era. In this case the event symbolized 1977 and the mistakes of its movement, and, more broadly, the ideological excesses and intolerance that characterized the 1970s and early 1980s. The PCI scheduled for that date a speech by Luciano Lama, a leading PCI figure and the secretary of the CGIL, to be held in the heart of the occupied university. This was regarded by many students as a provocation on the part of a political force that had lost the right to lecture anyone. From the start on the morning of 17 February the atmosphere was tense. A robust security squad from the PCI and the union guarded the speaker's platform. The area around the platform began to fill with students, many of them so-called *autonomi* well prepared for the opportunity. The 'Metropolitan Indians' were there too. The Indians, who specialized in irony, sang and danced around an effigy appended to a ladder, on which was hung a sign saying, 'The Lamas are in Tibet'. Students shouted out sarcastic slogans: 'Sacrifices, Sacrifices!', 'More churches, fewer houses!', 'More work, less salary!', and *'In Cile i carri armati, in Italia i sindacati'* ('In Chile, tanks, in Italy the unions'). Lama arrived, protected by an escort. He began his speech. He was hooted at and interrupted by the shouted slogans. A chorus of students yelled in unison, as the tension mounted: 'Idiot, idiot' and, referring to the PCI, *'Via, via la nuova polizia!'* ('Away with the new police!'). Lama continued to talk, but no one was listening. The PCI security service and the students pushed and shoved. Tussling began. A few missiles were hurled and the Indians threw water-filled balloons. Then, clubs, sticks of wood, metal wrenches, rocks and bottles, all obviously brought for the occasion, started to appear in the students' hands. Before long a full-scale battle broke out between the students and the workers. The Communist leader hurriedly concluded his speech and fled from the university before the advancing students. The *autonomi* spat on him. The students attacked and destroyed the platform from which he had been speaking and assaulted two vans of the organizers of the rally. Noncombatants took refuge in faculties of the university, as students and workers continued to engage in hand-to-hand combat with clubs and other weapons. Fifty persons were injured. Eventually, after a few hours of this fighting, the PCI and the union retreated in the face of what Lama called 'the new fascism'. The students overturned cars and set them afire. They barricaded the gates. In the afternoon, the police and *carabinieri* retook the university by force. The university was shut down, but the disorders were transplanted to the surrounding streets. In graffiti on a fountain in the university someone had echoed Mao: 'Great is the disorder under the heavens. The situation is thus excellent'.[1] Among the participants who were feeling exalted were a number of current or future members of the Red Brigades, including some who were to rise to lofty places.

The significance of the expulsion of Luciano Lama from the university escaped no one. It constituted a humiliation of the PCI and the CGIL and a rejection of their policy of moderation. It represented a sharp repudiation of democratic values and politics. The gap – chasm – between the official left and the extreme left had rarely been so plainly demonstrated as in this fighting between leftist students and Communists. The forces of violence clearly were more than a handful of isolated hotheads or provocateurs.

The movement that had thus broken out into the sunlight and that was to last for the rest of the year was unlike the student movement of '68 in a number of fundamental respects. Like *il sessantotto*, the movement of 1977 began in the schools and was overwhelmingly Marxist in orientation, but it was much more vehement and violent. There had been a certain élitism in '68, but now the movement was the instrument of the children of the middle and lower classes, many of whom, and many *autonomi* in particular, came from the metropolitan hinterlands, the sprawling quasi-ghettoes on the edges of the great cities that bred despair and desperation. These young people could perceive no future for themselves and could see no one within the established political order, not even within the PCI, willing to do anything truly serious about it.

The emotionality of this protest was *the* great difference between 1977 and 1968. The earlier movement had been political, with little room for the personal. In 1977, however, there was a strong existential impetus behind the movement; according to a famous slogan of the time, 'the personal is political'. This squared badly with formal Marxist analysis, but the contradiction did not matter to the protestors. To a notable degree, especially as concerned the *autonomi*, the movement of 1977 was irrational, nihilistic. 'History kills us', they said. The movement never troubled itself to elaborate any serious political program and it therefore could not but degenerate into emotional outbursts and decline into exhaustion.

The flight from reason was evident in a number of characteristics of the movement. There was the popularity of the 'theory of needs', which rejected work and postulated a revolutionary society that would satisfy all of every person's needs (how was never explained). One had to 're-appropriate life'. There was a self-defined 'creative' wing to the movement, the most conspicuous members of which, the Metropolitan Indians, painted their faces and dressed up like 'redskins', believing themselves to be as oppressed as the Indians in American history. The slogans yelled out in the marches and the graffitti painted on university walls were often clever, but behind their cleverness was a void. Here are some illustrations:

> 10–100–1000 Little Big Horns!
> The revolution is a holiday or it won't be made.
> We want shacks, not houses!
> Viva sacrifices!
> Re-discuss everything!
> We are realists. We ask the impossible – Revolution.

Intermingled with these were others of a less attractive tone:

> We create by destroying.
> Iron bars in '68, in '77 the P38 [a handgun]!
> Let's shoot the bosses!
> Let's organize our rage!
> PCI and police, we'll sweep you away![2]

As in 1968, the movement functioned through assemblies. But the *autonomi* tried to control these assemblies through intimidation. Outside the assemblies, the *autonomi* practiced a series of tactics that had not been seen in 1968, but that had made their appearance during the 1970s. There were housing occupations. There were 'proletarian expropriations' or 'proletarian shopping': groups of youths would invade supermarkets or shops and take food or stylish clothing or luxury goods without paying. There were *auto-riduzioni*, self-allotted discounts. A frequent target of *auto-riduzioni* were movie theatres, where groups of youths would enter together, paying some laughably low figure or nothing at all. This was all child's play, though, compared to what took place during marches and demonstrations. The violence that had occurred from time to time in past years now grew both in severity and in frequency. The following scenario is typical of what seemed to be occurring every week. It is a Saturday in Rome. 'Lotta Continua', 'Proletarian Democracy' and other legal groups of the movement have called a demonstration to protest against neo-Fascist violence, government educational policy and official repression. A large crowd arrives, including 3–4000 *autonomi*. The *autonomi* have come prepared. They bring rocks, wooden clubs, metal bars, wrenches, sacks filled with molotov cocktails, ski masks and bandanas and pistols. They raise their arms and salute with a closed fist, or with their fingers arranged (thumb straight up, index and middle fingers extended and last two fingers curled into the palm) in the sign of the P38 handgun, which became a sign of the times. At a suitable point in the march, near an office of the PCI or DC or a newspaper, the *autonomi*, in accordance with a pre-determined plan, break from the line of march. With their faces now covered, they, in groups of hundreds, throw rocks and launch the molotovs against the political or newspaper offices, buildings and cars and buses and the forces of law and order. As the streets fill with fire and smoke, shopowners try to bring down the grates protecting their property and by-standers scream and flee in terror. The *autonomi* force drivers out of their cars, overturn the cars and set them afire. They hijack buses and trams, eject the frightened passengers and turn the vehicles sideways to block the street and impede the advance of the forces of law and order. The *autonomi* run riot through the streets, smashing up cars and store windows and going 'shopping' and sacking in boutiques and shops. They break into weapons stores and make off with guns. They beat up real or imagined neo-Fascists or other class enemies with clubs or wrenches. Fugitively, they attack the police and *carabinieri*, throwing rocks, pieces of asphalt and molotov cocktails and firing pistols. The streets fill with tear gas, white clouds hang over the piazze and the police and *carabinieri* advance in ranks, dressed in full battle gear that eerily makes them seem creatures from a strange planet. The *autonomi* disperse, regroup elsewhere and the rondo begins again. After several hours of this, the *autonomi* scurry away, losing themselves in the side-streets and by-ways of Trastevere or the *centro storico*. They leave behind much property damage and, often, police or passersby wounded or dead.

In the heyday of the movement, the University of Rome was, in the words of the Questore of the city, 'a no man's land' controlled by the *autonomi*. The university was held to be simply beyond the authority of the police, towards whose investigatory efforts there was much hostility. At the university the spirit of a not insignificant part of the student body and of young people who frequented the campus for political reasons was reflected in slogans painted on the walls that threatened magistrates and government officials by name. These slogans remained there for over a year because, out of fear, no company would accept a contract to do the cleaning work.[3]

Who were these *autonomi*? In part, they were young people from the *borgate* of the cities who had no clear philosophy other than a belief in revolutionary violence and a disgust with the PCI and all the new left groups. These *autonomi* rejected sophisticated political analysis and relied upon slogans. They wanted a social as well as a political revolution. They believed in the mystique of the P38.

In part, the *autonomi* were also members of a more or less clearly-defined group, 'Autonomia Operaia' ('Workers' Autonomy'), a key player in the complex events of 1977. In the early 1970s, in the wake of the upheaval in the workers' movement, revolutionary dissidents had broken away from the PCI and other leftist groups and formed self-described 'autonomous' collectives and assemblies at Alfa Romeo, the huge industrial complex at Porto Marghera, and so on. In 1972, workers and students in Rome had created the 'Autonomous Workers' Committees', which, headquartered in the eventually notorious Via dei Volsci, became a center of allegiance for many collectives from the metropolitan area of Rome. In 1973 the new left group 'Workers' Power' had dissolved as its leaders squabbled over revolutionary strategy. All of these various tributaries came together to make up 'Autonomia Operaia'. 'Autonomia' (later called 'Autonomia Operaia Organizzata') was a national co-ordinating organization for the various collectives and committees, the most important of which were to be found in Rome, Milan, Bologna and the Veneto.[4]

'Autonomia' defined itself by its rejection of capitalist work. It wanted to undermine the capitalist economic system, and thus advocated a guaranteed salary equal for all regardless of merit, 'organized insubordination' and 'construction of armed workers' power against the power of the masters'.[5] It not only condemned the PCI and the unions, but the various new left groups as well, which it considered safety valves through which the will to revolt of the masses could be harmlessly dispersed. The new left groups were 'the guard dogs of democratic "legality" and union and social-democratic repression'.[6]

Beginning in 1974–5, there had been a marked increase in 'Autonomia's' concern for the *sociale*, the sphere of social life, and by the time the movement of 1977 came to life 'Autonomia' had become the principal philosophical influence on the movement's extreme wing. It conducted campaigns for the 're-appropriation of life', 'self-valorization' and 're-appropriation of social wealth': *auto-riduzioni* on the means of transport, of rent and utility bills; occupation of unrented housing, sometimes for months; 'political shopping' in supermarkets and stores. 'Autonomia' concerned itself with the 'ghetto-ization' of a 'youth proletariat' in Rome and the other metropoli. It related the need for revolution to the 'new needs' of these new 'social subjects'. It spoke of the fulfilment through communism of social, personal and sexual roles. It announced to the heavens: enough with this society of living to work! 'Autonomia' communicated these ideas through many journals, like *Red* and *Without Truce*, and via radio stations, Radio Red Wave and Radio City of the Future in Rome, Radio Alice in Bologna and Radio Sherwood in the Veneto. The

names of these stations reveal the literary infantilism that characterized 'Autonomia', an infantilism that, however, could not conceal 'Autonomia's' profound connivance in violence. These two
sides – poetic license and a license for violence – were frequently to
be seen combined in 'Autonomia's' acts and words. For example:

> Fascists and Christian Democracy today present the dirtiest face
> of power: they must be swept away. Necessarily, but without
> fanaticism: as it is necessary, to live, to have the house clean and
> to kill any cockroaches that infest it. But the house becomes
> beautiful, once swept, if flowers and clarity are put there: the
> flowers of struggle and the clarity of project.[7]

'Autonomia's' central concept concerned the role of the masses
in the revolution. 'Autonomia' believed that the revolution should
be achieved by means of the illegality of the masses, and it was
opposed to clandestine, military élites that pretended to represent
the masses by way of a delegation of power. The 'party must
develop workers' autonomy and not substitute itself for it; the
party must sink its roots in it'.[8] This basic principle set 'Autonomia'
apart from the Red Brigades.[9] To 'Autonomia' the *brigatisti* were
Marxist-Leninists lacking an adequate class analysis, an avant-
garde that had usurped a role that belonged to the masses
themselves. It was not that 'Autonomia' was against the BR's
violence. 'Normally when it is said that the *brigatisti* are comrades
who err, it is said that they are comrades who err tactically.
According to us, the *brigatisti* instead are proletarians who err
strategically'.[10]

Terrorism in a narrow sense and political violence in a broad
sense would not have spread so widely nor lasted so long in Italy
had it not been for the influence of many *cattivi maestri* ('bad
teachers'). These professors and intellectuals went far beyond the
debate and criticism of the nation's weaknesses that are part of the
intellectual's role in a democratic society. In the 1960s these
intellectuals had learned to loathe bourgeois society, the middle
class, the Christian Democrats, the very state itself. In the class-
rooms, in newspapers, books and journals, in pamphlets put out
by the Feltrinelli company and other trendy leftist publishers, and
in the many left-wing magazines that had sprouted since the 1960s,
the intellectuals conducted a fierce diatribe against the state.
Revolution was the only hope, they said, and they went on for

years beating this drum, justifying in windy theoretical expositions revolution and the establishment of a socialist society. They proved very effective propagandists, ideally suited to magnifying and prolonging in Italy the unrest that dissipated quickly elsewhere. Revolution became imperative, a high moral obligation, an emotion-charged, spiritual idea; and young people bought the idea and all the spurious trappings, as these 'bad teachers' hoped they would, and the young people made the state tremble and blood flow. The subversives in carpet slippers, the self-appointed spokesmen for the working class, thus have a very heavy share of the blame for the disaster that befell Italy, a moral if not a legal responsibility.

'Autonomia' is an excellent case in point. At the top, 'Autonomia' was a den of extremist intellectuals, professors, journalists, persons of culture and learning, some of whom, in 1983, after the devastation wrought by terrorism, while denying any connection to terrorism as such, admitted, without the slightest discomfiture, indeed with a kind of perverse pride, to having been subversives.[11] From a moral perspective, though, it is not a simple matter to separate advocacy of subversion from advocacy of terrorism; the terrorists, after all, never thought of themselves as such, but rather as revolutionaries. The chief of these subversive thinkers, one of the famous names of the 1970s, the most prominent and influential of the many 'bad teachers', was Professor Antonio Negri. Negri came from a family with ties to the Socialists. He started out in Catholic Action in the early 1950s, but left because of dissatisfaction with the rigidity of Pius XII and the failure of the church to involve itself actively in efforts at social betterment. Toni became a Socialist and was elected a city counsellor in Padua. Gifted and intelligent, he became a professor in 1958 at the age of 25 and obtained a post teaching political science at the University of Padua, and the way seemed open to a brilliant university career. He became a confirmed Marxist and his many writings often concerned some aspect of Marxist doctrine, about which he wrote in an extremely complex, abstruse and obscure manner. His interests were not purely academic, though, for he became increasingly preoccupied by the world of the factory and the application of his ideas in that world. He abandoned the Socialist Party and entered the circle of intellectuals who were trying to revitalize left-wing ideology in the swiftly changing reality of northern Italy in the 1960s. This was the time of the various new left journals, like *Red Notebooks* and *Working Class*, which were attempting to strike out on different paths from that of the PCI, to put the industrial worker and his problems at the center of intellectual attention and at the top of the political agenda of the left. Negri collaborated on several of these journals.[12] He became one of the leaders and chief theoreticians of 'Workers' Power' where he expressed ideas about the revolution as the work of the masses, about the need to 'subvert the capitalistic articulation of the command over social labor', about a political program of 'generalized appropriation, of the direction by the masses of the attack upon social wealth'.[13] When 'Workers' Power' dissolved in 1973, the professor became a leader of 'Autonomia'. He collaborated on the journal *Red*, headed up a covey of intellectuals of 'Autonomia' at the University of Padua and became the chief philosopher of 'Autonomia' in the country. In January 1978 he published a famous pamphlet with a resonant title, *Il dominio e il sabotaggio* ('Dominion and Sabotage').[14] While he theorized revolution through the illegality of the masses, he continued to teach at Padua and in Paris, and to acquire the prestige accorded at the time to cultivated intellectuals who advocated the destruction of the bourgeois state.

Negri's theorizing and his organizational involvements were sufficiently worrisome to the authorities as eventually to land the professor in a great deal of trouble. He would be indicted (in the famous 'April 7 case') and charged with being a leading terrorist, the organizer of an 'armed band', and one of those principally responsible for the violence in Italy in these years. The precise extent of his activity and the proper response thereto of the criminal justice system remain subjects of controversy. He certainly wrote incendiary things, had ties to terrorists, met with Renato Curcio, and so on. At trial he would be found guilty and sentenced to 30 years in jail. Some years later, the sentence would be reduced to 12 years, but his efforts to have himself totally exonerated would fail.

For all the importance of the *autonomi*, it would be an error to reduce the whole of the movement of 1977 to its most violent component. The *autonomi* were always a minority in the movement, though a significant minority that made itself disproportionately felt. Most of the young people of the movement were members or sympathizers of 'Il Manifesto', 'Workers' Avant-garde' and other new left groups, or young people without fixed loyalties or political histories. 'Lotta Continua' was the most influential and representative of the groups of the movement. Though LC was dead as a formal organization, it continued, through some of its local offices and especially through the daily newspaper, the unofficial bible of the movement, to live on as a rallying point for revolutionary change. But neither 'Lotta Continua' nor any other group could discipline the movement or lead it to any serious effect. Desperation and rage ran too deep. These would push even greater segments of the movement under the wing of the *autonomi* and/or into the ranks of the organized terrorist groups like the BR.

THE MOVEMENT'S DAYS OF GLORY

In early March, a few weeks after the expulsion of Lama from the university, there were more serious disturbances in Rome. In Bologna on 11 March, during street battles between *carabinieri* and students near the university, a young militant of 'Lotta Continua' was fatally shot, apparently by the police. For the next few days the city was rocked by violence in answer to the killing. Police stations were assaulted with molotovs, stores were damaged, cars set ablaze, the train station and an office of the Christian Democrats attacked and police agents wounded. Barricades were set up in the streets and the students and police exchanged molotovs and tear gas. The principal rebels were the *autonomi*, who had been causing havoc in Bologna for months.[15]

On Saturday, 12 March, a march of 50 000 students was held in Rome in protest against the educational reform program, unemployment and official brutality. Present were 'Lotta Continua' and other new left groups and, of course, the *autonomi*. Among the slogans shouted out or appearing on banners were 'Proletarian Violence' and, referring to the Minister of the Interior, '*Cossiga boia, è ora che tu muoia*' ('Cossiga, executioner, it's time for you to die'). After a lengthy march through the city, the demonstration broke down when the crowd reached Piazza del Gesù in the heart of the *centro storico*, where the national headquarters of the Christian Democratic Party is located. The headquarters was attacked with molotovs. The police fired back with tear-gas and chaos followed. Roving bands of rioters formed. Throughout much of Rome's historic center, stores, bars, hotels, banks, political offices and businesses were attacked and devastated, buses were overturned and set aflame, hundreds of cars were burned, armories were plundered, police and *carabinieri* posts attacked. Gunfire was traded between the rioters and the police. In the center of the city, *Corriere della Sera* reported, there was 'an atmosphere almost of a state of siege'. There was even shooting out at DaVinci airport. This went on for hours. In Turin, too, the *autonomi* went wild and someone assassinated a police officer, and in Milan, there was guerrilla warfare.[16]

In Bologna the authorities were forced to pour in four thousand police and *carabinieri*, and on 13 March tanks and armored vehicles rolled through the center of the beautiful old city, followed by police and *carabinieri* in full war gear. After clashes with the ultras and more tear-gas in the center, the forces of law and order thus retook the university from the radicals. Radio Alice was shut down. The police confiscated 100 guns.[17] The extent of the force required to re-establish a semblance of order, the sight of tanks and armed men retaking the streets of the city as though in wartime, were profoundly shocking. So too was the fact that this virtual uprising had occurred, of all places, in Bologna, the Communist capital of Italy, the 'red' city *par excellence*, and, in one of those contradictions typical of Italian life, a stable city of businessmen, enterprise, fine food and considerable wealth. The unrest had turned deadly by accident, but some such accident was probably inevitable, and, in any case, the fact that so deep a rejection of the existing social order had been manifested in the heart of Communist country was an unmistakeable indicator of the gravity of the crisis.

The University of Rome reopened, but its functioning was purely formal. Professors were insulted by *autonomi*, threatened and prevented from teaching and, on occasion, beaten. The head of the science faculty said: 'It's not possible to work anymore . . . The intimidations of teachers and students are countless'.[18] An activist described the situation thus: 'By now there are three types of students: those who are afraid and do not come to the University anymore, those who turn the other cheek and those who buy a revolver'.[19]

On 21 April the police and *carabinieri* once again had to be called into the university. In subsequent rioting, the *autonomi* fired guns, wounding two policemen and a reporter and killing another officer. Interior Minister Cossiga issued a ban on all demonstrations in the capital for a month. On 12 May, 'Lotta Continua' and other groups attempted to defy the ban by holding a rally in Piazza

Navona. The result was more guerrilla warfare in the *centro storico*, during which a 19-year-old girl, a bystander, was shot to death. More grievous disorders followed in cities around the country.

In July a group of French intellectuals, led by Foucault and the inevitable Sartre, opened a controversy with a predictable and simplistic denunciation of 'repression in Italy'. A somewhat similar, but less forgiveable ideological blindness was to be noted in some leaders of the movement. The main groups, like 'Lotta Continua', condemned the violence of the *autonomi*, but refused to disown them or bar them from the marches. They were 'comrades, even if they err'.[20]

From 23 to 25 September the movement held a convention in Bologna on the questions of repression and revolution. In the streets and piazze, there was a happening: there were Metropolitan Indians and hippies, the faithful selling revolutionary papers and mini-journals, militants eating and listening to music. Inside the meeting places the climate was not so benign. At the Palace of Sports two-thirds of the 10 000 or so in attendance, according to a journalist present, were more or less reasonable people from 'Lotta Continua' and the like. About a third were *autonomi*. The latter did rhythmic signalling with the handsign of the P38. There were placards reading such things as 'Red Brigades' and 'Free our comrades or we'll burn the city'. There was a great deal of talk. The crowd showed little patience for lengthy theoretical analyses and extreme statements by *autonomi* were apt to be shouted down. Insults and sometimes fists flew among the people of the revolution. As a whole, the convention was not a training session for the apprentices of terrorism, but there were some such apprentices present and the crowd itself showed an ambiguous attitude toward the armed struggle. One journalist detected in the crowd indifference towards proposals for the use of arms and yet solidarity towards those who had used them. When a representative of 'Autonomia' urged illegal action and referred to Renato Curcio, the BR and NAP as 'organized comrades', half the hall yelled back, 'Free Curcio, free Curcio!' The suggestion that the jails all be destroyed received large and convinced applause, as did a letter from an imprisoned *brigatista*.

The convention ended with a peaceful march of 35 000 young people through the city. The convention had been a success in the sense that it had produced little violence. But, in another sense, from the point of view of the movement, it had been a failure: the people of the city had turned their backs on the event and it is hard to make a revolution when the people are against you.[21]

On 30 September another member of 'Lotta Continua' was shot to death in Rome, this time by a group of neo-Fascists, which produced much counter-violence. In Turin, among the places attacked with molotovs was the 'Blue Angel' bar, believed to be a hangout for neo-Fascists. A young man uninvolved in politics unfortunately chanced to be in the bar at the time and was burned alive in the conflagration. The violence persisted through the year's end, provoking the closing down of the offices of the Roman *autonomi* in Via dei Volsci and Via di Donna Olimpia, while the terrorists continued to demonstrate how well they could disturb the pusillanimous bourgeoisie, a success that was attracting adherents to the cause of the armed struggle.

IN THE FRONT LINE

This decisive period in the history of terrorism in Italy saw the foundation of the second most important terrorist group that Italy produced. In late 1976, radical dissidents from 'Lotta Continua' and others took part in a number of acts of violence. In May 1977 the radicals formed a group at a meeting in Florence. Thus 'Prima Linea' (PL) ('Front Line') came to be. Many *autonomi* or dissenters from 'Lotta Continua' began to join or drift towards this new organization, and more would do so afterwards, when the movement of 1977 was effectively finished. 'Front Line' would have a much shorter life than the BR, but would make up for that by its vigor.

'Front Line' was an alternative to the BR and never had good relations with them. The first point of discord was the great issue in the revolutionary area, that which separately generated and kept separate 'Autonomia', 'Front Line' and the Red Brigades and which was to torment the BR itself – the issue of revolutionary élite versus revolutionary expression of the masses. 'Front Line' was of the opinion that the BR, in their obsession with efficiency and militarism, had lost touch with the masses. Protestations to the contrary notwithstanding, the BR pursued, according to a PL leader, Marco Donat Cattin (who was, by the way, the son of an important DC figure and frequent government minister), a theory of revolutionary uprising in the short term, a philosophy of 'hour

X', whereas 'Front Line' was firmly committed to the idea of a civil war of long duration to be brought about by the gradual spread of the practice of armed action among the masses. PL opposed the BR's principle of the 'attack upon the heart of the State', preferring to regard the enemy not simply as national political institutions and the men who ran them, but as the establishment in the broadest sense. PL also believed, however, in wounding and killing selected enemies of the people. Consistent with these strands of thought, PL opposed the BR on the central matter of the party. Whereas the BR's goals were the establishment of a Marxist-Leninist politico-military party and a Stalinist state, 'Front Line' was not concerned with building the party, and conceived of itself as an avant-garde that lived and breathed within the wide area of revolutionary desire, within the movement. PL's was, Donat Cattin admitted, a Utopian vision, an idea of a Communist society that had yet to be created anywhere on earth.[22] The absurdity of attempting to destroy what existed in order to replace it with something that no one had ever seen and no one could convincingly describe would unfortunately only become obvious when it was too late, after a great many crimes had been done and the militants of PL found themselves behind some very non-abstract prison bars.

The theoretical divisions between PL and the Red Brigades were reflected in differences in structure and in the conception of the revolutionary life. 'Front Line', unlike the BR, was not organized into rigid territorial columns. 'Front Line' had, of course, a national command, but its tentacles among the masses, the 'proletarian squads', 'patrols' and the so-called 'groups of fire', were in theory more flexible than the BR's columns. Unlike the BR, 'Front Line' on occasion used other names than its own to claim revolutionary acts. The militants did not live in total clandestinity, as did the BR's regulars, and thus, in theory, the PL member would be better able than a BR regular to undertake 'political activity' of propaganda, recruitment and the like in the factories and neighborhoods. Thus, Marco Donat Cattin held a job as a librarian in a high school (where he did not fail to proselytize among the students on behalf of the armed struggle) and would take days off from school now and again when he had to go out to shoot someone.[23]

THE RED BRIGADES AND THE MOVEMENT

The events of 1977 were very important to the BR, and not only because of the recruits who came forth from them. After a period of some discouragement, the BR saw the volcanic activity of 1977 as proof that their seismic readings had been accurate. They had not been wrong in perceiving that Italy was ripe for a revolutionary process. The student rising of '68 had been the first clear sign that the inevitable revolution was dawning and the subsequent rising of the workers had provided the necessary working-class coloration to this process. Now the revolution had taken further critical steps forward. The economy was in a shambles and the revolutionary idea was everywhere dominant. And now there was in existence a people's movement, vast and armed, that could serve as an important base upon which to build the revolution. The role of the revolutionary avant-garde and the task of building the party of the people had become more demanding and more critical, but more promising, than ever before. Mario Moretti and his friends were therefore encouraged. Of course, as in their interpretation of *il sessantotto*, the BR tended to sidestep theoretical inconveniences – that the movement of 1977 was a very strange creature, that it was heavily a movement of students rather than workers, that it was criss-crossed by contradictions and non-Marxist impulses. Still, the din it let out was great – the number of incidents of political violence went from 786 in 1974 to 1806 in 1977, including 23 deaths and 38 woundings[24] – and the BR were happy.

For their part, the BR continued to advance in their conduct of the armed struggle, increasing both the frequency and the brutality of their interventions. In 1977 they ambushed and wounded the director of the Ministry of Justice, nine officials of Fiat and other companies, three nationally-known journalists on three successive days in June, a professor at the University of Rome, an officer of a religious group and five Christian Democratic politicians. One of the businessmen wounded was a member of the PCI. A police officer was shot to death by a *brigatista* at a highway checkpoint. As for planned assassinations, the BR committed two. One victim was a journalist who was shot several times in the head because his conservatism and critical attitude did not set well with the BR. The other was the 75-year-old head of the Order of Attorneys of Turin, who was responsible for providing a defense for Curcio and the other *brigatisti* on trial there. This murder came just as a second attempt to begin the trial was being made. Prospective jurors then began to file certificates of 'depressive syndrome' and other illnesses. With the court unable to convene a jury, the trial lasted just 60 seconds, time enough for the court to postpone it to an undetermined date. The BR, in other words, had a good year in 1977. And, while the mole of the revolution was digging, the *brigatisti* were secretly preparing an operation that would catch the attention of the whole world in the spring of 1978.

7

The Spring Campaign

After its difficult birth in August 1976, the Andreotti government of 'non-no confidence' adopted a policy of austerity in an attempt to master the nation's economic problems. The initiatives, however, fell short of a complete rationalization of affairs, while the situation in the field of public security deteriorated spectacularly. The governmental formula started to weaken. The PCI, concerned about the political cost of supporting a policy of austerity, sought in compensation a greater role for itself, but its desires, which were backed by the Socialist leader, Bettino Craxi, were resisted by DC moderates and conservatives. In the nervous summer of 1977, the leaders of the parties whose non-opposition allowed the government to survive did succeed in agreeing upon a common political program. The credit was largely due to Aldo Moro, then President of the DC. Once again the PCI took a step forward. Once again the abyss was narrowly avoided.

In November Berlinguer gave a speech in Moscow that was notable for its independence. The speech impressed Ugo LaMalfa, the President of the Republican Party, who announced that the evolution of the PCI had gone so far that it should be admitted to an emergency government, the formation of which LaMalfa deemed necessary because of the gravity of the economic situation and the breakdown of law and order. Early in December, the various parties, including the PCI – and that was the important novelty – agreed upon a joint statement on foreign policy that reiterated Italy's customary positions. Then Berlinguer, needing to assuage his restless followers, demanded the formation of an emergency government in which the PCI would have a formal part. Because of disagreements about the proper course among the parties of the 'non-no confidence', Andreotti's government collapsed.

Thus, in January 1978, opened the most serious political crisis in the history of the Republic. The PCI's demand was strenuously opposed by a good part of the DC (indeed eight out of ten DC deputies, Andreotti was reliably informed),[1] and this position was encouraged, as had historically been the case, by the attitudes of the United States. Though having hinted at some kind of departure from the hawkishness of Kissinger, the Carter administration, fearing that the Communists were about to take power, issued a statement on 12 January 1978 that repeated traditional American policy: the United States did not favor PCI participation in the Italian government and indeed preferred to see a reduction in the influence of Communist parties in Western Europe.[2] A stalemate seemed to be looming.[3]

Aldo Moro, however, wanted no stalemate. Though as DC President his formal power was less than that of Prime Minister Andreotti or the DC Secretary, Benigno Zaccagnini, Moro's experience, prestige and political skills made him far and away the most considerable player in this drama. Moro again set to work to carry out his strategy of a 'third phase' in Italian political life (after the centrist and center-left phases) against the objections of political enemies foreign and domestic.

As is the practice in Italy, much of the struggle occurred in meetings behind closed doors. In an important encounter with Berlinguer on 16 February, Moro presented the case for a mutually advantageous 'third phase'.[4] Principally through Moro's efforts, a proposed solution began to emerge: (a) a common program of political and economic measures to meet the emergency; (b) affirmative votes by the other parties for the government (as against the previous abstentions); and (c) a pledge to cooperate in promptly enacting the program. The PCI would become a formal part of the parliamentary majority sustaining the government, but would not actually enter the government (in the sense of occupying ministries); the distinction was that between a parliamentary majority and a political majority.

The most important development in the whole crisis came when Moro gave a speech at a meeting of the DC Members of Parliament at the end of February. The coalition could not pass parliament or, even if it did, could not function to any effect unless the opposition inside the DC could be subdued. There were many moderate 'Fanfaniani' and members of the 'Doroteo' faction who were at best uneasy with the solution being developed. More uncooperative was the strongly anti-Communist 'Group of 100', which claimed a membership of 100 DC parliamentarians. Opposition and misgivings were expressed by these forces at the meeting and, even after Andreotti had had his say, the impression in the corridors was that the suggested governmental formula was in danger of being rejected.[5] At this point, the podium was turned over to Moro. Reading the text of his address,[6] you find no rhetorical flourishes to underscore the drama of the moment, the gravity of which indeed hardly required emphasis. Characteristically, Moro relied instead upon a calm and reasoned analysis of the situation and the options available. He noted that since prior to the 1976 elections the traditional political alignments had been wearing down, as proven by the DC's defeat in the 1974 divorce referendum, the PCI victory in the 1975 administrative elections, the abandonment by the Socialists of the center-left and the difficulty of governing since then. Though the DC had done well in the 1976 elections, so had the PCI and 'two winners in a battle certainly create problems'.[7] Now, in 1978, with the country mired in an extraordinary, perhaps decisive, crisis, it would not be responsible to call new elections. What, then, was to be done? Moro emphasized that the Directorate of the DC had already decided to reject the emergency government demanded by the PCI (had rejected, that is, a generalized partnership with the PCI). What the DC deputies were called upon to consider was thus a limited proposal – the PCI's convergence on a common political program and a change in its parliamentary posture from abstention to approval. Arguing in favor of this narrow innovation was the gravity of the crisis. In addition to the economic problems, there was, Moro observed, a kind of 'spreading anarchism', a worrisome 'rejection of authority, [a] rejection of limits, [a] deformation of liberty'.[8] It was here that the PCI could be of help. What would happen, Moro asked his colleagues, if, in the depths of these difficulties, in this nation of 'a constantly passionate nature and fragile structures', the system were to be confronted daily with an unrestrained opposition from the left?[9]

This was the predicament and it had to be faced honestly. The future was uncertain. This year, Moro said with tragically prophetic acuity, we may well have reason to fear surprises. If we could somehow skip over this period, we all would. But we cannot. '[W]hat is required is that we be courageous and confident at the same time, living the time that has been given us with all its difficulties'.[10] Concluding, Moro emphasized the central role of the DC in this effort and reminded his quarrelsome colleagues of the need to preserve the unity of the party.

Moro's pragmatism carried the day, and (a somewhat grudging) peace was restored to the house of the DC. On 1 March the various DC factions approved the proposed solution.[11] A few days later the parties agreed on a common political program and on a formula – a cabinet of Christian Democrats to be supported in Parliament by the DC, the Socialists, the lay parties and the PCI. Andreotti announced his ministers and the deliberations of Parliament on the new cabinet were set down for 16 March.[12] Moro had tried to minimize the new development when talking to his colleagues, but the truth was that a decades-old taboo was being shattered. For the first time in 30 years the Communist Party was to become part of a government majority.

Everyone recognized that Moro's mediation had been decisive. He was, as a prominent commentator observed, the true leader of the DC, which meant the most important and influential politician in the country. Only he could placate and persuade the naturally divisive political parties. The commentator wrote:

> Perhaps not even DeGasperi ever had such prestige and such responsibilities. No one, obviously, can know if Moro will bring the Italian people through this passage, so difficult and perhaps decisive for the very survival of our democracy. But from this point on, we can be certain of one thing. Either Moro succeeds, . or no one will.[13]

BEWARE THE IDES OF MARCH

What was the President of the DC thinking that morning? After church he would go to the Chamber of Deputies downtown, where Andreotti would present the new government, and the parliamentary debate would begin. There Moro would see his handiwork unveiled and hear the applause. A pleasant prospect. Perhaps he mentally caressed the notion of the significance of this event. If the PCI co-operated, this 16th of March would be a day for the history books and no one would have done more to bring it about than he. And as he was, despite his manner, an ambitious man, he may have had other thoughts. In December, the term of the President of the Republic would end, and Moro was now the leading candidate for the succession. This would be a wonderful way to cap his career: seven years as head of state, free from the rigors of the daily political battle (which his wife for years had been asking him to abandon), and with the assurance of a further section in the history books, as well as a chance to do some good as guardian of the nation's political fortunes. As far as the political part of his life was concerned – and that had always been a great part of it – this promised to be among the more satisfying days of his life.

Having saluted his grandson, Luca, he went downstairs and settled into the back seat of his dark blue, official car, amidst the newspapers and his briefcases. At the wheel was Domenico Ricci, *carabiniere*, and next to him, *carabiniere* marshall Oreste Leonardi. These two were fixtures in Moro's life. For 15 years Ricci had been his driver. For a little longer Leonardi had been head of his squad of bodyguards, companion on his daily walks and on his trips, *alter ego* and friend. The rest of the security detail that Leonardi supervised that morning consisted of police officers Giulio Rivera, the driver of the white escort vehicle, and Raffaele Iozzino and Francesco Zizzi. Zizzi was substituting for the regular guard, who had the day off.[14]

The President of the DC lived in a comfortable, middle-class residential zone of Monte Mario, a peaceful quarter of modern apartment buildings covered with green vines. The little caravan left Moro's home and headed towards Via della Camilluccia, which would take them to Piazza dei Giochi Delfici and the church of Santa Chiara. At about 8.55 a.m. the two vehicles were passing through Via Mario Fani. Via Fani runs into Via Stresa, where the driver Ricci would make a right-hand turn and proceed a short distance to the intersection with the heavily-traveled Camilluccia. The two cars proceeded down Via Fani close together at a sustained speed. Everything seemed normal. Hanging about outside the former bar 'Olivetti' were what seemed four pilots waiting for a ride to the airport. One thing out of the ordinary was that the flower vendor, who every morning sold his wares at the corner of Via Fani-Via Stresa, was nowhere to be seen. Someone had slashed the tyres of his van in the night.

The two official vehicles approached the intersection with Via Stresa, preceded by a white Fiat 128 bearing diplomatic plates. At the corner, the 128 braked suddenly without reason or warning (the rear brake lights had been disabled). Driver Ricci tried to swerve, but the president's car hit the rear right-hand corner of the diplomatic vehicle, and the escort car ran into the rear of Moro's sedan. In an instant, the ambush unfolded from two directions simultaneously. The two 'diplomats', one of whom, the driver, was Mario Moretti, jumped out of the 128. The four Alitalia 'pilots' extracted guns from large black bags. With other comrades acting as cover, the *brigatisti* began shooting at the police agents, taking great care not to hit the president. There was a storm of fire from three automatic weapons and three semi-automatic pistols: 91 shots, of which 45 hit their targets. The agents barely had time to realize what was occurring before they were riddled with bullets. All were immobilized in their seats, save for officer Iozzino. He was able to grab his pistol, jump out of the escort vehicle and get off two shots before he was felled. Four of the agents were dead within moments and the last, Zizzi, died within a few hours.[15]

The president was dragged to one of the BR's several cars. The *brigatisti* had equipped their cars with sirens and had brought along the pallets used by the police to stop traffic. With sirens wailing and waving the pallets at other drivers, the *brigatisti* could be sure of making a rapid escape through the crowded morning traffic. Only the first portion of the escape route has been established beyond doubt. Moro was transferred to another vehicle, perhaps two, perhaps in an underground garage, and the majority opinion is that he was taken to a carefully prepared safehouse in Via Montalcini 8 in Rome and held there for the duration of the affair.[16] Wherever the prison was, the *brigatisti* had chosen it with extreme care, aware of the intensity of the manhunt that would follow.

Back in Via Fani, witnesses, the curious and the first police to arrive surveyed the site of the ambush. No one who was there would ever forget the horrific scene. There were bullet shells and glass lying all around the street. One of the *brigatisti* had left behind one of the airline caps, a bag, a false moustache and a cartridge for an automatic weapon. Pages of the president's newspapers blew in the unearthly breeze, never to be read, but to be used instead to cover the bodies. The three automobiles involved in the ambush nestled up to one another, like strange animals frozen in time. Neither the president's car nor the escort vehicle was bullet-proof. The escort vehicle was perforated by bullet holes and the glass of the cars was either filled with the marks of the bullets or shattered. Inside the vehicles, glass, papers and blood were everywhere. The bodies had been damaged gruesomely. Agent Iozzino lay on the ground near the escort car, his young face turned upward, legs crossed, arms spread wide, a rivulet of red dribbling from under his head and rolling, eerily, towards the precise spot where his pistol lay a few feet away in the gutter. What struck the observer were the efficiency and cruelty of the operation and the unreality of such devastation in this quiet part of the city.

The alarm was received at police headquarters quickly, at 9.03 a.m. Countless police cars, sirens screaming, raced into the area. Roadblocks were in place within 45 minutes on the beltway surrounding the city, on major roads and on the entrances and exits of the *autostrade* outside Rome. Not long after, roadblocks and emergency surveillance measures were instituted nationwide and searches were begun of buildings in the area around Via Fani.

In the political offices downtown everyone was aghast and thunder-struck at the news. Politicians wept, took ill and struggled to accept what seemed unbelievable but which the police assured them was all too true. Some few called for the death penalty. The leaders of the political parties, Zaccagnini, Berlinguer, Craxi and the others, agreed that no sign of weakness should be given and that the vote of confidence on the government should be accelerated. Andreotti, after recovering from a fit of vomiting, gave an abbreviated version of his address to parliament, which, within hours, with the votes of the PCI, approved the formation of the new government. That evening Andreotti spoke to the nation on TV, urging calm and affirming the government's intention to meet the challenge that was before it.

The news of what had happened was rushed out to the public. Within short order, special editions of the TV and radio news were on the air and special editions of the newspapers on the streets. It was not certain who had carried out the crime, but suspicion immediately centered on the Red Brigades. As they looked at the film and photos of the carnage in Via Fani, the citizens felt anger towards the killers and great pity for the five policemen and their families. The convictions of the BR were so strong as to have adversely affected their judgement, a problem that was to plague them continually; thus, they had failed to anticipate the public reaction to the annihilation of Moro's guards. The BR regarded these five men as traitors to the working class who deserved to die. The public reacted differently. Everyone knew that the police and *carabinieri* obtained a large share of their recruits from among the children of poor southern families, who, in an effort to better themselves, were willing to serve a state that had so often misgoverned their region. These members of the lower class risked their lives in return for an attractive uniform and an inadequate salary. These were Moro's guards (apart from Leonardi), most of them young men into the bargain: two in their 20s, one 30, one in his early 40s and Leonardi, a vigorous 51. The BR had simply murdered five poor souls who had been doing their best. It was impossible for the public, watching the joint funeral on 18 March, to comprehend how these murders could better anything in Italy.

Shocked though it was, the public could still register its disapproval. On 16 March the union federation called a nationwide strike until midnight. Factories and business activity of all kinds came to a halt, and even the cinemas, theaters, nightclubs and watering holes closed. Millions marched into the streets in cities around the country. In Rome, in Piazza San Giovanni in Laterano, a huge crowd of Christian Democrats, Socialists and Communists gathered to listen to condemnations of the attack in Via Fani and praise of the democratic system, and among the crowd were banners rarely seen together in the same demonstration, the symbol of the DC, the cross and shield, mixing with the hammer and sickle of the Communists. The public unity was not perfect or bottomlessly deep, but it was substantial, and in view of it the Red Brigades ought to have been concerned about the chances for the revolution.

This unity had little to do with strong feelings of affection for Moro personally. He was regarded with at best respectful detachment by the public at large, which generally has little esteem for the occupants of the 'Palace'. Only rarely does a political figure attract great public affection and Moro did not possess the gift for making himself widely loved. If this said something about Moro as a public figure, it also revealed that the reaction of the public had in large part been determined by a rejection of the ideas of the BR and continued faith in the values of the Republic.

On one issue there was much baseless speculation in the aftermath of the slaughter in Via Fani. With a sense of inferiority, many Italians refused to believe that the ambush had been the work of Italian terrorists only. It was too efficient, it was said, to have been engineered without the help of German terrorists,[17] who had recently brought off a very similar kidnapping of the business leader, Hans Martin Schleyer. In truth, however, this was an Italian project from first to last. That should have come as no surprise given the BR's past. Nor should it have been impossible for the public and the security forces to have realized that the BR would not let the political rituals of March 1978 pass without making their voice heard.

PREPARING TO KILL THE KING

In December 1975, Mario Moretti, using the false name of engineer Mario Borghi, took an apartment in Via Gradoli in Rome. He was there to build a BR column, previous attempts to do so having failed. That the BR's leading member had undertaken this task was a mark of the importance the group attached to the idea of a column in the capital. In 1976 and 1977, with the assistance of the Reggiano, Franco Bonisoli (who had entered the BR's Executive Committee along with Moretti after the arrests of Curcio and Franceschini in 1974),[18] Moretti worked on developing contacts in the pullulating universe of the extremist groups: ex-militants of the disbanded 'Workers' Power', members of the numerous extremist committees in the neighborhoods of the great city, armed squads connected to collectives of radical leftists, and so on. Moretti sought to exploit the longing for revolutionary action, the anxiety to be and to do, of the fringes of the movement of 1977. Moretti recruited Valerio Morucci and Adriana Faranda, former leaders of 'Workers' Power'; Barbara Balzarani and other ex-militants of 'Workers' Power' from the Tiburtino section of Rome (nicknamed the 'Tiburtaros'); and members of 'autonomous committees' such as Bruno Seghetti, Antonio Savasta and Emilia Libera from Primavalle, Cinecittà, Centocelle and other zones of the city. All these individuals would participate in some aspect of the Moro operation. Faranda purchased the 'aviator' caps in a shop in Rome. Balzarani and Morucci were members of the commando squad in Via Fani. Seghetti drove the car that carried off Moro.

The 'autonomous area' not only was a foundation for the Rome column, but would furnish recruits for the BR in Rome and elsewhere for long afterwards. Coming to these committees and collectives, in many instances from more docile organizations (for example, 'Lotta Continua'), the young extremists found encouragement for their longing for violence. Though the theoretical differences seemed vast to those involved, it was, in practical terms, not a great step for a budding revolutionary experienced in conducting 'proletarian expropriations' in supermarkets and shooting pistols during demonstrations to join the more organized and efficient BR. The result of this transfusion into the veins of the BR was that the Rome column had a substantially different spirit than the original columns of the North. Rome is not a major center of industry and the Rome column members in general lacked an industrial working-class background, the supposed basis of the avant-garde of the proletariat. Over the years ahead there would be constant friction within the BR between those who had imbibed the 'autonomous' spirit and those who considered themselves the heirs and defenders of the historic Communist working-class and factory orientation.[19]

Moretti's efforts produced a column of about 35–40 members, between regulars and irregulars, with four brigades in different parts of the city, and a handful of satellites, 'little clandestine nuclei' that were armed by the BR and treated by them as embryos of revolutionary organisms of the proletariat.[20] There was also a network of sympathizers in the 'autonomous area' who were in contact with the *brigatisti*.[21]

In January 1977 the Reggiano Prospero Gallinari escaped from jail and rejoined his comrades. A central figure in the Moro affair, Gallinari later became head of the Rome column when Moretti returned to his post in the national leadership. Beginning in December 1976, the Rome column began to undertake revolutionary actions, burning automobiles of individuals linked to the Christian Democrats. Between February 1977 and January 1978 the Roman *brigatisti* 'knee-capped' an official of the Justice Ministry, the director of the leading national TV news program, a professor of economics at the University of Rome, an official of a Catholic social action organization, a member of the Lazio regional government and an official of the state-run telephone company.

The idea of kidnapping a significant person as a way to strike at the heart of the state went back to the period after the Sossi affair in 1974, when Franceschini had stalked Andreotti in the streets of Rome, but the idea had been abandoned after the arrests of Curcio and Franceschini. The idea had resurfaced in 1976 as a possible counter-measure to the trial of the historic nucleus in Turin, but this time the critical shortage of personnel had rendered the idea impracticable. In the early period of the Rome column's construction, the organization studied the possibility of bringing off such a kidnapping. At the outset the leading candidate was Andreotti, both because he was then Prime Minister and because he had been in the front rank of the DC for 30 years. The *brigatisti* therefore undertook an *inchiesta*, meaning an inquiry into a possible victim's political or professional activities and his personal habits to determine whether it would be ideologically appropriate and physically possible to 'knee-cap', kidnap or assassinate him. In the course of this, Moro's name came up and he entered the lists as a possible target. As Prime Minister, Andreotti was under a brighter spotlight, but it was obvious that Moro, then, as ever, a key figure in the DC and in the state, was right for kidnapping. Nevertheless, the BR leadership concluded that the organization still lacked the strength to conduct such a demanding operation and the *inchieste* were suspended.[22]

Enriched by 1.5 billion lire paid in ransom for a very wealthy kidnap victim, enriched by the infusion of support from ultra-radicals disillusioned with the movement, with the Rome column well established, the BR, in the fall of 1977, could again turn their attention to serious planning for a momentous attack on the heart of the state, the need for which was suggested, apart from the general policy of the BR, by two facts. The first was the evolution in the political situation, the emerging 'historic compromise' that would represent the nadir of the PCI as the party of the working class. The second was the reopening, or, to be precise, the state's attempt to reopen, not too far in the future (the date eventually fixed was 9 March 1978), the thus-far aborted trial of the historic nucleus in Turin. Having been twice defeated, the state could be expected to go all out to complete this trial. The *inchieste* on Andreotti and Moro were therefore re-opened, and the BR also took a look at the situation of Senate President and former Prime Minister, Amintore Fanfani. The Andreotti inquiry showed him to be well-guarded and the Fanfani inquiry was unproductive. As to Moro, two weak points were found – the church of Santa Chiara and Via Fani. The study also produced a rapid change in the BR's estimation of Moro's political importance. He had, of course, been regarded as a highly representative figure of the DC, but after his selection as DC president in 1976, and in view of the political situation of the moment, Moro had become more politically significant than Andreotti. The *brigatisti* were aiming, first, to attack the DC, the party of the 'regime', the expression of the repressive capitalistic state in the international imperialist system, and, secondly, to strike at the politics of national solidarity, of *rapprochement* between DC and PCI. On both scores Moro stood as the central figure. He was, in the words of Mario Moretti, 'the demiurge of bourgeois power, present in the decisive moments, mediations, choices'.[23] To the *brigatisti*, and, they supposed, to the public, Andreotti represented the old, cynical DC, the DC of the countless grasping factions, the clientelism and the corruption. Moro, on the other hand, represented the cause of reform and of a serious effort at resolving the national crisis, and only Moro stood a chance of succeeding.[24] To attack the DC, the BR came to believe, meant to attack Aldo Moro. In the fall of 1977 Moretti, on behalf of the Executive Committee, gave the order to proceed.[25]

The selection of Moro says something interesting about the nature of the BR and other forces like it. Whereas in the early days the BR chose their targets because these targets were Fascists or notorious reactionaries like Sossi and because they were for these reasons likely to receive little support or sympathy from the public, Moro's very virtues – his intelligence, his devotion to high standards, his integrity, his seriousness of purpose, his concern for the needs of the country – had become reasons for his condemnation. Since in theory the ultimate objective of the revolutionaries was to be a more humane society and since the oppression and exploitation of the capitalist system constituted the reasons for revolt, it might be supposed that the revolutionaries would have consistently chosen for their victims the most backward, most oppressive, least sympathetic of the representatives of this society. But, paradoxically, the fact that the victim was a man of distinction and progressive views made him a greater adversary and a more desirable target than the craven or self-serving or corrupt official. In fact, other victims of the BR and other groups were selected on the basis of such reasoning. And this paradox has operated elsewhere on other occasions. It was, for instance, the comparatively enlightened and progressive Czar Alexander II rather than some of his predecessors who was assassinated. It is not merely that the leader with scruples allows the revolutionaries greater opportunity to reach him than does the ruthless and cruel leader. It is that the leader has the power to reform society and ameliorate the injustices of the system, thus postponing the day of reckoning. In so thinking, though, the BR and others like them lacked faith in their own creed, in that portion of it that states that capitalist democracy is doomed and socialism inevitable.

The selection of Moro illustrates how symbolism submerges feelings of humanity in revolutionaries. To the revolutionary, the individual human being has no absolute value; what matters is the collectivity, the abstractions of ideology, the proletariat. In the process of making the revolution, the end – the morally justified and historically determined end of a socialist society – justifies all manner of individual cruelties. And in the carrying out of those cruelties, symbolism – the relation between the act committed or the person on whom judgement is inflicted and the abstractions of ideology – altogether outweighs every other consideration, including considerations of humanity. In the thinking of the BR, Moro was not Aldo Moro the man, the professor, the father and husband, the habitually worried southerner, but the physical incarnation of the DC, the shrewd and skilful agent of the oppressive capitalist system.

The BR were especially meticulous in planning for 'Operation Fritz' (from an Italian word used to describe the patch of white hair on Moro's head). Moro's movements – to political meetings, to his office in Via Savoia, to the university, where he taught a course in law, to and from his home – were followed closely. The BR were not above acting like believers and trailing him into church on several occasions, while outside a comrade checked out Moro's car and ascertained that it was not bullet-proof.[26] It was originally thought that Moro might be captured while in church and the guards disarmed but not killed, but the idea was not workable. (Perhaps it was also considered that such an act in such a place would seem excessively sacrilegious, even for the BR.) Via Fani was settled on instead and, cavalierly, the fate of the guards altered.[27] The mechanics of an attack in Via Fani were worked out and when the time was right, the necessary cars were stolen and equipped with sirens and false license plates, including, for additional security, the diplomatic plates on the Fiat 128 that was to initiate the chain of violence. The most able and experienced *brigatisti* were designated to form the assassination squad. Much more care was taken than usual in weapons training, although there was only so much of this the BR could do as they had to run the risk of practicing in grottoes or isolated open areas.[28]

The *brigatisti* did not, however, plan and carry out the operation perfectly. Prior to 16 March a BR vehicle so conspicuously tailed the Moro caravan that it became noticed (though without, as it turned out, adverse consequences for 'Operation Fritz').[29] The white Fiat 128 with diplomatic plates was observed by several witnesses to make strange maneuvers, like sudden departures at full speed and unnecessary braking and stopping, in Via Fani and the vicinity of the Moro home.[30] A half-hour prior to the ambush and near the fatal corner, one of the cars to be used in the action would not start so two *brigatisti* had to push it to get it going. When the shooting began, one of the comrades pressed the trigger of his weapon without effect and realized that he had forgotten to release the safety catch. During the shooting machine-guns used by Valerio Morucci and one of the other 'pilots' jammed and they had to use pistols. Despite these errors and misfortunes, the *brigatisti* succeeded, and did so for two reasons in addition to their preparation. The first was that they had the great advantage of surprise.[31] They needed only a brief span of time – 10, 15 seconds? – after the collision of Moro's vehicle with the Fiat 128 in which to open fire and, with many *brigatisti* strategically placed in a street adapted to an ambush, the guards would have had little chance no matter how alert they had been. And – the second reason – alert they were not.

It is a tragic fact that the escort was negligent. The escort's deficiencies had contributed to the BR's selection of Moro over Andreotti as the chief target of the 'spring campaign' and helped to make the ambush work.[32] No one in the security detail did anything about the strange maneuvers and presences in the vicinity of the Moro home.[33] No one compelled Moro to vary the hour of his departure for church, which occurred each morning at around 9 a.m. None of the members of the security squad was ever given any special training (for example, in defensive driving). To judge from Moro's other escort (which alternated turns with the one wiped out on 16 March), the guards were only very vaguely familiar with the instructions for an escort described in an official booklet that had been prepared after the Schleyer kidnapping in Germany. The members of the escort were supposed to take weekly shooting practice, but no one did. Weapons should have been at hand, but Marshall Leonardi's pistol was found inside a bag at his feet and that of driver Ricci in a bag wrapped in plastic and stowed away in a compartment located between the front seats.[34] In addition to pistols, the escort of the president had a single machine-gun. In such weapons practice as the guards did do, the machine-gun was never used. No one appears to have checked regularly on how the gun functioned, and its maintenance was inadequate, which lends credibility to the assertion by a *brigatista* that the gun, which the assassins made off with, was found to be rusty and virtually unusable.[35] There was little or no supervision of the escort by anyone in charge of providing security for government officials and politicians. Marshall Leonardi was personally able and attentive, as the BR discovered when they watched the impressive performance of the escort under Leonardi's direction at the university. It seems, however, that he regarded public events or appearances, especially at the turbulent university, as likely occasions for an attack, but discounted as a serious possibility an ambush directed at the president while traveling in his car. The vehicle containing the three police officers always followed Moro's car at a very close distance, often bumping into it. The escort feared that, in the crowded traffic of Rome, a menacing vehicle could insert itself between the two cars. The rules that the escort was supposed to follow, however, required that the second vehicle keep a certain distance from that of the person being guarded in order to be able to perceive and react to a threat and not to be caught in a simultaneous attack upon target and escort, as occurred in Via Fani. The greatest error of all concerned the routes traveled by the president. Those most in a position to know, namely, the surviving driver of the escort vehicle and the two surviving commanders thereof (one of whom had taken 16 March off) concurred that the president, instead of arbitrarily changing routes from day to day, always traveled through Via Fani except when traffic was unusually heavy in the direction of Via della Camilluccia, in which case the motorcade would take one alternate route. Anyone who wanted to attack the president need only have planted himself at the intersection of Via Fani and Via Stresa and been patient. The parliamentary committee that looked into the Moro affair concluded that 'there did not exist a sufficient awareness of the precautions to adopt' in order to protect the president adequately.[36]

The political violence in the first two months of 1978 was in itself a reason for attentive precautions. There were days of guerrilla warfare in the streets of Rome, Milan and Bologna and a number of political murders. At Padua in January there were 12 different incidents of firebombing on a single day and 15 on another. The Red Brigades shot and wounded the chief of a Fiat factory section in Turin, a telephone company official in Rome, a provincial leader of the DC in Genoa and an official of Sit-Siemens in Milan. In early March there were firebombings in Bologna.

On 9 March the trial of the historic nucleus was to begin and the

BR attempted both to intimidate prospective jurors and attorneys once again and to file a bloody protest against the conditions of life for their comrades in the 'laagers' of the state. Thus it was that on 15 February, the *brigatisti* of the Rome column assassinated magistrate Riccardo Palma, whose crime was that he had supervised the building and maintenance of the prisons, including the special high-security bunker that had been prepared as the site for the trial. This murder, of course, increased fear in Turin. There, several thousand police and *carabinieri* with guns, battle gear and armored vehicles were deployed to maintain security in the no man's land around the court and to keep the strange, highly-charged peace that obtained. Laboriously, despite a flood of illnesses, psychological and otherwise, a jury was being selected. At the beginning of March there was an 'unnatural tranquility' in Turin.[37] Finally, with a courageous group of jurors assembled, the trial opened on 9 March. There in the courtroom were the by-now familiar faces – Curcio, Franceschini, and so on – and, in short order, the *brigatisti* gave vent to the usual ideological rantings and threats. No one took the warnings lightly, or if anyone did, he quickly changed his mind. On 10 March the 'Mara Cagol' column of the BR assassinated in Turin the marshal of police, Rosario Berardi. The *brigatisti* at the trial claimed 'credit' for this murder and sang the praises of the violence of the proletariat.

PROFILE OF A CHRISTIAN DEMOCRAT

Aldo Moro was a man of the South, and this had much to do with his character.[38] Not so much the South of humanity, laughter and song, as the South of solitude, religious fervor and sadness. He was born in the province of Lecce in 1916, son of a school official and an elementary school teacher. The family moved to Bari when Aldo was a teenager. He was intelligent and an able student, the classic bookworm. He attended the University of Bari, where he did well. There he became active in the Italian Catholic University Federation (FUCI), an organization of Catholic university students, and, in 1937, became FUCI president in Bari. The following year he took his degree in jurisprudence and in 1939 was named national president of FUCI. It was at this time that Moro crossed paths with several persons whose lives would repeatedly touch his own. One was a young Roman named Giulio Andreotti, who helped Moro at the FUCI and succeeded him as president in 1942. Another was the spiritual counsellor of FUCI, Monsignor Giovanni Battista Montini, later Pope Paul VI. At the age of 25 Moro obtained a post as a professor of law at the University of Bari. Moro took his responsibilities as a teacher seriously, evidently both needing and enjoying the intellectual stimulation university life afforded. He was to continue teaching, later switching to the University of Rome, up to March 1978.

The war years were not Moro's best period. He kept his anti-war or anti-Fascist views to himself, if he had any. When drafted he served his time in an administrative post near Bari. After the surrender of Italy in September 1943 he simply returned to his career in Bari. In 1944 he joined the Christian Democratic Party and, on the recommendation of Msgr Montini, was named by the Pope national secretary of the Movement of Catholic University Graduates and director of its magazine. Moro also involved himself in a journal put out by a group of young intellectuals. His ideas were still in a formative stage. In 1945 he married Eleonora, a teacher active in Catholic Action. They were to have three daughters and a son. As a moderate, a prominent young professor, a faithful Catholic, Moro seemed a good prospect to the emerging DC. With the support of the local church hierarchy Moro was elected, in June 1946, a DC member of the Constituent Assembly, which was to draft the constitution of the new Republic. Andreotti was struck at the time by Moro's lack of zest for political affairs and believed that he had become a candidate in obedience to the wishes of the hierarchy.[39] Thereafter, from time to time Moro seemed to exhibit distaste for political life. Certainly his personality was unsuited to the aggressive combat of Italian politics, and given his deep and severe Catholicism, he probably did feel compelled to participate as a matter of religious duty. But that cannot be the entire explanation. He would not have continued at it for over 30 years, over the objections of his family, had political activity not satisfied some profound need in him – perhaps a need to count, to have the practical influence to which he believed his intellectual and personal qualities entitled him. However that may be, in 1946 he took himself off to Rome.

In the Constituent Assembly Moro found himself thrown among some of the most important political figures in the nation, many from backgrounds markedly different from his own: Palmiro Togliatti of the PCI, Lelio Basso of the PSI, the progressive

Catholics led by Giuseppe Dossetti and including Giorgio LaPira and Amintore Fanfani, and so on. Moro held his own. His legal background, retiring manner and a talent for mediation allowed him to become influential. Ideologically Moro gradually became close to, though independent of, Dossetti's progressives, an orientation that Moro was to maintain, with some backing and filling, throughout his career. His maturation and success in Rome were signalled clearly in July 1947, when he was elected vice-president of the DC group in the Assembly.

With the Constitution in place, Moro returned to Bari to run for the Chamber of Deputies in the April 1948 elections. He won easily. Under DeGasperi, he was under-secretary in the Foreign Ministry. In 1953 and 1955, Moro was elected president of the DC group in the Chamber of Deputies (defeating on both occasions Giulio Andreotti). In 1955 Moro was promoted to Minister of Justice and, in 1957, he became Minister of Public Instruction. The consensus is that, despite having the requisite background, Moro was not a great success in either ministerial post, primarily for reasons of temperament that were also, with more serious consequences, to affect adversely his leadership as prime minister. Still, in personal terms his record was one of unbroken success.

In 1959 Moro was chosen party secretary. Apparently the faction of the 'Dorotei', which was then emerging as the most powerful in the party, chose Moro because he was considered respectable but malleable. It was assumed he could not last long, but he had other ideas. Revealing an unexpected tenacity, he out-maneuvered everyone else and remained as the DC secretary for almost five years, which, by Italian standards, is a long tenure. Moro's main goal was to achieve a 'second phase' in the nation's political history – the incorporation of the Socialists in a government alliance. This would reinforce the coalition and strengthen the DC's hold on the main levers of power, but it would also bring into government reformist energies of the kind Moro favored, while isolating the Socialists' former allies, the Communists. Aware that his progressivism was not yet in vogue in his party, Moro pressed ahead cautiously, while spreading reassurance through vocal displays of anti-communism. At the party congress in October 1959, for instance, Moro said of the PCI that 'we remain irreconcilable adversaries'.[40]

Characteristically, as he was to do in 1978, Moro pressed his case by emphasizing realism, contending that the old coalition formula was dead, that there was no alternative and that the risks of the new course were being exaggerated. The mechanics used were also a harbinger of what was to come in 1978. The Socialists were not permitted to enter the government immediately; they were allowed only slowly to sidle up to it. The process began with a DC government on the vote for which the Socialists abstained. A phrase was coined to describe this government, a phrase incorrectly attributed to Moro by the common wisdom, which laughed at the geometrical absurdity – the government of 'parallel convergences'. It was not until December 1963 that the DC finally unveiled a government of which the Socialists were a formal part.

Between December 1963 and June 1968 there were three center-left governments with full Socialist participation. As the philosopher of the center-left Moro was thought the right man to preside over these governments. And since the allies had, until lately, been enemies, who better than the conciliatory Moro to contain the inevitable squabbling? Moro's success at holding the various destructive forces in check is demonstrated by the statistics – he remained at Palazzo Chigi for a longer consecutive period than anyone since DeGasperi, and his third government survived longer than any single coalition until the Craxi government of the 1980's. Stability in government is an achievement anywhere, but especially in a country with a system like Italy's (if there is another such). Temperamentally, however, Moro was not an ideal prime minister, as the substantive record of the center-left governments demonstrates. There were, to be sure, great obstacles. Still, what had made Moro successful as party secretary and what allowed him to hang on for so long as prime minister – his ability at effecting and his disposition towards compromise – was also his weakness. He could square differences and promise, with sincerity, the grand reforms desired by the Socialists and the DC left; what he could not do was battle to put the grand reforms into effect.

Moro had no Churchillian gusto for the administration of public affairs (Moro had no Churchillian gusto for anything; it is hard to think of two political leaders less alike) and showed little interest in the details of policy needed to respond to the problems confronting the nation. In his speeches Moro rarely analyzed specific social or economic problems and even less often recommended concrete measures for solutions thereof; he was content to argue for the pursuit of general goals. He had, instead, a limitless interest in the formulae of coalition government. He attempted to look into the future, but always in terms of arrangements for coalitions, the balance of power among the parties and the effects thereof on the configuration of cabinets.

In the 1968 elections the coalition was weakened, so Moro was thrown overboard by the DC powerbrokers. After more than 20 years of an uninterrupted rise to power, Moro found himself a mere Member of Parliament. It rankled. He did not, however, flee the political arena (which confirms that an abstract sense of duty was not the only thing that kept him there), nor did he allow himself to be overcome by a bitterness he did feel. Instead, after months of isolation and silence, he returned to the fray with an address in November 1968.[41] He called upon the party to listen to the cries for change that were coming from young people and to adapt. While asserting that 'a common direction of power by us and the Communist Party ... is not conceivable', he argued that 'attentive consideration' should be given to the desires for change represented by the PCI.[42] Though he was vague about the needed solutions, he at least had the open-mindedness and sensitivity to attend to the turmoil in society, while the 'Dorotei' remained deaf and unsympathetic. Recognizing the distance that separated him from the powers in the party, Moro took the significant step of forming a little faction, commonly known as the 'Morotei', to reflect his version of DC progressivism.

In mid-1969, Moro returned to official influence as Foreign Minister, a position he held in several governments in the next years. The reigning powers in the DC were showing themselves incapable of dealing with the nation's problems. As his competitors fell exhausted by the wayside, Moro increasingly took on the aspect of a wise, thoughtful and powerful statesman.

In October 1974 he once more became Prime Minister. The following June the Communists made their historic advance in the administrative elections. Moro was candid about the damage suffered by the DC in those elections (and in the 1974 divorce referendum) and sought to force the DC to face the reasons for the disaster, namely, that the party had lost the confidence of the public.[43] Moro's political diagnosis was that 'the future is in part no longer in our hands',[44] which was meant as a solemn warning of the extent of the DC's difficulties, but also revealed the DC's exalted sense of its role in the country's life. In Moro's view a 'third phase' had begun in the political history of the nation after the years of centrism and the period of Moro's other brainchild, the center-left. Moro believed that the party would have to increase its attention to the ferment in society and profoundly reform itself. To improve its image, after the elections the DC installed as its secretary Benigno Zaccagnini, Moro's friend and follower, a man regarded as progressive and honourable (his nickname was 'honest Zac'). In his own mind Moro came gradually to the conclusion that the base of support for Italy's troubled institutions should be broadened by the inclusion of the voters of the PCI. This was, he came to believe, important both to insure the safe passage of the country through the tempest and to accelerate the process of change within the Communist orbit. Moro, however, was not certain, even as late as a few days before 16 March 1978, what the ultimate, permanent shape of the 'third phase' would be; he only knew that such a phase was inevitable and was underway.[45] Starting from very different premises, Moro and Berlinguer were moving towards one another.

The political situation was growing more troubled. In January 1976 Moro's government fell. He immediately headed another, but this was short lived. His role now became that of party strategist. In October 1976 he was chosen President of the National Council of the DC. Directly, and through 'honest Zac', Moro's was now the central voice in the party, and he shaped the governmental expressions of the 'national solidarity'. The BR were right in thinking him both the most influential figure in the DC and the embodiment of its most progressive spirit.

Aldo Moro was a complex person. He was dignified, serious, intelligent. He was also timid and melancholy and very much given to worrying. His photographs usually showed him looking grim or dour or distracted. He lacked Italian fantasy or sense of style. On public occasions he was aloof, even at festive events like receptions among Italians living abroad. He always carried with him a briefcase filled with medicines in case of any eventualities, which was certainly an extraordinary exercise in precaution, if not a tacit confession of a negative outlook on life. In fact, something of a negative outlook he did have. He was, or seemed to be,[46] the archetypal fatalistic southerner, who has inherited a sense of defeat, who is fundamentally pessimistic about the nature of man and about how much good can be accomplished even with the best of intentions. This may explain Moro's proverbial patience, his preference for security over risky undertakings, for peaceful compromises over hard-fought but total victories. He did not exude energy or intensity, was slow-moving and lethargic, although he somehow managed to get a lot of work done. He tended to become enmeshed in matters that interested him, often ignoring those that did not. This, as well as his ambition and desire for control, are illustrated by his habit during his years as party secretary of spending an hour or more every evening personally correcting articles that were to appear in the next day's party newspaper, although he usually left untouched pieces on matters economic, a subject that, despite its importance for the nation in the 1960s and 1970s, bored him.[47] Personally honest, he was extremely faithful to friendships, even some that caused him considerable embarrassment.

Though Moro seemed lacking in self-esteem, in fact he had a high opinion of his merits and his political role. He had, a collaborator observed, a 'proud interior certitude, even when modestly denied'.[48] Profound though his respect was for the values of the DC and the millions who supported it, his public façade of formality concealed views often very critical of the competence or moral stature of some of his fellow Christian Democrats.

Moro's style won him little sympathy from the general public, who considered him skilled and intelligent but remote. Andreotti had a reputation as a man who had seen everything and knew where all the skeletons were buried, but at least he had the gift of the quick and witty phrase, often directed at himself. Moro had no such gift. Nor did he project the humanity of a Zaccagnini. Andreotti noticed that even on social occasions among people he knew, Moro rarely if ever broke through his 'serious and splendid isolation'; he would never indulge in any kind of frivolity nor engage in other than professional conversations.[49] Although in private talk the obscurities and complexities of his style of communication disappeared,[50] Moro's public image was fixed – that of the complicated, depressed, pessimistic southerner.

Henry Kissinger had occasion to work with Moro over the years. An antipathy between the domineering Kissinger and the cautious Moro was natural. Rendering their relationship more difficult was Kissinger's opposition to Moro's ideas about the role of the left in Italy. Moro, on the other hand, was intent on resisting what he and other Italians perceived, with more than a little justification, as an American inclination to think of Italy as though it were Rhode

Island. The two leaders got on badly, and this no doubt affected the opinion Kissinger formed of Moro's personal and professional qualities. In Kissinger's view Moro was the most formidable of the DC prime ministers of his time. However, he also found Moro taciturn, prone to unnecessarily complex discourse and apt to fall asleep during meetings. According to Kissinger Moro was an able party strategist, but was uninterested in foreign affairs and had assumed the job only as a power base.[51]

One of Moro's collaborators at the Foreign Ministry has vigorously disputed Dr Kissinger's portrait, with respect both to Moro's behavior in meetings and his general interest in foreign affairs. Although, according to this diplomat, Moro did not have the innate affinity for foreign affairs he had for political maneuvering, he carried out the job of Foreign Minister with a sense of duty and investment of hard work very rarely seen in the direction of Italian foreign affairs. What Dr Kissinger interpreted as indifference may have been Moro's skepticism about his and Italy's ability to count for much in international circles.[52]

The Moro the public saw was, to a surprising degree, the one his family knew. One of his daughters, Maria Fida, has written a detailed description of him.[53] To his children he had about him a 'shadow of sadness that seemed never to leave him, even when he played around irresistibly', as though 'he carried on his shoulders the weight of the world'.[54] He believed in *tempi lunghi*, that one could not force history and that man must be taken as one found him. Even in the family circle he tended to speak in a complex manner. He was austere, 'an extremely silent and reserved person and very few were able to understand what he was thinking in a given moment and how he really judged men and events'.[55] He did not tell lies, but was very able at talking on and on without ever saying what he did not want to say, a talent that was to be of use to him when in the hands of the BR. For all the severity of his character, he enjoyed movies and was an admirer of the comedian, Totò. With his children Moro was affectionate, kind, patient and indulgent. He developed an extraordinarily close bond with his young grandson, Maria Fida's son, Luca. These emotional attachments were very deep and sacred to Moro – so deep and so sacred that he never spoke of them. His religious commitment was firm and sincere. In his daughter's opinion he was extremely tolerant and went out of his way not to cause offense, so much so that it was almost a defect of character. He was silent when offended or injured by someone and thus drove his daughter crazy.

Because of politics Maria Fida had always felt that a future tragedy was hanging over her family. Her mother loathed politics and tried to get Aldo to confine himself to teaching. In the days prior to 16 March 1978 Maria Fida had a strong presentiment that something horrible was impending, which was followed by a deep depression that kept her awake at night. That morning her father offered to take his beloved grandson with him to church and bring him back afterward. Something told her Luca should not go and he did not. Moro put on his shoes, caressed the boy and left. Later, when her mother returned home, having already heard the news and having seen the terrible sight in Via Fani, she said: 'It's my fault. I ought not to have let him involve himself in politics'.[56]

8

The Justice of the People

ALDO MORO AND THE SIM

Led by Interior Minister Francesco Cossiga, the forces of law and order undertook the biggest manhunt in the nation's history and surely one of the biggest ever pursued anywhere. Thousands of police, *carabinieri* and finance guard officers (and later units of the army) were deployed in roadblocks around the country, in surveillance at airports, at the frontiers, on the trains and along the coasts and in an intense searching of apartments in suspected areas. About 1300 roadblocks daily nationwide (and 160 in Rome alone) brought millions of Italians into direct contact with the tragedy. Tens of thousands of homes were searched, mostly in Rome. Specific grounds for belief that an apartment might conceal Moro were not required to justify the searches. Thus, thousands of innocent persons were compelled to submit to the intrusions of armed and nervous officers during these days. According to their detailed, written rules of comportment, *brigatisti* in clandestinity were obliged to conduct themselves as model tenants, paying bills on time, adhering strictly to an apparently normal work schedule, dressing conventionally, being courteous to other tenants, and so on. The police and *carabinieri* therefore could not rely upon assurances from tenants or doormen that Signor X was a respectable young man. The authorities, of course, could not expect the *brigatisti* to be anxious to open their doors to them. What then to do about the apartments where no one answered the bell? The practice followed was not consistent, but a good many persons out at work when the police came to call found their doors smashed in on their return home.[1] A substantial number of telephones – of newspaper offices, of the Moro family and friends, of possible intermediaries for messages from the BR – were tapped by the forces of law and order in the hope of getting a lead.

Initial public patience with these intrusions in time began to wear thin. Observers wondered if these efforts were not just the crude gropings of a giant pachyderm that was lumbering about in the dark, searching whoever or whatever it chanced to bump into. It is certain that the roadblocks, apartment searches, and so on, did not stop the kidnappers. The *brigatisti* were able repeatedly to prepare bulletins in the operations headquarters of the Executive Committee, distribute them to the columns in Rome, Turin, Genoa and Milan and, at an appointed time, deliver them simultaneously to newspapers in the four cities. None of the 'mailmen' was ever captured. And the *brigatisti* did even worse things at virtually no cost to themselves. Still, even if disappointing, the colossal application of military force did make life uncomfortable for the *brigatisti*. The original plan of the BR had been to hold Moro for months, until as late as September 1978, and to magnify the gravity of the assault by kidnapping a high-level industrialist. Under the pressure of the forces of law and order, however, the idea of a second, simultaneous kidnapping had to be abandoned, and the duration of the Moro operation reduced.[2]

The attack upon Moro was immediately judged an attempt to undermine the democratic state. The reaction of the establishment was swift. On the morning of 16 March the cabinet and the party secretaries agreed with Andreotti that, in the event of some kind of ransom demand (which seemed probable since the terrorists could easily have killed Moro in Via Fani had that been their purpose), the state would make no concessions. Misgivings about, or outright opposition to, the Andreotti government inside the DC and PCI had been silenced by the national emergency. For the time being at least the majority was firm and united. What came to be known as the *linea della fermezza* ('policy of firmness') was thus already in place just hours after the kidnapping, and it was supported by the non-revolutionary press and the establishment generally. Andreotti, so fortified, was convinced that the democratic state, which perhaps appeared weak, was in fact strong and would triumph in the end.[3] Among the questions to be answered were how long it would be before this inevitable victory occurred and what price would have to be paid between now and then.

Aldo Moro, meanwhile, was in the BR prison under the care of his jailer, Prospero Gallinari, who was assisted by Anna Laura Braghetti, the proprietor of the apartment-prison in Via Montalcini 8 and an unsuspectable irregular. In future, after a bloody career as a revolutionary, she would become Gallinari's wife (a marriage made, not in heaven, but in jail).[4] The operation was being directly run by Mario Moretti and the other members of the Executive Committee. The Committee apparently functioned out of a base in or near Florence that had been furnished by Tuscan supporters.[5] Moretti delivered the Committee's communiqués to Valerio Morucci and Adriana Faranda of the Rome column, who in turn delivered them to the press.[6] On 18 March the first communiqué reached the press, and of course obtained the huge publicity the *brigatisti* expected and desired.[7]

Beyond the formal claim of the attack on Moro, the chief point of interest in the communiqué was the confirmation of what everyone suspected, that Moro was to be tried before a People's Tribunal, the results of which proceedings the BR promised to make public. It was obvious that the accused would be found 'guilty', but as to what the sentence could be, the *brigatisti* said nothing, the better to disorient the bourgeoisie. Together with this document, the BR delivered a photograph of Moro which was published in all the papers. In it Moro was shown in a shirt and without a tie, sitting against the backdrop of a banner of the terrorists that bore the name *Brigate Rosse* and the five-pointed star. It was a tremendous, a terrible image. There was an enigmatic, eerie, otherworldly expression on Moro's face: it seemed, at one glance, the image of a man at peace with himself, and the next, that of someone who had suddenly discovered that there was no hope in life. How was he holding up? The shock of the kidnapping, of the sudden intrusion of violence into his life; the fall from the very heights among the great and powerful of the world to this position of utter deprivation and humiliation; the loss of his ability to control even the most mundane things, like clothes and food; his loss of contact with his family, his unspeakable isolation; probably the oppressive silence of a soundproof room; and, of course, the fear – all these things he was likely to be enduring. For anyone this would have been an immensely trying situation, but it had to be worse for one like Moro, unused to physical privation, with no experience of violence, whose life had been free of sudden tragedies or misadventures, whose temperament was not the best adapted to a possibly protracted psychological struggle with the fallen angel of despair. For his daughter the most appalling thing about that photograph, which she saw in a newspaper held by a stranger in a crowd, was a seeming detail. Her father was a formal man; hence the jokes to the effect that he would even go to the beach in the summertime in suit and tie. Now here he was like this.

Nothing in all these long days made such an impression on her as that photograph. 'Never, never would papà have voluntarily appeared in shirtsleeves, and this fact, apparently so innocuous, turned my stomach'.[8]

The days passed without word of the illustrious prisoner. At the Turin trial the defendants publicly rejoiced at the kidnapping. By way of aggravating the situation, the BR column in Turin, in the street in broad daylight, shot and wounded in the legs a former DC mayor of Turin.

On 25 March Morucci and Faranda in Rome, and other *brigatisti* in the other leading cities passed to the press a second message which described Moro's career at the service of the imperialist bourgeoisie. Four days later a third communiqué vaguely summarized the progress of the interrogation, which was said to be advancing 'with the complete co-operation of the prisoner'. After yet another unsettling silence, on 4 April the BR issued a fourth communiqué.[9] It was only at this point that the political analysis that had inspired the BR in this operation became clear. The enlightenment, such as it was, came from a lengthy pamphlet that accompanied Communiqué no. 4. The pamphlet was the Strategic Resolution of February 1978,[10] which had been written by the Strategic Direction, the central committee of what the *brigatisti* were now calling, in an unintentional validation of Orwell, the 'Organization'. It said something about the preparation of the BR that the Resolution had been printed in a printing house.

The Resolution was an elaboration on a central concept, the grand fixation of the Red Brigades, which had already been sketched in the Resolution of April 1975. The evil of the current epoch, this Resolution now stated, was the imperialism of the multinationals, the phase of imperialism in which the multinationals, principally of the United States and Germany, dominate and control all forms of capital on the globe. This multinational imperialism gave rise in Italy to the Imperialist State of the Multinationals. The SIM had to restructure itself, and was doing so, in order to escape from the economic crisis. The DC was the keystone of this process; it was endeavoring to renew itself in order to fulfil its function as the domestic branch of the 'greatest multinational of crime that humanity has ever known'.[11]

The proletariat is on the march, the BR asserted. The response of the SIM was to try to bribe the proletariat with a politics of reform and to annihilate those who declined to be bribed. As to the current economic crisis, the authors of the Resolution asserted with unqualified confidence, there is no possibility of recovery. Imperialism of the multinationals, the BR wrote, is imperialism in 'the historic phase of its decline, of its putrefaction, [and] has nothing more ... to offer'.[12] The state's effort to restructure itself into the SIM in order to escape its fate presented the metropolitan proletariat with the immediate challenge of the question of power. The only way Italy could free itself from the imperialist chain and from the crisis was by destroying the state and installing the dictatorship of the proletariat. The action of the proletariat to this end must, the Strategic Direction wrote, proceed in stages. At present revolutionary action meant the 'disarticulation' of the forces of the enemy, which was to say, propagandizing the armed struggle while beginning to employ the tactical principle of the next phase, namely, the destruction of the forces of the enemy, with, as an immediate aim, an attack upon the DC. This stage would then lead to that of revolutionary civil war. In concrete terms the revolutionary project had to pass from 'demonstrative' actions to those unequivocally destructive of the enemy. This process would correspond to the building of the Fighting Communist Party to develop the class war of long duration for the conquest of power.

This was a clear reflection of the profound preoccupation of the *brigatisti* with the construction of a 'combatant party', of which they clearly considered themselves the precursors. In recent years, but especially in 1977, class antagonism, the BR wrote, had become more widespread and radical. This introduced the concept of the Proletarian Offensive Movement of Resistance (MRPO). The BR said that the MRPO, which was roughly equivalent to the most extreme elements in the movement of 1977, had to be united, which could be done only through the organizational efforts of a party of the avant-garde of the proletariat. The priority for revolutionaries, therefore, was to build the organization that the BR called 'the Fighting Communist Party'. These were virtually magical words to the *brigatisti* for they constituted the main aim of the group's actions. Thus, the documents of the BR throughout the Moro case and in innumerable other instances in later years made ritual bows to the concept, in such oft-repeated slogans as 'Reunify the Revolutionary Movement Building the Fighting Communist Party'.

In this analysis the BR were crossing swords with two competing tendencies on the extreme left. One was an 'economistic' tendency, one that, despite radical rhetoric, was willing to settle for concessions from the enemy. The *brigatisti* condemned this surrender by those with a petit-bourgeois vision of class struggle, undoubtedly referring to the journalists of *Lotta Continua* and others who advocated revolution but opposed the violent tactics of military élites such as the BR.[13] The other tendency, though not identified by name, was clearly that of the theorists of 'Autonomia'. The BR recognized and deplored the fact that the movement was extremely fragmented, but, they noted angrily, 'some notorious opportunists' have actually theorized just such 'diffused terrorism' and 'armed spontaneity'.[14] It is here, the BR indicated, that, as instructed by elementary Leninism, the party is critical. To transform a dispersed, disorganized, creeping civil war into a general offensive with a unified design, these tendencies must be fought and the Fighting Party built. The proletariat (including that of the South, where the 'barrier' to revolutionary activity must be broken down), which is 'objectively' united by the imperialism of the multinationals, must be united 'subjectively'. The Red Brigades are not themselves the Fighting Communist Party, the Resolution concluded, but an armed avant-garde that labors within the metropolitan proletariat for its construction.

With this theoretical basis in mind, you can understand the overlapping explanations of the BR's motives in the Moro action given years later by Mario Moretti and Franco Bonisoli. One objective was to achieve the acme of armed propaganda, an echo, the vast resonance of which would drive ultra-leftists into the embrace of the BR, permitting the BR to dominate and organize the movement of 1977 and to make, in short order, the 'leap' to the establishment of the revolutionary party. The other was, in effect, to obtain a recognition of the BR as a representative political force through mediation over the question of an 'exchange of political prisoners'.[15]

This summary of the characteristically prolix Resolution is inevitably reductive. In fact, the Resolution is more elaborate and sophisticated than the foregoing would suggest. It demonstrated that, whatever their psychological problems, the *brigatisti* were not simply psychotics. The Resolution also dispelled any lingering doubts among the fairminded about the political identity of the *brigatisti*. They were revolutionaries, in the grand tradition. The BR's indebtedness to Lenin, for instance, was explicitly acknowledged: '[O]ur theoretical-practical reconsideration of the Fighting

Communist Party', the Strategic Direction wrote, 'in fact is not other than the reproduction of the substance of the Leninist experience, and of its developments with the Chinese Revolution . . . For this reason, we define ourselves "Marxist-Leninists"'.[16]

The four communiqués explained Moro's relation to these ideas. He was the most prominent spokesman for the restructuring of the SIM. Moro and the party of which he is the highest expression, the *brigatisti* wrote, are responsible for the repression and exploitation of the workers, the misery of entire sectors of the proletariat, and the armed counter-revolution against the proletariat's effort to liberate itself. The judgement of 'the people' at the end of the 'trial' would be one of 'foreseeable harshness'.[17]

LETTERS, LETTERS

The most insidious novelty of these first 20 days of Moro's imprisonment was the letters that began to flow out of the people's prison. (Morucci, posing as 'Dr Niccolai', made phone calls to associates of Moro and informed them of the places in the city where these messages had been hidden.) The letters were critical to the shaping of the political dimensions of the affair, which became enormous, but it was as exhibits in a story of human affliction that the letters had the greatest impact. It all began when Moro wrote a letter to his family and another to Interior Minister Cossiga,[18] his friend and political ally. Moro had hoped to open a secret channel of communication, but because the letter to Cossiga offered enticing possibilities for a great deal of highly disruptive publicity, or because, as the *brigatisti* preferred to put it, 'nothing must remain hidden from the people and this is our custom',[19] the BR gave the Cossiga letter to the press and it was published on 30 March. Two weeks after the kidnapping, Moro's voice was being heard, and it was causing surprise.

In the letter Moro proposed to speak unemotionally. He was, he wrote:

a political prisoner, subjected, as President of the DC, to a trial directed at ascertaining my thirty years of responsibility . . . In truth, all of us of the leadership group are involved in this case and it is our collective work that is under accusation and for which I must respond.

Anticipating what the BR were likely to do and what the DC leaders were apt to be thinking, he raised an issue that the *brigatisti* had not mentioned in their two previous communiqués. Moro believed, or said he did, that the 'reason of State' favored the taking of action on his behalf:

I find myself under a complete and uncontrolled dominion, subjected to a popular trial that can be graduated, [and] I am in this state having all the knowledge and delicacy that derive from long experience, with the risk of being called on or induced to talk in a manner that could be unpleasant and dangerous in particular situations.

While a kidnapping should not be allowed to produce benefits to the kidnapper, that general rule cannot apply in a political case where injuries to the individual and to the state are 'sure and incalculable'. 'The sacrifice of innocents in the name of an abstract principle of legality', Moro wrote, 'is inadmissible when an indisputable state of necessity must induce their being saved'. Almost every country, he noted, behaved accordingly. And there should be no talk of the state's losing face, Moro said, when it 'has not known how or been able to impede the kidnapping of a high personality who means something in the life of the state'. It is necessary now to 'look lucidly at the worst that can happen. These are the ups and downs of a guerrilla war, which must be evaluated with coldness, blocking emotionality and reflecting on the political facts'.

For his family, affections were not mired in the complexities of politics:

My dearest Noretta,
    I desire that there reach you on Easter day, you and everyone, the most fervent and affectionate wishes with much tenderness for the family and the little one [his grandson, Luca] in particular. Remember me to Anna, whom I ought to have seen today. I pray Agnese to keep you company at night. I am fairly well, well fed and assisted with attention.
    I bless you. I send many dear things to all and a strong hug.
                                                                        Aldo

The members of the Rome column, Morucci and Faranda, had

opposed the release of the letter to Cossiga out of fear that publishing the letter at this delicate stage, when the political forces were forming their views on the fundamental issues raised, would inevitably cause the politicians to assume a position of rigidity from which it would be difficult to dislodge them later on. Moretti, always the hard-liner, was unpersuaded. The decision of the Executive Committee must be followed.[20]

In the early period after Via Fani the country was in a state of uncertainty, which led to an excess of speculation of all kinds. The press was not at its best, as it filled page after page with supposed hot items of scant value or with little basis in fact, or both. There were countless manifestations of the Italian passion for plots and wild imaginings about the real political coloration of the *brigatisti*, which at this point amounted to an indefensible unwillingness to accept the truth. The Ministry of the Interior consulted experts in terrorism, psychologists and handwriting analysts, not always with useful results. The press consulted other experts in these fields and produced rivers of hypotheses, some more or less reasonable, a great deal absurd or silly. This orgy of wild conjecture fed on the absence of news or developments, and, on the days when the *brigatisti* allowed some news out, it fed on that news too, calculated and tendentious though it was. As on the matter of the trial, the announcement of a 'people's trial' generated a 'debate' of very dubious value over how Moro would or might comport himself, which intensified with the revelation in Communiqué no. 3 of his purported 'collaboration'. Would he give away national secrets? Would they use force to make him do so? Would they drug him? Could he negotiate his way out of his predicament?

The arrival of the first letter stirred up further all these speculative energies, which came to focus on the political dilemma being created for the government and the DC by the posture Moro at least seemed to be adopting and on the person Aldo Moro as revealed in the letter. It was, as Andreotti said, 'a personal drama for everyone', especially for Cossiga and Zaccagnini, who were so close to the imprisoned leader. Andreotti felt that they all had to combine 'affection for Aldo and the sense of the state' and that Moro's situation was such as to deprive anything he wrote of 'moral validity'. At a 30 March meeting the other DC leaders agreed. There could be no backing away from the 'policy of firmness' without gravely imperiling the political system.[21]

And so the DC was embarked on a course directly contrary to

the one being urged upon it by its imprisoned president. There was considerable surprise in some quarters that the DC had not, as in other difficult circumstances, equivocated or dissembled or simply succumbed. The 'sense of the state', this phrase of common currency in those days, was not one of the DC's conspicuous virtues, this DC with its endless squabbling, its scandals, its compromising, its inefficient handling of the nation's business. 'It is a new image', wrote one observer.[22] 'From these Christian Democratic leaders from whom the Italians have heard half-words, half-truths and half-promises for so many years, there now seem to come, and on such a tragically difficult topic, accents of unusual firmness'. The DC found itself in the unaccustomed position of being almost universally applauded for its resolution and integrity.

When Moro had been silent, it had been easy to praise his behavior and everyone had done so. The first letter had changed everything. A debate, rather a one-sided one, began over the issue of the 'real' versus the 'false' Moro. The Moro of the letter was not the taciturn, shrewd figure to whom the press and public were accustomed. Nor was his analysis of the 'reason of state' what was expected from the Christian Democrat most regardful of the 'sense of the state'. Such was the emotional pitch of those days that the explanations proffered tended to be highly simplistic. The *Corriere della Sera* reflected the prevalent thinking when, in an editorial after the arrival of the letter, it stated that either Moro was no longer master of himself or the letter had been pried out of him by means of force or drugs.[23]

Meanwhile, copies of the BR communiqués were being distributed by the *brigatisti* at various places they considered fertile ground for the armed struggle, such as the state telephone company and the University of Rome. On 3 April the police undertook a wave of searches on the extreme left and brought many in for questioning, which set off a furore among the radicals but turned up no suspects. The same day the government majority's 'policy of firmness' was reconfirmed.[24] At the Turin trial the *brigatisti* complained about the prison system and the conditions therein for 'political prisoners'. In his diatribe on this matter, Renato Curcio referred to Moro. Curcio said:

> We assure you that this representative of your class, in whom we recognize the dignity of an individual, is not treated with the means you use ... [W]e also say to the public that the prisoners

of the people, from Amerio to the Fascist Labate to Moro, have never undergone any form of violence when they were imprisoned by the proletariat. They were simply interrogated about their responsibilities.[25]

Very reassuring, certainly!

On 4 April another letter from Moro[26] appeared. Moro this time wrote to Zaccagnini, intending to address himself to all the key DC leaders. The themes that he had set forth in his first letter reappeared here, but the tone was different. The *brigatisti* were either furnishing him with a version of what was occurring on the outside or permitting him to look at the newspapers, and he did not like what he heard or saw. He could not reconcile himself to the cruel unfairness of his position, and on this his mind dwelled morbidly during the interminable hours. He had worked all his life for the good of his party and his country and nevertheless was being asked now to pay for sins that were not his, or his only in part, sins in any case outweighed by the good he had done. It was a bitter reward. The DC owed him a special obligation because of

my extreme, reiterated and motivated reluctance to assume the position of president that you were offering me and that now tears me from my family, while it has the greatest need of me. Morally you are in my place, where physically I am, [the place of] a political prisoner who is put in an insupportable position by your brusque decision to close off any discussion concerning other persons similarly detained.

What Moro wanted was 'the only positive solution . . . the liberation of prisoners on both sides . . . To be tough may appear more appropriate, but a concession is not only fair, but also politically useful'. If the other political parties had not the courage to follow this course, the DC must have it. Otherwise,

you will have wished it and – I say it without animosity – the inevitable consequences will fall upon the party and persons. Then will begin another cycle, more terrible and equally without solution'.

Moro was aware of the debate about his mental capacity. He stated that what he had said, he had said in full lucidity and without having undergone any coercion of the person; such lucidity, at least, as one can have who for 15 days has been in an exceptional situation, who cannot have anyone to console him, who knows what awaits him.

And the proof, he said, was that he had expressed these same ideas about the humane solution of cases of kidnapping in the past. Feeling 'somewhat abandoned by you', he closed:

> If I did not have a family so much in need of me, it would be a bit different. But as it is, one needs courage indeed, having always given with generosity, to pay for the whole of the DC. May God illumine you and soon, as is necessary.

That evening the DC leaders met for another sorrowful and depressing examination of a situation that, in its human elements, was deteriorating. It was agreed that negotiations with the terrorists for some kind of 'prisoner exchange' in the event the *brigatisti* were to demand the same could not be entertained (though legal, humanitarian efforts could and should be explored). The next day the DC party paper rejected negotiations and wrote that Moro's latest letter was not morally ascribable to him. The sorely tried Zaccagnini paid a tormented call on the Moro family. The family told him that Moro was entirely lucid and that the DC must force the government to negotiate. The DC leaders discussed the family's position, but concluded that nothing could be done.[27] From this point on relations between the Moro family and the party leaders broke down rapidly, until in the end the family's sentiments toward the leaders (with very few exceptions) were those of bitterness and anger. At its most extreme, the position of the family (expressed publicly only afterward) was that the DC's unmoveability was a cruel, morally indefensible error, the result of cowardice, malignancy, envy or the desire to reap rewards for the party by the exploitation of an illustrious cadaver.[28]

Moro's letter, even more than its predecessor, was a bombshell. There was in its tone something petulant and self-pitying. The debate about the 'real' versus the 'false' Moro intensified. Moro, it was said, was being drugged, or brainwashed, or forced to sign letters dictated to him. This was no longer Moro.[29] Rather, the country was assisting, as the *Corriere della Sera* put it, at the physical, psychological and moral destruction of a man.[30] A few, mostly Moro's friends, deserted the chorus.[31] They contended that Moro had always been capable of critical, even harsh judgements about his political allies and adversaries, and, more important, that for him the paramount political consideration had always been man, not some abstraction like the 'reason of state', that a gentle, Christian conception of political life had animated all his activity since the days of the FUCI.

NEITHER WITH THE STATE NOR WITH THE BR

Ten days after the ambush in Via Fani the weekly *L'Espresso* observed that most people recognized that the community was being threatened and must defend itself.[32] There were, however, a few dissenters. A few days after Via Fani Alberto Moravia, the famous novelist, wrote that he felt like a stranger in his own country, 'extraneous' *vis-à-vis* the BR and *vis-à-vis* the ruling class.[33] This was the opening salvo in what was to become a fierce rhetorical war[34] the protagonist of which was the writer Leonardo Sciascia. Sciascia had no sympathy for the BR. But he could not be a member of a jury in a terrorism case, he said, because he felt no duty to the state. For Sciascia, the heart of the problem, scathingly delineated in his *Todo Modo* and other novels, was that the Christian Democratic Party, by virtue of its corruption, connivance with organized crime, hypocrisy and mismanagement, had tainted the state beyond all hope of redemption. In a book about the Moro affair, he wrote:

> It is as if a dying man were to get out of bed, jump up and grab on to a chandelier like Tarzan to the vines, launch himself through the window, landing, healthy and agile, on the road. The Italian State is revived! The Italian State is alive, strong, secure and tough! For a century, for more than a century, it has lived together with the Sicilian Mafia, the Neapolitan Camorra, Sardinian banditry. For 30 years it has cultivated corruption and incompetence, wasting public money in rivers and brooks of unpunished embezzlements and frauds. For 10 years, it has tranquilly accepted ... occupied and devastated schools, the violence of young people among themselves and toward the teachers. But now, in the face of Moro, prisoner of the Red Brigades, the Italian State raises itself strong and solemn. Who

dares doubt its force, its solemnity? No one must doubt: and least of all Moro, in the 'prison of the people'.[35]

The extra-parliamentary left had arrived at a loathing for the state by a different route. Though in many instances critical of the Moro operation, the extreme left had no intention of rallying around the state. The journal *Lotta Continua* was representative. One of the reasons for its anger at the BR was precisely because the BR's action reinforced the state. The state, according to *Lotta Continua*, used the excuse the BR furnished it to engage in repression and violence, a 'state terrorism'.[36] The journal here had in mind vast searches without warrants, the calling out of the army, the enactment of 'special' laws, the, in its view, criminalization of dissent whereby anyone 'who does not kiss the flag of order of Cossiga and [Communist Senator] Pecchioli is treated as an accomplice of the Red Brigades'.[37] As the BR's action reinforced the state, so the repression of the state in turn fed the flames of terrorism. Marco Boato, a leader of 'Lotta Continua', wrote that the acts of the BR had nothing to do with true Marxism, mass revolutionary movements, the class struggle born out of the events of 1968–9.[38] The objective must be a non-clandestine, mass, revolutionary opposition to the state. The guiding principle for *Lotta Continua* in the great national drama, and a slogan widely used on the far left and reflective of its thinking was, therefore, 'neither with the state nor with the BR'.[39]

These two positions show some of the difficulties the state faced in the spring of 1978. Looking back from a distance of years, you can see that Sciascia, Moravia and other such non-revolutionary dissenters were wrong, even downright irresponsible. As between the state and the *brigatisti* who aimed to destroy it, 'extraneousness' was an indefensible posture. The state, it was true, was inefficient; the political machinery was jammed; the political class was distant, arrogant and often astonishingly corrupt. And yet there could be no doubt as to which situation was preferable. This state, with all its failings, was democratic and it could be changed. Certainly there was a genuine alternative – the PCI – and there was nothing to prevent it from taking power if it could win allies and convince the necessary voters finally to sweep out the DC. What, on the other hand, did the BR believe in? Not democracy but ideas whose systematic expression, demonstrated in decades of experience, was immobile, monolithic, crushing of the human spirit. No one could deny the right of Sciascia and other dissenters to criticize the DC and the state; this was a democratic state, after all, not one controlled by the dictatorship of the proletariat. But this particular criticism was not only unfounded in its equation of the evils of the state with those of the BR; Sciascia and others also erred in creating a false choice of alternatives. The only options were *not* either siding with the BR or joining a universal chorus of mindless hosannas in praise of the DC. One could remain justly independent and critical of the DC and its ways, while backing the state in its battle against its greater enemy.

These observations apply as well to the extra-parliamentarians. But the extra-parliamentary left also bore an added responsibility for its violent cousins, the terrorists. The BR were born and developed in an age of ideology in Italy, when the professors of revolution extolled revolt and intolerance towards opposing views, when, according to progressives, the only intellectually and morally sound position was to favor the Marxist revolution of the masses against the contemptible bourgeois state, when the *brigatisti* were only 'comrades who err'. Supporters of 'Lotta Continua' and the like believed that the revolution could be brought off in the foreseeable future and that the force that would be required could be employed surgically, in a non-repulsive and limited way. Force, however, is a dangerous thing when used without democratic constraints. When they came to articulate the view that the revolution should be pursued without recourse to the violence of small armed sects such as the BR, 'Lotta Continua' and like groups should hardly have been surprised to encounter dissent on this question of method, and to discover that the aim of revolution was generally accepted but that not a few wished to hurry things along by using greater violence and using it now. When *brigatisti* are asked now how they could have killed a journalist or an industrialist without considering the inhumanity of such acts, their response is apt to be that, as one described it, they were living within a particular 'logic' – the logic of revolutionary violence – or that, as another put it, they looked at the world and at men through the 'glasses of ideology'. According to this 'logic', this ideology, to kill a man was no crime if done in the name of the proletariat. 'Lotta Continua' and others on the extreme left had contributed to the actions of the *brigatisti* by contributing to the accreditation of the ideology, the 'logic', of the anti-capitalist revolution. That 'Lotta Continua's' responsibility was indeed real was demonstrated irrefutably by the legions of former militants who eventually ended up as members of the terrorist groups.

Then there was the PCI. The PCI, to be sure, never supported the terrorists and, from 1977 on, took a very hard line towards left-wing violence. During the Moro affair the PCI distinguished itself by its rejection of any kind of dealing with the *brigatisti*. Berlinguer would have deserted the coalition, despite all the difficulties the PCI had had to overcome to get there, had the government begun negotiations with the *brigatisti*.[40]

Nevertheless, since 1921 the PCI had advocated a revolution against capitalism and the creation of a workers' Utopia, and it had greatly helped to make a culture of the left a powerful force in Italian life. And what (questions of method apart, important though they were) did the BR believe in? The intellectual paternity of the Strategic Resolution was clear. The central idea of the SIM, fantastical though it was, did not, the *brigatisti* Franco Bonisoli said,

> grow up out of nowhere. It was the ideologized and extreme fruit of that cultural baggage, including the centrality of the working class, the taking of power, the dictatorship of the proletariat, that the whole left, if in diverse ways, drew upon in those years.[41]

As a former Communist and prominent figure on the new left put it, looking at the terrorists was like leafing through a 'family album'. When some impertinent observations were made along these lines during the Moro affair,[42] the PCI lamely responded by reiterating its opposition to terrorism and arguing that terrorism conflicted with the teachings of Marx and Lenin.[43] And the PCI produced yet further examples of its wilful misreading of the BR. Because it was hardly possible to contend any longer that the *brigatisti* were merely neo-Fascists in disguise, the PCI fell back to a new line of defense. The *brigatisti* were leftists, the PCI would acknowledge hurriedly, while passing on to the main point. They are, the PCI would say, 'maneuvered' or 'manipulated' by reactionary plotters, that is, as Berlinguer put it, 'powerful forces, internal and international, that move the strings of this pitiless attack against the state and republican liberties'.[44] The principal international conspirator the PCI had in mind was the United States. As there was no proof of this conspiracy the PCI relied upon a deduction – the fact that the BR struck at the birth of the new government majority meant that their purpose was to damage the left; therefore, the plotters in charge were reactionaries. Thus, the influential PCI figure Emanuele Macaluso:

> The Red Brigades and violent extremism have not been set on their feet by a foreign secret service; but since their strategy tends explicitly to destabilize the democracy and to create the conditions for the coming of an authoritarian regime, it seems to us legitimate to think that certain forces, national and international, are trying to reach by a different road the objective they have thus far failed to achieve.[45]

And an editorial in *L'Unità*:

> What is the terrorism that is here today in Italy? Raniero LaValle in Paese Sera has given to this question a response that we agree with. He observed that the BR are only the iceberg of a powerful adversary that plays on many tables, not all clandestine ones, that re-emerges 'on the left' after having been beaten on the right, that not only uses false identity cards but also uses false names, false jargon and declares false objectives ... [T]errorism exists; it is a real phenomenon ... it uses fanatic, trained followers. But this said, it is absurd to believe all that one reads in the raving 'ideological' documents of the BR ... [This terrorism is] an instrument of provocation and destabilization.[46]

The PCI would continue thereafter to make, and still today makes, this kind of argument, which seriously distorts the nature and origins of terrorism of the left in Italy.

Furthermore, in the early years the PCI failed to exert its vast influence upon the working class to prevent the *brigatisti* from entering the factories and polluting labor-management relations, and the PCI failed to expel the *brigatisti* once they had entered or otherwise to discipline them. The union movement in general and the other leading force in the movement, the Socialist Party, share the blame. This policy favored the BR in several ways. Some workers left to become BR regulars. Others remained in the factories as BR irregulars, spying on management and the unions, identifying targets for revolutionary actions, distributing BR messages and searching for other workers to recruit to the cause. Some became sympathizers. Finally, among the workers were a not insignificant number who, though unwilling themselves to lend a hand to the BR, were equally unwilling to defend the 'regime', who considered it immoral to report on a fellow worker even if he were known to be a *brigatista*, who were not distressed if the foreman or a company officer were beaten up or 'knee-capped' by the terrorists. Even at the time of the Moro kidnapping, when the reality of subversive forces on the factory floors was clear, the subject was played down. During the kidnapping, day after day *L'Unità* overflowed with articles about the active and total opposition of the working class to the BR. But BR 'mailmen' found recipients for their bulletins in the factories and *brigatisti* were even elected union delegates, and if a representative of management or the forces of law and order were to denounce the presence of extremists in the factories, he was likely to be accused of dishonesty or worse. There were workers and others who refused to participate in the marches protesting against the Via Fani attack, or took part out of sympathy for the dead guards or to show opposition to a possible right-wing coup rather than because of solidarity with Moro and the establishment. Moro was a man of the 'Palace'. Why sympathize with him? Did the 'Palace' ever sympathize with us workers? In return for power and glory he ran some risks; it was part of his job. And anyway the DC, true to form, would, after a week or two of unctuous pieties about the sanctity of the state, descend to secret negotiations with the *brigatisti*, Moro would be freed to resume his maneuvering, and the whole business would be covered up by the silence of the politicians or the secrecy of state.[47] The *brigatista* Franco Bonisoli says:

In all our history we always had an area of consensus around us. Otherwise such an organization would never have been able to live and develop itself for ten years as happened. There are hundreds of episodes in one's memory, episodes that stimulated us quite a lot then because they had their origins in the common people. Bulletins that were passed from hand to hand, small groups of discussion in workplaces, concierges who warned comrades that the police had come to make an inspection of the building, the toasts of many members of the PCI base at the news of the [Moro] kidnapping ... Many saw in that action a shock in the direction of a possibility of a positive change in society. And then there should not be forgotten the resentment existing in large sectors of the population towards the DC and its

thirty-year-long direction of power. In substance, for many
people Moro in that moment was a little like the emperor
unhorsed.[48]

VERDICT

On 10 April the *brigatisti* delivered to the press another of their
communiqués (no. 5)[49] and a manuscript written by Moro.[50] The
latter was an attack on Senator and former Interior Minister
Taviani, guilty, according to Moro, of an error in denying Moro's
assertion of his opposition to a hard line in the Sossi case. Moro
insisted that his position had been then what it was now. Beyond
considerations of humanitarianism and wisdom, there were political reasons that supported this position. In cases of guerrilla
warfare such as this, he said, the state had to be willing to engage
in 'an exchange of prisoners' in order to save innocent lives, to give
some respite to 'combatants, even if they are on the other side of
the barricade', to prevent tension from growing and the state from
losing credit or force. The bulk of the document was startling,
consisting of a very sarcastic and unflattering description of
Taviani's political career.

   This latest effort did not have the results Moro hoped for. A
group of his political friends declared 'unrecognizable' the Moro
who had written this text.[51] Sen. Taviani remained unmoved,
while Prime Minister Andreotti was influenced by what he said
was documentary evidence in government files that showed that
Moro had been opposed to negotiations with the BR in the Sossi
case.[52] The DC reiterated its stance – it would not negotiate,
though it would leave no humane and legal solution unexplored.
Unfortunately the collection of 'political prisoners' in the jails of
the state increased by one as a result of tragic circumstances. On 11
April, after having 'knee-capped' an important businessman in
Genoa four days before, the BR shot and killed a guard in the jail
where the *brigatisti* on trial in Turin were being held. The symbolism of this crime was unmistakeable. One of the *brigatisti* was
wounded in this action and was left by his comrades in front of a
hospital. He was Cristoforo Piancone, who turned out to be a
former worker at Fiat.

   A few days later came the announcement, in Communiqué
no. 6,[53] that the interrogation of Moro was over. Moro had con-

firmed, the BR wrote, what the proletariat had always known – that the bourgeois state produced nothing but exploitation and misery for the proletariat. There were therefore no 'clamorous revelations' to disclose. Moro's trial was over and a verdict had been reached: 'Aldo Moro is guilty and is therefore condemned to death'.

The notice had been expected, but not for that was it any the less tremendous. Now clearly threatened, perhaps imminent, was what would be, if carried out, one of the greatest political crimes in recent Italian history and in the history of post-war Europe. Though Moro and his family seemed not to admit the possibility, the dilemma of the DC leaders was an awful one. Zaccagnini and Cossiga were sincerely attached to Moro. While under the threats of the BR he berated them and while they were being attacked by Mrs Moro, they struggled with their sentiments and their convictions. The BR had thus far made no demands. Surely they would not simply kill Moro without attempting to gain something for him. There might yet be time. Perhaps some way could be found to save Moro without conceding to or negotiating with the *brigatisti*. A *via umanitaria*?

OF COVES AND LAKES AND DEADLINES

18 April. The 30th anniversary of the DC's greatest electoral victory. Finally, after what had become an embarassingly futile investigation, the police had some real evidence in their hands. Unfortunately for the image of the police, the acquisition of this evidence had not been a masterwork of criminal investigation.

Water leaking through the ceiling of one of the tenants in Via Gradoli 96 in Rome had caused an intervention by the firemen, who entered the apartment above. The firemen found the source of the trouble – a running shower – and something more – that they were in a BR hideout. In short order, and with a lot of noise that drew a crowd, the police and *carabinieri* arrived. This was not just any BR cove. Among the documents, weapons and other material discovered was evidence linking the apartment to Via Fani, such as the original license plate of the Fiat 128 that had initiated the accident. It seemed as if this apartment, a relatively short distance by car from Via Fani, may have been the headquarters for the Moro operation. The handwriting on the rental contract found there was that of Mario Moretti. A pair of eyeglasses were identified as belonging to Barbara Balzarani, battle-name 'Sara'. Moretti had narrowly avoided capture. He had returned unsuspectingly to Via Gradoli after the firemen had arrived, but, alerted by the hullaballoo, had made off unnoticed.[54] The mass of material in the hands of the authorities was certainly useful.[55] But it did not provide indications of where 'Engineer Borghi' and 'Comrade Sara' were now. Nor did it contain any concrete lead to the prison of Aldo Moro or even the sector in which he was being held. If, that is, he was in Rome.[56]

The same day, a purported new communiqué was delivered to a newspaper in Rome.[57] It announced the execution of Aldo Moro ('through "suicide"') and that the body was to be found in the Lago della Duchessa. The horror and distress at this piece of news were international. There were big headlines in all the world's papers, special bulletins on the radio, special programs on the TV. Zaccagnini rushed to the Moro home to offer solidarity, but was allowed to speak only with two of Moro's long-time collaborators. Mrs Moro was convinced that all was over.[58] And yet there were reasons for thinking the Communiqué no. 7 false. It was, first of all, simply unlikely that the BR would end the match in this fashion, without even an effort to free Curcio *et al.* Secondly, the message in content and tone was suspiciously unlike the BR. There was none of the expected 'political analysis'. There were none of the slogans (for example, 'Build the Fighting Communist Party') with which the BR always closed their bulletins, and the style was unlike that of the BR. Thirdly, a mere glance at a map suggested that the small Lago della Duchessa was a very unlikely place in which to have discarded Moro's body. The lake is located at an altitude of about 1800 meters in the mountains not far from Rome. As was immediately obvious upon a hurried check of the place, there was no chance Moro's body was in that lake. There was snow on the ground and there were no tracks to indicate that anyone had been in that isolated area for days. Bringing a body up there, in the snow and wind and cold, would have been difficult. Why would the BR have chosen that of all places? It violated the BR's criteria of practicality and political symbolism. Moreover, the lake was frozen over with thick ice and had been so for months. Nevertheless, the lake and the surrounding area were searched, with divers laboriously inserted into the icy waters through holes chopped in the solid crust. The work was anxiously followed by the press and the

Moro family. Moro was not found. The communiqué had been a fraud.[59]

On 20 April the BR embellished their work when the vice-commander of the guards of the prison of San Vittore was assassinated by the 'Walter Alasia column' of Milan. (The column was named after a young ex-militant of 'Lotta Continua' who had joined the BR and been shot dead by the police, though only after having killed two policemen himself.) Later that day the *brigatisti* distributed the genuine Communiqué no. 7.[60] It described, at some length, the BR's vision of the treatment inflicted on Curcio and comrades, a universe of 'special laws, special tribunals, concentration camps', torture, political, psychological and physical annihilation, prolonged isolation. Whereas Aldo Moro was being treated 'scrupulously, like a political prisoner and with the rights that that status confers on him', political genocide had been carried out by the DC against fighting Communist militants and more of the same was planned for the future. Despite this, wrote the BR, the revolutionary movement would make no humanitarian appeal; its only appeal was for the destruction of the state:

> As far as Aldo Moro is concerned, we repeat ... that he is a political prisoner condemned to death because responsible in the highest degree for 30 years of Christian Democratic power in the running of the state and of all that that has meant for the proletariat. The problem to which the DC must respond is political and not one of humanitarianism – humanitarianism which it does not possess and which cannot constitute a façade behind which to hide itself, and which, claimed by its bosses, sounds like an insult.

Therefore, the members of the Executive Committee insisted, the 'release of the prisoner Aldo Moro can be taken into consideration only in relation to the liberation of Communist prisoners'. The DC would have to give a 'clear and definitive response' if it intended to follow this course; no other possibilities existed. The DC and 'its government' were given 48 hours, until 3 p.m. on 22 April, after which hour the *brigatisti* would carry out the sentence issued by the Tribunal of the People.

The hours after the false communiqué of 18 April, when it seemed that the worst had happened, had amplified the desire of all to prevent that worst from truly taking place. At the initiative of the Moro family, a group of public figures of diverse backgrounds (Heinrich Boll, Dario Fo, two prominent Communists and others) had issued an appeal, published in *Lotta Continua*,[61] urging both the state and the BR to take the steps necessary to free Moro. Numerous other intellectuals joined this appeal in subsequent days. For its part, *Lotta Continua*, which from the outset had supported the idea of a 'prisoner exchange',[62] had criticized the rigidity of the state, 'which in death, in war and in fear seeks to gain the force it does not have, the authority it does not have, the legitimization it does not have'.[63] Zaccagnini on TV had spoken of the DC's support for legal efforts to free Moro. Now, however, the critical hours had been reached. Moro was alive. That was certain because the *brigatisti* had delivered a photograph of him, the second, to a newspaper in Rome together with the latest communiqué. The photo showed him sitting in front of the usual flag with the five-pointed star and the words 'Brigate Rosse'. He wore a shirt open at the neck and in his hands was a copy of the previous day's *La Repubblica*, which carried the headline, 'Moro assassinated?' He did not seem physically ruined, as you might have expected from the tone of his letters, but rather tired and sad, and there was that distant, indecipherable expression on his face, that supreme weariness about the eyes and mouth. Moreover, the communiqué had for the first time broached the idea that his life might be saved. And by not stating any specific demands about the nature of the 'prisoner exchange', the communiqué had left some room for maneuver, for the DC and the *brigatisti* alike.

On the other hand, the BR had ruled out with clarity any humanitarian gestures. This had been foreseeable, for the BR were acting out of political belief and it was natural that they would listen only to a political interlocutor. And since they regarded the DC as the player on the other side of this chessboard, it was natural that they would consider valid only moves made by the DC. Thus in doubt were various humanitarian initiatives that had been launched by the government and the Moro family. Amnesty International issued an appeal in which it expressed willingness to talk with the BR about the detention of Moro. Later Amnesty obtained permission from the government to visit the jails in the hope that this focus on a matter of expressed concern to the *brigatisti* – prison conditions – might lead to a dialogue, or, at least, a slowing down of the machinery of death. The International Red Cross was approached by the government, but nothing came of this because of juridical limitations on the powers of the organization. At the request of the family Andreotti wrote a letter to Marshall Tito, seeking his intervention with other governments, and Tito in fact wrote to Castro, Gheddafi and Boumedienne.[64] UN Secretary General Waldheim on two occasions made appeals for the release of Moro. None of these efforts produced any results.[65]

Thus, over a month after it had so badly begun, the sequestration of Aldo Moro seemed at a turning point. There were but 48 hours to save him. To his family, the path to his salvation appeared blocked by a DC stubbornly and, they believed, inhumanely unwilling to compromise. For the DC, the opportunities to do something other than issue press statements full of pious hopes were narrowing. Someone would have to make a move to respond to those terrible appeals coming from the prison of the BR. It was obvious that the BR's threat had to be taken seriously. There was another bitter irony here. The BR, who vaunted a sense of humanity and a loftiness of ideals unknown to the DC and the rest of the bankrupt bourgeois democratic system, believed in the death penalty for their 'convicts', whereas the 'regime' of the DC had outlawed the death penalty and had refrained from using it against any criminal. In the justice of the proletariat, no such consideration could be accorded to such a one as Aldo Moro.

9

The Politics of Life and Death

THE PARTY OF FIRMNESS AND THE PARTY OF NEGOTIATION

On 21 April 1978, the day after the arrival of Communiqué no. 7, the Socialist daily *Avanti* announced that Moro's life had to be saved, that 'principles must be at the service of men, not men at the service of abstract principles'.[1] The PSI Directorate, though ruling out an exchange of prisoners on grounds of both principle and practicality, stated its dissatisfaction with what it called

> a sort of prejudicial and absolute immobilism . . . that goes so far as to exclude even the search for a reasonable and legitimate possibility. Between the extremes of giving in to blackmail and prejudicial refusal, other paths may exist, which, in diverse forms, diverse democratic states have not hesitated to explore. That that be done in the dramatic circumstances that have occurred is the firm request of the Socialist Party.[2]

This statement seemed a not-so-thinly-veiled critique of the DC, though it remained unclear what the Socialists had in mind as an alternative, as that other path to explore.

Previously Secretary Craxi and other Socialists had conducted a series of meetings with Giannino Guiso, attorney for Renato Curcio and other *brigatisti*. Guiso had warned the Socialists, on the basis of conversations with his clients, that a concession to the BR in the form of the release of detained revolutionaries would have to be made or else Moro would be killed. As to the details of a negotiation, the state, the *brigatisti* said, should 'dialogue with Moro'.[3]

In the past the *brigatisti* in jail had been critical of Moretti and the others for neglecting the problems of the prison and for failing to obtain their release. Word had been smuggled to the detainees prior to 16 March that an important, but otherwise unidentified operation would be put in motion to help to get them out. The jailed *brigatisti* had not dreamed that the BR would be so ambitious. Now, they believed, decisions about Moro rested with the members of the Executive Committee, who alone knew all the relevant facts. Moreover, circumstances made the contacts of the jailed *brigatisti* with Moretti *et al.* highly problematic. Thus, the ability of the jailed *brigatisti* to help the Socialists was limited. And there certainly was no particular sympathy for Moro on the part of the jailed *brigatisti*. Curcio and the others were not opposed to the killing of Moro on principle. Although it does not square well with Guiso's account of his discussions with the jailed *brigatisti*, Alberto Franceschini now claims that he, Curcio and the others were open to discussions that could have led to a declaration by the jailed *brigatisti* that Moro should be freed in exchange for concessions, such as the closing of Asinara and other special prisons. The possibility of such discussions was not pursued, however, because, according to Franceschini, the 'historic compromise' was too strong to permit it.[4]

At an early stage the Socialists realized that the Guiso contact would yield only general interpretations of the BR's thinking. Later the Socialists did locate an actual channel to the BR (or rather to a part thereof) in the persons of the prominent *autonomi*, Lanfranco Pace and Franco Piperno. Pace, it appears, had been a *brigatista* for a time. Craxi and other Socialists met with these individuals both to canvas the views of the 'autonomous area' and to find a solution to the kidnapping. The encounters proved of no help to the Socialist initiative. The contacts of Piperno and Pace, Valerio Morucci and Adriana Faranda, were then fighting an uphill battle to persuade the majority of the Organization to recognize that the killing of Moro would harm the cause of the armed struggle.[5]

At the beginning Craxi did not clearly articulate in public the change in his party's attitude to the government line. Confusion over the Socialist position, disagreement with it, the tension of the moment, and suspicion of the Socialists' motives combined to produce the greatest controversy of the period. On one side was the 'party of firmness': the DC, the Communists, and the two small lay parties of the majority (as well as the Liberals). On the other, the (inaccurately named) 'party of negotiation': the Socialists, the Moro family and friends, certain intellectuals and public figures and, most important of all, Moro himself. In the last phase of this crisis there was a continuous cross-fire of bitter charges between the two sides, accusations of disloyalty to the dead in Via Fani, of responsibility for the encouragement of terrorism and of a desire to reap partisan gain from the tragedy. The most notable charges along this last line were made by the sorely tried prisoner. This discord was widely perceived as a breakdown in the government's 'policy of firmness', or at least in the unanimity thereof.

The clearest point in defense of the 'policy of firmness' was that the freeing of jailed *brigatisti* would have violated the laws of the state. The power to dispose of accused or convicted terrorists did not even belong to the government, but to the independent magistrates. Moreover, the concession of freedom to jailed *brigatisti* would have been an enormous humiliation and political defeat for the state. A success for the BR would have confirmed the Organization's political strategy and reinforced the belief of the leadership and members in the future of the revolution. It would also have given the BR many recruits. A culture of the armed struggle and an extensive practise of it on a small scale were already widespread on the extreme left and young extremists were already being seduced by the image of the now world-famous BR. Here was one group that was demonstrating literally before the eyes of the whole world that it was serious about revolution. A triumph for the BR in the Moro duel would have greatly accelerated this process of conversion to the armed struggle. The question of the invigoration of the image of the state or that of the BR was not an inconsequential abstraction.

Ceding to the BR would also have aggravated the cynicism with which the state was all too often regarded by the public, proving that, whatever happened to others, the politicians would always find a way to save themselves. Similarly, it would have damaged the resolve of the forces of law and order. The commander of the *carabinieri* in 1978 has stated that he believed that protests or unrest would have taken place in the ranks of the police and *carabinieri* had the government negotiated with the BR.[6] Why should the *carabinieri*, police and prison guards put their lives on the line if the *brigatisti* they captured were then to be set free again? And no one could doubt that, if the state surrendered here, the country would face a rash of kidnappings, more freed terrorists and more political victories for the BR, the cumulative effect of which, at a time of political instability and economic crisis, could have been devastating. If the state bargained for Moro, then it would have to bargain for all future victims, whatever their political or social rank. Nor could exile for the freed *brigatisti*, which Moro suggested, be of much help. It was unlikely that, once freed, they would take up painting. They would return to their homeland to carry on the armed struggle, as had the terrorists in a famous German case of 'prisoner exchange' cited by Moro. Moro predicted a conflagration if his solution was not adopted; conversely, a 'prisoner exchange' would facilitate 'the gradual calming of the [terrorist] phenomenon',[7] a truce in the war. The BR, however, were uninterested in a truce; they *wanted* a war, as they stated clearly in the Strategic Resolution. The primary purpose behind 'Operation Fritz' was to inflame and to achieve hegemony over the groups of the movement and thus to build the Fighting Communist Party and lead the proletariat to a revolutionary civil war.

The Socialists were the most objective and responsible proponents of a different solution. Like Moro, they believed that the first duty of the state was to protect human life and that the government must act with this duty in mind in instances of political kidnapping. The idea that eventually emerged from the reflection of the Socialists – an autonomous, humanitarian initiative (which, however, fell short of the negotiated exchange demanded by Moro and his family) – would not have transgressed the constitutional order, though there would have been a departure from custom in pressure being brought to bear in favor of the beneficiary. The Socialists did not ignore the specter of a flood of kidnappings, but judged that risk more remote than that of the death of Moro. Like Moro, the Socialists were influenced by cases of prisoner exchanges in other countries. Not all of these, however, were happy precedents. In an instance to which Moro referred, Italy had expelled Palestinians caught red-handed in an attempt to carry out a terrorist attack. The expulsion had been negotiated by Foreign Minister Moro as part of an understanding by which Italy was to have been spared from being the site of future such activities. The feeling had been that this was an acceptable arrangement if peace inside Italy could be achieved thereby, even though the terrorists might very well go and kill elsewhere. But the BR were Italy's problem, which could only be resolved by an eventual confrontation between the terrorists and the state.

Most of the political forces and the press backed the government. So did the public, as a poll showed.[8] The developments in the case, including the repeated attacks, mortal and not, on others by the BR, contributed to a growing consensus that the BR were intolerably brutal and very dangerous and that the government could have no dealings with them. Although the debate – to negotiate or not – has never completely ended, there has been no sign of any great change of heart on the part of the public in the years since the end of the terrible 'spring campaign'. All the blood that has been spilled since has only confirmed that no serious compromise with these revolutionaries was then, or could ever be, possible or productive.

Along with the photograph and the communiqué setting forth the 48-hour deadline, 21 April saw the arrival of another Moro letter,[9] the most dramatic and pitiful to date. In the letter, addressed to Zaccagnini, Moro charged that the DC was seeking to deal with the problems posed by his case with 'indifference' and 'cynicism'. Dissent had been silenced, as had the voice of his family, which had been unable to 'shout out desperately its suffering and its need of me'. If nothing is done, he wrote, the death penalty would be reintroduced through 'inertia, insensitivity and blind respect for the reason of state'. He had worked hard to bring the government crisis to an end, not thinking

> either of my security or my rest. The government is on its feet and this is the recognition that is paid me for this as for many other efforts. The removal from my family without farewell, the solitary end, without the consolation of a caress, of the political prisoner condemned to death.

If he died, a terrible spiral would follow that would overthrow the DC leadership; an irreparable breach would open in the party, led by the humanitarian forces of the country, his friends, 'the many, many Christian Democrats who have been accustomed for years to identifying the party with my person'. 'I say it clearly: for my part, I will not absolve or justify anyone'. My blood, he said, 'will fall upon you, on the party, on the country'.

Moro would acknowledge no principle in the DC's position. In another letter to his wife,[10] he criticized the DC leaders for their failure to realize how much trouble would come 'after' and that a prisoner exchange was the lesser evil. All this rigor 'in a mixed-up country like Italy. Face is saved, but tomorrow honest men will

weep for the crime committed, and above all the Christian Democrats'.

> Naturally I cannot but underline the wickedness of all the
> Christian Democrats who wanted me, though I was unwilling, to
> take up a post, which, if necessary for the Party, ought to have
> been saved for me by the acceptance of an exchange of prison-
> ers. I am convinced that would have been the wisest thing. In
> this supreme moment, there remains my profound personal
> bitterness. Was no one found who would dissociate himself? . . .
> No one has repented of having pushed me to this pass that I
> clearly did not want? And Zaccagnini? How can he remain
> tranquil at his post? And Cossiga, who did not know how to
> imagine any defense for me? My blood will fall on them.

And the other great theme of the letters – his family:

> But it is not of this I want to speak; but of you whom I love and
> will always love, of the gratitude that I owe you, of the
> unspeakable joy that you have given me in life, of the little one
> whom I loved to watch and will try to watch until the last. If only
> I had your hands, your photos, your kisses. The Christian
> Democrats . . . take this also from me.

Moro also wrote to the Pope.[11] Recalling their past dealings
going back to the days of the FUCI, Moro asked the Pope to use his
influence to persuade the Italian government to accept a 'prisoner
exchange'.

The hours ticked on toward the deadline. On 21 April, the day
before the expiration of the deadline, while the Socialists disclosed
their discomfiture with official policy, the DC issued a statement
that, in tortuous style, proposed Caritas, the Catholic charitable
organization, as a channel of information to the BR.[12] Thereafter,
the radio and television broadcast phone numbers by which the BR
could contact Caritas to make their desires known. The hours
passed without result.

On Saturday, 22 April, the Vatican released an appeal from the
Pope to the Red Brigades.[13] The appeal had been prepared by the
Pope personally, in his own hand. In it, dispensing with the
customary papal 'we', the Pope begged the BR 'on my knees' to
free Aldo Moro, this friend since student days, this 'worthy and

innocent man'. This was an unusual and impressive act on the
Pope's part. There was, however, a feeling among those attuned to
the manner of thinking of the BR that it might have been wiser had
the Pope not made mention of a release of Moro 'without conditions'. The hours passed. The deadline of 22 April went by. From
the *brigatisti* there came only an ominous silence.

ULTIMATUM

On 24 April the silence was broken. The only good thing about
Communiqué no. 8[14] was that it indicated that Moro was still alive.
Otherwise it attacked the DC for having failed to give the clear
statement of position that the BR had demanded and rejected all
humanitarian appeals. The only thing that could restore Moro to
freedom would be the release of Communist prisoners, specifically
13 individuals: three from the group XXII October, three from
NAP, one common criminal turned revolutionary and six *brigatisti*.
The BR were thinking big; they wanted no less than Renato Curcio,
Alberto Franceschini, Maurizio Ferrari and Roberto Ognibene of
the historic nucleus, along with Paola Besuschio and even Cristoforo Piancone, the *brigatista* wounded in the recent 'battle' with
(that is, assassination of) the prison guard. In the absence of an
'immediate and positive response' by the DC, Moro would be
executed.

Later that day, continuing their masterly orchestration of this
national ordeal, the BR arranged for the delivery of another letter
from Moro to Zaccagnini.[15] After repeating many of the points
made previously, the letter concluded with terrible and severe
words:

I repeat that I do not accept the iniquitous and ungrateful
sentence of the DC. I repeat: I will not absolve and will not
justify anyone. No political and moral reason can drive me to do
it. Joined with mine is the cry of my family, wounded to death,
which I hope can autonomously speak its word. The DC must
not think that it has ended its problem, liquidating Moro. I will
be there still as an indomitable point of contestation and of
alternative, to prevent the DC's becoming what is made of it
today. For this reason, for an evident incompatibility, I ask that
at my funeral neither authorities of state nor party men take part.

I ask to be followed by the few who have truly loved me and are worthy therefore of accompanying me with their prayer and with their love.

It would have been hard for the *brigatisti* to have made a more provocative demand. Craxi was upset. The Socialist Party announced its rejection of the blackmail and so did the government and the rest of the political establishment. Further reminders of the peril the BR represented came on 26 and 27 April, when the Rome column shot a DC politician in the legs and the Turin column 'knee-capped' a Fiat official.

On 29 April a series of letters from Moro arrived, one directed to the Christian Democratic Party,[16] others to the President of the Republic, Andreotti, Craxi, Senate President Amintore Fanfani and others.[17] Everything continued to depend on recognition of the justness of a 'prisoner exchange'. In the letter to the DC Moro wrote:

Upon what basis can it be deduced that the state will go to ruin if, once in a while, an innocent survives and, in compensation, another person goes, instead of into prison, into exile? The whole matter is here. Behind this position, which condemns to death all the prisoners of the BR (and it is foreseeable that there will be prisoners), the government has taken refuge, the DC has stubbornly taken refuge, the parties in general have taken refuge, with some reservation on the part of the PSI, a reservation which it is hoped can be clarified urgently and positively, given that there is no time to lose. In a situation of this type, the Socialists could have a decisive function. But when? There will be trouble, my dear Craxi, if your initiative were to fail.

The 'obstinate, unmovable men of the DC', stuck on their 'questionable principles', were doing nothing to prevent

one of [the DC's] prestigious exponents, a faithful militant, from being brought to death. A man who had closed his career with the sincere renunciation of the leadership of the government, and was literally torn by Zaccagnini ... from his post of pure reflection and study to assume the equivocal role of President of the Party.

He lamented the absence of a formal debate inside the DC. Accordingly he would use his power as president to call an urgent meeting of the DC National Council and delegated the job of presiding over it to an ally. Again his thoughts turned to his family:

It is known that the very grave problems of my family are the fundamental reason for my struggle against death. Over many years and many events, my desires have fallen away and my spirit has been purified. And I believe I have, though with many faults, lived with hidden generosity and delicate intentions. I die, if my party will so decide, in the fullness of my Christian faith and in the immense love for an exemplary family that I adore and hope to watch over from on high in heaven ... But this bath of blood will not go well for Zaccagnini, nor for Andreotti, nor for the DC, nor for the country. Each will carry his responsibility. I do not want, I repeat, the men of power around me. I want near me those who have truly loved me and who will continue to love me and pray for me. If all this is decided, may the will of God be done. But let no one responsible hide behind the fulfilment of a presumed duty. Things will be clear, they will be clear soon.

The letters from prison certainly revealed a Moro to whom the public was unaccustomed, and, as each additional letter arrived, the controversy about the identity of Moro and the propriety of his conduct grew more intense. Some of the speculation about this Moro and these letters was far off the mark. He was not being drugged. The BR did not use physical force to get him to write those letters. It was said that psychological violence was employed, but the *brigatisti* have insisted since, and it is probably true, that it was Moro who conceived the arguments, drafted the letters and selected the addressees.[18] (Mrs Moro has specifically recognized her husband's style of expression and thought in the letters.) It is then comprehensible that Moro was irked by the widespread refusal to accept the documents as his and the refusal to grapple with the substance of his argument:

And I must say that I have been profoundly saddened ... that some friends ... without either knowing or imagining my suffering, not detached from lucidity and freedom of spirit, have doubted the authenticity of what I was maintaining, as if I wrote under the dictation of the Red Brigades. Why this certainty about my presumed non-authenticity? But between the Red Brigades and me there is not the minimum communality of views![19]

Of course the chromatics of the letters were disorienting to the public. The words were very harsh and embittered. The overwhelming fact was, however, that Moro was in prison, under threat of death, and had been so now for almost a month and a half. His knowledge of the events in the world outside was incomplete. In all likelihood his interrogator during his 'trial', Mario Moretti, and his jailer, Gallinari, made it a point to keep distant from him emotionally speaking, so that he was utterly alone (is it possible to be more alone?). He had every reason to be, as he put it, 'not in a happy state of mind'.[20] He was depressed and afraid. Who could blame him given the circumstances? As a result he dropped a curtain of formality and politeness that had concealed a darker side, one that, like the darker sides of all of us, did not entirely do honor to him. He did not repudiate the values of the DC, but the leadership, the 'men of power'. He had, it seems, long concealed a disdain for many of the leaders of the DC, to whom he felt superior. He had nevertheless worked with these men because he had wanted to practise politics and they were there. Evidently he had believed he could lead them, or at least restrain them, while through the party he put his Christian values to work in society. For many years, he had succeeded. Now, at this most difficult moment, he could not move them.

He was also prey, in those interminable days, to an underestimation of the value of the state as idea. All his career he had been a prodigious practitioner of the arts of political analysis and maneuver. Less successful had he been in the administration of the state and in the development of public policy. This divarication was a reflection of what he, pessimist that he was, believed possible in 'a mixed-up country like Italy'. In his prison he could not but sense a confirmation of this pessimism. So he gave vent to his darker feelings, even though they could have done him no good, either with the DC or with the BR.

Yet all of this is only a part of the story of Moro the prisoner. As the affair entered its decisive phase, it was to be noted that the *brigatisti* had failed to carry out their promise to spread far and wide the admissions they had purportedly forced out of the 'accused' during his 'interrogation'. This was one of those silences that speak volumes. Some months afterward, the *carabinieri* found the so-called 'memoriale' of Moro in a BR base in Milan.[21] This document appears to have been compiled by the splicing together into an uneven whole of excerpts of notes written by Moro in connection with his 'interrogation' or statements made by him during his questioning by Moretti. The document contains observations by Moro on abuses of the secret services, the formation and troubled lives of the center-left governments and the government of national solidarity, his experiences in the DC and other matters. The *brigatisti* clearly had selected what they judged the most damaging bits and pieces with the intention of distributing the same to the movement. They took their time assembling the document, however, and never did distribute it before it fell into the enemy's hands. The reason is clear: the interrogation of Moro was a great disappointment. Moro continued, as ever, to maneuver. Whatever the feelings against his friends in the DC that pressure and worry had unleashed in Moro, he was not about to give the BR anything with which to undermine the country or the DC itself. Thus he revealed no national secrets. He talked about the DC's problems with corruption without providing any evidence of corruption. He talked about the 'strategy of tension', but offered no spectacular revelations. He was vague about the 'regime' of the DC, though portraying the party's internal life as extremely turbulent and competitive. He said nothing that might have bolstered the BR's theory of the Imperialist State of the Multinationals. Indeed, on this subject fundamental to the BR's thinking, Moro was so imprecise that the *brigatisti* suspected he was trying to hide something. Tragically, it is only recently that it has occurred to the *brigatisti* that Moro may have been so taciturn because the SIM was a fantasy about which there simply was nothing to be said.[22] Moro did have a few extremely unkind observations to make about the talents and qualities of some leading Christian Democrats. Zaccagnini was 'the worst secretary the DC has had'. Flaminio Piccoli 'has always been wrong and will always be wrong'. Moro's venom was reserved especially for Andreotti: 'cold, inscrutable, without doubts, without feelings, without ever a moment of human pity', a man for whom Moro confessed an 'innate, forty-year long, irreducible distrust'.[23] But, at most, the public release of these phrases by the BR would have caused passing embarrassment to a few politicians. The *brigatisti* had expected a great deal more from the 'people's trial'.

Moro's vagueness and prevarication seem to have been no

accident. A *brigatista* has reported what he had been told by one of the BR leaders: 'Immediately after the kidnapping [Moro] asked for a bible and received it. In his way, Moro declared himself a political prisoner and did not offer any type of collaboration with the Red Brigades'. Moro was 'a very consistent and dignified and courageous person'.[24] Another *brigatista* was told the same by Valerio Morucci: 'The conduct of Moro was courageous and very dignified notwithstanding the awareness on the part of the parliamentarian of the impending danger to his life'.[25] Yet another reported having been told by Mario Moretti that Moro had shown 'much lucidity' and 'firmness in defending the political line of the Christian Democratic Party'.[26] Franco Bonisoli of the BR Executive Committee, to whom Moretti surely reported everything that was happening inside the 'people's prison', said that the *brigatisti*, whose opinions of the capacities, character and honesty of DC politicians and of the political class in general could not have been lower, were struck by Moro's intelligence and surprised by the sincerity of his religious faith.[27] His attachment to his family was profound and he spoke of them often. He passed his days as a prisoner writing, reading the Bible and responding to the questions put to him in the 'interrogation', which became, however, after the first few days, a discussion or debate in which Moro presented his version of facts and ideas in a free form, while also listening to Moretti and trying to understand the *brigatisti* and their highly ideological view of the world. The *brigatisti* were impressed by Moro's desire to comprehend the phenomenon of Italian revolutionaries and to understand why he had been selected as their victim. Immediately after his capture, astonished, he had asked the *brigatisti* why they had kidnapped him of all people, he who had always tried to bring right and left together, to calm inter-party discord, to heal and pacify. Moro held to his principles. 'His attitude in these interrogations', said Bonisoli, 'was like that of a great patriarch who does not unload onto others responsibilities that, as a father of the system, he felt to be his above all. And in this we always respected him'. Moro intervened with his letters, confident at the beginning that he could persuade the DC to see things his way, as he had always done, though having doubts about the PCI. But then, to his surprise, came the rejection of any negotiation. 'When he felt himself abandoned also by his friends in the party, he went through dramatic moments. But he always maintained a very dignified manner'.

THE SEARCH FOR A HAPPY ENDING

With Moro's life now in the balance, the Socialists pressed ahead with their initiative. A small group of legal experts was established to try to identify some 'political detainees', *brigatisti*, members of NAP or other revolutionaries, who had not killed or wounded anyone, whose legal position permitted some kind of intervention and who, because females with children or persons afflicted by health problems, were deserving of sympathy. The Socialists hoped that an indulgence – for example, a presidential pardon or a judicial order of conditional liberty – given such a person by the state, independently and without negotiation, as a humanitarian gesture, would permit the *brigatisti* to pretend to have won and lead to Moro's release.[28] Because of their prominence, all but one of the 13 names in Communiqué no. 8 were missing from the list under study by the group of experts. The one name in common, however, offered interesting possibilities: Paola Besuschio, a *brigatista* of some importance, a female who had spilled no blood and who suffered from health problems. Another name, not on the BR's list but still interesting, was that of Alfredo Buonoconto, a *nappista* who had been in jail for several years, who had committed no crimes against the person and who was tormented by psychological disturbances.

On 26 April, Craxi publicly sketched out his idea. That same day, after listening to Craxi, Zaccagnini expressed the DC's interest in exploring the possibilities for a humanitarian initiative that would respect the laws of the state. The Republicans and the Communists were extremely uneasy about the Socialist project, which they believed risked becoming a concession to the terrorists disguised as something else. For this reason the PCI openly criticized the suggested extension of executive clemency or provisional liberty.

Meanwhile, inside the fort of the BR, deliberations were underway about what to do with Moro. In keeping with the principle that all revolutionaries were equal (a principle denied in practice by the manner in which the BR were structured and functioned), the Executive Committee canvassed the Organization. The only ones not in favor of executing Moro were a small minority of the Rome column led by Valerio Morucci and Adriana Faranda. They argued that the movement within the Socialist Party, appeals by Amnesty International and the group of intellectuals in *Lotta Continua*, signs of possible softness on the part of Senate President

Fanfani and other events demanded flexibility from the BR.[29] Morucci and Faranda wanted Moro freed without conditions. They opposed the murdering of defenseless prisoners and in fact were in disagreement with the conduct of the entire 'Operation Fritz', believing that the armed struggle should be linked to the larger social struggles of the movement.[30] The discord was another instance of the great philosophical quarrel within the revolutionary area: that between supporters of the armed struggle within the movement, such as the leaders of 'Autonomia', on the one hand, and, on the other, advocates of the armed struggle led by an armed avant-garde, the nucleus of the party, the most prominent advocates of which were the BR.

Moretti insisted, however, that the intervention, or failure to intervene, of the DC would be decisive. The discovery of the base in Via Gradoli had caused a marked increase in the obduracy of Moretti and the Executive Committee, which was reflected in Communiqués nos 7 and 8. On 24 April Morucci met with the *autonomo* Lanfranco Pace, who reported on his contacts with the Socialists. Morucci informed him that Moretti was interested only in a direct recognition of the BR by the Christian Democrats.[31] Time was growing short. Moretti told Morucci towards the end of April that the affair would have to be brought to a quick end. One of the reasons Moretti gave for this change in plan was that a recent sweep by the police had come perilously close to the 'people's prison'.[32] Faranda told Moretti that the demand for the release of those particular 13 had been virtually a provocation. She and Morucci tried to persuade Moretti that the appeal of the UN Secretary General (25 April) constituted a political recognition sufficient to justify releasing Moro. Moretti was unmoveable.[33]

The arguments of Morucci and Faranda did persuade Moretti to make a small concession, a special warning to underscore the importance of an accommodative decision by the DC. On 30 April, from an underground passage in the Termini Station in Rome, in the presence of Morucci and Faranda, Mario Moretti placed a telephone call to the home of Aldo Moro.[34] As the Moro phone was tapped, the call was recorded by the authorities[35]; later this icy conversation was to be played for the nation on radio and TV. Mrs Moro answered the phone. The normally imperturbable Moretti mistook her for one of her daughters:

Eleonora: This is Nora Moro.

Moretti: Listen, I am one of those who have something to do with your father. I must give you a final communication.

Eleonora: Yes?

Moretti: We make this phone call out of scrupulousness, because your father insists upon saying that you have been a bit misled and probably you are reasoning on the basis of a misunderstanding, no? And up to now, all the things you have done are ... they are of absolutely no use.

Eleonora: Yes?

Moretti: We believe that, instead – by now the games are over, and we have already taken a decision. In the coming hours we cannot do anything other than carry out what we have said in Communiqué no. 8. So we believe only this: that an intervention, immediate and clarifying in this sense, by Zaccagnini is needed. If that doesn't happen, you must realize that we can't do anything but this. Understand? Have you understood me exactly?

Eleonora: Yes, I understand very well.

Moretti: Look, only this is possible. We have done this simply out of scrupulousness, in the sense that, you know, a sentence of death is not a thing that can be taken lightly, not even on our part. We are willing to bear the responsibilities that fall, that fall on us, and we would like exactly, since your father insists, believes, that in fact you have not intervened directly because you are badly advised ...

Eleonora: No, we have done what we could ...

Moretti: But look, the problem is ...

Eleonora: ... they even keep us prisoners.

Moretti: No, but the problem is political, so at this point Christian Democracy must intervene. We have insisted on this very much because it is the only way by which a negotiation can eventually be reached. If this doesn't happen ... No, I can't discuss it. I'm not authorized to do so. I can only give you this communication. Only a direct, immediate and clarifying and precise intervention of Zaccagnini can modify the situation. We have already taken the decision. In the coming hours the inevitable will happen. We can't do otherwise. I don't have anything else to tell you.

A volley of telephone calls from the family followed this 'scrupulous' message, including one to President Giovanni Leone. That same day, the family issued a public statement[36] that broke with the DC, whose position the family regarded as ratifying the death of Moro.

OF GERUNDS AND OTHER MATTERS

On 2 May Craxi met with Andreotti to illustrate his idea, mentioning Paola Besuschio as a possible beneficiary. Though not rejecting the autonomous solution in principle, the prime minister opposed the freeing of Besuschio and was worried that a concession would not necessarily lead to Moro's release. Craxi expressed optimism, but of course it was impossible to know for certain, especially in the absence of negotiations (which he ruled out), what the BR's inclinations were in this regard. Craxi also met with Berlinguer, who likewise opposed the extension of any benefits to Besuschio.[37]

In a meeting with the DC committee that was managing the crisis, a Socialist delegation presented the idea of an autonomous, humanitarian gesture. Though the meeting seems to have been heated, Craxi felt that the positions of the two sides were converging.[38] One of the DC leaders described the PSI's initiative as a proposed 'path that, in the abstract, is practicable, but which it is necessary to examine in concrete terms case by case'.[39] Zaccagnini consulted the other parties about their reactions to a humanitarian solution involving Buonoconto (without mentioning that name) and found that they were not opposed.[40] (Zaccagnini thought that he had not found absolute opposition on the part of the PCI, but that may well have been wishful thinking.) The DC issued a communiqué formally referring the proposal to the government. Shortly thereafter it was announced that the Central Directorate of the DC would meet on 9 May to discuss the situation and to re-examine all legally acceptable solutions. On that date a decision would be taken on Moro's request for the urgent convocation of the DC National Council.

A few hours after the release of the DC's communiqué the government expressed itself.[41] The Socialist proposal would be considered at a meeting of the Interministerial Committee on Security that would take place 'in the coming days'. However, government policy is 'not to hypothesize even the most minimal departure from the laws of the state and not to forget the moral duty of respect for the suffering of the families that mourn the tragic consequences of the criminal operations of the adversary'. From the perspective of anyone who favored considering an autonomous gesture by the state, as Andreotti apparently did,[42] the wording of this document was unfortunate. To *brigatisti* observing cynically from the outside, the postponement to an uncertain date and that concluding phrase appeared to be diplomatically-worded indifference to the BR's demands.

With a dénouement approaching, the family and allies of Moro increased the pressure on Zaccagnini and other key figures. Mrs Moro called Andreotti and pleaded desperately. At least a pardon of some terrorist should be tried, she implored. She asked as much in calls to President Leone and Justice Minister Bonifacio.[43]

The Besuschio option had in the meantime been set aside for technical legal reasons and because one of the factors that made her case appealing to the Socialists – that she was on the list of the 13 – made it very unappealing to the government. But the Socialist idea was gaining converts. The group of legal sages now concentrated on the case of the *nappista* Alfredo Buonoconto, which was brought to the attention of the Minister of Justice, while, to further fecundate the atmosphere with signs of reasonableness, the government granted a request by Amnesty International to inspect the much-criticized prisons. The release of Buonoconto from jail for health reasons was a matter for a judge, but the Justice Minister did request of the court speedy consideration of a motion for provisional liberty presented by the attorney for the *nappista* on 8 May. That same day, as a signal of the government's good intentions, Buonoconto was ordered to be transferred to Naples to be near his physician.[44]

To Moretti and the Executive Committee of the BR, this flurry of activity still fell short of the necessary public commitment to negotiations by the DC. The visit of Amnesty concerned a subsidiary issue. The Socialist initiative offered an outcome far from what the BR had demanded, was vague, and was being developed too slowly and too quietly. The DC continued, as the BR saw it, to dissemble. The government was unmovable. The BR therefore sent another of their messages of impatience written in the style congenial to them. On 4 May they 'knee-capped' two businessmen, one in Genoa and one in Milan.

The next afternoon Moretti brought the decision of the Executive Committee. He met Morucci and Faranda in Piazza Barberini in Rome and turned over to them for delivery to the press the BR's Communiqué no. 9 – the notice of impending death. There in the piazza, at the bottom of the fashionable Via Veneto, amidst the crowds coming and going in their private pursuits and the tourists thinking of Bernini and Respighi and the fountains of Rome, a strange, animated conversation ensued. Morucci and Faranda, who had taken part in the operation even to the extent of, in Morucci's case, firing on Moro's bodyguards in Via Fani, now argued on Moro's behalf. They contended that the various steps taken in response to the BR's action represented a victory for the revolution, that the BR had effectively been recognized as a political force by the interventions of the Pope and Waldheim and by the statement of the DC after the meeting with the Socialists on 2 May. They told Moretti that killing Moro would represent a political watershed highly damaging to the revolutionary move-ment, that it would create an escalating military struggle with which the BR could not cope. As usual the iron-willed Moretti could not be dissuaded. Moro must die! Moretti agreed only to postpone the execution until after the customary Sunday political discourses, against the extremely remote possibility that some desperate action would be taken by the politicians to save Moro's life.[45] 7 May would tell the tale.

The haste to conclude of Moretti and the Executive Committee remains one of the mysteries of the Moro kidnapping. You can understand easily enough why the *brigatisti* would have been dissatisfied with the steps taken or hinted at by the bourgeoisie. What is hard to understand is how the *brigatisti* could have failed to perceive that there was indeed real movement on the other side of the barricades. If they had held on a little longer, something closer to their desires might have been effected. The original plan, after all, had contemplated many months of imprisonment for Moro. Why such hurry now? Could they not have waited until the meeting of the DC Directorate on 9 May? Was it, as suggested in that comment of Moretti to Morucci at the end of April, fear that the police were drawing close to the prison where Moro was held? Or was it that Moretti and the hardliners were afraid that a kind of humanitarianism would, like a pestilence, infect the Organization? True, there was a division within the BR, but Morucci, Faranda and their followers represented a distinct minority. Was it that Moretti foresaw that a peaceful solution was possible if the hand of the executioner were stayed for some days or weeks longer, but that Moretti did not want such a solution, did not want to miss this wonderful opportunity for a qualitative leap towards the construction of the party and the rallying round it of the movement, an opportunity that might never present itself again? Now there predominates among the jailed *brigatisti* an interest in presenting an image of the BR as rational, but still no convincing explanation has come forth from them as to why they were in such a rush to see Moro dead.[46]

On 5 May Morucci and Faranda distributed Communiqué no. 9 to the press.[47] It was destructive of many hopes:

The so-called 'humanitarian proposals' of Craxi, whatever these might be, since they exclude the liberation of the 13 sequestered comrades, qualify themselves as maneuvers to throw smoke in the eyes, and figure in the games of power, in party or electoral interests, which do not concern us. The only clear thing is that on the exchange of prisoners the position of the PSI is the same, of obtuse rejection, as that of the DC and of its government, and this is enough for us.

In words we have nothing further to say to the DC, to its government and to the accomplices that sustain it. The only language that the slaves of imperialism have shown they know how to understand is that of arms, and it is with this that the proletariat is learning how to talk.

We thus conclude the battle begun 16 March, executing the sentence to which Aldo Moro has been condemned.

For the family, the nadir of despair had been reached. Only a slim strand of hope remained, that fixed to the gerund – 'executing' – used by the BR. That meant that the worst had not yet happened. The family could still plead and pray.

The Socialists did not abandon their effort despite the icy water thrown on it by the communiqué. On 6 May a leading Socialist met with Senate President Fanfani, a man of prestige and influence in the DC and a long-time competitor of Moro in the trench warfare inside the party, and tried to persuade him to endorse the PSI proposal. Fanfani, who was also being pressed by Mrs Moro, decided to have an ally of his make a public statement as a signal to the BR not to precipitate the situation. Unfortunately, the ally's effort, a speech on Sunday, 7 May, fell absurdly flat, amounting to no more than a vague restatement of past positions of the DC. Fanfani himself then made a public foray. Unfortunately he was a master of meaningless verbosity, and his statement on 8 May was convoluted and almost incomprehensible, which defeated the purpose.[48]

The uncertainty was magnified by the government. Shortly before the arrival of Communiqué no. 9, the Interministerial Committee on Security met, as promised, to consider the idea of an autonomous gesture. A statement issued by the Committee seemed to imply a rejection of the idea.[49] 'The concession of pardons', the statement said, 'is connected to humanitarian norms of clemency. Other, different connections would offend the legal system and the public conscience'. All other possible initiatives to free Moro, it continued, would be explored. Despite the appearance of intransigence on the part of the Committee, the case of Buonoconto was even then being studied. The signals being sent might not have been sufficient in any case, but it did not help their efficacy that they were being crossed.

In the desolation of his prison Moro was aware that his situation was almost hopeless. It will never be known whether his bitterness, his regret at having chosen a political life ('How much does the spectacle of apparent greatness cost!'),[50] his sense of the absurdity of what was happening to him because no one wished to trade a terrorist or two for his life, reached such depths as to become spiritual despair, the antithesis of the Christian faith that had sustained him through all the vicissitudes of his life prior to this most extreme one. At least from what the *brigatisti* say and some of what he wrote (for example, 'I accept what the Lord sends me'),[51] it would appear that in this he was resilient. The BR told him he was to die. He wrote a final time, to his wife.[52]

After a moment of very slim optimism, due perhaps to my misunderstanding what was being said to me, we are by now, I believe, at the conclusive moment. It doesn't seem to me worthwhile to discuss the thing in itself and the unbelievability of a sanction that falls upon my meekness and my moderation. Certainly I was mistaken, for good ends, in defining the direction of my life. But it is not possible to change now. It remains only to recognize that you were right. It can only be said that perhaps we would have been punished in some other way, we and our little ones. I would like the full responsibility of the DC, with its absurd and incredible behavior, to remain very clear. This must be said with firmness, just as any eventual medal that it is desired to give in this case must be refused. It's also true that very many friends ... either misled by the idea that speaking would damage me or preoccupied by their personal positions, did not move as they ought to have done. Only a hundred signatures collected would have forced a negotiation. But this is all in the past. For the future, there is in this moment an infinite tenderness towards you, the recollection of all and of each, a great, great love full of memories apparently insignificant and in reality precious. United in my memory you live together. It will seem to me to be among you ... Be strong, my sweetest, in this absurd and incomprehensible trial. These are the ways of the Lord. Remember me to all our relatives and friends with immense affection and to you and to all a very warm embrace full of eternal love ...

Now suddenly, when some small hope seemed to stand out, there comes, incomprehensibly, the order of execution. Noretta, sweetest, I am in God's hands and yours. Pray for me, remember me gently, caress the sweet little ones, all. May God help you all. A kiss of love to all.

Aldo

On 8 May the military secret service intercepted a message that it claimed originated with the *brigatisti*. The message seemed to have a hidden meaning. The text was *'il manderino è marcio'* ('the mandarine is rotten'). Studied by experts in deciphering, however, the message became distinctly more sinister: *'il cane morirà domani'* ('the dog will die tomorrow').[53]

OF FINAL THINGS

On the morning of Tuesday, 9 May, the Directorate of the DC met at party headquarters in Piazza del Gesù. The request for the release of Alfredo Buonoconto was being considered by the court, and the official order for Buonoconto's transfer was in the pipeline. Fanfani, who had been importuned the previous evening by Craxi and who was much affected by the appeals of Mrs Moro, intended this morning to try to persuade his colleagues that something further should be done for the President of the DC.[54] Fanfani began to explain his dissatisfaction with the actions taken thus far. It was then that Interior Minister Cossiga phoned Andreotti and told him that Moro had been found. For a second or two, Andreotti thought that perhaps they had located the prison and liberated Aldo. But Cossiga quickly disillusioned him – Aldo Moro was dead.[55]

That morning, Moretti had contacted Morucci and Faranda and told them to call and announce that the sentence had been carried out. Just after midday Morucci had gone to Termini Station and placed a call to Professor Franco Tritto, Moro's assistant at the university.[56] Morucci, as 'Dr Niccolai', had told Tritto that he should go to the Moro family to advise them where they could find Moro's body: in a red Renault-4 parked in Via Caetani. The police had been listening in on this call, but they had been too late to catch 'Dr Niccolai', who had slipped away into the crowds of unsuspecting travelers.

Via Michelangelo Caetani is a small, insignificant street in the heart of the Eternal City. What made it an ideal place for the grisly ending of this drama was that it was nearby both DC headquarters in Piazza del Gesù and PCI headquarters in Via delle Botteghe Oscure. The BR had driven across the city to one of the most heavily guarded areas of all, with the body in the back of the car. The extent of the risk taken was a demonstration of the importance the BR attached to the way 'Operation Fritz' was brought to a close. This last act, like so many others of the BR in the past and in the future, had to unfold according to a scenario drenched with symbolism, had to have, and be seen to have, a political meaning: the defiance of the DC and the PCI, the challenge to the 'historic compromise', the humiliation of the bourgeois system, and, Moretti emphasizes, an assignment of responsibility for the tragic outcome.[57] Not even a cadaver was immune from ideological exploitation by the BR.

There in Via Caetani the police found the red Renault. In the rear, under a blanket, was the body of Aldo Moro. The body, dressed in a suit, was curled up in a small space. Moro's right hand rested on his abdomen. His head was turned toward the left. His face was unshaven. His eyes were partly open. His overcoat was there and a bag containing his personal effects. As a priest gave the last rites, police and officials gathered. Private citizens came to look too, but were held back by the police. The forensic experts performed their ritual. Photographers shot pictures. The photos of the rear of the red Renault were destined to be spread around the entire world, to become infamous records of the grimmest era in the post-war life of the nation. Notwithstanding their elaborate theories, this was what the *brigatisti* stood for. This was not, as the *brigatisti* had thought, a political scene; it was, above all, a human one, as had been the one in Via Fani 54 days before. That was not an important politician in the back of the car, but simply a man, and it was the family of a man, not a politician, that was being shattered. The inconceivable had now happened, and for a good part of the country the truth about the Red Brigades was seen in all its vileness.

On the fringes of the movement, though, there were young extremists who were attracted by the BR's importance, by their determination, by their willingness to practise the armed struggle *alla grande*. For some young radicals, the kidnapping and assassination were a demonstration of the revolutionary rigor of the BR and gave the group a kind of glamour. The Moro operation generated a significant spurt of recruits, thus inspired and convinced that the BR were the only truly serious revolutionary option.[58] Apart from this military consequence of the 'spring campaign', however, this, which appeared the greatest victory of the BR, was in fact a defeat, the beginning of their decline. They had failed to take over and galvanize the movement, much of which instead condemned their actions. They had failed to break the DC or to shatter the majority of national solidarity, which, for all the controversy between the 'party of firmness' and the 'party of negotiation', had remained united. They had even achieved this – the transformation of public revulsion at what had been done into a substantial success for the DC (42.5 per cent) in partial administrative elections held on 14–15 May. Unfortunately, the decline of the BR would be slow, filled with many horrifying variants on the scene in Via Caetani. Valerio Morucci some years afterward said this:

The armed struggle, as a project of power or of subversion in an advanced society, was born with a cancer inside it. The metastasis exploded with the killing of Aldo Moro and from then on it has only been death. The more the armed struggle died, the more it tried, with a practise of homicide, devoid of any ethical and social sense, to exorcize its destiny.[59]

If the assassination of Moro ultimately proved a political disaster for the *brigatisti* and the whole revolutionary area, it did have one major political consequence that pleased the most enthusiastic of the terrorists. The murder of Moro was the removal from the scene, at a moment of unprecedented difficulty in the life of the Republic, of the premier political strategist. Moro's dire predictions for the future – of collapse, of the destruction of the DC, of a division in public opinion over the issue of negotiation with the terrorists – did not come true, for the state and its institutions were stronger than he had imagined, and the public much less tolerant of the terrorists than might have been feared or than was thought by the *brigatisti*. His predictions did come true to this extent, though – his absence changed things dramatically. With his death there was no one who could stitch together a coalition as he had been able to do, no one who could inspire the same confidence among the Communists while reassuring the DC and the other parties. It is possible that the 'third phase' he had foreseen would in any case have proved short-lived, that a compromise between the DC and the Communists was so much an intermingling of opposites as to have meant inevitable rupture. But if there had been any chance of success for Moro's vision, that had virtually been destroyed by his death. And, in fact, notwithstanding the great motive for unity represented by the continuing threat from the BR and the other terrorists, as well as the persistence of grave economic problems, the experiment in national solidarity ended in early 1979 with the PCI's abandonment of the majority. The majority had withstood the challenge posed to it and to the democratic system itself by the 54 days. But political differences were too great, and the price being paid by the PCI leadership within the party for the compromise with the enemy, the DC, was too high, and Moro was not there to smooth things over.

The President of the DC had been killed between 9 and 10 a.m. He had been shot 11 times, by Prospero Gallinari, who, almost a decade after the founding of the 'Group of the Apartment' in Reggio Emilia, now took a place in the gallery of the nation's most prominent murderers. Eleven shots had been necessary, Barbara Balzarani explained later to a fellow *brigatista*, because 'when you shoot someone in the heart, he doesn't cease to live immediately'.[60] Ten of the shots came from a Skorpion 7.65 automatic machine pistol that Valerio Morucci had brought with him into the BR and that had been used to assassinate magistrate Coco in 1976 and

Judge Palma weeks before Moro was kidnapped (a murder also done by Gallinari). One of the shots had come from a caliber 9 pistol. The shots had been fired at very close range while the president was lying in the rear of the red Renault. The bullets had hit Moro in the chest but missed his heart. He had lost consciousness within seconds, but did not die for some 15 minutes, as the result of vast loss of blood. Gallinari, probably with the help of his future wife, Anna Laura Braghetti, had stopped up the wounds with handkerchiefs to contain the bleeding. Moro's clothes had been put in order and the body covered with the blanket. Gallinari and Braghetti had then driven the red Renault off to its appointed destination in Via Caetani.[61]

The majority opinion is that the killing took place in the garage of the apartment in Via Montalcini (the two weapons having been furnished with silencers for at least 9 of the 11 shots).[62] Another matter not definitively resolved concerns Moro's state of mind as he climbed into the rear of the Renault. Did he think he was on his way to his death? His last letter to his wife so suggests. But some *brigatisti* have testified that 'humanitarianism' prevailed and there is a reference in Moro's 'memoriale' that seems to bear this out. The scene described is poignant. Moro was misled at the end. He was advised that he would be released rather than killed. He told Gallinari to send his regards to 'the other one', meaning the *brigatista* who had questioned him, Mario Moretti. He got into the back of the car with a lightness of spirit he had not known in almost two months. The surprise and the pain could have been felt only very briefly before he lost consciousness.[63]

The Moro family issued a statement in the late afternoon of 9 May:

> The family desires that the precise wish of Aldo Moro be fully respected by the authorities of state and of party. That means: no public manifestations or ceremony or discourse; no national mourning, nor state funeral or medal of commemoration. The family closes itself in silence and asks for silence. Of the life and death of Aldo Moro, history will be the judge.[64]

The next day, after deceiving the press about their intentions, the family took the body to Torrita Tiberina, a small town near Rome where the Moros kept a retreat from the difficulties of public life. There, with a simple rite, and followed only by family and friends from the village, Aldo Moro was buried.

On 14 May, despite the family's statement, an official memorial service for Moro was held at San Giovanni in Laterano conducted by the Pope and attended by the high and the mighty of Italian public life and by delegations from abroad. Moro's brother and sister were the only family members present. A few days later the family offered a r ɪss for Moro to which a small group of friends and, among politicians, only Craxi and Fanfani were invited. There Mrs Moro offered a prayer for the executioners of the crime and their supporters, and a prayer for those 'who, for reasons of jealousy, cowardice, fear, stupidity, ratified the condemnation to death of an innocent man'.[65] In the years since, she has not forgiven the leadership of the DC.

Could Moro have been saved other than by a total concession to the demand for the release of the 13? According to Valerio Morucci, 'a sign of openness of the DC and liberation of a single Communist prisoner' would have put the BR's backs to the wall, would, that is, have made the execution unacceptable.[66] Franco Bonisoli of the Executive Committee asserts that Moro could have been released had Paola Besuschio and Buonoconto been freed and the DC made some kind of formal recognition of the BR; and, further, he claims that the mere release of Besuschio would have prevented the BR from killing Moro (though the kidnapping might have gone on for some time afterward).[67] No less than Mario Moretti now claims, though evasively, that the outcome might have been different had the DC made a small gesture, provided, however, 'that it was clearly in the sense of the assumption of responsibility for the problem of the political prisoners', and provided that any eventual mediation was conducted in the view of the whole revolutionary area.[68]

Assuming that there had been some room for a deal on terms vastly less demanding than those of Communiqué no. 8, can the DC be criticized for having failed to have done more to explore the possibilities? What the DC could have done was limited not only by its sense of the responsibilities of a party and government under attack by the likes of the Red Brigades (as well as, it should not be forgotten, by other terrorist groups and the broader, but still unruly and often violent movement), but also by the positions of the other parties, the press and the public.[69] The DC, for example, would have been hard pressed to accept a situation in which it was being reproved for an inadequate defense of the democratic system by the Communists. Still, despite the great passion that marked the clash over the issue of negotiation, the differences in the end between the Socialists and the DC and the government were not so very wide. While the Socialists rejected a negotiation for the release of the 13, the DC and the government were making moves in the direction of an autonomous, humanitarian gesture. The policy adopted by the DC and the government was censurable, then, only by someone who favored the solution urged by Moro, or, at the opposite end of the spectrum, by someone who felt that even a humanitarian gesture was an inadmissable concession to the terrorists. The execution of this policy was a different matter. Although, of course, the government and DC were obliged not to give any appearance of irresolution, they seem to have moved too slowly, and certainly moved with insufficient clarity in the application of this policy. It may – may – be tragically true, assuming that there truly was some flexibility in Mario Moretti's cold heart, that Moro might have been saved had the BR's haste to end the affair not intertwined with these factors. You cannot be certain, however. You must be very cautious in weighing the after-the-fact claims of the *brigatisti*, for it suits their interests, even those of the unrepentant *brigatisti*, to shift the blame for Moro's death off themselves onto their enemy, the DC. The determination reflected in the communiqués issued during the 54 days and in the careers of Mario Moretti and the other leading *brigatisti* does not inspire confidence that a bloodless finish to an affair begun in blood was ever possible. Certainly, if the BR had been open to a solution that was practicable, they did not do much to show it. It is now convenient for the jailed *brigatisti* to imply that their adamantine communiqués were merely the public expression of ferocity done for the purpose of reinforcing image and internal discipline, but that behind the fierce words was flexibility. This is difficult to reconcile with, for instance, the demand for the release of the 13, clearly provocative both in its scope and for the identity of the personalities embraced in it. Apart from Curcio and Franceschini, whom it was obvious the state simply could not release, how could the BR not have recognized that the demand for freedom for the just-captured murderer Piancone would not only be rejected, but would be considered evidence of utter intractability on the part of the BR? Franco Bonisoli, who was in a position to know, now claims that the BR's demand for the release of the 13 had primarily a symbolic, political value and that they hoped for the release, not of all 13, but of one at least.[70] It is surely not fair, however, to put the blame for the misinterpretation of the BR's intentions (if that is what it was) upon those who read the messages for what they literally contained rather than those who wrote them that way. Moreover, the BR did not respond to any of the signals of flexibility sent their way. Just when some signs of movement by the bourgeoisie were detectable, as Morucci and Faranda were pointing out, Moretti and the Executive Committee (in Communiqué no. 9) repeated the demand for the 13 and heaped scorn on Craxi's initiative. The 30th April telephone call by Moretti to Mrs Moro showed a willingness to delay for a few days, but only so that the DC might concede to the *brigatisti*'s terms. On the substance of the issue the BR seemed only to want to be intransigent.

No final answer to this question will ever be arrived at. It is difficult to know where in these fervent revolutionaries the broad boundaries of faith ended and the narrow vestiges of a common sense of humanity began. This was exemplified on the day after the finding of Moro's body in Via Caetani, when Renato Curcio, founder, philosopher and guiding spirit of the BR, philosophized during the trial in Turin that 'the act of revolutionary justice exercised in regard to Aldo Moro is the highest act of humanity possible in this society divided in classes'.[71] Or, in the words of Mario Moretti: 'We did not kidnap and kill Moro the man, but his function. We reject the accusation of political homicide'.[72]

10

The Emergency, Phase One

GOOD INTENTIONS, MEAGRE RESULTS

Among other things the Moro affair revealed to the nation was the disheartening lack of preparation of the forces of law and order. The blunders began very soon after the shooting stopped in Via Fani. An official in the Interior Ministry sent an order to police offices around the country that they put into immediate effect the emergency 'plan zero'; unfortunately, the plan did not exist. Three automobiles used by the *brigatisti* in Via Fani were discovered in a street not far away – but only on three separate occasions over four days. The Interior Ministry released photographs of individuals believed to be *brigatisti* possibly involved in the crime and these were given wide publicity. It turned out, however, among other things, that two of the individuals in question were already in jail and two photos were of the same person under different names. Another of those shown was Marco Pisetta, who was in hiding from the BR. A few names were on the mark – Moretti, Gallinari and Bonisoli, for example.[1] But there were also other names of persons who were not even *brigatisti*, let alone involved in the case. And as to all of the individuals, the authorities had no hard proof.

Moreover, the police had few clear notions about where to look for their suspects and did not pursue all such notions as they did have. They suspected that the 'autonomous area' in Rome was in communication with, if not linked to, the *brigatisti*, but they did not tail the leaders of 'Autonomia', some of whom were indeed in contact with *brigatisti* during the 54 days.

Days after Moro's body was found the police entered the BR's printing shop in Rome and arrested the Organization's printer and other *brigatisti*. The investigators, however, had been slow in acting on the information that had eventually led them to the shop. Furthermore, though originally intending to delay an intervention in the hope of catching Moretti, they had gone ahead anyway even though Moro was by then dead. Graver still, afterwards they abandoned detailed surveillance, so that, when Moretti arrived and found the place shut up, he was able, upon learning from a neighbor that the printer had been arrested, to make another of his famous escapes.[2]

The most serious incident of all had to do with the hideout in Via Gradoli. The police searched Via Gradoli, no. 96, on 18 March 1978, that is, two days after Moro's capture. When they came to apartment number 11, no one answered the bell. The neighbors 'described Engineer Borghi and his girlfriend as quiet, respectable people. Though orders for that area were that the police should either enter vacant apartments by force or await the tenants' return, the police, satisfied, went away and no later visit was made to confirm what they had been told about Engineer Borghi, which information was of no value whatsoever by way of reassurance. Moreover, two tenants living in an apartment across the hall stated that they had told the police on 18 March that they had heard strange noises the night before, like the sounds of morse code.[3] Had the police entered the apartment on 18 March they would have uncovered the BR's operations center. They might then have put surveillance on the inhabitants, one of whom, Moretti, would have led them, within days of Via Fani, to the prison where Moro was held.[4]

The Moro case also brought to light a serious shortage of the means needed to conduct an effective counter-offensive against terrorism. There was no centralized, comprehensive memory-bank of data on the terrorists, as in West Germany. To maintain control over weapons traffic, the Interior Ministry possessed but a single file kept by hand.[5] The magistrate who took charge of the investigation on 16 March discovered that the information on known or suspected terrorists was inadequate and that no experts were available to assist him. A huge commitment of forces was made to countless roadblocks, which were of secondary utility in view of the BR's sophistication. The large-scale searching of homes was conducted without a clear plan. The authorities, in the words of no less than the Prosecutor General,[6] gave precedence to spectacular 'parade-like operations' over a search that was well thought out. With regard to the criminal investigation, the magistrate was somewhat overwhelmed by the dimensions of the case. The burden fell to him because he chanced to be on duty on 16 March. No group of magistrates was assigned to the case. Indeed, there were no magistrates who were expert in left-wing terrorism. The magistrate in charge was not relieved of his normal duties and had to work simultaneously on one of the most important criminal cases of the century and on motorcycle thefts and the like. He did not have adequate staff assistance nor sufficient co-operation from the police. He did not even have a phone in his office.[7]

In addition, the direction of the great man-hunt was confused and ineffective. No single individual or small group of individuals was really in charge. Each of the several police forces (public security police, *carabinieri* and finance guard), the jurisdictions of which overlap and which are given to rivalry, pursued its own course without real co-ordination. Co-ordination was, in theory, to have been provided by a committee of the chiefs of these forces and other important officials, which met daily under the leadership of Interior Minister Cossiga or his deputy. But the lesson to be drawn from the work of the committee was, according to the Moro Commission, a negative one: 'in effect, the Committee co-ordinated nothing, but rather revealed itself as the place in which the frustrations deriving from failure were poured out'.[8]

The record was also dismal as regards the collection of intelligence on suspected terrorists. It will be recalled that, in 1974, after the Sossi kidnapping, special anti-terrorism groups had been established, General Dalla Chiesa's *carabinieri* unit and the 'Anti-terrorism' of Emilio Santillo. Dalla Chiesa's group, however, had been dissolved some months after when those in higher authority decided that the BR had been destroyed.[9] Santillo's group had lasted slightly longer, having been transformed in July 1976 into the Security Service (SDS), an operational information-gathering organ with nuclei around the country. One result of these unjustified bureaucratic decisions was that experienced officers were transferred, with the loss of precious expertise.

A second series of mis-steps began in early 1978. Because of past abuses by the military secret service (SID), the parliament in October of 1977 had ordered an overhaul. The SID was to be abolished, and so was the SDS of Santillo. A new structure of the secret services was created: a military secret service, the 'Servizio per le Informazioni e la Sicurezza Militare' (SISMI) ('Military Information and Security Service'), in charge of espionage and counter-espionage; and an information service charged with internal security, the 'Servizio per le Informazioni e la Sicurezza Democratica' (SISDE) ('Democratic Information and Security Service'). To provide co-ordination and supervision, a committee was set up in the office of the Prime Minister, the 'Comitato Esecutivo per i Servizi di Informazione e di Sicurezza' (CESIS) ('Executive Committee for the Information and Security Services'). Contemporaneously, the Interior Minister created new police squads in the major cities. Certainly parliament's decision to reform the secret services was reasonable. The difficulties came in the timing and the implementation of the reforms. The new secret services were to begin operations in May 1978. Their predecessors, however, for reasons that remain obscure, were dissolved early, in January 1978. Though SISMI took over much of the personnel and apparatus of its predecessor (which was strange in view of the purpose behind the reform), it was not fully operational as of 16 March. SISDE, the service that was intended to be in the forefront of the anti-terrorist struggle, was, at the time of Via Fani, still months away from an operational condition. It had but 10–12 men and, as its chief admitted, was able to furnish only 'extremely limited' assistance in the Moro case.[10] CESIS was virtually non-existent. As a result of all these changes there had been considerable shuffling of personnel prior to 16 March, with inevitable confusion and ineffectiveness, which principally affected SISDE. Beyond that, individuals with experience in anti-terrorism operations were dispatched to jobs with unrelated responsibilities, which constituted once again a waste of priceless knowledge.[11] The means by which the state gathered and distributed intelligence on terrorism and the BR were thus probably at the lowest level of efficiency ever, just at the moment when the need was greatest.

The picture that emerges is of a state profoundly unprepared for what befell it in March 1978. Interior Minister Cossiga and all those who had held positions of responsibility among the forces of law and order in the spring of 1978 later acknowledged as much.[12] Why such imпреparation in the face of a phenomenon that was hardly new? With important exceptions (for example, Dalla Chiesa and his collaborators), there was complacency, and a lack of understanding of the terrorist phenomenon among the politicians and the bureaucracy. On a superficial view, the system seemed more or less to be coping and the warnings of the better-informed few were dismissed as excessively pessimistic. Among some, as we have seen, there was a refusal to accept that the BR were the leftists they claimed to be. The foregoing horrors have to do with the structure and the direction of the anti-terrorist effort, and it was on these points that the authorities should have been laboring prior to

1978. But their planning and organization had been founded on the assumption that the primary threat facing the state came, not from terrorism by military élites, but from widespread disturbances of public order, such as engaged in by 'Autonomia' in Rome or the Veneto. In so thinking, the authorities had erred, though they had not been simply wildly irresponsible: the BR had indeed been almost finished at the beginning of 1976 and 1977 had been the year of the movement and of the P38. In addition, the leaders were distracted from organizational questions, seduced by the idea, which commonly captures governments in times of special social unrest, that the answer to the problems of law and order lay in new legislation that increased criminal penalties and expanded the powers of the police. While young policemen who were without instruction in the ideology, strategy and tactics of the terrorists and who had not even had adequate training in how to use the guns given them were sent out to hunt and fight a crafty and by now experienced enemy, while anti-terrorist squads were dissolved and men were transferred without sufficient care, while Dalla Chiesa was denied complete co-operation from rival services and from rivals within his own service, the political leadership and the leaders of the forces of law and order spent time, energy and political capital trying to obtain such supposedly decisive weapons as the much-heralded *fermo di polizia* (a right of the police to stop and detain suspects). But it was less the 'get tough' laws that were to defeat the terrorists, than it was hard and unglamorous things – intelligent organization and direction of police forces, co-ordination, patient study of the enemy, determination.

GETTING TOUGH

The massacre of Via Fani and its aftermath sharply posed the dilemma that faces a democracy under terrorist attack – how to respond effectively without ceasing to be democratic. Uruguay and Argentina are two examples of the disasters that can occur. Although the primary focus of the BR was the pursuit of the early stages of the civil war of long duration against capitalism, the BR also occasionally, as in the Strategic Resolution of 1978, expressed a thought that could be summarized in the slogan 'the worse things are, the better'. In the Resolution, the BR stated that, while they longed for a war with the bourgeoisie, they also wished to unveil and provoke the imperialist counter-revolution that was hidden by the trappings of democracy, this on the theory that state repression would feed the discontent of the proletariat. An overreaction would set the BR's hearts aglow.

The whole course of the anti-terrorist effort from 1975 on was profoundly marked by the struggle with this problem. The result of the contention between perceived need and principle was a body of actions and enactments that, in varying degrees, contributed to the defeat of the terrorists, but at a price high enough to be worth recalling and reflecting on. There are lessons for all democrats in how Italy handled what everyone called 'the emergency'.

The late 1960s-early 1970s were a period of reform in the field of criminal justice.[13] A defendant's right to counsel was broadened; limits were set on 'preventive detention', that is, incarceration prior to the issuance of a definitive sentence in a case (four years in the most serious cases); a major reform of the prison system was enacted that aimed to reduce the harshness of prison life, broaden the detainee's opportunities for education and job-training, increase contact with the outside world and generally favor the detainee's reintegration into the law-abiding community.[14]

Under the pressure of rising violence, a reversal of course began in 1974. The judicial machinery was moving too slowly. Many accused, even if already convicted at a first or second stage in the proceedings, were in a position to be released because of the limits on preventive detention. To address this danger, parliament undid one of its recent reforms, doubling the maximum period of preventive detention (to eight years).[15]

In the spring of 1975 the *Legge Reale* was enacted.[16] The law considerably reduced the instances in which provisional liberty (that is, liberty pending a final ruling) could be granted. This, together with the extension of preventive detention, translated into a significant increase in the amount of time that could be spent in jail by a defendant not definitively adjudicated. A second area affected was that of police powers, which the law broadened notably. It accorded a right to search the persons and vehicles of individuals whose 'attitude' or presence in a particular place 'do not appear justifiable', and a right to stop and hold individuals against whom evidence of guilt was thought to exist. It enlarged the circumstances of immunity for a police officer who resorted to the use of a gun in the line of duty. The rigor of the law became the basis for heated controversy over the next several years, as did the shield it provided, in the view of some, for policemen quick on the draw.[17] The law won the support of 75 per cent of the voters in a referendum in June 1978. As a weapon against left-wing terrorism, however, the law was of limited utility.

As 'the emergency' grew worse, the jails were leaking like Etruscan goblets. Hundreds of detainees escaped, among them Renato Curcio and Prospero Gallinari.[18] In addition, there were many disturbances in the prisons and jailed terrorists were able to organize political collectives and convert the common criminals. Such conditions were intolerable and, therefore, in May 1977, the Minister of Justice ordered that General Dalla Chiesa be given responsibility for prison security.[19] Dalla Chiesa established the 'special' prison (or branch in an ordinary prison), in which the terrorists were held under an exceptionally strict security regime: isolation, body searches, surveillance cameras, limitations on phonecalls, visits and packages, control over the persons present during the recreation period and the like. One of the measures most hated by the 'politicals' might seem almost innocuous. Glass dividers were installed in visiting rooms to prevent weapons or messages from being smuggled in and to prevent the terrorists from smuggling out orders or theoretical documents. The result was that the detainee could not touch or caress his son or wife or girlfriend. These were the measures to which the harangues of the *brigatisti* on trial in Turin in 1978 referred, and to which the BR Executive Committee referred in Communiqués nos 7 and 8 during the Moro affair.

The special prisons were no doubt harsher than they need have been. Nevertheless, it is impossible to deny the gravity of the problems Dalla Chiesa faced in May 1977. Some critics ignored the fact that even after the special security measures had been imposed, unacceptable things still happened in the jails, such as the infiltration into and distribution out of the prisons of BR documents several hundred pages in length, the introduction into the prisons of explosives disguised as candy and other things, the completion of more than one beastly execution of a supposed informer by his fellow revolutionaries. The much-criticized glass dividers had not been installed out of pure cruelty; it was a fact that certain visiting family members and attorneys served as messengers for the BR. It was regrettable that special measures had to be taken, if for no other reason than that they brought to a brusque halt the movement towards long-overdue reform of the prison system.[20] The responsibility for this retrogression belongs, yes, in part to the government, but in much greater part to the *brigatisti* and other like-minded revolutionaries, who were more interested in destroying the prisons than in reforming them.

It was unrealistic to expect that the 54 days of the Moro affair would pass by without leaving a mark on the country's legislation. Five days after Via Fani, the Andreotti cabinet issued an emergency decree-law.[21] It created a new crime, kidnapping 'for the purpose of terrorism or subversion'. Consideration of the terrorist purpose as an element of the offense was a device that was to be broadly used during the later stages of 'the emergency'. One problem was that the term 'terrorism' was not defined. Prior to this law the police had been allowed to interrogate those arrested or stopped provided defense counsel was present. The law now authorized the police to conduct a species of mini-interrogation without the presence of defense counsel in which undefined 'summary information' could be elicited. The decree-law also expanded the power of the authorities to tap telephones, which was extensively done during the 54 days. Finally, the law provided that anyone who sold or rented a house or apartment had to report the fact and the identities of the parties to the transaction to the police within 48 hours. This measure terrified the BR, who feared that all their coves would be discovered. In fact, concern over this danger contributed to their abandonment of their plan to kidnap and hold along with Moro an important industrialist in Milan.[22] This fear was exaggerated because of bureaucratic obstacles to the complete utilization of this provision, as well as some lack of co-operation on the part of sellers and landlords ignorant of their obligations or reluctant to reveal their business dealings to the police. Still, the law had a useful destabilizing effect on the *brigatisti*, and it was instructive of how the battle against them might be won.

The other major innovation in the immediate wake of the Moro case was an organizational one. It was clear that something had to be done about the inefficiency of the anti-terrorism effort. In August 1978 an order was signed giving General Dalla Chiesa another special job. He was to build a national anti-terrorist squad and was to be given complete control over it, being obliged to report only to the Minister of the Interior himself. Because these powers were very broad and unusual, Dalla Chiesa's mandate was to last only a year (later briefly extended).

Dalla Chiesa carefully selected 180 *carabinieri* and 50 members of the police for his squad. He set his men to work studying BR documents, checking housing and public identification records, conducting stake-outs and tailing and hunting for suspected terrorists. These efforts were concentrated in Milan and Turin in 1978 and 1979. As usual with Dalla Chiesa, the results were not long in coming.

11

The Program of Annihilation: 1978–80

DISORDER AT LARGE

Although Mario Moretti and the other BR leaders believed that the Moro affair had been a political success (its failure would be recognized only in retrospect), they realized that operations at such a lofty level could not easily be repeated. What the BR could do, however, and proceeded to do, was to make constant and relentless the program of 'disarticulation' described in the 1978 Strategic Resolution and other documents. Agitated as 1977 had been (1806 acts of political violence), the data were much worse for 1978 (2725) and 1979 (2139). To have a sense of what these numbers meant to the texture of daily life, you need only calculate that, on average, there were over seven incidents of political violence every day, most of them in Rome, Milan, Turin and certain other areas of North-Central Italy. In 1978–9 almost 80 people were murdered for political reasons and 88 were wounded in ambushes, or, since the terrorists took August off, about two such crimes every week during the working year. The rapid acceleration in 1978 in what seemed to have been a decade-long descent into chaos was clearly linked to the irruption of 1977 and to some of its characteristics. That link is also evident in the pestilential proliferation of terrorist groups in 1977–9, for the BR were but the oldest and most important of an entire universe of active subversives. Between 1969 and 1976, 28 terrorist organizations, most of them leftist, had claimed acts of political violence, but now the number of such organizations shot up alarmingly: to 91 in 1977, then 209 in 1978, and then 269 in 1979.[1] The great majority of these groups too were leftist. Some of these existed in name only as flags of convenience unfurled by 'Front Line' or other formations to confuse the police, but a good part of what looked to be mushrooming subversion was just that, the spawning of new groups to respond to the impetus towards diffused, existential terrorism in the 'autonomous area'.

The authorities, then, in 1978–9, faced a difficult and complicated challenge: the terrorism of the BR, 'Front Line' and their imitators; the diffused terrorism of the organizations and collectives connected to the 'autonomous area'; and the Saturdays of mass violence, which continued to haunt, above all, Rome, Milan and Bologna. The *autonomi* were particularly disruptive in the Veneto, in and around Padua, where, as it happened, Professor Toni Negri and his allies were teaching and writing about *autonomia operaia* and the revolution. Here occurred the 'nights of fire', when squads of *autonomi* would, simultaneously in a number of localities, set off bombs under the cars or at the front doors of political figures, throw molotovs at the offices of DC exponents or magistrates, fire guns at the compounds of the *carabinieri*, and otherwise give vent to an uncontainable desire for violence.

The malevolence of the *autonomi* was displayed with an especial ignobility in the schools and universities. At Naples there was a hit list of 'reactionary' professors. At the University of Rome the 'Volsciviki' (from Via dei Volsci) and other *autonomi* continued to make normal pedagogical activity 'problematic'. On a typical day a squad of 50 ultra-leftists ran through the University of Florence, sacking and destroying, interrupting lessons, and beating up professors. At a professional institute in Milan, students insulted and assaulted teachers who refused to give out a *6 politico*, a passing grade to be awarded to all. When journalists went round to a student assembly, they were hooted at and insulted as 'capitalists' and 'bourgeois'. On the walls were graffiti with statements like these: 'Watch out, we'll kill you' and 'I'll shoot you in the mouth'.[2]

At the prestigious University of Padua, which had been founded in the thirteenth century, and had numbered Galileo among its professors, especially at the Faculty of Political Science, general quarters for Professor Negri and friends, the *autonomi* created a climate of intolerance and fear between 1977 and 1979. They demanded the right to run seminars, and insisted upon 'political' grades. These 'reforms' were not-so-distant relatives of some of those demanded by the Student Movement in the late 1960s, but the methods used by the *autonomi* to lobby on behalf of their ideas were quite a different matter. Among the venomous things on campus walls were 'To shoot at professors is our right' and '*Autonomia operaia non si tocca, docenti X e Y vi spareremo in bocca*'

('Autonomia operaia is not to be touched; teachers X and Y, we'll shoot you in the mouth'.) Professors who refused to concede were repeatedly interrupted in class, harassed and physically threatened. The threats were not idle. Professors were held prisoner, were beaten with wrenches, had their offices burned and were shot in the knees. In comparison with such things, 1968 seemed a fond memory.

Antonio Savasta was a Roman, born in 1955, the son of a policeman, of all things. He grew up in Centocelle, one of those huge working-class residential zones on the outskirts of Rome. It was the conditions of life there that first stimulated political resentment in the future *brigatista* :

Naturally I was part of the various collectives in the neighborhood that were born in the wake of the struggles of 1969–70.

The problem of entrance in such a collective is simply [having] the will and the political knowledge of certain problems. Above all, inside Roman neighborhoods like Prenestino and Centocelle, the ghettoization of the neighborhood is much felt and it weighs heavily on the shoulders of even very young boys (this is why there is a ready conscription of young *brigatisti*) – the political and also social impossibility of being able to be a force for the change of anything at all, inside a rather complex structure where it is almost impossible for youngsters to count for anything.

However, my real political leap forward occurred as a result of the huge wave of social struggles over the problem of housing. I can easily date the event, because it was from that point that a type of escalation began, that is, passage from a legal committee to an armed one. What was involved was the occupation of housing in the San Basilio area [in 1975]. In that situation, we were aware that we were carrying forward a struggle that was not simply that of students or one connected to the problems of the environment for young people inside the neighborhoods. It was a struggle that directly tied this reality with the much larger social reality that was the occupation of housing.

I recall that in this struggle I took part in three days of clashes with the police: in these encounters there was a response that demonstrated to us the line of argument that the BR already had been pressing for some time, that is, that forms of legal struggle absolutely no longer served to affirm the will for and the possibility of change in this country. On an emotional level, the death of a comrade who was trying to make this right to housing count for something, a comrade of the autonomous collectives of Tivoli, greatly affected me.

It was within a very brief time that the very face of the autonomous collectives changed. The third day, the night after the death of this young man, there were shootouts with the police; and from then on [came] the adaptation of this political structure to such encounters and therefore [came] weapons and therefore [came] clandestinity, as a political and logical consequence of an elevation of the intensity of the battle . . .

Naturally, from that point on, the passage was very brief. The armed squads within the committees already assumed a clandestine aspect in relation to the autonomous committees themselves, in which there was a separation between the military and the political, although a member of the military squads was also a political exponent of the committees. From here, then, the first experiences.

[T]his is the crux of the matter – that is, the fact that legal movements no longer had – at least so we thought – any political space to achieve change. Therefore, taking up arms was a very logical political consequence.[3]

He agreed with the BR's position – that the low-level violence of the movement would encounter a natural upper limit that would suffocate the revolutionary initiative unless the state was attacked at its heart. And so he became an irregular in the BR and the head of the Centocelle Brigade and the University Brigade. At the university, where he was a student, he took part in the expulsion of Luciano Lama and other violence. He conducted surveillance of Aldo Moro at the university a month or two prior to the operation in Via Fani. During the Moro affair he distributed BR bulletins at the university, took part in a 'knee-capping' and, along with several others, took charge of the red Renault until his superiors had need of it. His zeal and other qualities allowed him to get on in the BR; in September 1978 he became a member of the Directorate of the Rome column; early in 1981 he would reach Olympus, becoming a member of the Executive Committee and of the Strategic Direction. He had a hand in some of the most important operations of the BR after the Moro affair. He was, for instance, in on one of the boldest of all, when, in May 1979, 16 *brigatisti* ransacked, shot up and bombed the offices of the Rome committee of the Christian Democrats. Two police officers were shot to death and another was gravely wounded, while the BR got away unscathed. Not long afterwards, in July 1979, Savasta committed his first murder, gunning down Antonio Varisco, a lieutenant colonel of the *carabinieri*, in the streets of Rome.[4]

Strengthened by new recruits after Moro, the BR carried on the armed struggle into early 1980 under Moretti's leadership. During the same period 'Front Line' and other formations conducted their own particular versions of the armed struggle for communism, killing, wounding, robbing, and so on. The victims of the BR's assassinations and 'knee-cappings' in this period were often local officials of the number one enemy, the DC, executives or foremen of Fiat and Alfa, as well as some other businessmen. It is not possible neatly to divide the political from the military as far as the BR are concerned. Nevertheless, there was a clear step-up in the military aspect of the revolutionary struggle, no doubt partly a function of the arrival of a generation of *brigatisti* like Savasta, who, having grown to political 'maturity' in and around 'Autonomia' and its influences, were more vehement, less rational, less intellectual than had been the early *brigatisti*. More than ever before the struggle was one between opposing armed camps, the BR on the one side, and the police, *carabinieri* and magistrates, on the other. It goes without saying that the BR observed no code of conduct in the prosecution of this war. They assassinated an ex-anti-terrorism officer on a bus (June 1978), a magistrate in charge of penal affairs in the Justice Ministry (October 1978), two police officers on prison guard duty (December 1978), two *carabinieri* as they stood drinking coffee (November 1978), and three police officers in Rome (November–December 1979).

In January 1979 the BR assassinated Guido Rossa, a factory worker, union delegate and PCI member, in retaliation for his having reported on a BR 'mailman' he had discovered in his factory. For the BR, the murder was a political disaster. The task of inciting an entire working class to revolt when the workers were more interested in job security and material comforts than in the Stages of the March of History was already a challenge, but the problems were magnified manyfold when the BR included in their tactical armory the murder of Communists and workers. Roberto Sandalo of 'Front Line' thought that this murder was the worst error in the whole history of the armed struggle. Previously, he said, there had been a nucleus of the BR or 'Front Line' in almost every major factory in the North. The workers and union leaders had not reported the revolutionaries to the authorities. There had even been cases such as that of Lorenzo Betassa, an important *brigatista* who had been a union delegate at Fiat but had never been denounced. No one had reported on Sandalo though he was known to be a 'Front Line' member.[5] The murder of Rossa dealt a serious blow to this code of silence, as was apparent at Rossa's funeral. On a wet day in Genoa, a gigantic throng showed up, 200–250 000 people, and they yelled out slogans such as these: *'Brigate rosse non vincerete mai, contro di voi ci sono gli operai'* ('Red Brigades, you will never win; the workers are against you') and *'La lotta al terrorismo sarà più dura, la classe operaia non ha paura'* ('The struggle against terrorism will be harder; the working class is not afraid').[6]

The pools of sympathy in which the fish of the BR and other terrorists swam did not, however, dry up completely nor immediately. In the fall of 1979 Fiat executives complained that a minority of workers was supplying the BR and other groups with information and support and creating an intolerable state of violence in the factories.[7] There were four BR brigades in the Fiat factories,[8] but when Fiat shortly thereafter fired 61 workers for violence, the unions immediately sided with the workers. At Alfa Romeo BR bulletins were being regularly distributed inside the plant, where the Walter Alasia column had a brigade. Though much reduced and declining, the complicity and sympathy were to continue into 1980 and beyond, as the adventures of the Alasia were to illustrate.

Meanwhile, Morucci, Faranda and a few friends were still lobbying against the authoritarianism of the BR leadership, the militarization, the attempt to create a Leninist party that would control all social tensions within the movement and transform them into military struggle led by the BR hierarchy. At a certain point it became clear to Morucci and Faranda that the BR's 'blind and bloody "strategy"', as Morucci called it, could not be changed.[9] They were made to undergo a species of trial, led by Moretti. Before a final verdict was issued against them, in February 1979, the couple fled, taking with them documents, money and weapons, including the Skorpion that Morucci had brought into the Organization and that had been used to kill Aldo Moro. The *brigatisti* were very upset at the disobedience and what they regarded as the theft of the Organization's property.[10]

Morucci and Faranda, who were joined by a few other defectors, set up their own group. They did not last long, however. In May 1979 Morucci and Faranda were arrested in an apartment in Rome and their trove of treasure was confiscated by the police.

The dissension became public knowledge in the summer of 1979 with an exchange of communiqués between the Morucci–Faranda group and Renato Curcio *et al.*[11] Morucci–Faranda attacked the BR for rigidity, arrogance, excessive centralization and militarization. In their view the BR should have put themselves at the service of the movement and the proletariat, rather than have tried to dominate them. Also, the BR, Morucci–Faranda contended, had viewed the Moro operation as a trampoline from which they were making an adventuristic leap into war, which was a policy of sheer folly. Apart from insults ('poor fools used by the counter-revolution', and so on),[12] the historic nucleus responded to this 'movementist' critique by simply denying that any breach existed between the BR and the movement. The historic nucleus asserted that the real issue before the BR now, with the Proletarian Offensive Movement of Resistance assuming mass dimensions, was that of the 'leap to the party'. This – the role of the party – was the heart of the disagreement.

Morucci and Faranda knew that, from the early days in Trent on, the BR had always believed in a Marxist–Leninist interpretation of history and that, in this view, the party is fundamental to the achievement of communism. For the BR there were only two choices in Italy: to be a revisionist Berlingueriano or to be a serious revolutionary, a Leninist, a man of the party. To challenge the conception of the party was to hit at something central. Moreover, Morucci and Faranda knew that the BR, having history behind them, were certain of their course and intolerant of dissent, that once a policy was decided upon, the principle of democratic centralism stilled all debate. Because they challenged the BR both substantively and procedurally, the couple could not expect other than punishment. This discord – and the more serious disagreements that plagued the group in later years – were inevitable given the BR's ideas. These ideas could only produce a heavy-handed leadership and unquestionable positions on policy and tactics, and, in time, discontent with the one and the other. Morucci and

Faranda learned, as had others before them, how hard it is to reconcile Marxist–Leninism with the smallest expressions of independent thought.

The escalating violence of the BR and other groups over 1978–9 occurred simultaneously with, and in part was a response to, the improvement in the state's anti-terrorism effort led by Dalla Chiesa. As the battle came to a head, the number of victims grew, but the jails also began to fill up. Among the *brigatisti* captured were the Reggiani Lauro Azzolini and Franco Bonisoli of the Executive Committee, Prospero Gallinari, various workers and even Enrico Fenzi, a professor of Italian literature at the University of Genoa. But, despite these and other successes, much remained to be done, as people continued to die.

DESERTING THE CAUSE

On the day itself Patrizio Peci would not eat because he could not keep his food down. During the action, on the other hand, he was calm and confident. Afterward, his emotions varied according to the type of action. After a 'knee-capping' the tension passed quickly. He and his comrades did not dwell upon the human aspects; all that mattered was the contribution to the cause of the revolution. After an assassination, though, things were different. For several days after he was prey to a vague discontent that he could not conquer. He thought at the time that it was a question of stress. Only afterward did he recognize that it had all along been remorse at the obliteration of a human life.

Patrizio Peci was born in 1953 in a modest home in the Marche and grew up in a summer resort town on the Adriatic. Because his mother's father had had trouble with the Fascists, she believed nothing good could come out of politics and forbade any mention of it in the family circle. Patrizio was not a good student and never received his diploma. Instead he worked, in the summers serving as a waiter in a tourist hotel. He began to interest himself in politics at around age 17. *Il sessantotto* was over by that point, though its influence continued to be strongly felt. A few local agitations – housing occupations, for instance – persuaded him to think about political problems and led him to the conviction that there were grave injustices in the social order. 'Lotta Continua' was very important in the town and Patrizio involved himself in its activities for a time. But the group clearly was not radical enough, and Patrizio and his friends became interested in the emerging Red Brigades.

The problems faced by the metropolitan proletariat were absent from this non-industrial area, but Patrizio and his friends did have a powerful emotional bond with the BR – anti-fascism. Those were the years of neo-Fascist violence and plots, and it was common for the young leftists of the area, who were the majority, to fall into fights with young neo-Fascists. Patrizio and a few of his friends formed a little group and held clandestine meetings, burned cars and beat up real or imagined neo-Fascists.

Word got out and the little group was approached by drummers for the BR. They discussed the great issues. Gradually Patrizio and some others opened up to the larger themes and concluded that, as the BR said, the principal enemy was the state (in the form of the DC), that the state would have to be overthrown and communism installed if there were to be any justice in Italy, and that the PCI had betrayed the revolutionary cause, having fallen hopelessly under the spell of revisionism.

Patrizio's evolution was also affected by some reading. He began with the Communist Manifesto. Then he read pamphlets of 'Workers' Power' and 'Lotta Continua', the thoughts of Mao and some works of Stalin, who was a hero to him at the time. As he drew closer to the armed struggle, Patrizio read materials on the Tupamaros, the Irish Republican Army and other terrorist groups.

Patrizio wanted to join the BR. The choice to fight for the revolution was one compelled by altruism and by a sense of adventure: he wanted to risk all for others in a just cause and was fascinated by the image of the armed struggle of a small band against the many for the triumph of an ideal. He had no idea what the real life of a *brigatista* might be, but this very leaping into the dark was also a motive. If his expectations were deluded, he reasoned, he could always return to a life of legality, as some actually did. Since the military activities of the BR were then limited, he did not think there was a risk of death or truly serious criminal punishment in being a *brigatista*. For these reasons Patrizio accepted a BR invitation and, in autumn 1974, departed for Milan and the armed struggle.

Patrizio disliked Milan but not the Organization. He took part in his first action, a robbery of the Study Center of the Confederation of Industry, the leading national business organization. He had trained for this operation not in the Palestinian camps about which so many have speculated, but in an isolated area outside the city. The operation went off perfectly, and he was struck by how easy an armed action was if prepared with care and directed with determination. The contrast between the squalid reality of the small factory where he was working and the exhilaration of the armed action induced him to abandon all residue of doubt. After some interim steps he became a regular. In a little over two years he was to advance rapidly, becoming eventually the 'column commander' of the Turin column 'Mara Cagol', and a member of the national Logistic Front and the Strategic Direction.

Transferred to Turin, he took part in many activities. He 'knee-capped' a number of enemies of the proletariat and was a member of nuclei that committed several murders. It was his good fortune, though, never himself to fire the fatal bullets.

In time he came to realize that the life of a *brigatista* was not what he had expected. Apart from the chronic tension that comes with being sought by the police, the life was one of adversity. The regular could live only with his fellow regulars and have dealings only with other *brigatisti*. Much of the time he was at work on the revolution or else talking about it. He could never escape this burden. He could not have friends outside the Organization and his contacts with his family were reduced to an occasional telephone call. The Organization favored relations between male and female *brigatisti* provided they were regulars. Although there were, curiously, a large number of women in the BR, there were not enough to go around. (In the BR, there was, incidentally, considerable freedom for women, many of whom, such as Barbara Balzarani or Nadia Ponti or Pasqua Aurora Betti, reached the ranks of the leaders. Many women distinguished themselves for their icy nerves and cruelty. According to Patrizio, by reason of the disorientation created by, or the novelty of, equality, the women exaggerated, becoming inordinately aggressive and intolerant, even in political discussions with the men.) There were clashes of personality. There were shortages of money. When Patrizio became column commander in 1979, each regular received a monthly salary of 250 000 lire (about $250). Although the Organization provided lodging, the salary was small, the cost of living in Milan or Turin was high, and the regulars frequently complained. They could ask for more when needed, but it was annoying and humiliating for a 25- to 30-year-old revolutionary to have to ask for money to buy a pair of pants. Living underground was also often simply boring. The *brigatista* spent much time at the movies (second run; the first run films cost too much) or at 'home' (he never could have a home that was truly his) watching television or reading. This sort of existence was endured for years. Patrizio was underground for three years and some *brigatisti* lived in clandestinity for as long as eight or nine years.

In 1979 Patrizio became column commander when his predecessor was captured. With the new post came new responsibilities and more pressure. When the vacation ended that summer Patrizio was in the throes of a full-scale psychological crisis. He still longed for the revolution, but he was spiritually tired. Moreover, since having risen in the Organization, he had become aware of, and had come to resent, the constant pressure of the members of the historic nucleus on the leadership in order that it liberate them even at the risk of destroying the Organization. More important, from on high he could now see, for the first time, that, compared to the state, the Organization was a paltry thing and that it was not succeeding in spreading in the factories or among the proletariat generally. Insidiously, there came to him more and more often the thought that the BR had committed a fatal error in believing that there was substantial support for a violent Communist revolution among the Italian people. There were injustices, but not the insupportable repression and exploitation without which no revolution was possible. But he had no choices left. What alternative was there once you had committed a serious crime? Jail or exile or carrying on were the options. You were out of this world.[13]

In December 1979 General Dalla Chiesa's mandate as leader of the emergency anti-terrorist squad expired. He was given command of the *carabinieri* division headquartered in Milan with responsibility for all of northern Italy. In practical terms, he remained the leader of the anti-terrorism campaign in the part of the country where terrorism was most entrenched and menacing. He continued to wear down the BR.

In Turin Dalla Chiesa succeeded in placing an informant in the orbit of the BR irregulars and thus, in November–December 1979, his men came into contact with nine or ten *brigatisti*, among them Peci. A round-up began, but Peci escaped it. He hid out, passing long, depressing days locked up in his safehouse. In February 1980 he made one of his rare ventures outdoors, to a meeting with a member of the Executive Committee. The *carabinieri* were there also and the two *brigatisti* were captured.[14]

Peci was put into isolation, as his crisis reached its culmination. He was not tortured, as BR doctrine had led him to expect, but he suffered. His mind, already strained, dwelled morbidly on the decades of jail that lay before him. He came to realize that the state was large and strong, that the BR could never overturn the state, and that the working class would never sufficiently support the BR. That once-fugitive thought now assailed him – the BR were politically and militarily doomed.

Battered by these terrible ideas, Patrizio began to consider collaborating, a matter he discussed with Dalla Chiesa, whose humanity impressed him. Given all he had done and all he was responsible for as column commander, would he ever get out? He was through with all commitment to revolutionary violence. It was, however, a large step from there to the denunciation of his comrades. He recalled the shared illusions and shared difficulties of their life together, and he felt distaste for what was sought of him. There were two opposing considerations: first, that they would all end up in jail sooner or later anyway, and he might save them from a worse fate; and secondly, that he would be saving those his comrades would otherwise have shot, thereby repaying a part of the debt he owed humanity for the blood he had directly and indirectly spilled. With this reasoning – or so he claimed – he decided that he would talk.

The extent of his revelations was stunning. Patrizio confessed his own crimes. He explained the BR's structure and rules, the planning and execution of actions, the sources of their weapons, their international ties, and so on. He identified *brigatisti* and BR bases. He spoke about the Moro case. Although he incriminated many, he also exculpated some who had been wrongly suspected. He provided, in short, such an abundance of invaluable information that his decision to co-operate must be reckoned an event that decisively affected the history of the Red Brigades and of terrorism in Italy.[15] In the days, weeks and months that followed, Peci's information led, by Dalla Chiesa's count,[16] to the arrest of 85 *brigatisti* and the discovery of numerous bases, as well as the establishment of legal cases against many *brigatisti*. The Turin column 'Mara Cagol' was demolished and the Genoa and Milan columns gravely damaged. The Veneto column was new (1979) and somewhat fragile, a Naples column was but in the process of formation, which left only the Rome column near full strength. Moretti had his work cut out for him.[17]

Peci's collaboration also had other important consequences. For one thing, his testimony destroyed the myth of the BR's supreme efficiency, with no doubt considerable damage to the confidence of the *brigatisti* and of those who might have been contemplating signing on. Conversely, this was a great boost to the morale of the forces of law and order and the public. Secondly, Peci broke the code of silence that had shielded the BR. He was the first important *brigatista* to co-operate with the authorities; after him, with the help of legislative incentives, would come many others. Dalla Chiesa had been shrewd in perceiving that the apparently solid BR could be undermined from within.

Credit was also due to Peci for having contributed, indirectly, to the liquidation of 'Front Line'. Dalla Chiesa calculated that Peci, by providing a trail to an important member of the group, led to the arrest of 100 'Front Line' militants and the discovery of bases.[18] By the spring of 1980 the strategy of this group had broken down. The lure of violence had been the only influence left inside 'Front Line', which had undertaken actions devoid of political value, what the militant Roberto Sandalo called 'truly insane' violence.[19] As defeat had become apparent, a siege mentality had taken hold and the group had lashed out wildly. The cumulative effect of internal decay and the arrests was devastating, and by the end of 1980 'Front Line' had virtually ceased to be.

Thus, in 1980 the Red Brigades reeled, while 'Front Line' was suffering its quietus. Many of the smaller groups were likewise in retreat. In the Veneto the terrorism of the autonomous collectives had begun to subside after arrests of the alleged brains behind the violence, including Professor Negri, in April and December 1979 (the 'April 7 case'). Still, the terrorists, especially the BR, were strong enough yet to kill and wound, and, as with 'Front Line', adversity produced not resignation, but an intensification of the war for the revolution. In 1980 there were 833 instances of political violence, a decrease of 60 per cent in comparison with the previous year, while the number of organizations claiming attacks declined by two-thirds (to 89). But these favorable developments were accompanied by an increase in gravity of the crimes committed: 334 citizens were wounded and 135 killed, by far the highest number of deaths in any year between 1969 and 1988.[20] The BR murdered six members of the forces of law and order, a prison health director, a DC politician, three businessmen and three magistrates. Three former fellow revolutionaries were also killed inside the jails. One of the magistrates was the vice-president of the national governing body of magistrates. He was gunned down in a corridor inside the University of Rome after teaching a class in a hall named in memory of Aldo Moro. There was also a string of 'knee-cappings'.

THE SUMMER IN BOLOGNA

On the morning of 2 August 1980, a bomb exploded in the second-class waiting room at the central train station in Bologna. The blast devastated the waiting-room, sent glass and metal flying in all directions and brought the roof of the left half of the station crashing down on the travelers below. 85 people were killed and 200 wounded, people of all ages and from many countries. Suspicion immediately fell upon the extreme right.

The year 1974 had been the beginning of a crisis for the far right. Over the next several years important criminal inquiries into illegal activities of the far right were begun and stunning information emerged on *Rosa dei venti* and other plots. Taking a lesson from the far left, new Fascists came to prominence whose strategy contemplated armed struggle against the state rather than a conspiratorial putsch. A generational change contributed to this alteration in strategy. Many of the older right-wing extremists had fled abroad to sunny places like Franco's Spain, replaced by a new generation with different concerns. These young people, despite their loathing for the prospering leftists, had in common with them a hatred for the alienating impersonality, the harshness and many other aspects of the society in which they lived. The result was, for example, the group 'Third Position', perhaps the leading spokesman for an ideology that combined traditional Fascist ideas with others connected to these new themes. Disgust with the establishment was so strong that some of the young extremists even proposed initiatives to be pursued in common with the radical left (with whom it was of course intended that accounts would be settled once the state was brought down).

The most important military expression of this new fascism, the practitioner of the right-wing armed struggle against the state, was the 'Armed Revolutionary Nuclei' (NAR), whose name, significantly, could easily be mistaken for that of a leftist group. NAR committed more terrorist acts than any other right-wing group.

NAR and other groups perpetrated numerous murders, bombings and other acts of violence, many directed against the state. By 1980, however, the revolutionary project was failing: the neo-Fascists had failed to rouse any significant part of the population or to build any solid political-military organization. The rightists either were unable to see this or simply were overwhelmed by an appetite for battle for its own sake.

The state's campaign against the right was far from ideal. A pendulum had swung, perhaps too far: once underestimated, leftist violence had become the overwhelming concern of the authorities in the late 1970s.[21] A single magistrate was given responsibility for anti-Fascist investigations. After he was assassinated by rightists, another magistrate was named to replace him. No other prosecutor in the Rome office helped him and he received little investigative assistance and no police escort. He felt isolated and outnumbered. But he was serious and got results, and so, in June 1980, he too was murdered by NAR. Not long afterward came the bombing in Bologna.

The Bologna investigation has proven to be at least as difficult as any of its predecessors. There are objective obstacles to finding the truth: bombings are easily done, destroy evidence and, unlike the acts of the left, are not proudly trumpeted by the group responsible. But there are also obstacles of another sort. The trial for the massacre began recently and the final verdict is years away. Among the defendants are several young killers from NAR. There hovers about the case the shade of the secret services. At one point, the investigations were derailed by a trail of evidence (including a suitcase containing weapons, explosives and documents 'found' on a train in Bologna) suggesting that the bombing had been done by French and German terrorists, a trail that was manufactured by deviated elements of the military secret service, the SISMI, which, it will be recalled, had been created in 1977 supposedly as a clean replacement for the by-then irremediably compromised SID. Several persons connected to SISMI, including a general, the former secretary-general of SISMI, and a colonel on the SISMI staff, are now defendants in the case. The allegations to be considered in these proceedings go far beyond this incident to a broad political conspiracy involving right-wing terrorists, misdirected segments of SISMI, and obscure individuals in the masonry with sinister aims and connections to people in lofty places. The allegations in this instance seem something more than paranoia.[22]

The Bologna case is a tragic illustration of the curse of ideology with which Italy had to live in the 1970s and early 1980s. And the nostalgia of the far right has been depressingly hardy: just before Christmas 1984 a bomb went off on a train in a tunnel along the much-bombed stretch between Florence and Bologna, leaving 15 dead and many more injured.

12

Evanescence

Despite the reversals, the BR remained convinced, as they put it in the Strategic Resolution of October 1980, that capitalism was a 'dying dinosaur'; 'its agony will be long, the blows of its tail tremendous. But the revolution will kill it'.[1] The emergence from the movement of 'revolutionary organisms of the masses' would be critical. These bodies, as the BR described them in another document from this period, 'The Twenty Final Theses', were to be political-military organisms through which the masses themselves (and not just an avant-garde) were to fight the police, the 'masters', and so on, 'on the terrain of the armed struggle'.[2] The principal tactical objective of the revolutionary effort had to be the construction of these organisms. On this point, Curcio, Franceschini *et al.*, the authors of the theses, took a slap at Moretti, asserting that a misunderstanding had occurred inside the Organization over the concept of annihilation. Speaking with cold detachment, the *brigatisti* wrote that in each act of annihilation, the political message had to be 'limpid' and the target selected with the maximum of 'political rigor' and the minimum of 'excesses'. Undoubtedly, Curcio and the others had in mind the killing of the worker, Guido Rossa, which had clearly not been 'limpid'.

In the resolution the BR displayed a not surprising interest in the prison, not surprising in view of the fact that many *brigatisti* and other revolutionaries were by now restrained therein. To the BR the prison was a place where the avant-garde of the proletariat could be neutralized. Asinara, the prison-island off the coast of Sardinia, and the other 'special' prisons were 'concentration camps for prisoners of war'.[3] Central to the BR's program were the liberation of proletarian prisoners and the disarticulation of the imperialist jail; preferred targets were the leadership of the Justice Ministry, the prison bureaucracy, prison guards, *carabinieri* and the 'war magistrates'. Asinara, the Monte Cristo of the *brigatisti*, was a place of isolation and torture, and therefore a first step in an immediate program against these concentration camps had to be to

199

'close Asinara by any means'.[4] A clear enough warning, it should have seemed.

These two documents were conspicuous for their abstraction and lack of realism, qualities that were to characterize the intellectual activity of the BR in their last phase, as though the more prospects for the revolution declined, the more the BR needed to hide that disagreeable fact behind thick clouds of theorization. The *brigatisti* did not confront the group's true condition, economic realities or the actual state of public opinion. For a decade the BR had been misinterpreting the state of mind of the workers. They were still doing so, as the signs of an economic sea-change became apparent to those not enchained by ideology. Despite considerable economic difficulties, the post-industrial era was dawning, in the North at least. The factory would become more mechanized, less oppressive, and the industrial working class would shrink. The economic crisis was certainly not a terminal illness. Marxist-Leninism increasingly came to seem a philosophy whose day had passed with the society that had given it birth. But the BR buried these realities beneath mounds of 'analysis', which consisted of incomplete facts misread in an ideological key. The flights of fantasy were truly astonishing. For instance, the purportedly critical and much-discussed 'revolutionary organisms of the masses' were wholly imaginary. In general, the BR, at very great length, elaborated obscure notions and cut complex distinctions totally unconnected to reality (for example, the 'Line of the Masses', which meant the organization's 'Program of Transition to Communism', which was divided into 'General Political Program' and 'Immediate Political Program'), and served up the whole in indigestible Marxist jargon. As society advanced, the *brigatisti* continued to rush dizzily backwards, in search of a gloomy past.

The threat implicit in the Strategic Resolution was carried out in December 1980, when the BR kidnapped Giovanni D'Urso, a magistrate with a high post in the Ministry of Justice. The BR demanded the closure of Asinara and it was closed, though the government insisted that the decision had been taken prior to the kidnapping. A revolt that followed in one of the 'special' prisons was put down by a *carabinieri* unit. The BR retaliated by assassinating the *carabinieri* general in charge of prison security, a friend and collaborator of Dalla Chiesa. D'Urso was released unharmed when a few papers published communiqués as demanded by the BR.

This case raised serious questions about the determination of the government. According to the Communists, who were now in opposition after the collapse of the government of 'national solidarity', the government had not displayed the requisite firmness. At least in appearances, this case differed notably from the Moro affair. The case also raised questions about the reconciliation of the press's obligations to report the news fully but not to serve as a microphone for terrorists. The BR, of course, judged the 'campaign' a success, claiming that they were now closer to the working class than ever before.[5]

The BR leaders could not, however, ignore the breakdown in the unity of the Organization. After the damage done the Walter Alasia column of Milan by Dalla Chiesa's men in winter 1978–9, Mario Moretti and Barbara Balzarani had succeeded in rebuilding it. By the end of 1979 the column was present in several major factories. By 1980, however, there was dissension. At a July meeting of BR leaders, the representatives of the Alasia attacked Moretti and Balzarani as inept and authoritarian and accused the Organization of having lost touch with the workers everywhere save in Milan. The members of the Alasia insisted that *they* were the only true *Brigate Rosse* and should take over the Organization.[6] The meeting ended in disarray and bad feelings.

In November 1980 the renegades of the Alasia assassinated two businessmen without permission of the Executive Committee. The national leaders disavowed these crimes. The members of the Alasia defied the national leaders, appropriating the name 'Red Brigades' for themselves. Outraged at this, the national leaders announced publicly that the Alasia was anti-party, guilty of 'opportunism' and in violation of the rules of democratic centralism and therefore they expelled it from the organization.[7]

Subsequently, the Alasia conducted its own version of the armed struggle centered on the factories in Milan, especially Alfa Romeo, and criticized the rest of the *brigatisti* for their 'subjectivism' and militarism. The Alasia emphasized that 'politics must guide the rifle towards clear perspectives and not vice versa'. It was an error, typical of the Morettiani, to engage in actions that were unclear, that confused primary enemies and secondary ones, that tended to heal the divisions in capitalist society, and that failed to take into account the limited political consciousness of the masses after centuries of slavery.[8]

The Executive Committee could not simply abandon the city where Curcio, Cagol, Moretti and the others had begun the long march years before. It fell to Moretti to set up a new column that would seize the initiative from the heretics. As a result of the pressure of the forces of law and order, the internal dissent and the growing inhospitability towards armed violence among the workers, the task proved difficult, to say the least. Perhaps, too, Moretti was simply tired after nine years of life underground. Whatever the reason, he carelessly trusted an aspiring *brigatista* about whom he knew little and who was an informer. Thus it was that in April 1981 the elusive Moretti was finally in the hands of the authorities. The day after, Eugenio Scalfari, the respected editor of the progressive daily, *La Repubblica*, wrote that 'the armed party ... is now finally destroyed. Its historic leaders, the militarist wing and the movementist one, the column heads, the respectable fellow-travelers, are now all in prison'.[9] The normally acute Scalfari was celebrating before the final battles had been won.

At this point began the ascendancy of Professor Giovanni Senzani. Senzani was born in 1940. After receiving a degree in sociology, he published a study in 1970 on juvenile detention facilities. Later, he taught at the University of Siena. A professor who knew him described him as intelligent, demanding, severe, given to ideological theorization. Criminology was his speciality, which made him the ideal person to lead the BR's Front of the Prisons. He was a collaborator of the Ministry of Justice, where he spied for the BR. He was married to the sister of fellow professor and *brigatista*, Enrico Fenzi. Senzani worked on an adult education project for textile workers in the town of Prato, just outside Florence, which may have added to his sympathy for the working class. In 1971 and 1974, he worked for a cultural center in Torre del Greco, near Naples, and thus learned a good deal about the economic and social problems of the South. In 1979 he obtained a post teaching criminology at the University of Florence. In March of that year he was arrested on charges of false testimony in connection with a terrorism inquiry, but was released shortly afterwards. In May 1979, purporting to go abroad to work on a government-funded research project, he went underground.

He was given charge of the BR's Front of the Prisons and put his imprint on the D'Urso 'campaign'. Senzani was then dispatched to take charge of the new Naples column. The BR wanted to expand southward, to 'knock down the barrier of the South', as they had put it in the Strategic Resolution of February 1978. It was in Naples that Senzani's ambitions burst all bounds.

On 27 April 1981 Senzani's group kidnapped near Naples Ciro Cirillo, Christian Democrat, the regional assessor for public housing and urban problems. Cirillo's bodyguard and driver were murdered and his secretary wounded. One of the *brigatisti* involved in the assault testified later that it was the professor himself who fired the fatal shots at the guard.[10] In leading this operation Senzani had failed to heed the Executive Committee's orders. Senzani's disobedience produced friction between him and the Executive Committee, but not a total collapse in relations.[11]

The novelty in this action lay in its 'political' content, which was a reflection of the 'movementist' concerns that set Senzani apart from the Morettiani. In November 1980 a powerful earthquake had devastated areas of the South, killing, injuring and making homeless many thousands of persons and adding new problems to the ancient woes of Naples. Cirillo headed a technical committee charged with the rebuilding effort and was thus, for the BR, a representative of what had been wrong with Naples and what was wrong with it in the aftermath of the quake. In their communiqués the BR complained about the many homeless and unemployed, the direction and pace of the rebuilding program, and the difficult life of displaced families living in trailer camps. In the eyes of the *brigatisti*, capital was attempting to restructure the labor market and deport the proletariat, and therefore the *brigatisti* launched the battle cries, 'Work everyone, work less!', 'Requisition the vacant houses of the masters!', and 'Build the revolutionary organisms of the masses!'

While the Cirillo kidnapping was in course, on 20 May the Veneto column of orthodox *brigatisti* kidnapped Giuseppe Taliercio, the director of the huge petrochemical plant of Montedison at Porto Marghera. The kidnapping was intended as the response of the 'militarists' to the criticisms of the Walter Alasia. On 4 June the Alasia column undertook an action of its own, kidnapping an official of Alfa Romeo. Finally, on 12 June *brigatisti* from Rome, adherents of Professor Senzani's faction, kidnapped Roberto Peci, the younger brother of the famous *pentito*. That made four. The Moro operation apart, the BR had never undertaken so demanding a set of initiatives as these concurrent kidnappings.

The Alfa Romeo kidnapping ended happily on 24 July when the victim was released unharmed. Taliercio was less fortunate. According to two *brigatisti*, Taliercio was uncooperative, was 'not sufficiently humble', was unrepentant about his choice of a profession, was courageous and firm, and ended up in an attitude of 'total opposition to any discussion'.[12] So Antonio Savasta, at the time head of the Veneto column, member of the Executive Committee and Strategic Direction, shot him.

The execution was as politically pointless as it was brutal. The support the BR had expected from the workers at Porto Marghera did not materialize. The Veneto column broke into two over the conduct of the operation. The operation was also condemned by Senzani and followers: 'A campaign lacking in political content is more counterproductive for the metropolitan proletariat than the blows of the counterrevolution'.[13]

The fragmentation of the BR was further accelerated by the manner in which Senzani chose to resolve the Cirillo kidnapping. The professor decided to free Cirillo in exchange for a large ransom (1.5 billion lire), which some have alleged was collected and paid by the DC. It later came to light that the secret services had again intervened. Astonishing though it is, this intervention consisted of nothing less than the dispatching of intermediaries to meet in jail with representatives of Raffaele Cutolo, the imprisoned boss of the camorra of Naples, to discuss efforts by Cutolo to help gain the release of Cirillo with the payment of a ransom.

The Executive Committee had opposed acceptance of a ransom because it would obliterate the political value of the 'campaign'. Senzani's action made for a final, total break between him and the Executive Committee.[14] Senzani claimed to see political gains in the Cirillo affair, but his critics were right. The acceptance of the ransom damaged the BR's credibility and undermined the political aspects of the 'campaign'. The *brigatisti* believed that conditions in the South were ripe for the spread of revolution,[15] but this belief was unfounded. The South was far behind the North and revolutionary consciousness was non-existent among the poor. None of the magical 'revolutionary organisms of the masses' developed among the Neapolitan proletariat. Though capable of spilling more blood, as it did, the Naples column was doomed to isolation and failure.

With Cirillo's release on 24 July only Roberto Peci remained to be disposed of. The BR extorted statements out of Roberto that falsely maligned himself and his brother. His family swallowed hard and confirmed the statements in the hope that that might assist his release. Senzani's group indicated that his life might be saved if the press were to publish his interrogation and other documents. The press, which had been restrained in coverage of the BR throughout this spring and summer of kidnapping, was generally unreceptive. Once again, the Socialists dissented, publishing letters and other documents in the party paper for humanitarian reasons.[16] Roberto's wife and sisters held press conferences and made telephone calls in a desperate effort to have the demands met.

Progress was being made in satisfying the BR's terms. Nevertheless, on 31 July the *brigatisti* issued a communiqué declaring that Roberto 'is a traitor and traitors must be annihilated'.[17] The inconsistency is readily explained: the decision to kill him, a *brigatista* has revealed, had been taken at the outset of the operation.[18] Roberto had to pay for the mistakes of his brother. Very early on the morning of 3 August they moved Roberto, blindfolded, from his jail in Rome to an abandoned, roofless house near the Via Appia on the outskirts of Rome. They made him lean against a wall, amidst the weeds and piles of refuse, beneath a sign reading 'Death to traitors'. They shot him at extremely close range. Eleven shots, including a *coup de grâce*. The body was left among the garbage, covered by a banner with the five-pointed star. More than ever before the *brigatisti* had sunk to the level of heartless and unprincipled common criminals. What 'political value' was there to justify this murder? It was a case of pure revenge, one that, with its symbolic mistreatment of the body, could have been done by the mafia. The *brigatisti* issued a picture showing the unlucky young man lying against the wall with a gun pointed at him a foot away from his chest. They even filmed his death. Ironically, one of those responsible for Roberto's death was believed later to have himself co-operated with the authorities, for which reason two of his comrades murdered him in jail in July 1982, in the style of the mafia.

At the end of 1981 two separate Strategic Resolutions were issued, one representing the views of the Executive Committee and the other the gospel according to Giovanni Senzani. The Resolution of the Executive Committee[19] emphasized the international context of the revolutionary struggle. The BR were seeking revitalization that they could not obtain at home by feeding off ferment in Europe over questions of NATO, disarmament, and so on. The revolution will be international, the *brigatisti* affirmed, or it will not be. Senzani and the 'movementists' criticized the 'subjectivism', opportunism and militarism of the orthodox group.[20] Senzani wanted the Organization to be closer to and more respon-

sive to the masses, to be, in a sense, a revolutionary movement
rather than a military élite. The Senzaniani announced the 'leap to
the Party'. The 'Party-Guerriglia of the Metropolitan Proletariat,
the Fighting Communist Party', they said, has been built – and it is
we.

The 'militarists' undertook the BR's first 'campaign' at the
expense of a foreign target, and a very potent target it was. Having
suffered such defeats as they had on the local stage, could the
brigatisti really expect better fortune against a larger, more powerful enemy? The answer was obvious, but they had gone too far to
turn back. As Antonio Savasta put it, 'We knew we had minimum
force, but we had to do this to recoup everything . . . Either you
went in that direction or you stayed home – the famous wager with
history'.[21]

On 17 December 1981 the 'militarists', led by Antonio Savasta,
kidnapped General James Dozier, one of the highest ranking
American officers in Italy. Dozier, who was kidnapped in Verona,
was held in an apartment in Padua, where he was kept for over a
month in a tent in the middle of the room, as rock music blasted
continually in his ears to prevent him from guessing anything
about his location. The rites of the kidnapping were performed –
ransom demands, ideological statements, photographs of the victim, and so on – while the police and *carabinieri* searched in vain.
Then surveillance and questioning of individuals believed to have
links to the subversive world produced solid leads, including the
confession of one of those who had helped to transport the trunk
containing General Dozier and the revelation by this participant of
where the prison was located. On 28 January 1982 a specially-
trained assault team smashed the door down and entered the BR
hideout. Inside the tent one of the *brigatisti* was pointing a pistol at
the general's temple. In an instant one of the members of the
assault team knocked the pistol away and immobilized the *brigatista*. The other four *brigatisti* had no time to react. The general was
safe. No shots had been fired. The operation had succeeded
splendidly.[22]

They had captured a regular from Florence, a railroad conductor
who had been a member of 'Lotta Continua' until joining the BR in
1977. Another captured regular had become a *brigatista* while
working in a large factory. The apartment belonged to the irregular, an unsuspectable 22-year-old, the daughter of a prosperous
physician from Padua. The remaining two *brigatisti* were Savasta

and his girlfriend, Emilia Libera, who had come out of the Centocelle quarter on the periphery of Rome and whose political experiences paralleled those of Savasta. The capture of all of these *brigatisti*, especially one of the caliber of Savasta, was a triumph in itself. But the achievement was much greater than the authorities realized as they packed Savasta and the rest off to headquarters. The month of January 1982 was a Waterloo, the beginning of the end for the Red Brigades. The *brigatisti* had lost their wager with history.

13

The Emergency, Phase Two

Under pressure to do something about the avalanche of violence of 1979, the government issued another major piece of 'emergency' legislation, the decree-law of 15 December 1979.[1] This law was something of a mixed bag: it granted benefits to repentant terrorists as a weapon against the terrorist organizations, but also, in certain aspects, passed the limits of the acceptable in its restrictions on civil liberties.

The law further broadened the powers of the police. It provided that the organs of public security could, in urgent situations, stop and hold for 48 hours suspicious persons, whom the law defined only very vaguely. Broad and vague as it was, this species of preventive arrest could have been a disaster, but it did not turn out to be so, nor did it become the powerful weapon its advocates had naïvely hoped. It proved to be an anti-terrorist weapon of very small value and it was rarely used. The provision existed for two years and then expired, and it was not missed.[2]

The cumulative effect of other articles of this law was quite different. The law expanded upon an idea launched in the decree-law issued during the Moro affair by employing for several ends the legal figure of the 'purpose of terrorism or subversion'. Again, the purpose was not defined. In the case of any crime committed for this purpose, the existing penalty was increased by a half, provisional liberty was, with few exceptions, denied the accused and the limits on preventive detention were extended by a third.

With a serious emergency facing the country, increasing the penalties for all crimes of terrorism was not a surprising step to take, though it was doubtful given the ideas of the terrorists that such a measure would have any deterrent effect whatever on their behavior. Some changes in the rules on 'bail' and preventive detention were likewise understandable. One of the problems with which the authorities had to contend was that terrorist defendants who were released from jail, either on 'bail' or because the limits on preventive detention had been reached, frequently, being true revolutionaries, went back underground at the first opportunity. Still, these two measures taken together worked an inordinate infringement on the rights of defendants. The limits on preventive detention, which had already been substantially increased because of 'the emergency', were extended further – over-extended – by the 1979 decree-law. For example, a defendant in the most serious cases of crimes committed for terrorist ends could legally be held in preventive custody for 10 years and 8 months, and, with the abolition of provisional liberty, no 'bail' was possible. This was a flagrant abuse of preventive detention not easily reconcilable with the constitutional principle (Art. 27) of the presumption of innocence prior to a final determination. The effect of these measures was deplorable even if the defendant was guilty, and was an outrage as far as an innocent defendant was concerned.

The Members of Parliament were not indifferent to these injustices; unfortunately they lacked the will to address the underlying problem – that the legal system was incapable of processing cases rapidly. Everywhere the pace of criminal justice is slow, but in Italy it is glacial. A defendant could easily languish in a prison – often a brutal, over-crowded, inhuman place – for three or five or eight years before a final ruling was reached in his case. Even the evidence-gathering phase prior to trial (the 'instruction') could last for years and a defendant in a terrorism case could arrive for his trial having already spent three years in jail. In 1984, of the 43 685 detainees in Italian prisons about 70 per cent were awaiting final disposition of their cases.[3] This was a problem of long standing, but it grew much worse under the onslaught of crime in the 1970s. In 1974–8 the number of pending criminal cases doubled, and it took over three years to complete merely the trial stage of the average case (after which lay an intermediate and a final appeal).[4]

One of the reasons for this state of affairs was the failure of parliament to furnish the necessary personnel and resources. There were, and still are, too few prosecutors, judges, secretaries and chancellors, too few offices, courtrooms, typewriters, and so on. Another reason was the extraordinary complexity of the criminal process. For years prior to the onset of 'the emergency', efforts were in course to replace the Code of Criminal Procedure (approved in 1930 under an administration not renowned for its progressivism) with a modern system of rules, but these efforts had always come to naught. Instead of enacting the necessary profound reforms, parliament fled from the problem, frequently resorting to amnesties to free up some space on the court dockets and some places in jail. When 'the emergency' arrived the legislators were in no mood for talk about reform; it was time to be tough and tough they were.

The guardians of the Constitution, the judges of the Constitutional Court, did not show themselves to be vigilant. In an opinion of 1982[5] the court dealt, *inter alia*, with the notorious case of Giuliano Naria. Naria had been in jail since October 1976 awaiting trial on terrorism charges. He had been due to be released in 1980 because the limits on preventive detention through the trial phase would have been exceeded. The intervening 1979 measure had extended the period of detention for the trial phase to five years and four months, meaning that Naria would stay inside until February 1982. Because of consequences such as this, the 1979 extension of preventive detention was attacked as a violation of the principle of innocence enshrined in Art. 27 of the Constitution. The Constitutional Court wrote:

> If one must admit that a system in which terrorism sows death – including through the pitiless assassination of innocent 'hostages' – and destruction, creating insecurity and, hence, the need to entrust the safety of life and goods to armed escorts and private police, is in a state of emergency, one must, however, agree that the emergency . . . is a condition certainly anomalous and grave, but also essentially temporary. It follows that this legitimizes, yes, unusual measures, but that these lose legitimacy if unjustifiably protracted in time.
>
> It must also be observed that, though in a regime of emergency, an excessively long extension of the limitations on preventive detention such as to lead to the substantial undermining of the guarantee would not be justified.[6]

From which you might conclude that the court found in Naria's favor. It did not. Despite these words of warning, the court concluded that the very long periods of preventive detention were reasonable in view of 'the emergency', and it refused to hold parliament to account for the ponderous pace of the legal machine. Naria stayed in jail until 1985, making for a total of nine years awaiting resolution of legal proceedings against him, while his health deteriorated.

The European Court on Human Rights was less indulgent. As a

signatory of the European Convention on Human Rights, Italy is obliged, among other things, to provide everyone accused of a criminal offense a trial within a 'reasonable' time (Art. 6), and to provide everyone in preventive detention with either a trial within a 'reasonable' time or release from jail (Art. 5). Interpreting the former provision in 1982, the court concluded that Italy had violated the Convention by failing to provide a reasonably prompt trial for the appellants.[7] As the appellants were not in preventive detention and as the longest of the time spans at issue was less than half the 10 years and 8 months allowed by the decree-law of 1979 in terrorism cases, Italy would surely have fared badly had it had to defend the decree-law before the European Court.

In or about 1981, as the contest between the forces of law and order and the BR entered its most intense phase, the season of the great terrorism trials opened in the courtrooms of the country. The atmosphere was very different from that which had attended the Turin trial of the BR in 1976–8. Now the state was in a position of considerable strength and confidence. The culture of 'the emergency' was at work to preserve this strength and confidence and could be seen in the way in which the trials were conducted, in the legal doctrines employed, in the results reached.

From a strictly physical point of view, the trials were impressive and disturbing. The typical setting was that of a 'courtroom-bunker': an ultra-modern, specially-designed, high security hall, encased in a kind of fortress, sometimes annexed to a prison, surrounded and protected by barbed wire, electronic security devices and *carabinieri* with guns and bullet-proof gear and dogs. Inside, the hall was often bright and sterile and not a little surreal. The most striking and unsettling features of the courtrooms were the large cages, with plenty of metal bars and wire mesh. The defendants were kept in these, guarded closely by platoons of *carabinieri*, and it was impossible not to think of the defendants as animals in a zoo. The almost Orwellian setting tended to stimulate misgivings about the content of the legal liturgy to be there performed, concern that the much-feared 'Germanization', as it was frequently put, might be being realized.

The trials were 'great' not merely because of their political and historical importance. Many were 'maxi-trials': trials of 50, 100 or even 200 defendants in a single case that embraced a myriad of crimes committed over a period of years, a legal proceeding so complex as to last for many months. The cages were therefore many, among which the defendants were distributed depending on whether they were 'movementists' or 'militarists' or *pentiti* or *dissociati* or something else. There was a grotesqueness to the appearance of these maxi-trials, to which the *brigatisti* added greatly. As in the past, they yelled out slogans, read communiqués, abandoned the courtroom whenever an 'infamous person' like Peci came to testify, and so on. The judges, however, ceased to tolerate such behavior, and many a defendant was expelled. When the *brigatisti* fired their attorneys, the judges promptly ordered the appointment of replacements and the trials went forward. In time the histrionics, increasingly forlorn and pathetic, became less frequent.

The elephantine nature of these proceedings raised serious questions of substance. Could justice be done with respect to each defendant in a case in which you needed a computer to keep track of the accused? Would the marginal defendant be lost in the crowd of defendants, their guilt infecting him? Even if he were guilty of something, would his sentence truly be determined on the basis of what *he* had done, or would it not inevitably be influenced by the months of testimony of terrible deeds committed by persons with whom he may once have associated and who were now there in the cages alongside him?

These questions became more troubling when you took account of the types of crimes at issue in these cases. The maxi-trials included numerous charges of specific crimes, but every case was also founded on charges of crimes of association, especially criminal association for the purposes of terrorism or subversion and *'banda armata'* ('armed band'). As noted, terrorism was not defined, which made for possible problems. Just who was a 'terrorist' as opposed to a mere radical and what standards were applied to differentiate the two? The creation or promotion of a terrorist association or an 'armed band' was a crime, but so was mere membership therein and the penalties therefore were substantial, and a person so accused would be compelled to submit to the combined effects of preventive detention, the unavailability of provisional liberty, and the extremely slow pace of justice. While Curcio, Moretti and other big names attracted the attention of the press, hundreds of obscure persons were charged with such crimes. Were they really irregulars or 'mailmen' or sympathizers who had lent their apartments or names to the work of the BR? Were they truly 'terrorists'? Or, as the critics alleged, were individuals arrested and convicted on the basis of an acquaintance with radicals, or an acquaintance with someone who turned out to be a terrorist, or naïve assistance to such a person, or even mere association with the associates of terrorists? To answer such questions definitively would require an impossibly detailed study of the cases in which crimes of association were prosecuted. But clearly it is fair to say that, given the objective conditions of the gargantuan maxi-trials, a not insignificant number of injustices may very well have been done. Surely many more errors were made at the expense of marginal defendants than would have been made in normal trials in normal times. The 'emergency' involved these things also – widespread use of allegations of crimes of association and, in consequence, the sowing of doubts about the fairness of this 'emergency' justice.

A source of similar disquiet was the not infrequent recourse of the judiciary to the concept of 'moral complicity' in acts of terrorism, a sort of spiritual participation of one person in an act done by another. Here, too, the problems of proof were serious. Occasionally the resolution of those problems was patently unsatisfactory, as when the *brigatista* Valerio Morucci, guilty, to be sure, of many things, was sentenced to nothing less than life imprisonment for 'moral complicity' in a crime the commission of which he had actively opposed inside the BR.

The 'emergency' also meant severe sentences for those found guilty. The typical maxi-trial ended in an avalanche of life sentences and sentences of 20 or 30 years, totalling hundreds of years in prison. Many a verdict was softened somewhat on appeal, in a later period when the political defeat of the terrorists had become manifest, but even then no one could say that the terrorists had been treated with velvet gloves.

The most important, and certainly the most controversial, legal innovation of 'the emergency' was the legal benefits granted to the *pentiti*, ex-terrorists who collaborated with the authorities. One critic has written, perhaps hyperbolically, that these measures caused 'the most serious laceration that the principles and practices of penal justice have known in the history of our Republic'.[8] The decree-law of December 1979 granted reductions in the sentence of a repentant terrorist under certain conditions. The case of Patrizio Peci suggested to the authorities the usefulness of encouraging defections from the terrorist groups and, it was hoped, the collapse of these groups from within. The murder of

Roberto Peci had the opposite effect from that intended by
Giovanni Senzani by giving an additional boost to the legal cause
of the *pentiti*. In May 1982 the major law on the *pentiti* was enacted
by parliament.[9] The law granted a one-third reduction in the
sentence of a terrorist defendant who repented, confessed his own
crimes, and worked effectively to reduce the harmful consequences thereof or impede the commission of new crimes, and a
reduction of one-half to a repentant defendant who confessed and
helped in the collection of decisive or important proof about the
crime and its authors. A defendant who made a contribution of
'exceptional importance' would be entitled to a reduction of
two-thirds of his sentence, provisional liberty and parole were
made available, and certain defendants could be exempt from
punishment altogether. Sometimes the complaint is made that the
terrorists were not truly remorseful about what they had done.
Many *pentiti* did experience spiritual crises and crises of political
faith, as the magistrates who worked with them, not a naïve group,
have indicated. Other *pentiti*, though, were no doubt more interested in helping themselves than in anything else. The problem
is that the substantial indulgences offered by the law created
temptations for arrested terrorists to bend the truth or lie outright
in order to get a discount or to be judged to have made the
contribution of 'exceptional importance' worthy of the greatest
benefit. The writer, Giorgio Bocca, one of the leading authorities on
Italian terrorism, whom no one could fairly accuse of being an
apologist for the terrorists, challenged the jurisprudence of repentance because of the chain of doubtful accusations it created.[10] But
this machine was not necessarily unsound; its proper running
depended upon the engineering of the magistrates.

   The magistrates were supposed to demand corroboration for the
pentito's testimony: the addresses of hideouts, information about
the group's weapons, and other information that could be physically checked; confirmation of the *pentito*'s account by disin-
terested witnesses, other *pentiti* or the physical evidence. Ideally,
the magistrates would constantly subject the testimony of the
pentito to evaluation of this sort. Did the magistrates remain faithful
to this ideal? Or was the verification an illusion? When a *pentito*'s
testimony was shown accurate in certain respects, was it taken for
accurate in all? As with the problems of the marginal defendant, a
definitive answer would require an investigation not here possible.
Some partial enlightenment, however, is available. Many of the

revelations of Peci and other *pentiti* have been confirmed by unequivocal evidence, including the testimony of terrorists who were not *pentiti*. Legal documents of the magistrates in some key cases reveal a reassuringly deliberate and painstaking evaluation of the proof. Furthermore, the accusations of the prosecutor were subject to the check of the 'indicting' magistrate (the judge of the 'instruction'). The trial, of course, provided a basic control upon the *pentiti*, who were called to testify and to respond to examination and challenge by the defense. The appeal stages provided important safeguards, particularly in the later phase of 'the emergency', when a more dispassionate evaluation was possible. It should also be recalled that Peci and a number of other *pentiti* co-operated with the authorities at great personal risk and before the measure that granted the greatest benefits (the 1982 law) had even been proposed.

On the other hand, it is clear that the dangers inherent in the law were not always circumvented. In a 1987 decision, the Court of Cassation overturned a guilty verdict because the lower court had failed to corroborate the testimony of two *pentiti*.[11] Undoubtedly there were other instances of this sort. The limits of the practice of building legal cases on the testimony of *pentiti* were also demonstrated spectacularly in the mid-1980s in a maxi-trial against hundreds of defendants, a case that involved organized crime but was instructive none the less. The sheer size of this case seemed to make the hope for justice illusory. That consideration apart, there was the dreary spectacle of the *pentiti*: the inherently doubtful, sometimes incredible charges, the contradictions between *pentiti* and within the accounts of each, the retractions, the retractions of retractions, the unsavory individuals with long histories of crime and dishonesty. Undoubtedly errors were made and injustices done, though whether there were so many as to have outweighed the undeniable benefits of the law is difficult to say. It is not difficult to say that the law was a very dangerous thing that required the greatest of care in its application and healthy skepticism toward the *pentiti* by the magistrates, and that a system of justice worthy of the name is far more likely to be created if such arrangements are avoided.

Two problems caused by the justice of the *pentiti* were not the fault of the magistrates. The laws created disparities of treatment which could have been reduced or eliminated had the laws been written with greater precision and more attention to possible side-effects. One disparity was that between the *pentito* and a terrorist with more or less equal penal responsibilities who did not repent. The latter would receive a tough, sometimes even ferociously harsh, sentence, while the former, though equally guilty, could receive a sentence two-thirds less severe. This disparity at least was remediable – the unrepentant terrorist could change his mind – but another disparity was not. Take the case of a minor member of the BR, guilty of mere participation in an 'armed band'. Because of this individual's low status in the hierarchy, and because of the extreme compartmentalization and secrecy that ruled inside the BR, such a defendant would have in his possession little information that he could provide the magistrates, however profound his remorse and sincere his repentance. Only someone higher up, with greater culpability, would know what the magistrates wanted, and only someone like a Peci could make the contribution of 'exceptional importance' that would yield the greatest discount. The more guilty you were, the better your chances of getting a break.

The law also produced discounts that were unjustifiable, however useful the contribution of the *pentito*. The case of Marco Barbone, which understandably caused a tremendous uproar, is emblematic of the excessive leniency of the law. Barbone, together with another member of his little revolutionary band, the Brigade 28 March, a rather squalid and pedestrian group of radicals who sought to imitate and impress the BR, shot and killed the young and distinguished Walter Tobagi of *Corriere della Sera* in 1980. Barbone quickly became a *pentito*. He was entitled under the 1982 law to a substantial discount and received a sentence of eight years and six months. It was also concluded that he met the law's tests for provisional liberty. After but three years in prison, the gates opened and the murderer of Tobagi was free. Defending these decisions, the magistrates responded that they were merely following the dictates of the law. The law, in other words, was intrinsically defective, for such a result as this was unjust, failing in respect for the value of a human life.

What has made the debate over the *pentiti* so tormented is the clear utility of the laws. After Patrizio Peci came others. Not long after the enactment of the 1982 law, 130 *pentiti* were collaborating with the authorities,[12] and that number grew until there was a virtual rush to abandon the listing ship. It is certain that many lives and many limbs were preserved in consequence, for the arrest and the building of legal cases against hundreds of terrorists would have been a very much longer process without the *pentiti*. It would be an oversimplification to say that the laws alone caused the political defeat of the BR and the other terrorists. Rather it was the legislation in combination with the growing recognition among the terrorists of the failure of the revolutionary idea that led to the collapse. And it is obvious that efficiency cannot be the only standard by which a legal system is judged; civil rights and due process of law will always interfere with efficiency. The intensity of the debate over 'the emergency' cannot, however, be understood without taking into account the defects of the legislation, but also the good produced by it, good measured above all by the lives saved from the cosmic vengeance of the Red Brigades.[13]

There is no gainsaying the repressiveness of 'the emergency'. Try as it did, Italy could not resist the impulse to deal with terrorism by 'special' and 'tough' legislation. In certain respects the Italian case offers cautionary lessons for the future, for in part the legislation was of doubtful utility or no utility at all, while it reversed progress in civil liberties and in the humanization of the prison system, and contributed to what was often called the 'barbarization of the process of criminal justice'. The record, in short, is not as glorious as the occasional sanguine politician likes to make it appear. It is useful that this be recognized. It is also important, however, if only to avoid disabling discouragement, to recognize what was *not* done during 'the emergency'. There were no death squads of state, no arbitrary arrests in the night, no hidden prisons, no *desaparecidos*. Torture was the rare exception, not the rule. The right to counsel and the right to a legal defense were preserved, as were the presumption of innocence, the independence of the *magistratura* and the other cardinal principles of the Constitution. Despite all the pressures and the maneuvering of certain extreme rightists, no leader on horseback arrived and, except among the small minority of fanatics, there was little nostalgia for the toughness of Fascist law and order. The press was not censored by the government, and though it sometimes censored itself, its self-censorship was not unanimous and was contained in time. With all the difficulties of the situation, the right to speak and write freely was preserved astonishingly well during the decade and a half of political discontent and violence. Like green things in the tropics, extremist journals and papers sprouted and flourished in uncountable numbers, all manner of outrageous notions were expressed and circulated, and it was possible for years, while a revolutionary struggle was actually in course, to spout quite incendiary ideas in favor of the revolution. The book *L'ape e il comunista* (Brigate Rosse, 1980d), the prescription for the revolution written by Curcio, Franceschini *et al.*, was, yes, prosecuted, but the verdict went in its favor. The democracy continued to function and fundamental political rights continued to be respected. Italian democracy resisted, avoided the trap of a reactionary response and, in the end, emerged strengthened, with renewed credibility. It had been by no means clear in the 1970s, in the grim 54 days of the Moro affair, that such an ending was possible. That the system weathered the hurricane as it did is an achievement of no small significance.

14

Connections

According to one version of the philosophy of the conspiracy theory (or *dietrologia*, from *dietro* for 'behind'), the BR were, for all practical purposes, a branch of the secret services of the USSR or an allied state. In another version the BR were leftists controlled by reactionary forces within or at the margins of the Italian state and by the CIA. These analyses distort the complex reality that was the BR.

FRIENDS ABROAD

Over the years there was cooperation between the BR and other Western European terrorist groups, which consisted primarily of ideological solidarity and logistical assistance. For example, in the early 1970s war *matérial* was stolen from deposits of the Swiss army. Hand grenades and other items from Switzerland were found in Via Gradoli and other BR bases, as well as in Barcelona and in hideouts of the Baader-Meinhof gang. In 1979 two members of the RAF, one arrested and one killed, were found to be in possession of identity cards that were part of a stock of blank cards stolen by the BR from an Italian city hall in 1972.[1]

In the early years the BR's interest in relations with other groups was substantial and Moretti worked on the subject. Over time, however, relations were reduced for political reasons. Patrizio Peci has reported that contacts with the IRA and the Basque group ETA came to very little because the two groups were primarily nationalistic and therefore interlocutors of scant value to the theoretically inclined *brigatisti*.[2] A few militants from 'Front Line' and 'Fighting Communist Formations' trained with the ETA in France and had contacts with a French radical group.[3]

The BR's closest allies in Western Europe were the Germans. In the early period, relations with the RAF were maintained by the Reggiano, Lauro Azzolini, whose interpreter, Ingeborg Kitzler, was later arrested in Italy on terrorism charges. These relations involved weapons exchanges and discussions of matters ideological. Alberto Franceschini speaks of the former exchanges as having been rather modest in early years and of the latter as having been the primary motivation behind the dealings. According to him, the groups exchanged documents and ideological statements and arranged for occasional meetings using the simple device of a post office box. After 1972 or so this relationship was broken off by the BR because the *brigatisti* concluded that the members of the RAF were obsessed by international issues at the expense of the problem of relations with the domestic working class. The BR found the attitudes of the German group '2nd of June' much closer to their own and pursued contacts with them instead.[4]

After Azzolini's arrest, Mario Moretti re-established relations with the RAF. In the fall of 1978 Moretti was in Paris with Anna Laura Braghetti to re-open contacts with the Germans. While there with them, another *brigatista*, on instructions, rented an apartment in his name for the Organization. Not long after, this *brigatista* and Braghetti procured a post office box in Rome that was to be used for contacts with the RAF. Moretti had dealings with Willy Peter Stoll, a leader of the RAF who was eventually shot to death by German police and on whose body were found documents relating to his Italian liaison. According to another *brigatista*, two members of the RAF were given hospitality in Milan for a long time and were in direct touch with Moretti. At a certain point the BR concluded for a second time that the association with the RAF was politically unsatisfactory. The BR believed that the RAF supinely deferred to Soviet foreign policy, whereas the BR, as their Resolutions showed, regarded the USSR as an advocate of 'social imperialism' and a practitioner of state capitalism, sins that made it little better than the US. More important, in the eyes of the BR the Germans still were unreasonably preoccupied by NATO and the Americans and had only a very limited relationship with the working class. (On the second point the Red Brigades were clearly right; the German terrorists never enjoyed anywhere near the level of support from the proletariat that the BR did.) Although, by 1980 anyway, the BR were not uninterested in NATO, the RAF's emphases in general were different from those of the BR. And despite all the feverish speculation at the time about the involvement of the RAF in the kidnapping of Moro, the evidence collected disproves any link of this kind. The speculation even gave rise to cynical laughter among the *brigatisti*.[5]

The BR had dealings with the powers of the East, but, it appears, rather fewer than suggested in the speculations repeatedly engaged in by various observers, from the President of the Republic on down. Czechoslovakia was on everyone's list of suspects. It was often asserted that the *brigatisti* were trained at special camps there, but Antonio Savasta, who was high enough up in the BR to know about such things, has denied this. He has also revealed, however, that after the kidnapping of General Dozier, the *brigatisti* were approached by agents of the Bulgarian secret services, who wanted information from the General, in return for which the BR would have received money and arms. The *brigatisti* were unenthusiastic about the Bulgarians' encroaching on the Dozier operation. Still, an appointment to talk the matter over was fixed with a representative of the Bulgarian embassy, who, however, did not appear. Shortly thereafter, the Dozier operation went disastrously wrong for the BR and that was the last that was heard of the Bulgarians. The Bulgarians, it will be recalled, were implicated in the plot to kill Pope John Paul II, although the judgement in the legal case was that sufficient proof was lacking to convict the Bulgarian defendants.[6]

The BR's dealings in the international arena were most substantial with the Palestinians. From 1978 Mario Moretti made frequent trips to Paris with Anna Laura Braghetti and others to meet with representatives of the PLO. A faction of the PLO, impressed by the military efficiency demonstrated by the BR, especially in 'Operation Fritz', was interested in arranging attacks on Israeli embassies and personnel in Europe and believed that the BR might be of help. Wishing to be useful to a cause that was congenial, the BR conducted an *inchiesta* on the Israeli military attaché in Rome. When the *brigatista*, Bruno Seghetti, was arrested in May 1980 in the aborted getaway attempt after an assassination in Naples, he was found in possession of a paper written in English, a language he did not know, which identified the addresses in Rome of the Israeli ambassador and the Israeli military attaché. The quid pro quo for the BR's commitment to help the Palestinian cause was weapons. One group of weapons was brought into Italy by the BR by land from France in 1978, and a second was delivered in August 1979 to Moretti and several other *brigatisti* who traveled to the waters off Lebanon in a sailboat for the purpose and brought the weapons back to Mestre. Among the weapons that came to the BR via the PLO were pistols, hand grenades, Sterling automatic weapons and Soviet AK47 Kalashnikovs. The Sterling guns had been delivered by the English manufacturer to Tunisia, a friend to the PLO. A part of the weapons was to be held for the future use of the PLO and, in fact, weapons discovered by the authorities in a BR cache had been wrapped up in an Arab newspaper. The BR were also offered military training in Lebanon, but rejected this offer because of the perils of travel across borders and probably also because the *brigatisti* realized they were doing just fine from the military point of view without such training. The *brigatisti* never did carry out their part of the contract with the PLO, apparently because of resistance inside the BR to the Organization's immersing itself in turbid international affairs unrelated to the primary objective and because of fear of the consequences of such involvement for the BR's security, and, as a result of this, relations with the PLO turned chilly.[7] Apparently on commission for a Middle Eastern group, though, the late BR assassinated the American, Leamon Hunt, director of the multinational peace-keeping force in the Sinai, in Rome in February 1984.

Another shipment of weapons, again including AK47's, came from the Middle East to 'Front Line', the BR and another group in the summer of 1978. The weapons were brought to Italy in another sailboat by Maurizio Folini. Folini was a mysterious figure with connections in the Middle East and, according to him, with Gheddafi and the KGB. Folini was only arrested in June 1987, so it will be some time, if ever, before the full truth about his role is discovered.[8]

A strange episode involves the Israeli secret service. Alberto Buonavita joined the Executive Committee in October 1974, at which time he was informed by Margherita Cagol of the secrets he would need to know as a BR leader. One concerned an approach made to the BR in 1972-3 by the Israeli secret service. An individual purporting to be an intermediary of the Israelis met with a representative of the BR and offered to supply the *brigatisti* with arms, training and information. In return, the Israelis wanted the BR to accelerate their military activities in Italy. The Israeli objective was to put pressure upon the United States to increase its support for Israel by weakening Italy and increasing the relative importance of Israel to the maintenance of US interests. The BR leadership rejected this proposal out of sympathy for the Palestinian cause and fear of the security risk that such an arrangement would present. As they had promised, the Israelis reappeared later and gave the *brigatisti* some information free of charge. The information turned out to be true, but the BR turned them down again, for the reasons previously given and because by then the *brigatisti* had remedied their financial and armament problems. Alberto Franceschini, who even more than Buonavita was in a position to know, has confirmed the essentials of Buonavita's account. Peci described a similar offer from the Israelis, though the motive he attributed to them was their fear of the prospect of PCI participation in the government.[9]

It is not clear what common interest Franceschini, Buonavita and Peci had to concoct this story. On the face of it, though, the motivations described by the putative Israeli agents are far-fetched. As to the motivation indicated by Peci, the contacts were said to have occurred in the early 1970s when the prospect of PCI participation in the government appeared remote, and, in any case, it is hard to see how destabilizing Italy would necessarily have reduced PCI influence over Italian political life. As for the other motivation, it is difficult to accept that Israel, which has not traditionally acted in this manner, would seek to generate additional American support by undermining a strategically-situated American ally. The Italian authorities rejected these claims of an Israeli approach to the BR, but the Moro Commission concluded that it was at least possible that such a contact had been made.[10]

Many a *brigatista* or other terrorist has had occasion to spend time in France and many are there still, some in retirement. Over the years and up to the present, French governments have been remarkably hostile to Italian requests to send back these visitors, even those against whom arrest warrants were outstanding. In explanation of this policy the French have invoked their tradition of hospitality towards political refugees, as well as skepticism about the justifiability of Italian accusations of subversive association and 'armed band', which, when appearing in Italian extradition requests, have tended to be considered 'political crimes' and therefore disregarded. Whatever the legal technicalities, this attitude is hard to justify. It is difficult to perceive what claim upon the sympathies of the French public members of the BR and like groups could have. Furthermore, it is clear that the countries of Western Europe have a common interest in opposing terrorist groups, even those that, like the BR, carry out their revolutionary activities primarily in their own countries. And it is beyond dispute that some of the Italian visitors to France were up to no good, such as Mario Moretti and other _brigatisti_ who aided him and took his place after his arrest.

A full understanding of what Moretti and his comrades were doing in France requires a brief journey back in time. In 1969 and early 1970 several radicals, led by one Corrado Simioni, split off from the Metropolitan Political Collective. Simioni and two others from the group, in appearance at least, abandoned radical politics in the early 1970s and went to Paris, where, together with others, they opened the Hyperion Institute, a language school. Moretti continued to maintain contact with Simioni and friends. According to a _pentito_ who testified to having discussed the subject with Moretti, the Hyperion provided aid and protection to terrorists on the run and served as a point of communication for various terrorist groups from other nations. It was through the Hyperion that Moretti conducted his conversations with the PLO. Antonio Savasta confirmed the key aspects of this testimony (though he was unfamiliar with the name Hyperion).[11]

The precise role of the institute remains to be discovered. In particular, it remains to be established or disproven what Savasta reported on the basis of his conversations with Moretti – that, as Moretti believed, the KGB was in touch with the institute in some way and thereby was aware of the discussions of arms traffic and acts of terrorism among Moretti, the representatives of the PLO, the RAF, and so on. In addition, in the summer of 1981 the first joint anti-NATO campaign by European terrorist groups was decided upon in Paris. Various actions followed in implementation of this plan. One of these was the Dozier operation.[12]

As far as the means needed to conduct the revolutionary struggle were concerned, kidnappings and bank robberies provided the BR with the necessary cash.[13] Weapons were obtained through flexible arrangements with the Palestinians, purchases on the wide-open arms market, purchases in gunshops using false or stolen licenses, and robberies of individual police officers and armories. Franceschini reports that, in the early years, the group obtained weapons by buying them from organized crime in Italy or on the market in Switzerland and Liechtenstein. Buying abroad was easy, though it did create the risk of capture when the weapons were brought into the country. Through research the *brigatisti* discovered border points that were not well controlled, learned to hide arms on trains, and sometimes simply used the post.[14] Thus, the fact that the *brigatisti* employed the notorious Czech Skorpion did not prove Czech assistance to the group.[15]

Over the years there have been many hypotheses and outright claims that the Italian terrorists were made into fighters during training sessions in Libya, Lebanon, Czechoslovakia and other countries. At least as a general rule, however, according to Morucci, Savasta and other well-placed *brigatisti*, the members of the *Brigate Rosse* did not receive training abroad. They did not need it, and weapons training appropriate to conditions in the Middle East would have been of little value in the cities of Italy. The Moro Commission looked into the matter and concluded that the training of the BR and other groups was very much an artisanal matter.[16] Patrizio Peci painted a very modest picture of his acquisition of experience with weapons. It was often suspected that Alberto Franceschini had been trained in a special camp in Czechoslovakia along with his fellow Reggiano, Fabrizio Pelli. The story that Franceschini recounts, however, is less spectacular, though very largely credible. Franceschini reports that he, Curcio and Margherita learned to shoot under the tutelage of their comrade, Alfredo Buonavita, who had learned about guns when he had gone hunting as a boy with his father and brothers. The *brigatisti* practiced in isolated grottoes. Franceschini claims that he and Renato were never very good as marksmen, but that Margherita showed real skill, which, however, did not suffice to save her life in the Cascina Spiotta.[17]

The foregoing appear to have been the principal ties between the BR and political forces abroad during the years of the BR's greatest activism. In the last few years the enfeebled BR have sought refuge and help abroad and have had dealings with the RAF, the French 'Action Directe' and the Belgian 'Fighting Communist' Cells, but this co-operation has been as much a part of the struggle for survival as a matter of conviction, and does not signify the abandonment of the battle inside Italy, where all the BR's crimes to date have occurred. Although there may have been an indirect relationship with the KGB (through the PLO and perhaps the Hyperion), the BR were not controlled by Soviet orders and had only rare contacts with the secret services of Eastern block countries. The most important international connections, with the RAF and the Palestinians, were circumscribed, as were the BR's alliances in France.

Ideological considerations and fear of being sold out motivated the distance the BR kept from the various secret services. Although as Leninists they believed in international cooperation with like-minded groups, and although their late ideological documents increasingly emphasized international cooperation, the primary concern of the *brigatisti* was always the revolutionary struggle inside Italy, their primary focus the Italian proletariat – the workers in the factories in Milan or Turin or Porto Marghera, young people in the Roman *borgate*, the underclass of Naples. It was not until near the end of their most active phase that the BR attacked their first foreign target. Furthermore, the *brigatisti* were in disagreement with bureaucratic, non-revolutionary, stultified socialism *à la* Breshnev (recall their disagreement with Feltrinelli on this point as far back as the early 1970s), and they had an interest in not getting too close to the possibly crushing embrace of the Russian bear. Nor were the BR's needs so pressing as to compel them to run the risk. The BR, in short, were an independent group, domestically oriented for the most part. There was no *grande vecchio*, no sinister brain running the Organization from somewhere above the Strategic Direction.

FRIENDS AT HOME

In March 1981 investigators unexpectedly discovered some surprising evidence at the offices and villa of one Licio Gelli, businessman. The consequence was the greatest scandal in Italian post-war history (which is saying something). The principal piece of evidence was a membership list of the 'Propaganda Due' ('P2'), a masonic lodge of which Gelli was the Venerable Master. This may not seem disturbing, but, as subsequent investigation showed, the P2 was no ordinary fraternal lodge. First, it was kept completely secret both from other organs of freemasonry and from the public and the authorities despite a law banning secret organizations. Secondly, on the list of 953 names were those of many of the high and the powerful in government, business, finance and, most important of all, the military. There were 195 military officers on the list, many of a high rank. There were five ministers or ex-ministers, a party secretary, 16 magistrates, 422 individuals from government or public agencies, 36 Members of Parliament, important businessmen and bankers (including the 'bankrupters'

Michele Sindona and Roberto Calvi) and leading figures of journalism, publishing and television. Many of these were individuals of unprogressive political tendencies. Prominent on the list were representatives of the secret services: Gen. Vito Miceli, head of SID (1970–4), Gen. Giuseppe Santovito, head of SISMI (1978–81), Gen. Giulio Grassini, head of SISDE (1978–81) and the head of CESIS (from 1978), Walter Pelosi. Also present were a number of officers suspected of involvement in right-wing political conspiracies and high-level officers from the finance guard who were indicted on charges of corruption in a massive fraudulent scheme involving oil imports. Financial activities by P2 members led to the take-over of the Rizzoli publishing empire and the *Corriere della Sera* and almost to the destruction of both. Sindona and Calvi's fraudulent businesses eventually collapsed. The former died under strange circumstances, poisoned in his jail cell, and the latter, even more bizarrely, 'committed suicide' by hanging under a bridge in London.[18] What was Gelli up to? What was the P2?

While the precise contours of the danger represented by the P2 remain to be defined, the group's secrecy, the special character of its membership, and evidence accumulated about its activities, suggest that Gelli, his P2 and many of those linked to them, were enemies of Italian democracy. The Parliamentary Commission of Investigation on the P2 uncovered an extraordinarily complex network of relationships, including relationships of subordination to Gelli on the part of P2 members, and illicit and immoral dealings. But the lodge had a larger aim beyond matters of greed – to condition the political system in a reactionary direction. Gelli, whose earlier career prefigured his imprint on the P2 (during the war he had been an ardent Fascist until the victory of fascism had become in doubt, at which point he had started to work for both sides simultaneously), had right-wing sympathies. Up to the mid-1970s the P2 was involved in subversive, ultra-rightist activity. From 1975 the Venerable Master's strategy changed and the P2 came to prefer spreading its influence over positions of official power, especially military power, in other words, a strategy of occupation of the system through control of appointments to the posts of command.

The magistrates who investigated the Bologna bombing assembled a mass of further evidence about Gelli and the P2, the secret services, and right-wing extremism. The magistrates charged that there was a subversive association that was responsible for various bombings and violent acts, including the Bologna bombing. Gelli was accused of being the force behind this association, the misdeeds of which the secret services, directed by P2 members, attempted to cover up. It was at Gelli's initiative, the magistrates concluded, that agents of SISMI, on instructions from high SISMI officers, created the false trail of proof of international complicity in the Bologna bombing, in order to distract the attention of the investigators from those truly responsible, Gelli and the others.

Although it remains to be seen whether the Bologna accusations stick through the final appeal, enough has been said to add useful details to the portrait of the decade and a half of political violence in Italy and to clarify somewhat more the plotting of the far-right from Piazza Fontana onward. All was not *dietrologia*. That said, however, the story of Gelli and his friends also needs looking into because of the possibility of a more direct connection to the BR and left-wing terrorism in Italy.

Some Communists have had a field day with this story. To them, the discovery of the P2 was proof of the rightist conspiracy they always knew lay behind the BR and the other leftist groups. With this new knowledge these Communists read a whole series of past events in, let us say, a creative light. Two books written under Communist auspices present these readings with relish.[19] They assert that occult forces manipulated the BR even in details of their operations. A movie, *Il caso Moro*, and a book by the same name,[20] recently presented a similar picture. It is claimed that the P2 and the secret services, which were linked together through P2 members at the head of the services, following directions received from Washington, manipulated and encouraged the terrorists, failed to arrest them or uproot them despite having the knowledge and opportunity to do so, and saw to it that Aldo Moro did not return alive, all this in order to destroy his political handiwork, the government of national solidarity, and end any chance of *rapprochement* with the Communists. These theorists offer conspiratorial explanations for many specific events in the story of the BR and terrorism. It is suggested, for example, that the discovery of the Via Gradoli base was brought about on purpose for obscure motives.

These works collect facts tendentiously and examine them with bias in order to confirm a conclusion already arrived at. Had there been an elaborate conspiracy as alleged, it ought to have left behind many traces, or at least some traces, but the P2 Commission concluded that there was very scarce proof of an intervention by

the P2 in left-wing terrorism, and much of the 'proof' relied upon
by these authors is inference or supposition or the very unobjective
interpretation of some admittedly unclear or mysterious points in
the Moro case and the history of terrorism. Furthermore, it is hard
to see how this conspiracy could have controlled or directed the
vast, anarchic violence of the left of those years. How could it have
controlled and manipulated the BR? And how could it have
brought about the obstruction of the Moro investigation? In order
to accept the existence of a conspiracy one must believe that the
leaders of the plot were extraordinarily clever, omnipresent, perfectly organized and supernaturally efficient. When one examines
the countless incidents that the theorists attribute to the intervention of plotters, one cannot help but wonder how any human being
could possess the resources needed to bring off so much without a
hitch and without leaving behind witnesses or evidence.

Nor is it clear how the conspiracy could have managed the
activities of the BR and other groups without any of the terrorists
becoming aware of what was being done to them, a manipulation
they would certainly have rejected angrily and bloodily. Renato
Curcio called these theories 'stupid ideas' and said: 'From its
beginnings, in the history of the Red Brigades there has never been
an intrusion, direct or indirect, by the secret services or of other
"occult powers"'.[21] And Mario Moretti is just as vehement:

> Never, not even once, was there any contact with the secret
> services of any type. Anyone who has had the patience to follow
> the extremely long and very tormented judicial process of which
> the BR are protagonists has been able to perceive that there does
> not exist a single episode to support such an invention.[22]

The inclination of the theorists is no doubt to respond that Curcio,
Moretti et al. do protest too much, which is perhaps a clever
rejoinder, but an altogether unpersuasive one. No one who has
any sense of what the BR were, what they believed in, and what
they wanted to do, could fail to understand that conspiracy
theories such as these are, to the brigatisti, libels of the worst
possible kind that can only evoke frustrated rage.

This methodology of the conspiracy theory is nowhere better
illustrated than in elaborate suspicions surrounding a visit by Aldo
Moro to the US in September 1974. It is asserted that Moro recieved
threatening invitations to change his political ideas from an impor-

tant political figure during this visit and it is suggested that that person was Secretary of State Kissinger, who, as we have seen, disagreed with what he took to be Moro's unjustifiably sanguine attitude toward the PCI. The implication seems to be that these threats had something to do with Moro's death. The proof of such a threat by a US representative is, to say the least, negligible (as the Moro Commission concluded)[23] and the whole idea is preposterous. Among other things, compromises with the PCI were not in the offing at the time of the visit. The majority of which the PCI was a member was constructed and Moro was kidnapped after Dr Kissinger was long gone, under the Carter Administration, which did not have a conception of the role of covert action in foreign policy. Moro and Kissinger did not even share a language. None of these difficulties has impeded some adventurous authors, however, who continue to refuse to accept the truth about the BR. The director of the film *Il caso Moro*, recognizing the problems in trying to pin the thing on Dr Kissinger, suggests that the threat may have been made at a diplomatic reception – by none other than Licio Gelli in person.[24]

A more responsible argument for a link between occult forces and left-wing terrorism is presented by the prominent political scientist, Giorgio Galli, although even he draws the ire of the outraged Curcio.[25] Professor Galli eschews fashionable 'explanations' founded upon involvement on the part of the CIA, and instead suggests that the plot was a domestic one led by elements in the secret services and well-placed reactionaries from the P2. In addition to the existence of the P2 and its particular membership, Galli relies upon what he regards as the demonstrated ability of the forces of law and order to infiltrate and arrest the terrorists. From the successes he deduces that the police and *carabinieri* always had the capacity to crush the terrorists and that they did not do so because someone did not want them to do so. The abolition of Dalla Chiesa's anti-terrorism unit in 1974 is but one of a series of events given a sinister cast.

The trouble with this analysis is that it seems too neat and simple. For instance, Dalla Chiesa's group was no longer thought necessary in 1974 because the BR were believed to have been destroyed. That turned out to have been a serious error in judgement. Yet the BR were indeed then very close to disappearing, and it was certainly possible for someone to have dissolved the General's group in good faith. It was also mistaken, but not absurd, for some authorities to have been more concerned at a later stage with the many and very serious disorders in the streets than with the activities of clandestine bands like the BR. As the Moro Commission found, the evidence shows very extensive disorganization in the forces of law and order at the time of the Moro affair, and a shortage of knowledge, personnel and resources. It is difficult to reconcile these conditions, described by everyone from Minister Cossiga on down, with the supposedly healthy state of the forces of law and order sketched by Galli. Furthermore, that left terrorism could have been given a 'free hand' at times, that it could have been turned on and off like a spigot, seems improbable. Even if that were possible, how could it have been done without coming to the attention of some of the very many persons above suspicion in the anti-terrorism fight, including Minister Cossiga, General Dalla Chiesa and Emilio Santillo? This thesis also appears to underestimate the amount of work involved in the efforts of Dalla Chiesa and others and ignores the occasional piece of sheer luck that took place (for example, the change of heart of Peci) and that was then exploited by the General.

In the clarity of retrospection everything seems both inevitable and much more easy than it could have been at the time. There is little concrete proof of this conspiracy, and though a conspiracy is, by its nature, secretive, that fact should not become an excuse for boundless inferences. Although it is possible to believe in misdeeds by hidden powers, the suggestion that, in effect, Aldo Moro, magistrates, police and *carabinieri* were allowed to die for reactionary political ends is sufficiently serious as to require more tangible proof than has thus far come to light.

15

We Are All *Dissociati*

After their capture, Antonio Savasta and the rest of the *brigatisti* involved in the Dozier operation (save one) began to confess in great detail. Savasta had recognized for some time that the position of the Organization was hopeless:

> The organization Red Brigades did not have the possibility of affecting Italian social reality. Its loss of a connection to the mass movements and to the class sectors to which [the BR] referred – the worker, the prisoner, the marginal person – this isolation we were seeing day after day. The political impossibility of having an effect did not derive, does not derive, simply from tactical errors, but from the very foundation of our political analysis, of the analysis of the State, of the analysis of the movements ... which led us to believe that the armed struggle was the only possible political expression of the avant-garde of the movements. This oversimplification caused us to read as imminent the possibility of civil war ... if not in temporal terms then in political terms, a possibility that might then effectively take root. This rooting has not occurred.[1]

Emilia Libera had come to the same conclusion. '[W]e made a somewhat superficial analysis', she said with notable understatement.[2]

On the basis of this and other information, the police and *carabinieri* made many arrests. By mid-March 1982 the number of leftist terrorists arrested just since the beginning of the Dozier operation reached 340, with 35 coves uncovered.[3] Savasta even furnished information on the hideout of Barbara Balzarani and the other leaders of the 'militarists' in Milan, but all but one escaped capture. This period also witnessed devastating setbacks for the Senzani faction, including the arrest of the professor himself. Among other things found in the professor's bases were four missiles. The 'movementists' had been planning an imminent

232

attack upon a meeting of the DC national congress. The *brigatisti* had intended to bombard the site with the missiles and bazookas and to send a trained commando group into the meeting, where hand grenades would be thrown and automatic weapons would be fired upon the delegates. Between police and Christian Democrats, 100 were to be killed, including, the *brigatisti* hoped, most of the leadership of the party.[4] Good *brigatista* that he was, the professor declared himself a 'political prisoner' and lapsed into a silence that he has maintained ever since.

Many other arrestees, however, abandoned the terrorist cause or, like Savasta, sang as loudly as they could. Over the next year or so the Red Brigades collapsed. The Turin and Genoa columns had previously been virtually destroyed. Arrests and defections now demolished the Veneto column. The organization of the 'militarists' in Milan was smashed and the Walter Alasia was hit severely. (Among the arrestees in 1982 were at least 12 factory union delegates who had been leading double lives as *brigatisti*.)[5] The Rome column was gravely damaged. With the arrest of Senzani the Naples column lost its spiritual leader, but it otherwise was the column least affected by the confessions and arrests after the Dozier fiasco. After a series of assassinations and other actions, the Naples column largely abandoned the unreceptive city for the North, for Turin, where an effort was made to re-establish a BR presence in this metropolis of the group's origins. In October in Turin, in one of the most cold-hearted of their crimes, the BR killed two guards during a bank robbery. The guards were made to lie face down on the ground, and, without provocation, were each given a bullet in the back of the head. But Turin was less hospitable to the BR than it had been in the early 1970s. By the end of 1982 many of the transplanted *brigatisti* were behind bars and the Organization was everywhere in retreat. 'Front Line' had broken up and the other terrorist groups were also fast disappearing. The whole terrorist universe was coming apart.

The statistics reveal the downward trend. The acts of political violence in 1981 were 368, less than half the number of the year before. In 1982 that figure declined to 174. The number of groups claiming these actions also declined sharply. The dead were 24 in 1981 and 30 in 1982.[6] In 1981–2, the once much-vaunted revolutionary praxis of the BR was but a brutal struggle for survival directed against police and traitors, the outcome of which was almost a total rout of the *brigatisti* by 1983.

More than ever before, the jail and the courtroom became the stages to which the *brigatisti* were restricted. In April 1982 the trial of Mario Moretti, Prospero Gallinari and other *brigatisti*, for the kidnapping and murder of Aldo Moro and the massacre of his guards, opened in Rome. By this time it was clear to all but the unrepentant *brigatisti* that the tide had turned. In the courtrooms there were cages for the *pentiti*, who were by now numerous, including Professor Fenzi, the brother-in-law of Professor Senzani and comrade-in-arms of Mario Moretti. There were cages for the *irriducibili* – those, like Moretti and Gallinari, whose belief in the cause was unshaken despite the scorched earth all around them. And there was the increasingly important new phenomenon, also separately caged, the *dissociati*. The *dissociati*, as the word suggests, dissociated themselves from the armed struggle and the practice of violence for political ends. They confessed their own crimes and explained the operations in which they had taken part, but they refused to identify anyone who had participated with them, at least anyone who had not already been identified by the authorities through other means. This position was determined by what the *dissociati* described as morality and a sense of honor.

Valerio Morucci and Adriana Faranda were paradigmatic *dissociati*. At first, they would not testify at the Moro trial or other proceedings, though neither would they join the rantings of Senzani and his followers or the 'militarists'. The two maintained a rather dignified silence. It was plain that they were developing a position that would separate them from the path of violence. In December 1983 they and a group of like-minded prisoners wrote of their recognition of the errors of the armed struggle and of its end, saying that if such opinions were dissociation, 'then we are all *dissociati*'.[7] By the time of the appeal in the Moro case in late 1984–early 1985, Morucci and Faranda were willing to help the state that they had once sought to overthrow. They testified in this and in other cases. The one thing they continued to refuse to do was to name names of former compatriots in the battle for communism.

The interior journey of Morucci and Faranda was traveled by hundreds within the span of but a few years. There were those who turned their weapons over to a cardinal. There was the little band that, already condemned to long sentences and having undergone a change of heart in prison, revealed to the man who had prosecuted them where they had hidden a cache of weapons.

There was Alberto Franceschini, who advised a fellow *brigatista* to give up the struggle: 'We have only been addicts of a particular type', said Franceschini, 'addicts of ideology. A fatal drug, worse than heroin. A few cubic centimeters of it and you're done for for life'.[8] There were innumerable individuals like Maria Teresa Zoni, who said in 1985:

> My journey of self-criticism with regard to the armed struggle is definitely finished: for this reason I assume my responsibilities. Today I am a different person. A cycle in my life is over. I no longer believe in destructive values, but in constructive ones.[9]

So-called 'homogeneous areas' were formed inside the 'special' prisons by groups of individuals who were breaking with their pasts. Interest in religion rose. Many former leaders and members of the BR, 'Front Line' and other groups launched appeals to young people urging them not to take up the ways of violence, and denouncing the occasional act of terrorism that, sadly, continued to occur. These *dissociati* undoubtedly hoped that something concrete might be done for them. The phenomenon of dissociation, however, would be grossly distorted were it viewed exclusively as the product of interested calculations. Between 1983 and 1986 a profound cultural change was in course among the terrorists. No longer did revolution seem a kind of mystical goal. Even those who did not wish to admit it – and naturally there were many who were reluctant to acknowledge that they had thrown their lives away – had a hard time escaping the fact that the effort to bring off a revolution had failed; indeed, that it had been counter-productive, crushing, as many a far-left critic of the BR lamented, all hopes for some kind of serious systemic change through means other than terroristic violence. Those were the sounds of ideology dying, freeing from its grasp the long-choked, misshapen idealism of young people, who were now no longer quite so young. Respect for human values and recognition of the significance of a human life resurfaced in the thoughts and words of the *brigatisti* and the other terrorists, and the reflections were often painful and apparently sincere. In 1986 Antonio Savasta sent a letter to the wife of Giuseppe Taliercio, the businessman Savasta had murdered five years before, after a kidnapping lasting a month and a half:

> Your husband in those days was as you described him – calm,

full of faith, incapable of hating us and very dignified. He lived serenely even though his thoughts and worries were about you. It was he who tried to explain to us what the meaning of life was, and I in particular did not understand, did not understand from where he gathered the force to be so serene, almost detached from earthly things. I know, signora, that this will not give you back very much, but please know that within me the word that your husband carried has won. It has won over me, I who only today succeed in comprehending something. It has won over all those who still today do not understand. And in those moments your husband gave love; it was a seed so powerful that not even I who fought against it succeeded in extinguishing it within me. This is a flower that I want to cultivate so that I too can give it.[10]

Lessons learned, unfortunately for the *brigatisti* and their victims, too late.

The authorities were pleased by this breakdown in the cohesion of the Organization and the other terrorist groups and wished to further it. This suggested that something be done for the *dissociati* by way of a reduction in their sentences, which by then were widely recognized to have been unnecessarily harsh as a consequence of the emotional climate of 'the emergency'. Benefits for the *dissociati* would be a means to recuperate a lost generation, the thousands of *brigatisti* and members of other groups who were in jail by the middle of the decade; a means also to make a contribution towards 'leaving "the emergency" behind', as the hope was commonly expressed, to send an official signal of interest in a new era for civil liberties and criminal justice. There were, of course, some objections. The image of the *dissociato* was purer than that of the *pentito*, but the latter was much the more useful to the cause of capturing and prosecuting the terrorists. There was also the argument about sincerity: clearly, not all the changes of heart were honorable ones. The matter was resolved after much debate with the enactment of a special law, and although the decision continued to be subject to criticism, it was surely the correct one. By this point the *brigatisti* and the others were politically defeated; there were no longer thousands of terrorists in circulation, and the priority therefore had to be to consolidate the victory over the various groups and buttress the psychological break with the armed struggle that had been taken by many former loyalists. Nor could society simply ignore the plight of so many young people living in very harsh conditions with very long sentences before them. The action of parliament was in keeping with an expanding public conviction that this awful chapter in the nation's history ought now to be closed (without, of course, abandoning the effort to find the terrorists who remained at large) and with as little irretrievable damage as possible for all those who had been involved in it.

In February 1987 a law was approved granting substantial reductions in sentences to those who had definitively abandoned violence as a method of political activity and had admitted their own crimes, or who would make a declaration to this effect in the form and within the time limits set by the law.[11] By July 1987 over 560 persons had made the requisite declaration, including some who had been on the run.[12]

Meanwhile, other steps were being taken to roll back some of the more questionable features of 'the emergency'. In 1984 parliament approved notable reductions in preventive detention.[13] The overall maximum permitted was reduced to six years, which, if still too long, was nevertheless a considerable improvement over the pre-existing limit. In addition, the same reform greatly broadened the availability of provisional liberty, which 'the emergency' had brought the legislators to deny to alleged terrorists. The reform, however, still did not address the underlying difficulties that make the wheels of justice turn so slowly in Italy.

The courts also took action on their own. Many severe sentences issued by trial courts were reduced on appeal. In the Moro case, for instance, the initial sentence – 32 life sentences and a total of 1245 years in prison for 59 defendants – was reduced on appeal by ten life sentences (the beneficiaries included Morucci and Faranda) and by a total of 786 years. Some of the more unappreciated security measures imposed on terrorist prisoners were revoked and the political community began once again to discuss proposals for prison reform and the implementation of the enlightened but never realized reform of 1975. The Court of Cassation drew a line in the sand over the use of the testimony of *pentiti* without adequate corroboration. In 1985 the high court issued a decision setting strict limits on the breadth of the concept of 'moral complicity'.[14] The unhappy 'emergency' was being brought to an end.

Though the *brigatisti* have been defeated, politically and militarily, more than a handful remain at large, enough to carry forward the revolutionary cause and, on occasion, to kill. The BR assassinated

the American diplomat Leamon Hunt (February 1984); Ezio Tarantelli, professor at the University of Rome and adviser on economics
to the CISL union confederation, was murdered inside the University (March 1985); Lando Conti, former mayor of Florence was
savagely gunned down in his car (February 1986); two policemen
were killed in a robbery of a postal truck in Rome in a manner
reminiscent of Via Fani (February 1987); and Licio Giorgieri, an air
force general, was assassinated while driving home from work
through the streets of Rome (March 1987). When, despite these
events, the press and others seemed to think that the menace had
finally disappeared for good, the BR resurfaced in April 1988 to
disabuse them of that illusion. The *brigatisti* assassinated Roberto
Ruffilli, professor at the University of Bologna and DC Senator.
Senator Ruffilli was selected as a target because the country in the
months prior to his death had been actively discussing proposals
for modifications to the political system, such as changes in the
rules governing admission of parties to parliament, modification of
parliamentary procedures and ideas about new institutional
mechanisms that would stabilize government coalitions. Sen.
Ruffilli had offered a widely-publicized proposal for reform and
was the principal adviser on the subject to Prime Minister Ciriaco
DeMita. Following the indications of their predecessors, who in
1974 had condemned discussions of institutional reform as an
anti-revolutionary 'neo-Gaullist' conspiracy, the latest *brigatisti*
contended in the inevitable communiqué that the Senator was a
factotum carrying out an anti-proletarian, imperialist design mas-
querading as reform.

The Hunt, Conti and Giorgieri murders had international overtones, and it seems that the Ruffilli assassination and other
operations may have been organized from BR bases in France.[15] It
is also believed that the BR held important discussions about the
future course of the revolutionary effort in Italy, in Paris in 1984.
The murder of General Giorgieri in particular appears to have been
conceived as the contribution of a BR faction to a joint European
terrorist offensive. On a number of occasions proof has surfaced of
cooperation between the RAF and the BR, as in the case of a failed
assassination attempt by the RAF in Germany late in 1988. In 1986,
an important businessman involved in defense work and his driver
were assassinated in Germany by the RAF's 'Mara Cagol Commando'. The BR have indicated that the driving idea behind this new
international cooperation is the desire to destroy NATO and

undermine the United States, though it is plain that the BR's weakness at home is a major factor in its course. This strategy has not, however, shielded the *brigatisti*, in a number of important cases, from discovery and arrest.

In June 1985 'Comrade Sara', Barbara Balzarani, one of the last links to the historic nucleus, was arrested in Rome after eight years underground. With her arrest, all hope of healing the dissension inside the BR came to an end. The much-shrunken BR were now split into two factions, the 'Fighting Communist Party' and the 'Union of Fighting Communists', the heirs of the 'militarists' and the 'movementists' respectively. The second of these factions murdered Gen. Giorgieri, has suffered many arrests, and is now bordering on extinction, while the former is more resilient and more clever, though it too has suffered arrests, including very recently those believed responsible for the murder of Sen. Ruffilli. For the *brigatisti* who remain, the strategy of the armed struggle must appear more troubled than it ever has. And more strenuous than ever before is the life of the revolutionary, who is hunted by the police, with money and safehouses very hard to come by, and allies difficult to find.

That the BR have lasted this long – over 18 years – is a remarkable thing. A magistrate expert in terrorism cases estimates that there are about 100 *brigatisti* left in Italy between regulars, irregulars and sympathizers (though it has been reported that the secret services put the number at about 400).[16] Probably the BR can go on at the present low level of manpower and activity for a considerable period yet, and this would permit them, if they are skilful, to bring off even a series of spectacular crimes. (Apparently the 'Fighting Communist Party' faction was recently studying the possibility of another Via Fani, the kidnapping or assassination of Prime Minister DeMita.) But can they rise again, like a phoenix? Can they become anything like what they once were? It would be imprudent for the authorities to rule this out, for the BR have been buried too hastily too many times before. If a prediction can, with this caveat, nevertheless be hazarded, it would be that the BR will not be able to rebuild and become what they once were. There is a great difference between the 1970s and the last few years. It is a cultural difference, even more profound than that which separates the 1960s in Britain and the United States from the climate of Thatcherism and Reaganism. There has been a metamorphosis in political thinking. Revolutionary ideology is a tiny shadow of its former self. The inflammatory journals have largely disappeared. The professors of revolution no longer preach about the need for violence and the destruction of the State. 'Lotta Continua' is gone and 'Autonomia' is a walking skeleton. There are no more 'nights of fire', no more Saturdays of urban guerrilla warfare in the streets of Rome or Milan. The factories have been generally peaceful and preoccupied with normal issues of industrial relations, and the occasional BR bulletin that turns up appears to elicit only rejection or indifference from the workers. The economic situation has very greatly improved. Inflation eventually came down to manageable levels and the rate of economic activity grew (though the public debt remains far too high). With the experiment at national solidarity having ended in 1979, the political parties rediscovered the equilibrium, in economic and other fields, that had been lost some years before. The stock market has been booming and millions have been investing there and elsewhere and enjoying the fruits of a new prosperity. The post-industrial transformation has continued at a brisk pace. Capitalism is no longer a pestilence, nor profit a dirty word. Conditions in the schools are still bad and youth unemployment is a very grave problem, and these are matters for concern in view of the history of the 1970s. Yet the schools are quiet and uninterested in political activity, so much so that great was the hand-wringing and press coverage in 1986 when some students for a month or so held a few rallies, directed not at overturning the bourgeois system, but at demanding more halls and books and studies. The consequences of the orgy of ideology of the late 1960s and 1970s are vivid still in the memories of almost everyone, and there is little wish to revisit that national disaster.

And the protagonists? In jail for the past 14 years, now a *dissociato*, Alberto Franceschini is facing a sentence that runs until 2022, but realistically looks forward to freedom well before then. Curcio is serving something like a 50-year sentence and Moretti and Balzarani several life sentences. Lately these three have begun to speak out. They admit that the armed struggle has failed, that 'a revolutionary experience [is] in fact now concluded'.[17] But they do not disown their activities and ideas and refuse to consider dissociation or any other disavowal of their past. For this reason they will not accept a pardon. They request an amnesty or other indulgence as the solution to what they still consider the problem of 'prisoners of conscience', a political resolution to what has been, for them, merely a political problem. Curcio says: 'I am content with myself, with what I am, with what I have been'.[18] And

> For what I have done, I do not believe I ought to undergo any type of punishment. I do not feel myself responsible for any crime. My initiatives as a revolutionary militant have all been part of a project and an organizational event of a political type. And it is in political terms that our problem must be addressed.[19]

Interesting as the evolution in thinking of Curcio, Moretti and Balzarani is, significant as it is in symbolizing the changed political climate, hopeful as it may be for a future free of a recrudescence of major terrorist activity, there is little likelihood that the three will soon get their way. Having been in jail for 13 years and never having killed anyone or directed an operation that cost human life, Curcio the theoretician stands the best chance of getting out before too long. You wonder, should that happen, where he will go and what he will do. What does a failed revolutionary do in a democratic society? With much blood on their hands, however, Moretti and Balzarani are hardly sympathetic characters, and there is no justification for according them any treatment other than the long sentence that is the desert of someone responsible for murder.

As for others, Professor Senzani and Gallinari, now serving several life sentences each, have no regrets. Savasta is in jail and will stay there for many years. Morucci and Faranda have spent some time out of jail on furlough and are hoping for permanent release in the very near future. Peci is out, living somewhere in Italy with his bodyguards. For all of these, their involvement in the violent experience of the years of terrorism has been, and will continue to be, the dominant fact of their lives. General Dalla Chiesa, however, had to move on to other challenges. He became vice-commander of the *carabinieri*, the highest rank open to a professional *carabiniere*. Then, because the government was desperate to inflict some damage on the mafia, he was sent to Sicily as Prefect of Palermo. He lasted but 100 days. He and his young second wife were savagely gunned down while driving home in their little car. Italy's victory over terrorism has left many historic problems unaltered and much ferocity uncountered.

16

Conclusion

Why the BR? Why terrorism in Italy? It is not easy to arrive at firm and comprehensive conclusions about this complex matter, but this book has endeavoured to present an accurate portrait of the 'years of lead' and to offer an explanation, or at least the beginnings of an understanding. Political violence and terrorism resulted from a complex series of influences. Among other factors were the extraordinary transformation that Italy had undergone by the late 1960s and was still undergoing, the trauma of the ending of a way of life and the crisis in values that followed, and the injustices and social problems created or aggravated or merely left unresolved by the recent economic miracle; the unrest in Third World countries and among students around the world and the accompanying intellectual ferment; the extent and heavily ideological nature of the student protest in Italy; the history of political violence in Italy; the myth of the Resistance; the deeply-rooted revolutionary tradition; the evolution of the PCI; the extent and ideological nature of labor unrest; the violence of a far right with strong roots in Italian history; and the peculiar nature and weaknesses of the Italian political system, the mistakes and failures of the politicians, especially the Christian Democratic Party, and the fact that the system was blocked, unable to offer a credible alternative.

It is obvious that other countries had been greatly changed by the post-war period, but few quite so dramatically as Italy. It is also true, of course, that other advanced industrialized societies felt the effects of strong youth unrest and yet did not suffer 'years of lead'. But the youth unrest in Italy was probably more diffused than elsewhere and surely was more profound, feeding off social problems that were more serious than in other countries and being propelled by a degree of ideologization without the like elsewhere. Although socialism has, of course, had a significant role in the history of other West European countries, in few other countries had the socialist ideal remained as strong. But in Italy, in the late

1960s–early 1970s, that tradition was considered as having been betrayed by its principal spokesman, the PCI. The violence of the young was thus in part a protest against the PCI and its strategy. As for the BR, one of the main planks in the armed party's platform from the very beginning was firm opposition to the PCI, and it set the BR apart from the Communists, as well as from much of the movement, that, as the *brigatisti* took pride in exclaiming, they acted while everyone else talked.

Clearly crucial to the violence was the labor unrest. It was crucial both that this discontent took place and that it took place just when it did, in conjunction with the rising of the students. Nothing comparable occurred in other countries, not even in France (where the situation was different in a number of ways). The effect of the upheaval and the continuing discontent in the factories was to provide a tremendous stimulus to young protestors and to the radicalization of their thinking. As far as the founding *brigatisti* were concerned, the labor unrest was a critical confirmation of the rightness of their worldview, and proof that revolution in Italy was not only possible but inevitable.

Governments in other countries not plagued by terrorism of course have their shortcomings, but the weaknesses of the Italian system are unique. The system had been dominated for decades by an inefficient, much-resented party. Attempts at reform had failed as the student unrest was beginning, and a period of especially serious instability and drift was underway. The system offered little possibility of an alternative to the DC and the only opposition was not only ineffectual but collaborationist. Therefore – to the barricades, to the P38! To the BR and the armed struggle for Communism!

It is true that the BR had begun to practice their revolutionary tactics during a period in which the PCI was benefiting from a substantial increase in popular support. But the *brigatisti* had already decided that, however well the PCI might be able to dupe the electorate, the party had no intention of bringing real change to Italy. The 'historic compromise', adopted by the party as its line as early as 1973, was indisputable proof of this. As we have seen, at a later point, after the PCI's electoral victory of 1976, the disillusionment with the PCI that the founding *brigatisti* had long felt became generalized in the movement, manifesting itself in the uproar of 1977.

To observe that social problems and sins of omission and

commission by the politicians contributed to political violence is not to justify the actions of the terrorists. It is not easy to define with precision what terrorism is. (Renato Curcio recently said, in a remark typical of BR thinking, that what the BR did was 'armed struggle, not terrorism', and that 'terrorism in the country was done by others, at Piazza della Loggia and Piazza Fontana'; the BR 'simply expressed an impulse present and widespread in the country'.)[1] But there was no doubt that the Italian system, for all its faults, was a vital, functioning democracy and this democracy had succeeded in producing a remarkable economic advance, however imperfectly distributed its benefits. There was no excuse for taking up arms to try, in defiance of the wishes of the great majority of the people, to destroy the democratic system and to replace it with something that could only be worse. It is here that the actions of the professors of revolution, the various Professor Negri's, can be seen to have greatly contributed to the development of serious political violence in Italy. They helped to disseminate disgust with the democratic mechanism, to undermine democratic values, to legitimate the idea of armed revolutionary struggle, and to create a climate of revolt out of which came chaos in the schools, violence in demonstrations and marches, the vituperation and threats heaped on teachers, the violent slogans, the intemperate journals, the radical radio stations, the revolutionary collectives and committees and so on, and out of which, too, came those who were intent upon putting all the fancy theories to work in the practice of systematic clandestine violence. The experience of the 'years of lead' teaches that, in order for a society to avoid the ravages of political violence, it is important that those with the power to shape the climate of ideas act responsibly, eschewing apocalyptic visions and promises of an impossible Utopia and recognizing the value of democratic processes and the right of everyone to hold whatever opinion most commends itself to him.

Among observers during the years of terrorism and political violence, objectivity was in too short supply. At first there was a failure to understand what the BR were and how dangerous they could become. At a later point, it became accepted that the BR truly were leftists, but even then emotion at the murders of innocents and ideological considerations led to unfounded analyses and arguments. The PCI continued its myopic approach, now in the modified form of complicated conspiracy theories. Furthermore, many politicians, commentators and members of the press misunderstood the BR in other ways and made claims about them that went far beyond the evidence. It was often asserted that the terrorists were madmen. Why one person rather than another should resort to violence in a democratic society to achieve his ends is a complex question that cannot be treated here. But the left-wing terrorists in general, though certainly very over-zealous and in the thrall of an authoritarian and absolutist ideology, were not simply psychotics. On this as on other points, the truth about the BR and the other terrorists was more complex than some were prepared to acknowledge, and more disturbing. Nor were the terrorists what some of their critics painted them – simply a handful of radicals in designer clothes, the rich or comfortable who were trying to exorcise private demons or obtain the vaunted solidarity with a working class with whom they had had little contact and about whom they knew nothing beyond the generalizations of the sacred texts. And the *brigatisti* and other terrorists were not afloat in a wholly hostile sea. This was a sharp contrast with terrorist groups in other countries, such as 'Action Directe' in France or even the RAF in Germany. The Red Brigades especially, but also 'Front Line', 'autonomous' collectives and other groups, had a social base. The base was always much smaller than the BR thought it was; capitalism was not dying and the democratic system was not repudiated by the citizenry. Yet, that base did exist, in the working class and among the new youth proletariat. Many *brigatisti* were students or young intellectuals, but many of them were far from privileged. Many other *brigatisti*, from Mario Moretti, Patrizio Peci, Alfredo Buonavita on down, were factory or office workers without university degrees or education, including union activists and even union delegates. There was, in addition, an area of sympathy: workers and others who approved and applauded what the Red Brigades did, especially in the early years, or who would not condemn the 'armed struggle' because to do so was to defend the Christian Democratic 'regime', and who would not condemn the *brigatisti* because they were 'comrades who err'.

One of the claims often made about the BR and the other Italian terrorists is that they were, in essence, the agents of the Soviet Union or its surrogates. There is to be sure, a fraternity among terrorists around the world to which the Soviet Union and other countries have links. This situation should not, however, be distorted or over-simplified. The BR were not a department of a terrorist multinational and did not take orders from an international board of directors. Nor is it accurate to reduce the BR and other groups to no more than pawns of obscure right-wing plotters. Here again, objectivity is often wanting. Instead, these conspiracy theories are built upon speculation, biased interpretation of evidence and purported 'logical' assumptions. It is difficult to address theories in which everything is explained by unseen plotters and convictions far outrun the hard evidence. The *brigatista* Antonio Savasta was correct, though:

[T]his whole game of roles, of the secret services, of the Great Old Man, acts as a mask upon a much clearer reality: that we are the children of the contradictions that the Italian political class itself has produced. It is much simpler to put the blame upon a Great Old Man who is part of the secret services than it is to go and analyze the historical and political reasons that have produced the guerrilla warfare.[2]

Misinterpretations have also been made about relationships among the various terrorist groups inside Italy. For some time, allegations were made, including officially, that a single terrorist organization controlled all of the left-wing terrorist groups inside Italy, and there was a great brouhaha about this matter in the Italian press. In the April 7 legal case, for instance, it was alleged that such an organization existed and that Professor Negri was one of its leaders, but years of legal proceedings, though resulting in the Professor's condemnation to prison for certain offenses, showed how full of holes such assertions were. There was no single terroristic corporation in Italy. On the contrary, the groups were often in bitter disagreement with one another. Though they both sought a revolution, 'Lotta Continua' and the BR disagreed on many things, as, for instance, in the Moro case. 'Lotta Continua' was, indeed, a way station on the road to the BR or other groups for many radicals, but this journey involved the rejection of 'Lotta Continua' in favor of something more violent, something truly terroristic. The BR and 'Autonomia' did not see eye to eye on fundamental points, such as the role of the party and the place of the masses in the revolutionary struggle. The *brigatisti* and the members of 'Front Line' were in sharp discord over such things as the centralization of the revolutionary campaign, the proper structure of a revolutionary group and the appropriate tactics and targets of the struggle. Even inside jail there was often very bad feeling between the militants of the BR and those of 'Front Line'. The *brigatisti* were sometimes skeptical of the skills of other revolutionaries or, as in the case of Feltrinelli, of their good judgement. It was, in other words, an error to believe that the revolutionary universe was a monolithic one, or even that the terroristic sub-universe thereof was such. The failure to keep a dispassionate mind on this question led to much misguided journalism and, more important, to some judicial errors. Some individuals were accused of being terrorists who were not and even Professor Negri was charged with things – such as direct participation in the Moro kidnapping – of which he was innocent.

In looking at the history of the Red Brigades, one is struck by the limited perspective of the terrorists on the question of the revolution. The documents of the BR are notable for their failure to analyze seriously the idea of the revolution. Just what would revolution mean for an advanced country like Italy? What did the people as a whole think of the condition of their lives? What did they actually want? Nothing prompted such questions at the outset of the armed struggle and nothing that occurred to the terrorists during their experience of it caused them to re-examine the foundations of their beliefs. As we have seen, within a very short time from the onset of the student unrest, revolution became the dominant idea for a substantial area of the left. Among, say, the followers of 'Lotta Continua' or 'Workers' Power' or 'Workers' Avant-garde', the BR or 'Front Line', and even factions within the BR itself, there were innumerable arguments about how to bring the revolution off, and impassioned discussions of fine points of revolutionary philosophy. What was lacking, however, was any attempt at an objective examination of Italian realities. For a large part of the left and of the intellectual community, the ideal of revolution had been validated by history and it was, politically and morally, a principle that could not be questioned. Once the great upheaval began, there was thereafter no room for the least openmindedness among so many of the young protagonists, those who ended up in the BR and like groups, and those who, luckily for themselves, stopped with 'Lotta Continua'.

One is also struck in studying the BR's documents by other lacunae. The BR's writings are full of complicated discussions of revolutionary tactics and strategy, of abstruse exegeses of the principal ideas of the *brigatisti* such as the Imperialist State of the Multinationals, of casuistry and of complex analyses of imagined realities such as the 'revolutionary organisms of the masses'. The BR, as shown in the Moro case and countless other instances, were very concerned about obtaining publicity for their actions and ideas. In this, the *brigatisti* were paying heed to one of the elementary imperatives that drive terrorist groups everywhere. The remarkable thing, though, is that the *brigatisti* were indifferent to the need to explain those actions and ideas in words that ordinary citizens could understand. It is strange that a group so conscious as the BR of their connection to the masses and so understanding of the importance of the press to the revolutionary project could have been so inept at crafting their message for the audience they wished to reach. But so unquestioning was the faith of the *brigatisti* in the idea of the revolution and of its inevitability that the BR felt themselves under no special obligation to persuade, which obligation is a democratic notion. So deeply had the *brigatisti* entered into the idea of the revolution, as into a dark cave, that they could no longer tell that there was a difference between jargon and ordinary language. So little did they truly understand the proletariat of whom they constantly spoke that they confused their own peculiar language with that of the proletariat. The BR also never seriously troubled themselves to explain what they planned to make of Italy once they had led the masses to victory in the civil war of long duration. One searches in vain in their pamphlets and communiqués for any exposition of what they wished for a post-revolutionary Italy. Everything suggests that they would have established a Stalinist system, but if they had another idea they did not let on what it was. This is a major silence, as well as, once again, a mark of the disdain the *brigatisti* felt for the audience at which they purportedly aimed; had they not felt disdain, they would have tried to describe for the masses just what it was those masses should risk all for. But the BR were certain that in revolution lay the answer to all problems.

The history of the Red Brigades is a parabola that may reflect the likely, or perhaps inevitable, fate of any small revolutionary group that seeks to overturn an advanced, industrialized democracy through systematic violence. In such a society it is not possible to practice a guerrilla war in the strict sense. Budding revolutionaries must therefore make of necessity a virtue, as the BR did, by undertaking the struggle in the metropolis. At first the metropolis seems likely to be fruitful ground, the heart, as it is, of the industrial system and the home of the working class, as well as the font of so much modern anguish and despair. But the metropolis is also a difficult place for revolutionaries. For one thing it is expensive and the solution of this problem creates risks for the radicals. For another, the size and anonymity of the metropolis make recruitment difficult. To draw members and to rally the proletariat the group will have to engage in serious, newsworthy actions. In a functioning democracy, tensions are accommodated and dissipated through the political process. Thus, despite Italy's many problems in the late 1960s and 1970s, there was no great national injustice pressing down unbearably on the working class and driving it to revolt. The ability of the revolutionaries to see that is distorted by ideology, so that, as the BR did, they overestimate the support that might be available to them. Excited by the revolutionary idea but frustrated by its slow progress, the revolutionaries will undertake increasingly violent and notorious actions. Such actions will perhaps achieve a marginal level of support. But the group's increasing activism will bring down upon it the attentions of the police. Whereas guerrillas can hide out in the mountains and defend themselves militarily, the metropolitan revolutionaries are vulnerable to discovery. They must go underground and institute rigid measures of internal secrecy in order to avoid capture.

Clandestinity, however, is both a weapon and a trap. The radicals can hope to escape the police for a time, but they will be unable to prevent the attenuation of their links to the masses, even if they succeed in infiltrating members into, or making converts in, the factories and offices and union councils. It was not long after the BR went underground in a serious way that this problem surfaced, and it remained a basic difficulty for the *brigatisti* throughout the later years. As the problem grows, disagreements will become more serious and increase in frequency over who best represents the masses and how links to the masses can best be maintained or even strengthened. Dissatisfaction will be aggravated because it will become plain that the group cannot succeed in clandestinity without a firm, centralized, authoritarian leadership. This leadership will provoke quarrels and resentments, both personal animosities and disagreements over strategy and tactics. Because ideological purity is critical to the radicals and their view of life, it will happen frequently, as occurred not only in the BR but in the whole of the revolutionary area in Italy, that there will be bitter splits over matters of philosophy complete with accusations of betrayal. The internal life of the group will become a minefield, there will be defections and expulsions and the connection to the masses will weaken.

There will be an escalation in the level of violence perpetrated by the group. As the experiences of the BR and 'Front Line' show, the revolutionaries come to see no option but a 'raising of the level of fire'. At the beginning the BR were wary of using excessive violence, conscious, no doubt, that unrestrained violence had at least as much power to alienate the masses as to galvanize them. But as time passed and the BR suffered setbacks, they became more ruthless. Certain of the justness of their cause, they would do what they had to do. Once embarked on this course it became very difficult to turn from it; as Morucci discovered, the machine of death acquired a momentum of its own. From a practical point of view it was difficult for the *brigatisti* to give up the fight, as it will be for any revolutionary who commits crimes of any significance. Thus it was that even though some terrorists were sincerely desirous of ending their revolutionary careers, and even though there were many who eventually became *pentiti* or *dissociati*, only a handful ever voluntarily gave themselves up to the police. Either they fled abroad, or they carried on with what they could see was a hopeless armed struggle. In addition, the failures of the armed struggle and the suffering of arrests and deaths will only create further incentives toward greater violence. Finally, the revolutionary will be committing acts that plainly disgust his potential followers and that are lacking in 'political content'.

Concomitant with the growing isolation and increasing bloody-mindedness of the terrorists is likely to be a sharp deterioration in the quality of the intellectual analysis at the center of the enterprise. At the outset the BR's documents, for all their many limitations, those mentioned above and others as well, were marked by a certain level of clarity and rationality. Curcio's poetic effusions notwithstanding, this particular flower did not bloom in the arid soil of clandestine life. Instead, their documents grew ever more abstract, convoluted and jargon-filled, the analyses more divorced from the realities of life in the country, and even less comprehensible to the ordinary person. By the time the 'militarists' and 'movementists' were firing off at one another interminable strategic resolutions, the writings of the BR had lost all influence and were of interest only to General Dalla Chiesa and his allies.

Paralleling the deterioration in the quality of the BR's argument was a change in its substance. This process occurred in other countries and it, too, may be inevitable. The BR's argument at first was a narrow Italian one and their victims tended to be easy targets, unpopular businessmen and neo-Fascists. Then the targets changed and the message grew more complex as the BR began their attack upon the heart of the state and started to elaborate upon ideas about the SIM. In both respects the BR were making trouble for themselves: it turned out that the state was not so easy a target as they had thought, nor was the message about the Imperialist State of the Multinationals so relevant to the concerns of the workers and attractive to them as the *brigatisti* had supposed. The BR then turned increasingly to international arguments, hoping to exploit public worries about armament levels and other international problems to gain the support they had not found by other means. This kind of change in strategy will surely fail, as it did for the BR, if there does not exist very great public discontent with some aspect of the international situation.

For a time it seemed as if the Italian system, like a rickety, untended house, was about to collapse. But as Professor Walter Laqueur has observed, terrorism, for all the dust it stirs up and the blood it spills, is a recipe for failure. Looking back now, with terrorism almost wiped out in Italy, and with the BR reduced to a shadow of what they once were, you can see that the revolutionary project had been doomed from the outset. The *brigatisti*, 'Front Line', NAP and the others were too marginal a force to succeed; the apparently inept and feeble state was more resilient than even its defenders suspected; and the Italian people, despite their past tendency to stand watching at the windows, were, at heart, opposed to the revolutionary project and loyal to the values of the democracy, the true values represented by the Resistance. The system had been tested and the public had decided – some things were worth defending.

Politicized as Italy is, and tormented and divided as it was by the violence of the 1970s, it is today remarkably united in its feelings about the experience of terrorism. There is spirited debate about many things: the 'emergency', the anti-terrorism activities of the state, connections between the far right and the state apparatus, and so on. But as to the use of violence as a political tool, and as to the overturning of the Republic as a political goal, there is a broad consensus. The political and intellectual climate is very greatly changed from that which prevailed in the 1970s. For the overwhelming majority of Italians the memory of those grim years is all too fresh and vivid, and the conviction is strong that what was done was terrible, arrogant and unjustifiable. The lesson has been learned.

There are further lessons. For one thing, a democratic society should act to avoid the development or persistence of conditions that can breed revolutionary groups. To help block the emergence of such groups and to weaken them should they emerge, a democratic society should bestir itself continually to hear, and at least attempt to respond to, legitimate demands for reform. The system should also offer an alternative to which the discontented can turn. The Italian democracy is, as Aldo Moro was wont to say, a 'difficult democracy'. The unbroken dominance of the DC and the lack of an alternative have been and remain weaknesses of the system in Italy. A formula that would temper accumulating social tensions would offer a political program that addresses the social ills of the nation and an institutional mechanism by which, from time to time, the public can throw the rascals out.

Another counsel the Italian experience offers is that, in the event that terrorism were to raise its dragon-like head, the nation afflicted should remain calm, and be realistic. Terrorism frequently creates panic and fury, as it often intends to do, and these can lead to ill-advised, ineffective or counter-productive responses. As noted earlier, some aspects of the Italian 'emergency' were of little use and others were unjustifiable. To call for the death penalty, as some normally thoughtful persons did in the immediate wake of Via Fani, is to do little good. Emergency measures may be needed to streamline legislation, or re-organize the police forces, or to fill gaps, but such measures should be enacted only with great care and applied with restraint. The problem of domestic terrorism in a democratic society is best confronted by the creation and mainte- nance of an efficient, well-equipped and well-organized police apparatus, by the collection and shrewd analysis of intelligence about the terrorist groups, and by the skilful administration of a carefully prepared anti-terrorism campaign. Gathering data, tailing suspects, conducting surveillance and the like will generate more results than many an angry speech in parliament or many a repressive law.

There is, finally, another kind of lesson that can be learned, a lesson both larger and more simple. Looking at what was done in the name of justice for the working class and an end to exploitation, one cannot help but be appalled by the evil that men can do their fellows when they allow human feeling, common decency and the democratic disposition to be overwhelmed by the rigidities and certitudes of ideology. But one also cannot help but be moved by the countless stories of courage on the part of police, *carabinieri*, magistrates and those on the terrorists' lists, and the many demonstrations of fortitude, affection and decency on the part of the victims who survived and the families of the victims. The suffering that was inflicted will endure for decades to come, and the lives of the children of those who were assassinated, and the lives of their children, will be unalterably affected. But amidst all the evil and all the suffering, there were also on display in those years some of the more noble qualities of which the human being is capable; and although terrorism is a political and social fact that must be understood as such, the demonstration of these qualities on the part of ordinary Italians was a fitting and sufficient response to all the elaborate theorizations of the *Brigate Rosse* and others who acted as they did.

Notes

Frontispiece

Aldo Moro (1979, pp. 334, 300).

Preface

On the statistics cited, see *La Repubblica*, 12 February 1987; *Corriere della Sera*, 10 October 1986, p. 5.

1 *Il Sessantotto*

1. On the student unrest at Trent, see, for example, Alessandro Silj (1977, pp. 33–68); Rossana Rossanda (1968, pp. 44–56); Soccorso Rosso (1976, pp. 11–34); Piero Agostini (1980, pp. 62–118); *Corriere della Sera*, 24 September 1974, p. 5.
2. Soccorso Rosso, op. cit., pp. 28–30.
3. For documents issued by the students during the unrest at Trent, see Movimento Studentesco (ed.) (1968, pp. 1–78); Autori vari (1968, pp. 7–81).
4. Rossana Rossanda, op. cit., pp. 16–32; Giorgio Bocca (1982, pp. 176–88); Gianni Statera (1975, pp. 97–108, 170–7, 219–30). See also note 3.
5. Walter Tobagi (1970, pp. 59–77).
6. On Curcio's personal background, see Yolanda Curcio (1975), (Part I), 4 August, pp. 6–11, and (Part II), 11 August, pp. 24–8.
7. Letter, 29 November 1974, in *Gente*, 4 August 1975, p. 10.
8. Bruno Caccia (1975, p. 236).
9. Yolanda Curcio, (Part II), op. cit., p. 26.
10. Renato Zampa (1976, pp. 4–8).
11. Letter of 29 November 1974, in *Gente*, 4 August 1975, p. 10.
12. Yolanda Curcio, (Part I), op. cit., p. 11.
13. Soccorso Rosso, op. cit., p. 32.
14. Silj, op. cit., p. 46.
15. Soccorso Rosso, op. cit., pp. 31–2.
16. On Margherita's background, see Milena Cagol (1975); Agostini, op. cit., pp. 1–62; Silj, op. cit., pp. 69–78; Sabino Acquaviva, *Corriere della Sera*, 23 June 1985, p. 1.
17. Milena Cagol, op. cit., p. 45.
18. Alberto Franceschini (1988, p. 19).
19. Milena Cagol, op. cit., p. 44.
20. Letter, 1968, in *Gente*, 18 August 1975, p. 28.
21. *L'Europeo*, 6 June 1975, p. 36.
22. On Reggio Emilia and the *brigatisti Reggiani*, see Franceschini, op. cit., and Alberto Franceschini (1987, pp. 42–7); Liano Fanti (1985); Silj, op. cit., pp. 3–32.

23. Franceschini (1987, p. 44).
24. 'Reggio 15', 7 July 1968, in Fanti, op. cit., p. 122.
25. Franceschini (1988, p. 27).
26. Franceschini (1987, pp. 44–5).
27. *Gazzetta di Reggio*, 14 January 1984, in Fanti, op. cit., p. 206.
28. Letter, 1 July 1969, in *Gente*, 11, 18 August 1975, p. 28.
29. Milena Cagol, op. cit., p. 44.
30. *Gente*, 18 August 1975, p. 28.

2 Progress and its Discontents

1. Shepard B. Clough (1964, p. 9).
2. The data in this paragraph are from Kevin Allen and Andrew Stevenson (1975, pp. 29–31, 34, 37).
3. Alberto Ronchey (1978a, pp. 12–23).
4. On the problems of the universities, see, for example, Rossanda (1968, pp. 13–16); Guido Martinotti (1969, pp. 179–87); Ronchey, op. cit., pp. 29–34; Statera (1975, pp. 71–2, 211–16).
5. Statera, op. cit., p. 20.
6. Rossanda, op. cit., pp. 15–16; Statera, op. cit., pp. 214, 279 n. 15.
7. On socialism and communism in Italy before and after fascism, see Adrian Lyttelton (1973); Denis Mack Smith (1982, pp. 14–94); Denis Mack Smith (1969, pp. 171–387, 489–98); Serge Hughes (1967); Giuseppe Mammarella (1978); Norman Kogan (1983, pp. 16–44, 161–86).
8. See Soccorso Rosso (1976, pp. 12–25).
9. See, for example, Kogan, op. cit., pp. 87–103, 176–7, 224–31; Norman Kogan (1978); Ugo Finetti (1978); Antonio Lombardo (ed.) (1978).
10. See Alberto Ronchey (1983); Jean-Francois Revel (1978, pp. 295–305); Luciano Pellicani (1978, pp. 154–64).
11. Finetti, op. cit., p. 60, quoting Giancarlo Pajetta.
12. Kogan (1978, p. 79).
13. For example, *Quaderni Piacentini*, *Classe Operaia* and *La Sinistra*.
14. Tobagi (1970); Giuseppe Vettori (1973). The Italian Communist Party (Marxist–Leninist) was perhaps the most important of the Maoist parties. It published a journal, titled, significantly, *Nuova Unità* (the PCI's daily paper is *L'Unità*). The Party had between 5000 and 10 000 members, but it was unable to attract many workers, in good part because of its rigid interpretation of democratic centralism, though it did enjoy the political and financial support of the Chinese. Its authoritarianism scuttled it in December 1968, when it split into irreconcilable factions (Tobagi, pp. 14–57, 79–95, 104, 123–41; Vettori, pp. 30–75).
15. Luigi Bobbio (1979, p. 61), quoting Adriano Sofri.

3 A Little Private War of Our Own

1. See Dominique Grisoni and Hugues Portelli (1977, pp. 71, 149); Sergio Turone (1981, pp. 337–433); Allen and Stevenson (1975, pp. 131–41).

2. Grisoni and Portelli, op. cit., pp. 82–3; Donald C. Templeman (1981, pp. 11–17).
3. Soccorso Rosso (1976a, p. 38).
4. Templeman, op. cit., pp. 13–14.
5. Turone, op. cit., pp. 432–3; Grisoni and Portelli, op. cit., pp. 173–4. In 1970, for instance, absenteeism at Fiat was at twice the level of 1965 (Turone, op. cit., p. 432).
6. See, for example, Ronchey (1978a, pp. 49–60).
7. Tobagi (1970, pp. 59–77, 111–21, 141–52); Luisa Cortese (ed.) (1973); Vettori (1973, pp. 75–133); Statera (1975, pp. 247–59).
8. On the history and activities of 'New Order', 'National Avant-garde' and like groups, see Rosario Minna (1984, pp. 19–72); Mario Battaglini (1986, pp. 27–41).
9. Mauro Galleni (ed.) (1981, p. 51).
10. Giuseppe DeLutiis (1984, pp. 61–89); Bocca (1982, pp. 158–60).
11. See, for example, Corrado Stajano and Marco Fini (1977).
12. For information on the mind-bogglingly complex legal proceedings and the final judgement of fact of the Court of Appeals of Bari of August 1985, see *La Repubblica*, 2 August 1985, p. 11; *Corriere della Sera*, 3 August 1985, p. 6. The Bari judgement was confirmed by the highest court, the Court of Cassation, in January 1987 (*La Repubblica*, 28 January 1987, p. 14).
13. *La Repubblica*, 31 July 1986, p. 4; *Corriere della Sera*, 31 July 1986, p. 4.
14. Agostini (1980, pp. 118–21).
15. 'Social Struggle and Organization in the Metropolis', in Soccorso Rosso, op. cit., pp. 46–53.
16. Vincenzo Tessandori (1977, p. 48).
17. Ibid., pp. 49–50.
18. Soccorso Rosso, op. cit., p. 71.
19. Letter, June 1971, in *Gente*, 18 August 1975, p. 28.
20. Milena Cagol (1975, p. 45).
21. Ibid; Yolanda Curcio (1975), (Part III), 4 August.
22. Actually the group briefly used the name *Brigata Rossa*.
23. Franceschini (1988, pp. 32, 62).
24. Soccorso Rosso, op. cit., p. 90.
25. Ibid., p. 81.
26. Tessandori, op. cit., pp. 63–4.
27. Soccorso Rosso, op. cit., pp. 110–11.
28. On this case, see Vittorio Borraccetti, 'Introduzione', in Borraccetti (1986b, p. 16); *La Repubblica*, 28 June 1986, p. 5; *Corriere della Sera*, 7 August 1986, p. 7. Right-wing defendants were found guilty and sentenced to life for carrying out the bombing, while four *carabinieri*, including a general and two colonels, were found guilty of having obstructed justice in the case by diverting the attention of the investigation toward innocent 'reds' (*La Repubblica*, 26 July 1987, p. 18).
29. Renato Curcio (1988). In July 1988, in a surprising move, several militants of 'Lotta Continua' were arrested and charged with the assassination, including Adriano Sofri, former leader of 'Lotta

Continua' and, as one commentator put it, 'one of the most prestigious protagonists of the youth revolt of Sessantotto' (*La Repubblica*, 29 July 1988, p. 1). The arrests were somewhat shocking because 'Lotta Continua' had not been known to have used such means as these in pursuit of its political ends. The case will be sure to prove highly contested as it unfolds.

30. Soccorso Rosso, op. cit., pp. 169–70.
31. Ibid., p. 172.
32. Franceschini, op. cit., pp. 79–80.
33. Paolo Emilio Taviani, *L'Espresso*, 1 September 1974, p. 13.
34. *L'Unità*, 20 April 1974, p. 1.
35. Franceschini, op. cit., p. 80.
36. See, for example, statements of *Paese Sera*, Camilla Cederna, Giuliano Spazzali and 'Il Manifesto', in *Corriere della Sera*, 17 March 1972.
37. On Feltrinelli's background, see Nino Mattioli (1972, pp. 1–10); Luigi Barzini (1972, pp. 35–40); Giorgio Bocca (1981a); *Corriere della Sera*, 17 March 1972, p. 1.
38. The three works are listed in the bibliography.
39. Jillian Becker (1977, pp. 153, 258).
40. 'Requisitoria Viola', in Guiso *et al.* **(1975, pp. 43–68).**
41. Giorgio Bocca (1985a, pp. 43–4, 80); 'Requisitoria Viola', op. cit., pp. 43–68.
42. Franceschini, op. cit., p. 46.
43. Marco Pisetta (1973).
44. *Lotta Continua*, 19 January 1973, pp. 2–3.
45. Ibid., pp. 2–3.
46. *L'Espresso*, 28 April 1974, p. 9 (interview with Umberto Federico D'Amato).
47. Bocca (1985a, p. 49), quoting Franceschini.
48. Soccorso Rosso, op. cit., p. 124 (from a BR document).
49. *Corriere della Sera*, 20 April 1974.
50. Brigate Rosse (1974).
51. *L'Unità*, 19 April 1974, p. 1.
52. For example, *Corriere della Sera*, 21 April 1974, p. 1.
53. Franceschini (1987, p. 47).
54. BR communiqué, *Corriere della Sera*, 24 May 1974, p. 1; BR Internal Memorandum, in Bruno Caccia (1975, pp. 313–15).
55. Galleni (ed.), op. cit., pp. 51, 101–7, 111, 118–23.

4   Getting to Know the General

1. Marco Nese and Ettore Serio (1982, pp 1–45); Antonio Ferrari and Giogio Bocca, in Pino Arlacchi *et al.* (1982).
2. Interview with Rita Dalla Chiesa, in Gigi Moncalvo (1985, pp. 57–96).
3. Roberto Chiarini and Paolo Corsini (1983, pp. 305–44); Mario Rotella (1986), and Vittorio Borraccetti, 'Introduzione', in Borraccetti (ed.) (1986b, pp. 16). On the 1985 verdict in the proceedings against Angelo Papa *et al.*, see *La Repubblica*, 20 April 1985, p. 16. On the later

verdict in proceedings against Cesare Ferri *et al.*, see *La Repubblica*, 24–25 May 1987, p. 15. The verdict of not guilty was affirmed by the Court of Cassation in September 1987.

4.   Galleni (ed.) (1981, pp. 296–7); Borraccetti, 'Introduzione', op. cit., p. 16. Sentenced to life in prison for this bombing were Luciano Franci and the notorious extremist, Mario Tuti (*La Repubblica*, 19 December 1986, p. 7).

5.   DeLutiis (1984, pp. 100–44); Giulio Andreotti (1986, pp. 60–1); Giulio Andreotti (1981, pp. 28–9); Gianfranco Viglietta (1986); Claudio Nunziata (1986); Giancarlo Scarpari (1986).

6.   In theory, the Inspectorate, headed by Emilio Santillo, was to encompass Dalla Chiesa's group, but in practice the former pursued right and some left terrorist groups, while Dalla Chiesa concentrated on the Red Brigades.

7.   Silvano Girotto (1975).

8.   Franceschini (1988, p. 19).

9.   Franceschini (1987, p. 45).

10. Franceschini (1988, pp. 103–12).

11. *Corriere della Sera*, 10 September 1974, p. 1; Testimony of General Carlo Alberto Dalla Chiesa, in Senato della Repubblica-Camera dei Deputati (1983) (Moro Commission), vol. 4, pp. 302–3 [references to testimony before the Moro Commission henceforth will take the form of 'Moro Comm.', preceded by the volume number and followed by the page number and, in parentheses, the witness's name]. See also *La Stampa*, 19 February 1975, p. 9. On the infiltration of Girotto and the arrests of Curcio and Franceschini, see Bruno Caccia (1975, pp. 264–86); Franceschini (1988, pp. 113–21); 'Dossier sulle Brigate Rosse', *Tempo*, 11, 18, 25 April 1975; Girotto, op. cit., pp. 367–83.

12. Alfredo Buonavita, 'Verbali', *Lotta Continua*, 26 March 1982, pp. 18–19; Alfredo Buonavita, 'Terrorismo – Lettera aperta di un capo BR', *L'Espresso*, 14 June 1981, p. 35.

13. Buonavita, 'Terrorismo', op. cit.

14. See the BR's internal document, 'Alcune questioni per la discussione sull "organizzazione",' in Caccia, op. cit., pp. 340–7; Giancarlo Caselli and Donatella della Porta (1984, pp. 156–73).

15. Piero Agostini (1980, pp. 144–5).

16. Ibid., pp. 151–3.

17. Testimony of General Dalla Chiesa, op. cit., p. 303.

18. *La Stampa*, 19–22 February 1975.

19. Brigate Rosse (1975).

20. Soccorso Rosso Napoletano (ed.) (1976); Romano Cantore *et al.* (1978, pp. 107–13); Silj (1977, pp. 99–137).

21. On the kidnapping and the gun battle, see *La Stampa*, 5 June 1975; *Tempo*, 20 June 1975. On the BR's version of what happened, see, for example, Bocca (1985a, pp. 114–16).

22. Milena Cagol (1975, p. 45).

23. Soccorso Rosso (1976, pp. 283–4).

24. Bocca (1985a, pp. 118–19).

5 Slouching Towards Disaster

1. Templeman (1981, pp. 14–15, 21).
2. Allen and Stevenson (1975, pp. 123–4).
3. Templeman, op. cit., pp. 4, 42–3.
4. Ibid., pp. 91–4, 146–8, 171, 212–16; Allen and Stevenson, op. cit., pp. 285–9.
5. By 1978, close to 80 per cent of the unemployed were aged 29 or younger (Templeman, op. cit., pp. 91–4, 140).
6. Enrico Berlinguer (1975, pp. 609–39), reprinted from *Rinascita*, 28 September, 5, 9 October 1973.
7. Enrico Berlinguer, op. cit., pp. 610–13.
8. Ibid., p. 617.
9. Arturo Gismondi (1986, p. 30).
10. These numbers refer to the regional elections. Voting for provincial and local offices produced similar results.
11. Giuseppe Are (1978, p. 135).
12. Tribunale di Torino (1982, p. 875); *Corriere della Sera*, 9 June 1976, pp. 1–2, and 10 June 1976, p. 1.
13. *Corriere della Sera*, 10 June 1976, p. 1.
14. The bulletin claiming responsibility is in *Corriere della Sera*, 10 June 1976, p. 2. One of the reasons given to justify the murder of Coco, a 'ferocious enemy of the proletariat and of its armed avant-garde', was the prosecutor's role in foiling the 'exchange of prisoners' during the Sossi kidnapping.
15. Bocca (1985a, pp. 122, 132). See also Statement of Enrico Fenzi in Sue Ellen Moran (ed.) (1986, pp. 161–2); Alfredo Buonavita, cited in Tribunale di Torino (1982, p. 916).
16. Tribunale di Torino (1982, pp. 899–930); Bocca (1985a, p. 144), quoting Lauro Azzolini.
17. Lia Moretti (1981).
18. On the trial, see Emilio R. Papa (1979); Tessandori (1977, pp. 17–19, 312–16).
19. Anonymous (1976, pp. 45–50).
20. *Corriere della Sera*, 10 June 1976, p. 2.
21. Andreotti (1981, p. 25).
22. Mammarella (1978, pp. 570–2).
23. Andreotti (1981, pp. 13–29); Andreotti (1986, pp. 219–39). See also Gismondi, op. cit., pp. 45–89.
24. Luigi Bobbio (1979, pp. 113–88).
25. See the typically stimulating article of Gianfranco Pasquino (1984a).

6 The Movement of 1977

1. *Corriere della Sera*, 19 February 1977.
2. Collettivo redazionale 'La Nuova Assemblea' (ed.) (1977, pp. 161–74).
3. 6 Moro Comm., pp. 14–16 (E. DeFrancesco).
4. Lucio Castellano (ed.) (1980); Comitati autonomi operai di Roma (ed.) (1976). The leading concentrations of 'Autonomia' were the

'Workers' Political Collectives' and the 'Communist Committees for Workers' Power' in Milan, linked to *Red* and *Without Truce* respectively; the collectives formed around the magazines *A/traverso* and *Zut* and around Radio Alice and Franco 'Bifo' Berardi, in Bologna; the collectives of Via dei Volsci and Via di Donna Olimpia, the Policlinico hospital and the university, in Rome; and the 'Political Collectives of the Veneto'.

5. 'Documento di confronto, Coordinamento nazionale delle Assemblee, dei Collettivi, dei Comitati autonomi operai', October 1974, in Comitati autonomi operai di Roma, op. cit., p. 79. See also Gruppo Gramsci, 'Una proposta per un diverso modo di fare politica', from *Rosso*, December 1973, in Lucio Castellano (ed.), op. cit., p. 90.

6. Volantone of Comitati comunisti proletari *et al.*, 'Capire subito, ricominciare', May 1977, in Castellano (ed.), op. cit., p. 161.

7. Coordinamento nazionale dell'Autonomia, 'Autonomia operaia contro le elezioni', in *Rosso*, June 1976, in Castellano (ed.), op. cit., p. 117.

8. Comitati autonomi operai di Roma, op. cit., p. 376.

9. Some legal authorities have contended that the differences between the BR and 'Autonomia' were less real than their theoretical documents suggest. The major such argument was the so-called 'therem of Calogero', named after the prosecutor in the 'April 7' case, who maintained that the BR and 'Autonomia' were branches of a single organization run by a single directorate. This part of the theorem did not survive the legal proceedings in the 'April 7' case. Calogero also asserted that 'Autonomia' did more than organize the spontaneity of the masses, that it also organized actual semi-clandestine armed bands. The verdict on appeal in this case was a general defeat for the theorem, though the court did find the existence of an 'armed band' (*Corriere della Sera*, 9 June 1987, p. 9).

10. 'L'autonomia organizzata di fronte al "dopo Moro"', in *Rosso*, May 1978, in Castellano (ed.), op. cit., pp. 192–3. See also 'Autonomia operaia: dalla lotta della classe il processo di organizzazione proletaria sul terreno della guerra civile', in *Rosso*, September 1977, in Castellano (ed.), op. cit., pp. 175–6. For other documents of 'Autonomia', see Gabriele Martignoni and Sergio Morandini (eds.) (1977).

11. Imputati del 7 Aprile (1983).

12. Mino Monicelli (1981, pp. 90–6).

13. Antonio Negri (1974, pp. 35, 42–3).

14. Subtitled *Sul metodo marxista della trasformazione sociale*, this work was published by Feltrinelli in its series of pamphlets on Marxism.

15. *Corriere della Sera*, 5, 6, 12 March 1977.

16. Ibid., 13 March 1977.

17. Ibid., 12–14 March 1977.

18. Ibid., 30 March 1977, p. 6.

19. Alberto Ronchey (1977b), quoting Enzo Modugno.

20. *Corriere della Sera*, 11 September 1977, p. 2, by Walter Tobagi, quoting Milanese leaders of 'Lotta Continua' and 'Workers' Movement for Socialism'.

21. Ibid., 24–26 September 1977.

22. 8 Moro Comm., pp. 366–7 (M. Donat Cattin).
23. Corrado Stajano (1982, pp. 1–134).
24. Galleni (ed.) (1981, p. 49).

7 The Spring Campaign

1. Andreotti (1981, p. 172).
2. Zbigniew Brzezinski (1983, pp. 311–12).
3. On the government of 'non-no confidence', its fall and the subsequent crisis, see, for example, Andreotti, op. cit., pp. 68–177; Gismondi (1986, pp. 91–206); Ugo LaMalfa (1978, pp. 476–88).
4. Andreotti (1986, p. 236); Gino Pallotta (1979, pp. 168–72); Italo Pietra (1983, pp. 195–210).
5. *Corriere della Sera*, 1 March 1978, pp. 1–2.
6. Gian Paolo Cresci *et al.* (eds.) (1982, pp. 9–26).
7. Ibid., p. 12.
8. Ibid., p. 23.
9. Ibid., pp. 23–4.
10. Ibid., p. 25.
11. *Corriere della Sera*, 1 March 1978, pp. 1–2.
12. The parliamentary majority was to encompass the DC, the Socialists, the Social Democrats, the Republicans and the PCI, but not the Liberals. The PCI, however, was not happy with the composition of Andreotti's cabinet, essentially unchanged from that of its immediate predecessor. It was not certain, therefore, that the PCI, when it came to it, would vote for Andreotti, but the betting was that, having taken the leap towards cooperation with the DC, the PCI would not reverse course so soon.
13. *Corriere della Sera*, 2 March 1978, p. 1 (commentary of Gianfranco Piazzesi).
14. On the ambush in Via Fani, see Senato della Repubblica-Camera dei Deputati (1983) (Moro Commission), Relazione, vol. 1 [hereafter cited as Relazione, Moro Comm.]; Corte di Assise di Roma (Prima) (1983) [hereafter cited as Sentenza, Moro I], especially at pp. 766–833; Corte di Assise di Appello di Roma (Prima) (1985) [hereafter Sentenza, Moro II]; Roberto Martinelli and Antonio Padellaro (1979, pp. 21–47).
15. It appears that the commando was composed of Moretti, Morucci, Gallinari, Bonisoli, Raffaele Fiore, Barbara Balzarani, Bruno Seghetti and two others (Sentenza, Moro II, pp. 60–2). Suspicion has since centered on Alessio Casimirri and Rita Algranati, both still at large, as the mysterious other two. It has, though, been suggested by some that in reality perhaps 15 or so were involved.
16. For example, Relazione, Moro Comm., pp. 63–6. For other views, see Giuseppe Zupo and Vincenzo Marini Recchia (1984, pp. 109–14); Mimmo Scarano and Maurizio DeLuca (1985, pp. 260–4).
17. Gino Pallotta (1978, pp. 10–11).
18. Franco Bonisoli (1985, p. 15).
19. Sentenza, Moro I, pp. 707–24; Relazione, Moro Comm., pp. 13–16.

The following are some of the members of ultra-left groups, committees and collectives in or around Rome who flowed into the BR. From the 'Tiburtaros' came Balzarani, Gabriella Mariani, Antonio Marini, Enrico Triaca, Teodoro Spadaccini; from 'Formazioni Armate Comuniste', Morucci and Faranda; from the 'Comitato Comunista Centocelle', Bruno Seghetti, Antonio Savasta, Anna Laura Braghetti, Emilia Libera; from 'Viva il Comunismo', Francesco Piccioni, Luigi Novelli, Marina and Stefano Petrella and Giulio Cacciotti (Sentenza, Moro II, pp. 44–5). This is something of a 'who's who' of the BR in their middle-late period.

20. Sentenza, Moro I, pp. 739–41.
21. By means of the so-called, rather nebulous *strutture di cerniera* (Corrado Incerti 1985, pp. 145–8, reporting the testimony of Valerio Morucci; Sentenza, Moro I, pp. 707–10).
22. Bonisoli, op. cit., p. 15.
23. Mario Moretti (1984, p. 6).
24. Bonisoli, op. cit., pp. 15–16; 9 Moro Comm., pp. 279–81 (Savasta).
25. Incerti, op. cit., p. 148.
26. Savasta Testimony, pp. 287–8; Sentenza, Moro I, pp. 761–2.
27. Incerti, op. cit., p. 148.
28. Bonisoli, op. cit.
29. 5 Moro Comm., p. 18 (Eleonora Moro).
30. Sentenza, Moro I, pp. 766–71.
31. Bonisoli, op. cit., p. 16.
32. Relazione, Moro Comm., pp. 27–30. See the testimony before the Commission of capiscorta Rocco Gentiluomo and Ferdinando Pallante (8, pp. 56–79), driver Otello Riccioni (8, pp. 79–82) and Guido Zecca, Director of the General Inspectorate of the Interior Ministry (6, pp. 65–79).
33. Zecca Testimony, p. 76.
34. Sentenza, Moro I, p. 920.
35. 7 Moro Comm., p. 220 (Peci).
36. Relazione, Moro Comm., p. 29. See also Sentenza, Moro I, pp. 915–20.
37. *Corriere della Sera*, 1 March 1978, p. 5.
38. On Moro's life and political ideas, see Gino Pallotta (1978, 1979); Antonio Rossano (1985); Aniello Coppola (1976); Italo Pietra, op. cit.; Andreotti (1986, pp. 50–67); Sandro Magister (1978, pp. 10–15).
39. Andreotti (1986, p. 54).
40. Aldo Moro (1979, p. 78).
41. Ibid., pp. 271–3.
42. Ibid., pp. 271, 272.
43. Pallotta (1979, pp. 160–4).
44. Ibid., p. 162.
45. Tullio Ancora (1988).
46. Corrado Augias (1978, p. 32); Pallotta (1979, p. 8).
47. Andreotti (1986, pp. 62–3); Sandro Magister, op. cit., p. 13.
48. Roberto Ducci (1982, p. 39).
49. Andreotti (1986, p. 64).

50. Giovanni Spadolini (1978, p. 28).
51. Henry Kissinger (1979, p. 101).
52. Ducci, op. cit., p. 45–54.
53. Maria Fida Moro (1982).
54. Ibid., pp. 33, 53.
55. Ibid., p. 72.
56. Ibid., p. 80.

8 The Justice of the People

1. Relazione, Moro Comm., pp. 35–6, 38–9.
2. 7 Moro Comm., pp. 224–5 (Peci); 8 Moro Comm., pp. 252–5 (Sandalo); 8 Moro Comm., pp. 334–6 (Donat Cattin).
3. Andreotti (1981, pp. 192–3); 3 Moro Comm., pp. 140–3 (Andreotti).
4. Neither Gallinari nor Braghetti has admitted this involvement in the operation, but the evidence points to them.
5. The supporters were the BR's Tuscan Revolutionary Committee, which was not an operational column, but a collective of active sympathizers and a base of logistic support.
6. Sentenza, Moro I, pp. 593; Sentenza, Moro II, pp. 64–6; Corrado Incerti (1985, pp. 152–4), reporting the testimony of Morucci.
7. Communiqué no. 1, in Giorgio Bocca (ed.) (1978a, pp. 34–6).
8. Maria Fida Moro (1982, pp. 86–7).
9. Giorgio Bocca (ed.), op. cit., pp. 37–48.
10. Ibid., pp. 49–112.
11. Ibid., p. 55.
12. Ibid., p. 91.
13. Ibid., p. 44 (Communiqué no. 3).
14. Strategic Resolution, ibid., p. 104.
15. Moretti (1984, pp. 6–11); Bonisoli (1985, p. 16).
16. Giorgio Bocca (ed.), op. cit., p. 53.
17. Communiqués nos. 3, 4.
18. The letters were transmitted via a letter to Moro's secretary, Nicola Rana (Senato della Repubblica-Camera dei Deputati (1983) (Moro Commission), Relazione Franchi, vol. 2, Allegati, pp. 91–2 [hereafter cited as Relazione Franchi, Moro Comm.]). The Moro letters are contained in this source and, with some additions, in Aldo Moro (1979).
19. Communiqué no. 3, p. 43.
20. Incerti, op. cit., p. 154.
21. Andreotti, op. cit., p. 197.
22. Augias (1978, p. 38).
23. 30 March 1978, p. 1.
24. Andreotti, op. cit., pp. 199–200; *Corriere della Sera*, 4 April 1978.
25. *Corriere della Sera*, 4 April 1978, p. 2.
26. Relazione Franchi, Moro Comm., pp. 93–4.
27. Andreotti, op. cit., p. 200–1.
28. See Robert Katz (1980).
29. See, for example, Augias, op. cit., p. 41; Gustavo Selva and Eugenio

Marcucci (1978, pp. 46–7); Spadolini (1978, pp. 19–27); William Murray (1978b, p. 72); 'Il vero e il falso Moro' (1978).

30. 4 April 1978.
31. For example, Vittorio Cervone (1979, pp. 48–9).
32. *L'Espresso*, 26 March 1978, p. 5.
33. *Corriere della Sera*, 20 March 1978, p. 3.
34. See Gilberto Polloni and Daniele Romano (eds.) (1978). Sciascia had already set off a firestorm of controversy with a statement in 1977 (*Corriere della Sera*, 12 May 1977, p. 1), in which, among other things, he said: 'I do not understand what the police and magistrates are defending ... To serve the democracy, to not give in, to not surrender ... these are only words'. See also Domenico Porzio (1977).
35. Sciascia (1978a, p. 63).
36. 18 March 1978, p. 1.
37. Ibid., 19–20 March 1978, p. 1.
38. Boato (1978, pp. 6–7).
39. 30 March 1978, p. 10.
40. 5 Moro Comm., pp. 351–2 (Berlinguer).
41. Bonisoli, op. cit., p. 15.
42. See, for example, the articles of Alberto Ronchey (1978b, 1978c).
43. For example, Aldo Tortorella (1978).
44. Berlinguer (1978).
45. Macaluso (1978).
46. Editorial (1978a). To like effect, see Flavio Michelini (1979); Alessandro Natta (1979); Romano Ledda (1978); Aldo Tortorella (1978); Pietro Ingrao (1978); Gian Mario Bravo (1982, pp. 91, 135, 143).
47. See Bruno Mantelli and Marco Revelli (eds.) (1979).
48. Bonisoli, op. cit., p. 16.
49. Giorgio Bocca (ed.), op. cit., pp. 115–17.
50. Relazione Franchi, Moro Comm., pp. 94–6.
51. *Corriere della Sera*, 11 April 1978.
52. Ibid.; Andreotti, op. cit., p. 204; 3 Moro Comm., pp. 144–5 (Andreotti).
53. Giorgio Bocca (ed.), op. cit., pp. 120–2.
54. 9 Moro Comm., pp. 330–1 (Savasta).
55. Relazione, Moro Comm., pp. 38–43; Martinelli and Padellaro (1979, pp. 118–24).
56. The unusual circumstances of the discovery of the apartment led to all manner of theories, frequently of the conspiratorial variety – for instance, that someone inside the BR, unhappy with the direction of the Organization by Moretti, revealed the existence of the place to the police, or even that Moretti himself, for some incomprehensible reason (incomprehensible especially in view of the importance of the evidence left in the apartment), set the shower running and in a way so as to make discovery of the apartment inevitable. Franco Bonisoli categorically rejects the proposed mystery. Other *brigatisti* have testified to having been informed that the apparent accident had been that in fact. *Brigatista* Enrico Fenzi was told by Moretti that

the discovery of the base had indeed been due to the accidental overflow of water (Sentenza, Moro I, pp. 843–4). This was not the only accident to befall the *brigatisti*.

57. Giorgio Bocca (ed.), op. cit., p. 123.
58. Andreotti (1981, pp. 208–9).
59. A member of the leftist group 'Revolutionary Action' testified that his group, feeling the pressure of the police, had fabricated the communiqué in order to divert attention from themselves, perhaps to buy time or to escape from the city. For a variety of reasons his testimony was not considered dispositive (8 Moro Comm., pp. 240–1 (Paghera)). More recently the same leftist has stated that this testimony was a lie done on the instructions of the secret services (Marcella Andreoli, 1988c, pp. 60–3). It is now thought that the false communiqué was written by a shadowy small-time Roman criminal with apparent links to the BR and to organized crime (Marcella Andreoli, 1988a, pp. 56–9; Enrico Deaglio, 1988, pp. 20–7).
60. Giorgio Bocca (ed.), op. cit., pp. 124–6.
61. 19 April 1978, p. 1.
62. 18 March 1978, p. 1.
63. 20 April 1978, p. 1.
64. Andreotti (1981, pp. 215, 217).
65. Relazione, Moro Comm., pp. 75–81.

9 The Politics of Life and Death

1. *L'Avanti*, 21 April 1978. See also 5 Moro Comm., pp. 479–585 (Craxi).
2. *L'Avanti*, 22 April 1978.
3. Relazione, Moro Comm., pp. 153–8; 6 Moro Comm., pp. 165–283 (Guiso); Giannino Guiso (1979); Craxi Testimony, pp. 480–3, 514–24.
4. 10 Moro Comm., pp. 581–9 (Buonavita); Relazione, Moro Comm., p. 157; Franceschini (1988, pp. 149, 155–61).
5. Relazione, Moro Comm., p. 159; Craxi Testimony, pp. 489–90; 6 Moro Comm., pp. 103–42 (Signorile); Franco Piperno (1984, pp. 28–31).
6. 3 Moro Comm., p. 412 (Corsini).
7. See the document cited at note 21, p. 135.
8. *L'Espresso*, 23 April 1978, p. 12. Just under 63 per cent believed the government should not negotiate a 'prisoner exchange'.
9. Relazione Franchi, Moro Comm., pp. 101–2.
10. Ibid., pp. 107–8.
11. Ibid., p. 116.
12. Andreotti (1981, pp. 211–12); *Corriere della Sera*, 22 April 1978.
13. *Corriere della Sera*, 23 April 1978, p. 1.
14. Giorgio Bocca (ed.) (1978a, pp. 131–3).
15. Relazione Franchi, Moro Comm., pp. 103–4.
16. Ibid., pp. 110–12. Two variations on this letter are at pp. 112–15.
17. Ibid., pp. 96–117.
18. Bonisoli (1985, pp. 16–17).
19. See note 16.

20. Ibid.
21. Found in Via Montenevoso 8 in October 1978. The document is Aldo Moro (1978).
22. Bonisoli, op. cit., p. 16.
23. Aldo Moro, op. cit., pp. 153–4. It appears that this section of the 'memoriale' was written or spoken after Moro had been told that he was to be freed ('I wish to acknowledge that it is to the generosity of the BR that . . . the salvation of my life and my restitution to freedom are owed'). Moro stated that he intended to renounce all future political positions and resign from the DC (Ibid., pp. 154–5).
24. *La Repubblica*, 28 January 1982, p. 8, reporting the testimony of *pentito* Carlo Bozzo (based on conversation with Riccardo Dura).
25. Ibid., reporting the testimony of Massimo Cianfanelli.
26. Sentenza, Moro I, p. 863 (testimony of Savasta).
27. Bonisoli, op. cit., p. 16.
28. Craxi Testimony, pp. 484–6; 6 Moro Comm., pp. 418–79 (Vassalli).
29. Corrado Incerti (1985, p. 154).
30. Valerio Morucci (1984, pp. 25–6); Valerio Morucci (1982, p. 8); 10 Moro Comm., pp. 80–116 (Cianfanelli).
31. *Corriere della Sera*, 11 March 1987, p. 5.
32. Ibid., 19 June 1985, p. 5.
33. Corrado Incerti, op. cit., p. 154.
34. Valerio Morucci (1984, pp. 25–6); Corrado Incerti, op. cit., p. 154.
35. Atti of the Moro Commission, quoted in Mimmo Scarano and Maurizio DeLuca (1985, pp. 211–12).
36. Giorgio Bocca (ed.), op. cit., p. 141.
37. Andreotti, op. cit., pp. 218–19; 3 Moro Comm., pp. 156–7 (Andreotti); 5 Moro Comm., pp. 362–3 (Berlinguer). The PCI was unaware of the Buonoconto hypothesis until after 9 May (Berlinguer Testimony, pp. 362–3).
38. Craxi Testimony, pp. 488–9.
39. *Corriere della Sera*, 3 May 1978, p. 1, quoting Giovanni Galloni.
40. 5 Moro Comm., pp. 306–11 (Zaccagnini).
41. *Corriere della Sera*, 4 May 1978.
42. Andreotti (1981, p. 221), referring to Andreotti's request of Justice Minister Bonifacio on 5 May that he examine the files on captured terrorists to see if there was a candidate for an autonomous, humanitarian act by the government. Bonifacio has confirmed discussing this subject with Andreotti and that the prime minister was in favor of what Bonifacio was doing in the Buonoconto case (3 Moro Comm., pp. 319, 332).
43. Andreotti (1981, p. 221).
44. Bonifacio Testimony, pp. 314–33; Andreotti (1981, p. 221); Relazione, Moro Comm., pp. 166–7.
45. Corrado Incerti, op. cit., p. 154.
46. The unsatisfactory explanation of Bonisoli is as follows. The Executive Committee perceived only total obstinacy on the part of the DC. There had been no response to the telephone call of 30 April. The proposals of the PSI seemed inconclusive and a waste of time in

view of the attitude of the other parties. Freeing Moro without receiving anything in exchange would not have permitted the so-much-desired 'leap to the party'. Therefore, after discussion and reflection on other possibilities, and taking into account the risk that the police might discover the prison, the Committee could see only one solution (Bonisoli, op. cit., p. 17).

47. Giorgio Bocca (ed.), op. cit., pp. 142–4.
48. Zupo and Recchia (1984, pp. 172–4). Another initiative involved contacts on 6 and 7 May between a magistrate and Daniele Pifano, a well-known leader of the 'autonomous' collective of Via dei Volsci in Rome. Pifano claimed to have received word from the BR through a chain of intermediaries that Moro could well be freed in exchange for the release of one of the terrorists on the list of 13. The government was informed of this, but the idea was rejected. There could be no ceding on the matter of the 13 and no negotiation with the BR (Bonifacio Testimony, pp. 318–22; 5 Moro Comm., pp. 130–73 (Vitalone)).
49. *Corriere della Sera*, 6 May 1978.
50. Letter to Sereno Freato, Relazione Franchi, Moro Comm., p. 122.
51. Letter to Nicola Rana, ibid., p. 121. Some of Moro's letters, such as this one, were never sent but were found later in the BR safehouse in Via Montenevoso 8 in Milan.
52. Letter to Mrs Moro, ibid., pp. 122–3.
53. See 4 Moro Comm., p. 177 (Santovito).
54. Craxi Testimony, pp. 490–1.
55. Andreotti (1981, p. 222).
56. Corrado Incerti, op. cit., p. 154. The text of the telephone call is in *Corriere della Sera*, 2 July 1978, p. 6.
57. Moretti (1984, p. 11).
58. 9 Moro Comm., p. 384 (Savasta). ('After Moro, there was a very great influx of comrades. After D'Urso, the same thing'.) See also Moretti, op. cit., p. 11. Among the many known to have joined the BR in this influx were Norma Andriani, Arnaldo Maj and Carlo Brogi, with Massimo Cianfanelli having signed up during the 54 days (Sentenza, Moro II, pp. 71–2).
59. Morucci (1984, p. 26).
60. Sentenza, Moro I, pp. 900–1.
61. Concerning autopsy findings, see Sentenza, Moro I, pp. 903–5; *Corriere della Sera*, 11 May 1978; Martinelli and Padellaro (1979, pp. 210–12).
62. Sentenza, Moro I, pp. 903–5. An alternative hypothesis is based upon the finding in Moro's shoes and clothes and in the car of sand and bits of vegetable matter originating from a specific area along the coast near Rome. It is suggested that Moro was held prisoner there, at least for a time (Zupo and Recchia, op. cit., pp. 109–14; Scarano and DeLuca, op. cit., pp. 260–4). Another mystery concerns the timing of the shots. The ballistics report indicated that the shots had been fired at two different times. The Zupo-Recchia book speculates that Moro may have been subjected to a ritual execution,

having been shot a second time, in a second place perhaps, after he was already dead. The book does not explain why the BR would have had an interest in carrying out such a bizarre ritual, which was hardly in keeping with their normal procedures and their philosophy.

63. Testimony of Peci, Sentenza, Moro I, p. 900; Valerio Morucci (1985b, p. 7).
64. Giorgio Bocca (ed.), op. cit., p. 145.
65. Augias (1978, p. 82).
66. Morucci (1982, p. 8).
67. Bonisoli, op. cit., p. 17.
68. Moretti, op. cit., pp. 9, 11.
69. The Chamber of Deputies approved the government's handling of the Moro case by a vote of 317 in favor, 36 opposed (*Corriere della Sera*, 20 May 1978).
70. Bonisoli, op. cit., p. 17.
71. *Corriere della Sera*, 11 May 1978, p. 1.
72. Moretti, op. cit., p. 8.

10 The Emergency, Phase One

1. 6 Moro Comm., pp. 82–7 (Fariello); Zupo and Recchia (1984, p. 74 n. 2).
2. Relazione, Moro Comm., pp. 46–9; 5 Moro Comm., pp. 429–78 (Spinella); Fariello Testimony, pp. 87–9.
3. 6 Moro Comm., pp. 2–33, 49 (DeFrancesco); 7 Moro Comm., pp. 125–7, 137–9 (Infelisi); 5 Moro Comm., pp. 84–96 (Lettieri); Relazione, Moro Comm., pp. 38–9.
4. The name Gradoli surfaced again in early April in another context. To pass the time in a country house, an important economist and friends played an occult game involving a plate supposedly made to spin and pick out words in response to questions. The answer to the question 'Where is Moro?' made such an impression that the economist felt compelled to refer what had been 'learned' to the authorities. On 5 April the Interior Ministry advised the police of this information and on the following day an appropriate search was made. The notice to the police was to search for an isolated house with a cantina along state highway 74 in the province of Viterbo, town of Gradoli (Lettieri Testimony; 8 Moro Comm., pp. 295–304 (Prodi) and pp. 304–24 (Friends); Relazione, Moro Comm., pp. 39–42). Given the unchallengeable integrity of the economist and his guests, this information was either the product of other-worldly forces or of an extraordinary coincidence. The search in the town of Gradoli was obviously to no avail. No one in authority recalled that a street by that name had been searched in Rome and thought to look into the matter again. Mrs Moro testified that, apprised of the incident of Gradoli village, she had asked one of the authorities if a street in Rome were not involved, that she had been advised in reply that no such street was listed in the phone directory

and that she had checked herself and found otherwise. She said at one point that she had spoken of this to Minister Cossiga, who denied any such discussion had ever occurred (Relazione, Moro Comm., p. 40).

5. Relazione, Moro Comm., p. 43.
6. 7 Moro Comm., p. 191 (Pascalino).
7. Infelisi Testimony, pp. 123–64; Relazione, Moro Comm., pp. 43–6. See also 7 Moro Comm., pp. 198–215 (DeMatteo).
8. Relazione, Moro Comm., p. 43.
9. 4 Moro Comm., pp. 291–2 (Dalla Chiesa).
10. 4 Moro Comm., pp. 195, 241 (Grassini).
11. Ibid., pp. 194–241; and Moro Comm.: vol. 4, pp. 465–89 (Santillo) & pp. 139–93 (Santovito); vol. 9, pp. 143–65 (Sparano); vol. 3, pp. 235–6 (Cossiga). See also DeLutiis (1984, pp. 201–7, 261–77).
12. Moro Comm.: Cossiga, p. 191; vol. 3, pp. 263–4 (Rognoni), p. 397 (Corsini) & p. 342 (Parlato); vol. 5, p. 73 (Lettieri); vol. 7, p. 103 (Coppola).
13. Vittorio Grevi (1984, pp. 17–20).
14. The prison reform law is that of 26 July 1975, no. 354. Related regulations are in Decree of Procedures and Regulations, 29 April 1976, no. 431.
15. Decree-Law, 11 April 1974, no. 99, converted by Law, 7 June 1974, no. 220.
16. Law, 22 May 1975, no. 152.
17. See, for example, Pier Vittorio Buffa and Mario Scialoja (1985, p. 6); Giorgio Bocca (1985b, p. 11).
18. In 1977, 431 detainees escaped and there were 16 murders in prison (Pier Vittorio Buffa and Franco Giustolisi, 1984a, p. 69).
19. Ministerial Decree, 4 May 1977.
20. The prison reform law itself contemplated the use of special security measures in emergencies. See the famous article 90 of the law.
21. Decree-Law, 21 March 1978, no. 59, converted with substantial modifications by Law, 18 May 1978, no. 191. A decree-law takes immediate effect, but ceases to be effective if not approved by parliament within 60 days.
22. 7 Moro Comm., p. 225 (Peci).

11 The Program of Annihilation: 1978–80

1. See Galleni (ed.) (1981, pp. 49, 175–92).
2. See a series of articles in *Corriere della Sera* beginning on 2 February 1978.
3. 9 Moro Comm., pp. 265–6 (omitting questions).
4. Ibid., pp. 266–74, 419–20.
5. Rino Genova (1985, pp. 48–9).
6. *Corriere della Sera*, 28 January 1979, p. 1.
7. Ibid., 7 October 1979, p. 2.
8. Patrizio Peci (1980, pp. 7–8).
9. Morucci (1984, p. 26).

10. Ibid.; 10 Moro Comm., pp. 657–60 (Morucci); Sentenza, Moro II, pp. 73–9.
11. *Lotta Continua*, 25 July 1979, pp. 9–14, and 11 August 1979, pp. 4–11.
12. Ibid., 11 August 1979, p. 4.
13. Patrizio Peci (1983).
14. 4 Moro Comm., pp. 250–2 (Dalla Chiesa); Peci (1983, pp. 174–7).
15. Early information provided by Peci led to an irruption in a BR cove in Genoa and the deaths of the occupants: Riccardo Dura, former proletarian leader of the Genoa column and member of the Strategic Direction; Lorenzo Betassa, ex-worker at Fiat, ex-union delegate, formerly Patrizio's comrade-in-arms in the Turin column and a member of the Strategic Direction; Piero Panciarelli, ex-worker at Lancia, another former comrade from the Turin column; and Anna Maria Ludmann, secretary, owner of the apartment and *prestanome* (that is, a person above suspicion who lends his name as a cover for the BR by renting or buying a home for their use as a cove).
16. 9 Moro Comm., pp. 228–35.
17. Dalla Chiesa Testimony, vol. 4, pp. 252–8; Peci (1983, pp. 177–99); Peci (1980, pp. 5–20); 7 Moro Comm., pp. 217–317 (Peci).
18. See note 16.
19. 8 Moro Comm., p. 261.
20. Galleni (ed.), op. cit., pp. 49, 175–6, 244–6.
21. Vittorio Borraccetti (1986a, p. 189).
22. On the new right, see the Borraccetti volume (1986b) and Rosario Minna (1984, pp. 21–72). On the Bologna bombing and the legal proceedings concerning it, see the requisitoria and sentenza-ordinanza of the Bologna magistrates collected in Giuseppe De-Lutiis (ed.) (1986a). At the end of the trial stage of the case, four neo-Fascists were sentenced to life imprisonment for the bombing and other defendants were found guilty of related crimes, including two officers of SISMI, an individual connected to SISMI and the head of the lodge P2, Licio Gelli (*La Repubblica*, 12 July 1988, p. 5).

12 Evanescence

1. Brigate Rosse (1980c, p. 1).
2. See Theses 1–5, in Brigate Rosse (1980d, pp. 269–87).
3. Brigate Rosse (1980c, p. 66).
4. Ibid., p. 81.
5. Brigate Rosse (1980/81).
6. Statement of Enrico Fenzi in Sue Ellen Moran (ed.) (1986, pp. 198–202, 206–16); Procura della Repubblica di Milano (1983, pp. 80–3, 103–5).
7. Brigate Rosse (1980e).
8. For example, Brigate Rosse (1981e).
9. *La Repubblica*, 4 April 1981, p. 1.
10. *La Nazione*, 7 December 1984, reporting the testimony of Giovanni Planzio.

11. 9 Moro Comm., pp. 372–6 (Savasta).
12. Procura della Repubblica di Venezia (1983, pp. 100–11).
13. *La Repubblica*, 10 July 1981, quoting from two BR bulletins found in Rome the day before.
14. Savasta Testimony, pp. 375–80.
15. Brigate Rosse (1981d, p. 137).
16. See, for example, *L'Avanti*, 3, 4, 8, 16, 18 July 1981.
17. *La Repubblica*, 1 August 1981.
18. *Corriere della Sera*, 18 July 1986, p. 4 (testimony of Roberto Buzzatti).
19. Brigate Rosse (1981g).
20. Brigate Rosse (1981f).
21. Savasta Testimony, p. 387.
22. This is the version of the Dozier liberation given by one of the police officials in charge (Genova, 1985, pp. 97–112, 152–5).

13 The Emergency, Phase Two

1. Decree-Law, no. 625, converted by law, 6 February 1980, no. 15.
2. Mario Chiavario (1981); Domenico Pulitanò (1981, pp. 77–86).
3. Camera dei Deputati (1985, p. 207).
4. Vittorio Vicini (1982, pp. 37–42), reporting data from the Consiglio Superiore della Magistratura.
5. Sentenza no. 15, 14 January 1982.
6. Ibid., in Camera dei Deputati, op. cit., p. 184.
7. Opinions in the Foti and Corigliano cases, 10 December 1982.
8. Mauro Mellini (1986, p. 12).
9. Law, 29 May 1982, no. 304.
10. Bocca (1981c; 1984; 1985a, p. 286; 1985d).
11. *Corriere della Sera*, 6 March 1987, p. 4.
12. Luciano Violante (1984, p. 257).
13. One of the cases in which the role of the *pentiti* was most criticized, the most controversial of all the legal cases of 'the emergency' for this and other reasons, was the 'April 7' case against Professor Negri and other intellectuals of 'Autonomia'. The moral responsibility of these persons for much of the political violence was clear, but whether they were criminally responsible, and, if so, for what was debatable. For facts and views, see Giorgio Bocca (1980); Ivan Palermo (1982); Francesco Leonetti and Enrico Rambaldi (eds.) (1983).

14 Connections

1. Sentenza, Moro I, pp. 245–6, 295; 3 Moro Comm., p.307 (Rognoni).
2. Sentenza, Moro I, pp. 976–82; Relazione, Moro Comm., pp. 129–30.
3. 8 Moro Comm., pp. 255–60 (Sandalo).
4. Franceschini (1988, pp. 71–3).
5. Sentenza, Moro I, pp. 627–9, 976–89; Relazione, Moro Comm., p. 129–30; 7 Moro Comm., pp. 230–1 (Peci).

6. 9 Moro Comm., pp. 398–413 (Savasta); Rognoni Testimony, p. 306; Relazione, Moro Comm., pp. 139–50.
7. Sentenza, Moro I, pp. 570–1, 602–4, 976–87; Procura della Repubblica di Venezia (1983, pp. 146–50); Relazione, Moro Comm., pp. 131–5; Report of CESIS, 'Implicazioni internazionali del terrorismo', March 1983, in 2 Moro Comm., pp. 378–80.
8. Sentenza, Moro I, p. 1000; Relazione, Moro Comm., pp. 146–7; Sandalo Testimony, pp. 255–60; *Corriere della Sera*, 23 June 1987, p. 5; *La Repubblica*, 23 June 1987, p. 20.
9. 10 Moro Comm., pp. 551–66 (Buonavita); Franceschini, op. cit., pp. 74–5; 7 Moro Comm., pp. 222–4 (Peci).
10. Relazione, pp. 141–4.
11. Buonavita Testimony, pp. 556–8; Franceschini, op. cit., pp. 42–4; Procura della Repubblica di Venezia, op. cit., pp. 136–52; Savasta Testimony, pp. 413–15; Relazione, Moro Comm., pp. 135–7.
12. CESIS Report, op. cit., pp. 382–3; Procura della Repubblica di Venezia, op. cit., pp. 136–41; Rosario Priore (1985).
13. Relazione, Moro Comm., p. 147.
14. Franceschini, op. cit., p. 74.
15. 4 Moro Comm., p. 147 (Santovito); Relazione, Moro Comm., p. 139.
16. Relazione, Moro Comm., pp. 137–40.
17. Franceschini, op. cit., pp. 10–11.
18. Vito Zincani and Sergio Castaldo (1986, pp. 306–9, 323); Senato della Repubblica-Camera dei Deputati (1984).
19. Zupo and Recchia (1984); Scarano and DeLuca (1985).
20. Armenia Balducci *et al.* (1987).
21. Renato Curcio (1987, p. 28).
22. Mario Moretti (1987, p. 18).
23. Relazione, pp. 19–22.
24. Armenia Balducci *et al.*, op. cit., pp. 230–1.
25. Galli (1986a).

15 We Are All *Dissociati*

1. Sentenza, Moro I, pp. 579–80.
2. Ibid., p. 612.
3. *La Repubblica*, 16 March 1982, p. 4.
4. Ibid., 13–14, 19–20 January 1982.
5. Ibid., 29 December 1982, p. 12.
6. Data from the PCI Section on Problems of the State, reported in *La Repubblica*, 13 January and 31 December 1982, and Donatella della Porta and Maurizio Rossi (1983, pp. 5–6).
7. 'Sono stati tempi difficili', in Daniele Repetto (ed.) (1984, p. 75).
8. Franceschini (1988, p. 204).
9. *Corriere della Sera*, 20 June 1985, p. 7.
10. Ibid., 6 July 1986, p. 5.
11. Law, 18 February 1987, no. 34, Gazzetta Ufficiale, no. 43, 21 February 1987, p. 3.
12. *La Repubblica*, 12 July 1987, p. 17.

13. Law, 28 July 1984, no. 398.
14. *Corriere della Sera*, 3 June 1985, p. 1.
15. Gian Paolo Rossetti *et al.* (1988, p. 34).
16. *La Repubblica*, 19 April 1988, p. 8; Rossetti, op. cit., p. 35.
17. *La Repubblica*, 22 January 1988, p. 2.
18. Pier Vittorio Buffa and Franco Giustolisi (1984b, p. 18).
19. Renato Curcio (1987, p. 28).

16 Conclusion

1. *La Repubblica*, 22 March 1988, p. 8.
2. 9 Moro Comm., p. 416.

References

ACQUAVIVA, SABINO (1979a) *Guerriglia e guerra rivoluzionaria in Italia* (Milan: Rizzoli).

ACQUAVIVA, SABINO (1979b) *Il seme religioso della rivolta* (Milan: Rusconi).

ADAMS, JAMES (1986) *The Financing of Terror* (New York: Simon & Schuster).

ADORNATO, FERDINANDO and GAD LERNER (1987) 'Il movimento del '77: Quell 'urlo lungo un anno', *L'Espresso*, 18 January 1987, pp. 88–107.

AGLIETTA, ADELAIDE (1979) *Diario di una giurata popolare al processo delle Brigate Rosse* (Milan: Milano Libri).

AGOSTINI, PIERO (1980) *Mara Cagol: una donna nelle prime Brigate Rosse* (Venice: Marsilio & Trent: TEMI).

ALBERONI, FRANCESCO (1976) *Italia in trasformazione* (Bologna: Il Mulino).

ALEXANDER, YONAH and KENNETH A. MYERS (eds) (1982) *Terrorism in Europe* (London: Croom Helm).

ALLEN, KEVIN and ANDREW STEVENSON (1975) *An Introduction to the Italian Economy* (New York: Harper & Row).

AMENDOLA, GIORGIO (1978) Interview by Fabio Mussi, 'Chi è responsabile della violenza politica', *Rinascita*, 7 April 1978, pp. 3–5.

ANCORA, TULLIO (1988) Interview by Guido Quaranta, 'L'erede immaginario', *L'Espresso*, 26 June 1988, p. 20.

ANDREOLI, MARCELLA (1988a) 'Prova Polaroid – Brigate Rosse e malavita nel sequestro Moro', *Panorama*, 12 June 1988, pp. 56–9.

ANDREOLI, MARCELLA (1988b) 'Caso Moro-P2 – La manovra contro Cossiga: Quirinal tango', *Panorama*, 19 June 1988, pp. 50–5.

ANDREOLI, MARCELLA (1988c) 'Sequestro Moro – Una manovra dei servizi: Paghera, dica 7', *Panorama*, 26 June 1988, pp. 60–3.

ANDREOTTI, GIULIO (1981) *Diari, 1976–1979 – Gli anni della solidarietà* (Milan: Rizzoli).

ANDREOTTI, GIULIO (1986) *Visti da vicino* (Milan: Rizzoli).

'Anni di piombo – Una vittima e una terrorista si scrivono: Perché mi volevi morto?', *Panorama*, 1 May 1988, pp. 226–31.

ANONYMOUS (1971) *Feltrinelli, il guerrigliero impotente* (Rome: Edizioni 'Documenti').

ANONYMOUS (1976) *Criminalizzazione e lotta armata* (Milan: Collettivo Editoriale Librirossi).

ANSELMI, TINA (1984) President of the Parliamentary Commission of Investigation on the P2, Relazione, *L'Espresso*, special insert, 20 May 1984, pp. 1–62.

ARE, GIUSEPPE (1978) 'La struttura politica del PCI dal 1968 al 1978', in Antonio Lombardo (ed.) (1978).

ARLACCHI, PINO *et al.* (1982) *Morte di un generale – L'assassinio di Carlo*

Alberto Dalla Chiesa, la mafia, la droga, il potere politico (Milan: Mondadori).

AUGIAS, CORRADO (1978) *1978 – Cronaca di un anno drammatico* (Rome: Editoriale L'Espresso).

AUTORI VARI (1968) *Università: l'ipotesi rivoluzionaria – Documenti delle lotte studentesche, Trento, Torino, Napoli, Pisa, Milano, Roma* (Padua: Marsilio).

BALDUCCI, ARMENIA, GIUSEPPE FERRARA and ROBERT KATZ (1987) *Il caso Moro* (Naples: Pironti).

BALESTRINI, NANNI (1987) *Gli invisibili* (Milan: Bompiani).

BARZINI, LUIGI (1972) 'Feltrinelli', *Encounter*, July 1972, pp. 35–40.

BATTAGLINI, MARIO (1986) 'Il movimento politico Ordine nuovo – Il processo di Roma del 1973', in Vittorio Borraccetti (ed.) (1986b), pp. 27–41.

BAUMANN, MICHAEL (1977) *Terror or Love?* (New York: Grove Press).

BECKER, JILLIAN (1977) *Hitler's Children – The Story of the Baader-Meinhof Terrorist Gang* (Philadelphia: J.B. Lippincott).

BELL, J. BOWYER (1978) *A Time of Terror – How Democratic Societies Respond to Revolutionary Violence* (New York: Basic Books).

BERLINGUER, ENRICO (1975) *La 'questione comunista', 1969–1975*, 2 (Rome: Riuniti).

BERLINGUER, ENRICO (1978) 'Unità e rigore', *L'Unità* 19 March 1978, p. 1.

BERNARDI, ANTONIO (1978) 'Reggio Emilia – Fucina delle Br?', *Rinascita*, 7 April 1978, p. 13.

BEVERE, ANTONIO (1984) 'Chiamata di correo e carcerazione preventiva: la miscela propellente del processo penale dell'eterna emergenza', *Critica del diritto*, no. 33, June 1984, pp. 27–42.

BIAGI, ENZO (1983) 'Le mie due ore con Patrizio Peci', *La Repubblica*, 27 April 1983, reprinted in 'Dieci anni – 1983', supplement to issue of 15 April 1986.

BOATO, MARCO (1978) 'Né con le BR né con lo stato. E poi?', *Lotta Continua*, 25 March 1978, pp. 6–7.

BOBBIO, LUIGI (1979) *Lotta Continua – Storia di una organizzazione rivoluzionaria* (Rome: Savelli).

BOCCA, GIORGIO (ed.) (1978a) *Moro – una tragedia italiana* (Milan: Bompiani).

BOCCA, GIORGIO (1978b) 'Violenza: BR e fascisti – Il terrore viaggia sul doppio binario', *L'Espresso*, 8 October 1978, pp. 33–4.

BOCCA, GIORGIO (1980) *Il caso 7 aprile* (Milan: Feltrinelli).

BOCCA, GIORGIO (1981a) *Il terrorismo italiano – 1970–1980* (Milan: Rizzoli).

BOCCA, GIORGIO (1981b) 'Il terrorismo a un bivio: ecco perché', *Epoca*, 18 April 1981, pp. 11–18.

BOCCA, GIORGIO (1981c) 'Ma chi sono questi pentiti?', *La Repubblica*, 1 September 1981, p. 5.

BOCCA, GIORGIO (1982) *Storia della repubblica italiana dalla caduta del fascismo a oggi* (Milan: Rizzoli).

BOCCA, GIORGIO (1984) 'L'antitaliano: I "pentiti" e la filosofia di Torquemada', *L'Espresso*, 25 November 1984, p. 15.

BOCCA, GIORGIO (1985a) *Noi terroristi* (Milan: Garzanti).

BOCCA, GIORGIO (1985b) 'L'antitaliano: Ma quelli erano anni di guerra', *L'Espresso*, 24 March 1985, p. 11.

BOCCA, GIORGIO (1985c) 'L'antitaliano: Una sentenza per uscire dagli anni di piombo', *L'Espresso*, 16 June 1985, p. 23.

BOCCA, GIORGIO (1985d) 'L'antitaliano: Continua con i pentiti la giustizia dell "emergenza"', *L'Espresso*, 6 October 1985, p. 33.

BOCCA, GIORGIO (1987) 'L'antitaliano: A Curcio e a Negri manca la modestia', *L'Espresso*, 25 January 1987, p. 23.

BOLOGNA, SERGIO (ed.) (1978) *La tribù delle talpe* (Milan: Feltrinelli).

BONANATE, LUIGI (1986) 'Discussioni: Ancora a proposito del libro sul terrorismo di Giorgio Galli – Un potere occulto non può essere "evidente"', *Corriere della Sera*, 4 June 1986, p. 3.

BONISOLI, FRANCO (1985) Interview by Fabio Cavalera, *Corriere della Sera*, 6 October 1985, pp. 15–17.

BORDIERI, FRANCO, *et al.* (1975) 'Chi sono le ragazze della guerriglia', *L'Europeo*, 6 June 1975, pp. 36–9.

BORRACCETTI, VITTORIO (1986a) 'Sul processo per la strage del 2 Agosto 1980', in Vittorio Borraccetti (1986b).

BORRACCETTI, VITTORIO (ed.) (1986b) *Eversione di destra, terrorismo, stragi – I fatti e l'intervento giudiziario* (Milan: Angeli).

BOZZO, CARLO (1984) Interview by Ennio Remondino, 'Moretti il doppio', *L'Espresso*, 9 December 1984, pp. 24–8.

BRAVO, GIAN MARIO (1982) *L'estremismo in Italia* (Rome: Riuniti).

BRIGATE ROSSE (1971) 'Autointervista', September 1971, in Vincenzo Tessandori (1977), pp. 375–80.

BRIGATE ROSSE (1973) 'Autointervista', January 1973, in Vincenzo Tessandori (1977), pp. 389–94.

BRIGATE ROSSE (1974) 'Contro il neogollismo portare l'attacco al cuore dello stato – Trasformare la crisi di regime in lotta armata per il comunismo', April 1974.

BRIGATE ROSSE (1975) 'Risoluzione della Direzione Strategica', April 1975, *Controinformazione*, no. 7–8, June 1976, pp. 144–50.

BRIGATE ROSSE (1976) 'Crisi e rivoluzione', *Controinformazione*, no. 7–8, June 1976.

BRIGATE ROSSE (1977) 'Risoluzione della Direzione Strategica, No. 4 – Attaccare, colpire, liquidare e disperdere la Democrazia Cristiana, asse portante della ristrutturazione dello Stato e della controrivoluzione imperialista', November 1977.

BRIGATE ROSSE (1979a) 'Marzo '79 – Campagna di primavera: cattura, processo, esecuzione del presidente della D.C. Aldo Moro'.

BRIGATE ROSSE (1979b) Historic Nucleus, Reply to Morucci and Faranda, *Lotta Continua*, 11 August 1979, pp. 4–11.

BRIGATE ROSSE (1980a) Collettivo Prigionieri Comunisti, 'L'Unione Sovietica è una formazione sociale di tipo capitalistico', *Corrispondenza Internazionale*, no. 14–15, May–September 1980, pp. 92–103.

BRIGATE ROSSE (1980b) Collettivo Prigionieri Comunisti, 'Per una discussione su "soggettivismo" e "militarismo"', *Corrispondenza Internazionale*, no. 14–15, May–September 1980.

BRIGATE ROSSE (1980c) Direzione Strategica, 'Conquistare le masse alla lotta armata per il comunismo. Costruire gli strumenti del potere proletario armato: il Partito Comunista Combattente e gli Organismi di Massa Rivoluzionari', October 1980.

BRIGATE ROSSE (1980d) Collettivo Prigionieri Comunisti, *L'ape e il comunista, Corrispondenza Internazionale* (Special Issue), no. 16–17, October–December 1980.

BRIGATE ROSSE (1980e) 'Battere l'opportunismo liquidazionista e l'ideologia della sconfitta. Rifiutare il frazionismo antipartito. Fare chiarezza sulla linea delle Brigate Rosse: Unire i comunisti nel partito combattente', December 1980.

BRIGATE ROSSE (1980/81) Campagna D'Urso, Opuscolo no. 11, 'Organizzare la liberazione dei proletari prigionieri', December 1980–January 1981.

BRIGATE ROSSE (1981a) Interrogatorio di Giovanni D'Urso, *L'Espresso*, 11 January 1981, pp. 74–90.

BRIGATE ROSSE (1981b) Interview by Mario Scialoja, 'Noi, brigatisti, raccontiamo che . . . ,' *L'Espresso*, 11 January 1981, pp. 91–8.

BRIGATE ROSSE (1981c) Fronte delle Carceri and Colonna di Napoli, '13 Tesi sulla sostanza dell 'agire da partito in questa congiuntura', May–June 1981.

BRIGATE ROSSE (1981d) 'Autointervista', June 1981, in Appendix to Dini and Manconi (1981), pp. 134–44.

BRIGATE ROSSE (1981e) Colonna Walter Alasia 'Luca', 'Contributo della Colonna Walter Alasia "Luca" alla elaborazione della linea politica per la fase di transizione alla guerra civile popolare di lunga durata e alla costruzione del partito comunista combattente' (Campagna Sandrucci, Document-Self-interview) July 1981.

BRIGATE ROSSE (Partito-Guerriglia) (1981f) 'Risoluzione della Direzione Strategica', December 1981, in 'Lotta armata per il comunismo', Giornale delle Brigate Rosse, no. 4.

BRIGATE ROSSE (per la costruzione del partito comunista combattente) (1981g) 'Risoluzione della Direzione Strategica', December 1981.

'Brigatisti rossi – Il Cattolico', (1978) *L'Espresso*, 9 April 1978, p. 20.

BRZEZINSKI, ZBIGNIEW (1983) *Power and Principle – Memoirs of the National Security Adviser, 1977–1981* (New York: Farrar, Straus & Giroux).

BUFFA, PIER VITTORIO and FRANCO GIUSTOLISI (1984a) *Al di là di quelle mura* (Milan: Rizzoli).

BUFFA, PIER VITTORIO and FRANCO GIUSTOLISI (1984b) 'Non sono pentito, sono stanco', *L'Espresso*, 8 April 1984, pp. 16–18.

BUFFA, PIER VITTORIO (1984c) 'Carceri: Giù le sbarre', *L'Espresso*, 26 August 1984, pp. 12–13.

BUFFA, PIER VITTORIO and MARIO SCIALOJA (1985) 'In nome della legge – Quando la polizia uccide', *L'Espresso*, 24 March 1985, pp. 6–9.

BUONAVITA, ALFREDO (1981) 'Terrorismo – Lettera aperta di un capo BR', *L'Espresso*, 14 June 1981, pp. 33–6.

BUONAVITA, ALFREDO (1982) 'Verbali', *Lotta Continua*, 26 March 1982, pp. 18–19.

CACCIA, BRUNO (1975) 'Requisitoria', in Giannino Guiso *et al.* (1975).

CAGOL, MILENA (1975) Interview, *L'Europeo*, 20 June 1975, pp. 42–5.

CALVI, GABRIELE and MASSIMO MARTINI (eds) (1982) *L'estremismo politico – Ricerche psicologiche sul terrorismo e sugli atteggiamenti radicali* (Milan: Angeli).

CAMERA DEI DEPUTATI (1985) *La carcerazione preventiva – Ordinamento italiano e esperienze giuridiche straniere* (Rome: Camera dei Deputati).

CANTORE, ROMANO (1987) 'Rivelazioni: Gli ultimi misteri del caso Moro – Quell 'altra prigione', *Panorama* 24 May 1987, pp. 54–6.

CANTORE, ROMANO, CARLO ROSELLA and CHIARA VALENTINI (1978) *Dall 'interno della guerriglia* (Milan: Mondadori).

CARLI, GUIDO (1976) 'Italy's Malaise', *Foreign Affairs*, 54(4), July 1976.

CARLUCCI, ANTONIO (1987) 'Rivelazioni: Italia e OLP da Moro alle Brigate Rosse – Arafat, cosa si fa per te', *Panorama*, 24 May 1987, pp. 58–61.

CARLUCCI, ANTONIO (1988a) 'Brigate Rosse – Perché l'uccisione di Ruffilli: Al cuore DeMita', *Panorama*, 1 May 1988, pp. 50–3.

CARLUCCI, ANTONIO (1988b) 'Brigate Rosse – Le immagini inedite dell'incontro tra Curcio e Frate Mitra: Dall'infiltrato speciale', *Panorama*, 12 June 1988, pp. 70–5.

CARRILLO, ELISA A. (1965) *Alcide DeGasperi: The Long Apprenticeship* (Notre Dame: University of Notre Dame Press).

CARSTEN, F.L. (1980) *The Rise of Fascism* (Berkeley: University of California Press).

CASELLI, GIAN CARLO and DONATELLA DELLA PORTA (1984) 'La storia delle Brigate rosse: strutture organizzative e strategie d'azione', in Donatella della Porta (ed.) (1984).

CASERTA, JOHN (1978) *The Red Brigades* (New York: Manor).

CASTELLANO LUCIO (ed.) (1980) *Aut. Op. – La storia e i documenti: da Potere operaio all'Autonomia organizzata* (Rome: Savelli).

CATALANO, FRANCO (1969) *I movimenti studenteschi e la scuola in Italia (1938–1968)* (Milan: Mondadori).

CAUTE, DAVID (1988) *The Year of the Barricades – A Journey Through 1968* (New York: Harper & Row).

CAVALERA, FABIO (1986) 'Ex BR ai nuovi BR: "Non sparate"', *Corriere della Sera*, 13 May 1986, p. 10.

CEDERNA, CAMILLA (1975) *Sparare a vista – Come la polizia del regime DC mantiene l'ordine pubblico* (Milan: Feltrinelli).

CEOLIN, CARLO (ed.) (1984) *Università, cultura, terrorismo* (Milan: Angeli).

CERVI, MARIO (1967) *La giustizia in Italia* (Milan: Longanesi).

CERVONE, VITTORIO (1979) *Ho fatto di tutto per salvare Moro* (Turin: Marietti).

CHABOD, FEDERICO (1963) *A History of Italian Fascism* (London: Weidenfeld & Nicolson).

CHIARINI, ROBERTO and PAOLO CORSINI (1983) *Da Salò a Piazza della Loggia* (Milan: Angeli).

CHIAROMONTE, GERARDO (1978) 'Le cose da fare subito', *Rinascita*, 24 March 1978, pp. 1–2.

CHIAVARIO, MARIO (1981) 'Un anno di fermo di polizia nelle relazioni del Ministro dell'Interno', *La legislazione penale*, no. 2, 1981, pp. 296–310.

CLINE, RAY S. and YONAH ALEXANDER (1984) *Terrorism: The Soviet*

Connection (New York: Crane, Russak).

CLOUGH, SHEPARD B. (1964) *The Economic History of Modern Italy* (New York: Columbia University Press).

CODRINI, GIANLUCA (1981) *Io, un ex-brigatista* (Naples: Fiorentino).

COLLETTIVO REDAZIONALE 'La Nuova Assemblea' (ed.) (1977) *Le radici di una rivolta – Il movimento studentesco a Roma: Interpretazioni, fatti e documenti, febbraio-aprile 1977* (Milan: Feltrinelli).

COMITATI AUTONOMI OPERAI DI ROMA (ed.) (1976) *Autonomia operaia* (Rome: Savelli).

COPPOLA, ANIELLO (1976) *Moro* (Milan: Feltrinelli).

CORTE DI ASSISE DI ROMA (Prima) (1983) Sentenza, in penal proceedings against Andriani Norma & 62 (Caso Moro), Judgement 24 January 1983, deposited 3 October 1983, no. 31/81.

CORTE DI ASSISE DI APPELLO DI ROMA (Prima) (1985) Sentenza, in penal proceedings against Andriani Norma & 58 (Caso Moro), Judgement 14 March 1985, deposited 10 June 1985, no. 20/84.

CORTE DI ASSISE DI APPELLO DI TORINO (1979) Sentenza, 8 December 1979, in penal proceedings against Basone Angelo & 30, no. 57/79.

CORTESE, LUISA (ed.) (1973) *Il movimento studentesco – Storia e documenti, 1968–1973* (Milan: Bompiani).

COWAN, SUZANNE (1980) 'Terrorism and the Italian Left', in Carl Boggs and D. Plotke (eds), *The Politics of Eurocommunism – Socialism in Transition* (Boston: South End Press), pp. 163–93.

COYLE, DOMINICK J. (1983) *Minorities in Revolt – Political Violence in Ireland, Italy, and Cyprus* (Rutherford, N.J.: Fairleigh Dickinson University Press).

CRAXI, BETTINO (1978) Interview by Raffaello Uboldi, 'Craxi: "Non sarà la morte di Moro a rendere lo stato più forte"', *Epoca*, 10 May 1978, pp. 34–5.

CRESCI, GIAN PAOLO *et al.* (eds) (1982) *Moro: i giorni del tormento* (Rome: Cinque Lune).

CROZIER, BRIAN (1973) *DeGaulle* (New York: Scribners).

CURCIO, RENATO (1975) Interview by Mario Scialoja, *L'Espresso*, 5 January 1975, p. 9.

CURCIO, RENATO (1976) 'L'ultrarevisionismo', *Controinformazione*, no. 7–8, June 1976, pp. 126–7.

CURCIO, RENATO (1984) *Wkhy* (Rome: Fatamorgana).

CURCIO, RENATO (1987) Interview by Mario Scialoja, "Non mi pento non rinnego", *L'Espresso*, 18 January 1987, pp. 24–8.

CURCIO, RENATO (1988) Interview by Mario Scialoja, 'Parla Curcio – Quando uccisero il commissario', *L'Espresso*, 16 October 1988, pp. 24–6.

CURCIO, RENATO and ALBERTO FRANCESCHINI (1982) *Gocce di sole nella città degli spettri* (Rome: Corrispondenza Internazionale).

CURCIO, RENATO and MAURO ROSTAGNO (1980) *Fuori dai denti* (Milan: Gammalibri).

CURCIO, YOLANDA (1975) Interview, *Gente*, 4, 11, 18 August 1975.

CUTOLO, EUGENIO (1980) *Aldo Moro – La vita, l'opera, l'eredità* (Milan: Teti).

DALLA CHIESA, CARLO ALBERTO (1981) Interview by Enzo Biagi,

280 *References*

'Generale, perché si pente un terrorista?', *Epoca*, 28 February 1981, pp. 28–31.

DALLA CHIESA, NANDO (1981) 'Del sessantotto e del terrorismo: cultura e politica tra continuità e rottura', *Il Mulino*, January–February 1981, pp. 53–94.

DEAGLIO, ENRICO, 'Dimenticare Moro', *Epoca*, 6 March 1988, pp. 20–7.

DELLA PORTA, DONATELLA (ed.) (1984) *Terrorismi in Italia* (Bologna: Il Mulino).

DELLA PORTA, DONATELLA and MAURIZIO ROSSI (1983) 'I terrorismi in Italia tra il 1969 e il 1982', *Cattaneo*, III (1).

DELLA PORTA, DONATELLA and SIDNEY TARROW (1986) 'Unwanted Children: Political Violence and the Cycle of Protest in Italy, 1966–1973', *European Journal of Political Research*, 14 (5–6), pp. 607–32.

DELUCA, MAURIZIO (1985) 'Terrorismo nero – Con i soldi della loggia', *L'Espresso*, 7 April 1985, pp. 20–1.

DELUTIIS, GIUSEPPE (1984) *Storia dei servizi segreti in Italia* (Rome: Riuniti).

DELUTIIS, GIUSEPPE (ed.) (1986a) *La strage – L'atto d'accusa dei giudici di Bologna* (Rome: Riuniti).

DELUTIIS, GIUSEPPE (1986b) 'Per una reale riforma dei servizi segreti', *Questione giustizia*, 2 (1986), pp. 307–17.

DINI, VITTORIO and LUIGI MANCONI (1981) *Il discorso delle armi – L'ideologia terroristica nel linguaggio delle Brigate Rosse e di Prima Linea* (Rome: Savelli).

'Discussioni – Ma noi della sinistra in che cosa abbiamo sbagliato?', *L'Espresso*, 9 April 1978, pp. 22–7.

DRAKE, RICHARD (1982) 'The Red Brigades and the Italian Political Tradition', in Yonah Alexander and Kenneth A. Myers (eds) (1982).

DUCCI, ROBERTO (1982) *I capintesta* (Milan: Rusconi).

EARLE, JOHN (1975) *Italy in the 1970s* (Newton Abbot: David & Charles).

ECO, UMBERTO (1983) *Sette anni di desiderio* (Milan: Bompiani).

Editorial (1978a) 'Terroristi o qualcosa di più?', *L'Unità*, 27 April 1978, p. 1.

Editorial (1978b) 'Non dare spazio al terrorismo', *L'Unità*, 28 April 1978, p. 1.

Editorial (1978c) 'Il loro disegno', *L'Unità*, 30 April 1978, p. 1.

Editorial (1978d) 'Limite invalicabile', *L'Unità*, 3 May 1978, p. 1.

Editorial (1978e) 'Una via non praticabile', *L'Unità*, 4 May 1978, p. 1.

Editorial (1981) 'The Smell of Fear', *The Economist*, 10 January 1981, p. 14.

EHRENREICH, BARBARA and JOHN (1969) *Long March, Short Spring: The Student Uprising at Home and Abroad* (New York: Monthly Review Press).

ELAD, SHLOMI and ARIEL MERARI (1984) *The Soviet Bloc and World Terrorism* (Tel Aviv: Jaffee Center for Strategic Studies).

FANTI, LIANO (1985) *S'avanza uno strano soldato – Genesi del brigatismo rosso reggiano* (Milan: Sugarco).

FARANDA, ADRIANA (1985) Interview by Enzo Biagi, *Corriere della Sera*, 20 October 1985, insert.

FELTRINELLI, GIANGIACOMO (1968) *Persiste la minaccia di un colpo di stato in Italia!* (Milan: Libreria Feltrinelli).

FELTRINELLI, GIANGIACOMO (1969) *Estate 1969 – La minaccia incombente di una svolta radicale e autoritaria a destra, di un colpo di Stato all'italiana* (Milan: Libreria Feltrinelli).

FELTRINELLI, GIANGIACOMO (1970) *Contro l'imperialismo e la coalizione delle destre – Proposte per una piattaforma politica della sinistra italiana seguite da saggi e tesi su problemi specifici dello sviluppo capitalistico* (Milan: Edizioni della Libreria).

'Feltrinelli – Scomodi da trent'anni', Tuttolibri, *La Stampa*, 21 September 1985, p. 3.

FERRACUTI, FRANCO and FRANCESCO BRUNO (1984) 'Psychiatric Aspects of Terrorism in Italy', in Israel L. Barak-Glantz and C.R. Huff (1981) *The Mad, the Bad, and the Different* (Lexington, Mass.: Lexington Books), pp. 199–213.

FERRARA, GIULIANO (1978) 'Il terrorismo non è soltanto un complotto', *L'Unità*, 24 March 1978, p. 2.

FERRARESI, FRANCO (1987) 'La destra eversiva alla sbarra – Quarant'anni di storia fra mistero, segreti e terrore', *Corriere della Sera*, 3, 5 March 1987.

FERRAROTTI, FRANCO (1976) 'Le origini di Curcio', *Paese Sera*, 4 February 1976, p. 3.

FERRAROTTI, FRANCO (1980) *L'ipnosi della violenza* (Milan: Rizzoli).

FICONERI, PIERLUIGI (1981a) 'Professore fuori ruolo', *L'Espresso*, 25 January 1981, pp. 16–17.

FICONERI, PIERLUIGI (1981b) 'Brigate Rosse – La colonna romana e i suoi colonnelli', *L'Espresso*, 1 February 1981, pp. 10–13.

FINETTI, UGO (1978) *Il dissenso nel PCI* (Milan: Sugarco).

FLAMIGNI, SERGIO (1988) 'Mistero per mistero', *L'Espresso*, 26 June 1988, pp. 38–42.

FORD, FRANKLIN L. (1985) *Political Murder – From Tyrannicide to Terrorism* (Cambridge, Mass.: Harvard University Press).

FORLANI, ARNALDO (1981) Interview by Raffaello Uboldi, 'In parlamento sono arrivati i farisei', *Epoca*, 31 January 1981, pp. 30–1.

FRANCESCHINI, ALBERTO (1987) Interview by Carmen Bertolazzi, 'Vent'anni buttati', *Panorama*, 1 March 1987, pp. 42–7.

FRANCESCHINI, ALBERTO (1988) *Mara Renato e io – Storia dei fondatori delle BR* (Milan: Mondadori).

FRASER, JOHN (1981) *Italy: Society in Crisis, Society in Transformation* (London: Routledge & Kegan Paul).

FURLONG, PAUL (1981) 'Political Terrorism in Italy: Responses, Reactions and Immobilism', in Juliet Lodge (ed.) (1981), pp. 57–90.

GALANTE, SEVERINO (1981) 'Alle origini del partito armato', *Il Mulino*, May–June 1981, pp. 444–87.

GALLENI, MAURO (ed.) (1981) *Rapporto sul terrorismo* (Milan: Rizzoli).

GALLI, GIORGIO (1984a) 'Quando i "servizi" capirono che le Br servivano', Interview by Rocco DiBlasi, *L'Unità*, 9 November 1984.

GALLI, GIORGIO (1984b) 'Per una storia del partito armato', *Panorama*, special insert, 12 November 1984, pp. 134–60.

GALLI, GIORGIO (1986a) *Storia del partito armato, 1968–1982* (Milan: Rizzoli).

GALLI, GIORGIO (1986b) 'Il governo invisibile dietro le Br', *Corriere della Sera*, 11 June 1986, p. 3.

GALLO, MAX (1973) *Mussolini's Italy – Twenty Years of the Fascist Era* (New York: Macmillan).

GANDUS, VALERIA (1986) 'Post terrorismo: Come si recupera una generazione perduta – Premiata Dissociati & C', *Panorama*, 16 November 1986, pp. 74–87.

GARDNER, RICHARD (1988) 'Non fu colpa Cia', Interview by Gianluigi Melega, *L'Espresso*, 27 March 1988, pp. 23–4.

GARRONE, ALESSANDRO GALANTE (1985) 'Caso Naria – Quando la giustizia è crudele', *L'Espresso*, 2 June 1985, p. 26.

GENOVA, RINO (1985) *Missione antiterrorismo* (Milan: Sugarco).

GIAI, FABRIZIO (1982) 'Verbali', *Lotta Continua*, 10 February 1982.

GIDONI, MASSIMO (1988) 'Io, i servizi e le Bierre', Interview by Carmen Bertolazzi, *Panorama*, 17 July 1988, pp. 60–2.

GIGLIOBIANCO, ALFREDO and MICHELE SALVATI (1980) *Il maggio francese e l'autunno caldo italiano: la risposta di due borghesie* (Bologna: Il Mulino).

GIORGIO (1981) *Memorie – Dalla clandestinità un terrorista non pentito si racconta* (Milan: Savelli).

GIROTTO, SILVANO (1975) *Padre Leone – La mia vita* (Milan: Sperling & Kupfer).

GISMONDI, ARTURO (1986) *Alle soglie del potere – Storia e cronaca della solidarietà nazionale: 1976–1979* (Milan: Sugarco).

GIUSTOLISI, FRANCO (1978) 'Storie di brigatisti: Il Guevarista Galeno', *L'Espresso*, 9 April 1978, p. 17.

GOMEZ, RAFFAELE (1969) *Università: il nocciolo della crisi* (L'Aquila: L.U. Japadre).

GORRESIO, VITTORIO (1978a) 'I passi perduti – Perché lo Stato non deve trattare con le Brigate rosse', *Epoca*, 12 April 1978, p. 15.

GORRESIO, VITTORIO (1978b) 'Moro: Una politica pensata sempre in anticipo sui tempi', *Epoca*, 17 May 1978, pp. 10–15.

GRESS, DAVID (1988) 'Talking Terrorism', *The New Criterion*, 6(8), April 1988.

GREVI, VITTORIO (1984) 'Sistema penale e leggi dell'emergenza: la risposta legislativa al terrorismo', in Gianfranco Pasquino (ed.) 1984b, pp. 17–74.

GRISONI, DOMINIQUE and HUGUES PORTELLI (1977) *Le lotte operaie in Italia dal 1960 al 1976* (Milan: Rizzoli).

GUISO, GIANNINO (1979) *La condanna di Aldo Moro* (Milan: Sugarco).

GUISO, GIANNINO et al. (1975) *Criminalizzazione della lotta di classe* (Verona: Bertani).

'The Happy Ending that May Mean Sad Ones to Come', (1981) *The Economist*, 17 January 1981, pp. 45–6.

HARVEY, ROBERT (1978) Survey, 'Italy – The Eternal Crisis', *The Economist*, 1 April 1978, pp. 7–38.

HAYCRAFT, JOHN (1985) *Italian Labyrinth – Italy in the 1980s* (London: Secker & Warburg).

HITCHENS, CHRISTOPHER (1986) 'Wanton Acts of Usage – Terrorism: A

Cliché in Search of a Meaning', *Harper's*, September 1986, pp. 66–70.

HOFMANN, PAUL (1987) 'It's Standing Room Only At Rome State', *New York Times, Education Supplement*, 4 January 1987, pp. 78–84.

HUGHES, H. STUART (1979) *The United States and Italy* (Cambridge, Mass.: Harvard University Press).

HUGHES, SERGE (1967) *The Fall and Rise of Modern Italy* (New York: Macmillan).

IMPOSIMATO, FERDINANDO (1986) 'La mina vagante del terrorismo', *Corriere della Sera*, 27 March 1986, p. 11.

IMPUTATI DEL 7 APRILE (1983) 'Do you remember revolution?', *Il Manifesto*, 20, 22 February 1983, p. 8.

INCERTI, CORRADO (1985) 'Processo Moro – Quei 55 giorni maledetti', *Panorama*, 20 January 1985, pp. 144–54.

INGRAO, PIETRO (1978) Interview by Alfredo Reichlin, 'La risposta del Paese al terrorismo', *L'Unità*, 22 March 1978, pp. 1–2.

'Italy's Terrorists – Guns on the Run', (1980) *The Economist*, 22 November 1980, pp. 54–5.

JANKE, PETER (1980) *Guerrilla and Terrorist Organizations: A World Directory and Bibliography* (Brighton: Harvester Press).

JARACH, ANDREA (1979) *Terrorismo internazionale – Gruppi, collegamenti, lotta antiterroristica* (Florence: Vallecchi).

KATZ, ROBERT (1980) *Days of Wrath* (Garden City, N.Y.: Doubleday).

KISSINGER, HENRY (1979) *White House Years* (Boston: Little, Brown).

KOGAN, NORMAN (1974) 'Socialism and Communism in Italian Political Life', in Edward R. Tannenbaum and Emiliana P. Noether (eds) (1974).

KOGAN, NORMAN (1978) 'The Italian Communist Party: The Modern Prince at the Crossroads', in Rudolf L. Tokes (ed.) (1978).

KOGAN, NORMAN (1983) *A Political History of Italy – The Postwar Years* (New York: Praeger).

LAMALFA, UGO (1978) 'Communism and Democracy in Italy', *Foreign Affairs*, 56(3), April, pp. 476–88.

LAPALOMBARA, JOSEPH (1987) *Democracy, Italian Style* (New Haven, Conn.: Yale University Press).

LAQUEUR, WALTER, (1987) *The Age of Terrorism* (Boston: Little, Brown).

LAQUEUR, WALTER (ed.) (1978) *The Terrorism Reader – A Historical Anthology* (New York: New American Library).

LEDDA, ROMANO (1978) 'Il disegno comincia a farsi più netto', *Rinascita*, 28 April 1978, pp. 4–5.

LEGA ITALIANA DEI DIRITTI DELL'UOMO (1978) Sezione Genova, *Il caso Coco – Processo a Giuliano Naria* (Milan: Collettivo editoriale Librirossi).

LEONETTI, FRANCESCO and ENRICO RAMBALDI (eds) (1983) *Il dibattito sul processo dell'Autonomia* (Milan: Multhipla).

LEONHARD, WOLFGANG (1978) *Eurocommunism – Challenge for East and West* (New York: Holt, Rinehart & Winston).

LODGE, JULIET (ed.) (1981) *Terrorism: A Challenge to the State* (Oxford: Robertson).

LOMBARDO, ANTONIO (ed.) (1978) *Le trasformazioni del comunismo italiano* (Milan: Rizzoli).

LONGO, LUIGI (1977) 'Basta con il terrorismo e l'inefficienza', *L'Unità*, 20 November 1977, p. 1.

LYTTELTON, ADRIAN (1973) *The Seizure of Power – Fascism in Italy, 1919–1929* (New York: Scribner's).

LYTTELTON, ADRIAN (1987) 'Murder in Rome', *New York Review of Books*, 25 June 1987, pp. 3–6.

MACALUSO, EMANUELE (1978) 'Chi indulge', *L'Unità*, 29 March 1978, p. 1.

MAFAI, MIRIAM (1984) *L'uomo che sognava la lotta armata – La storia di Pietro Secchia* (Milan: Rizzoli).

MAGISTER, SANDRO (1978) 'La tragedia Moro – Storia di un leader', *L'Espresso*, 14 May 1978, pp. 10–15.

MAGISTRATURA DEMOCRATICA (ed.) (1982) *La magistratura di fronte al terrorismo e all'eversione di sinistra* (Milan: Angeli).

MAMMARELLA, GIUSEPPE (1978) *L'Italia dalla caduta del fascismo ad oggi* (Bologna: Il Mulino).

MANCINI, FEDERICO (1981) *Terroristi e riformisti* (Bologna: Il Mulino).

MANCINI, GIACOMO (1982) *7 Aprile – Eclisse del diritto* (Rome: Lerici).

MANCUSO, LIBERO and ATTILIO DARDANI (1986) Sostituti Procuratori, 'Requisitoria, May 1986, Strage di Bologna', Chapter 6, in Giuseppe DeLutiis (ed.) (1986a), pp. 303–80.

MANDERINO, ENZO (1978) *55 giorni: W la morte W la vita* (Verona: Bertani).

MANTELLI, BRUNELLO and MARCO REVELLI (eds) (1979) *Operai senza politica – Il caso Moro alla Fiat e il 'qualunquismo operaio'* (Rome: Savelli).

MANZINI, GIORGIO (1978) *Indagine su un brigatista rosso* (Turin: Einaudi).

MARIGHELA, CARLOS (1971) *For the Liberation of Brazil* (Harmondsworth: Penguin).

MARIOTTI, CRISTINA (1987) 'Spari di stato', *L'Espresso*, 1 November 1987, pp. 36–40.

MARTIGNONI, GABRIELE and SERGIO MORANDINI (eds) (1977) *Il diritto all'odio – Dentro/fuori/ai bordi dell'area dell'autonomia* (Verona: Bertani).

MARTINELLI, ROBERTO and ANTONIO PADELLARO (1979) *Il delitto Moro* (Milan: Rizzoli).

MARTINOTTI, GUIDO (1969) 'The Positive Marginality: Notes on Italian Students in Periods of Political Mobilization', in Seymour Martin Lipset and Philip G. Altbach (eds) (1969) *Students in Revolt* (Boston: Houghton Mifflin).

MATTIOLI, NINO (1972), *Feltrinelli – Morte a Segrate* (Modena: Settedidenari).

MAZZETTI, ROBERTO (1979) *Genesi e sviluppo del terrorismo in Italia – Il maggio troppo lungo* (Rome: Armando).

McFORAN, DESMOND (1986) *The World Held Hostage – The War Waged by International Terrorism* (New York: St. Martin's).

MEHNERT, KLAUS (1976) *Twilight of the Young: The Radical Movements of the 1960's and Their Legacy* (New York: Holt, Rinehart & Winston).

MELLINI, MAURO (1986) *Il giudice e il pentito – Dalla giustizia dell'emergenza all'emergenza della giustizia* (Milan: Sugarco).

MELODIA, DAVIDE (1976) *Carceri: Riforma fantasma* (Milan: Sugarco).

'Memento Moro', *The Economist*, 20 December 1980, pp. 35–6.

MERKL, PETER H. (ed.) (1986) *Political Violence and Terror – Motifs and Motivations* (Berkeley: University of California Press).

MICHELINI, FLAVIO (1979) '"Non sanno come siamo fatti noi"', *Rinascita*, 2 February 1979, pp. 4–5.

MINNA, ROSARIO (1984) 'Il terrorismo di destra', in Donatella della Porta (ed.) (1984), pp. 21–72.

MINUCCI, ADALBERTO (1978) *Terrorismo e crisi italiana – Intervista di Jochen Kreimer* (Rome: Riuniti).

MINZOLINI, AUGUSTO and BRUNO RUGGIERO (1987) 'Caso Moro: Sondaggio tra politici e giudici – Eppure quel film c'è', *Panorama*, 24 May 1987, pp. 56–7.

MONCALVO, GIGI (1985) *Oltre la notte di piombo* (Rome: Paoline).

MONICELLI, MINO (1981) *La follia veneta – Come una regione bianca diviene culla del terrorismo* (Rome: Riuniti).

MORAN, SUE ELLEN (ed.) (1986) *Court Depositions of Three Red Brigadists* (Santa Monica: Rand Corp.).

MORETTI, LIA (1981) Interview by Claudio Fioretti and Pier Attilio Trivuizio, 'Parla la moglie di Moretti – Era bello, era buono', *Panorama*, 20 April 1981, pp. 47–52.

MORETTI, MARIO (1984) Interview by Giorgio Bocca, 'Io, Moro e le BR', *L'Espresso*, 2 December 1984, pp. 6–11.

MORETTI, MARIO (1987) Interview by Mario Scialoja, 'A nessun patto', *L'Espresso*, 10 May 1987, pp. 14–18.

MORI, ANNA MARIA (1978) *Il silenzio delle donne e il caso Moro* (Cosenza: Lerici).

MORO, ALDO (1979) *L'intelligenza e gli avvenimenti* (Milan: Garzanti).

MORO, ALDO (1978) 'Memoriale', in Senato della Repubblica-Camera dei Deputati (1983), Relazione Franchi, vol. 2, Allegato no. 2, pp. 125–75.

MORO, MARIA FIDA (1982) *La casa dei cento Natali* (Milan: Rizzoli).

MORUCCI, VALERIO (1979) Letter, *Lotta Continua*, 8 August 1979, p. 12.

MORUCCI, VALERIO (1982) Interview by Paolo Virno *et al.*, *Il Manifesto*, 20 November 1982.

MORUCCI, VALERIO (1983) 'Steady Cam', 'Per un nome', in Paolo Lapponi *et al.* (1983) *L'idea fissa* (Cosenza: Lerici).

MORUCCI, VALERIO (1984) Interview by Mario Scialoja, 'In quella prigione di Moro. . . .', *L'Espresso*, 25 March 1984, pp. 25–6.

MORUCCI, VALERIO (1985a) Interview by Luigi Manconi, 'Mai più quegli anni', *Il Messaggero*, 17 May 1985, p. 5.

MORUCCI, VALERIO (1985b) Interview by Roberto Martinelli, 'Quello che so di Moro', *La Stampa*, 30 November 1985, p. 7.

MORUCCI, VALERIO and ADRIANA FARANDA (1979) Statement of Dissent from the Brigate Rosse, *Lotta Continua*, 25 July 1979, pp. 9–14.

MOSCONI, GIUSEPPE (1982) 'Lo stereotipo del terrorista pentito: natura e funzione in relazione al decorso legislativo', *Critica del diritto*, no. 25–6, pp. 71–93.

MOSS, DAVID (1981) 'The Kidnapping and Murder of Aldo Moro', *European Journal of Sociology*, 22(2), pp. 265–93.

MOVIMENTO STUDENTESCO (ed.) (1968) *Documenti della rivolta universitaria* (Bari: Laterza).

MURRAY, WILLIAM (1978a) 'Letter from Rome', *The New Yorker*, 16 January 1978, pp. 72–82.

MURRAY, WILLIAM (1978b) 'Letter from Rome', *The New Yorker*, 17 July 1978, pp. 70–5.

MURRAY, WILLIAM (1980) 'Letter from Rome', *The New Yorker*, 15 September 1980, pp. 64–87.

MUSSI, FABIO (1978) 'Sulle teorie del "partito armato"', *Rinascita*, 20 January 1978, pp. 22–3.

MUSSI, FABIO (1978) 'Dal 1969, le dure prove della democrazia', *Rinascita*, 28 April 1978, pp. 3–5.

NAPOLITANO, GIORGIO (1977) Interview by Eric Hobsbawm, *The Italian Road to Socialism* (Westport: Lawrence Hill).

NATTA, ALESSANDRO (1979) Interview by Fabrizio D'Agostini, 'L'uso politico del "caso Moro" e la crisi di oggi', *Rinascita*, 16 February 1979, pp. 3–5.

NEGRI, ANTONIO (1974) *Crisi dello Stato-piano: Comunismo e organizzazione rivoluzionaria* (Milan: Feltrinelli).

NEGRI, ANTONIO (1980) *Il dominio e il sabotaggio* (Milan: Feltrinelli).

NESE, MARCO and ETTORE SERIO (1982) *Il generale Dalla Chiesa* (Rome: Adn Kronos).

NETANYAHU, BENJAMIN (ed.) (1986) *Terrorism: How the West Can Win* (New York: Farrar, Straus & Giroux).

NEWHOUSE, JOHN (1985) 'The Diplomatic Round – A Freemasonry of Terrorism', *The New Yorker*, 8 July 1985, pp. 46–63.

NICHOLS, PETER (1973) *Italia, Italia* (London: Macmillan).

NICHOLS, PETER (1981) 'Italy: The Crisis of Terrorism', *Spectator*, 17 January 1981, pp. 7–9.

NICOTRI, GIUSEPPE (1984) 'Terrorismo: Siamo stati noi', *L'Espresso*, 16 December 1984, pp. 22–4.

NUNZIATA, CLAUDIO (1986) '"Golpe Borghese" e "Rosa dei venti": come si svuota un processo', in Vittorio Borraccetti (ed.) (1986b), pp. 71–96.

OAKLEY, ROBERT (1986) 'International Terrorism', in 'America and the World 1986', *Foreign Affairs*, 65(3), pp. 611–29.

ORLANDO, FEDERICO (1978) *P38* (Milan: Editoriale Nuova).

OTTOLENGHI, FRANCO (1984) 'Prima e dopo il partito armato', *Rinascita*, 1 December 1984, p. 9.

OTTOLENGHI, SANDRO (1987) 'Miti infranti: Vent'anni dopo, la Francia seppellisce lo storico maggio – Sessantotto meno meno', *Panorama*, 24 May 1987, pp. 114–17.

PALANDRI, ENRICO et al. (eds) (1977) *Bologna, marzo 1977, fatti nostri* (Verona: Bertani).

PALERMO, IVAN (1982) *Condanna preventiva* (Naples: Pironti).

PALLOTTA, GINO (1978) *Obiettivo Moro: un attacco al cuore dello Stato* (Rome: Newton Compton).

PALLOTTA, GINO (1979) *Aldo Moro – L'uomo, la vita, le idee* (Milan: Massimo).

PANSA, GIAMPAOLO (1980) *Storie italiane di violenza e terrorismo* (Bari: Laterza).

PANSA, GIAMPAOLO (1988) 'Il Grande Vecchio e i piccoli giovani', *Panorama*, 1 May 1988, p. 57.

PAPA, EMILIO R. (1979) *Il processo alle Brigate Rosse – Brigate Rosse e difesa d'ufficio – Documenti* (Turin: Giappichelli).

PASQUINO, GIANFRANCO (1984a) 'Sistema politico bloccato e insorgenza del terrorismo: Ipotesi e prime verifiche', in Gianfranco Pasquino (ed.) (1984b), pp. 175–220.

PASQUINO, GIANFRANCO (ed.) (1984b) *La prova delle armi* (Bologna: Il Mulino).

PASQUINO, GIANFRANCO and DONATELLA DELLA PORTA (1986) 'Interpretations of Italian Left-Wing Terrorism', in Peter H. Merkl (ed.) (1986), pp. 169–89.

PATERNO, FRANCESCO (1985) 'Una vita in nero – Tre accusati di terrorismo di destra raccontono Nar e dintorni', *Il Manifesto*, 19 April 1985.

PECCHIOLI, UGO (1978) Interview by Raffaello Uboldi, 'Il dramma Moro – E se avessero rapito Berlinguer?', *Epoca*, 3 May 1978, pp. 38–9.

PECI, PATRIZIO (1980) 'Verbali', *Lotta Continua*, 7 May 1980, pp. 5–20.

PECI, PATRIZIO (1983) *Io, l'infame* (Milan: Mondadori).

PEDRAZZI, LUIGI (1973) *La politica scolastica del centro-sinistra* (Bologna: Il Mulino).

PELLICANI, LUCIANO (1978) 'La cultura politica del PCI: Leninismo e Gramscismo', in Antonio Lombardo (ed.) (1978).

PERTEGATO, GIANCARLO (1985) 'Tutti gli uomini dell'antiterrorismo – Come Emilio Santillo ha combattuto i nuclei armati rossi e neri', *Corriere della Sera*, 9 January 1985, p. 8.

PICCOLI, FLAMINIO (1988) 'Anni di piombo – Perdono di stato', Interview by Mario Scialoja, *L'Espresso*, 24 January 1988, pp. 24–6.

PIETRA, ITALO (1983) *Moro, fu vera gloria?* (Milan: Garzanti).

PIPERNO, FRANCO (1984) Interview by Mario Scialoja, 'E poi mi chiamò Craxi', *L'Espresso*, 23 December 1984, pp. 28–31.

PISANO, VITTORFRANCO S. (1979) 'A Survey of Terrorism of the Left in Italy: 1970–78', *Terrorism*, 2(3–4), pp. 171–212.

PISANO, VITTORFRANCO S. (1980) *The Red Brigades: A Challenge to Italian Democracy* (London: Institute for the Study of Conflict).

PISANO, VITTORFRANCO S. (1984) *Terrorism and Security: The Italian Experience*, Report of the Subcommittee on Security and Terrorism, Senate Judiciary Committee, 98th Cong., 2nd Sess., November 1984.

PISANO, VITTORFRANCO S. (1985) *Terrorism in Italy: An Update Report, 1983–1985*, Report of the Subcommittee on Security and Terrorism, Senate Judiciary Committee, 99th Cong., 1st Sess., October 1985.

PISANO, VITTORFRANCO S. (1987) *The Dynamics of Subversion and Violence in Contemporary Italy* (Stanford, Cal.: Hoover Institution Press).

PISETTA, MARCO (1973) 'Memoriale', *Il Borghese*, 14, 21, 28 January, 5 February 1973.

POLLONI, GILBERTO and DANIELE ROMANO (eds) (1978) *Le cicale e il caso Moro* (Rome: Edizioni delle Autonomie).

PORZIO, DOMENICO (1977) *Corragio e viltà degli intellettuali* (Milan: Mondadori).

PRIORE, ROSARIO (1985) Interview by Sandro Acciari, 'Prima o poi anche le BR . . .', *L'Espresso*, 17 February 1985, pp. 8–9.

PROCURA DELLA REPUBBLICA DI MILANO (1983) Requisitoria del Pubblico Ministero, Filippo Grisolia, Sostituto Procuratore, in penal proceedings against Adamoli Roberto & 96, no. 490/81F, 25 March 1983.

PROCURA DELLA REPUBBLICA DI NAPOLI (1983) Requisitoria del Pubblico Ministero, Gerardo Arcese and Olindo Ferrone, Sostituti Procuratori, in penal proceedings against Acanfora Mauro & 130, no. 981/81 etc., 1983.

PROCURA DELLA REPUBBLICA DI VENEZIA (1983) Requisitoria del Pubblico Ministero, Gabriele Ferrari, Sostituto Procuratore, in penal proceedings against Alunni Corrado & 122, no. 179/82-A, 18 July 1983.

PULITANÒ, DOMENICO (1981) 'Misure antiterrorismo – Un primo bilancio', *Democrazia e diritto*, nos 1–2, pp. 77–98.

QUARANTA, GUIDO and RENZO DIRIENZO (1981) 'Il caso D'Urso comincia adesso', *L'Espresso*, 25 January 1981, pp. 6–14.

RA'ANAN, URI *et al.* (eds) (1986) *Hydra of Carnage – The International Linkages of Terrorism and Other Low-Intensity Operations* (Lexington, Mass.: Lexington Books).

RAGGHIANTI, CARLO L. (1968) *Università in prima linea* (Florence: Vallecchi).

REPETTO, DANIELE (ed.) (1984) *Il clandestino è finito? – Contributi per un dibattito su terrorismo e soluzione politica* (Rome: Adn Kronos).

REVEL, JEAN-FRANCOIS (1978) 'The Myths of Eurocommunism', *Foreign Affairs*, January, pp. 295–305.

RONCHEY, ALBERTO (1977a) *Accadde in Italia, 1968–1977* (Milan: Garzanti).

RONCHEY, ALBERTO (1977b) 'Il terrorismo in Italia – che c'è dietro', *Corriere della Sera*, 8 May 1977, p. 1.

RONCHEY, ALBERTO (1978a) *Libro bianco sull'ultima generazione – Tra candore e terrore* (Milan: Garzanti).

RONCHEY, ALBERTO (1978b) 'L'oscuro complotto e il chiaro ritardo', *Corriere della Sera*, 1 April 1978, p. 1.

RONCHEY, ALBERTO (1978c) 'Fra le cause del terrorismo', *Corriere della Sera*, 9 April 1978, p. 1.

RONCHEY, ALBERTO (1983) *Chi vincerà in Italia?* (Milan: Mondadori).

ROSSANDA, ROSSANA (1968) *L'anno degli studenti* (Bari: DeDonato).

ROSSANO, ANTONIO (1985) *L'altro Moro* (Milan: Sugarco).

ROSSETTI, GIAN PAOLO *et al.* (1988) 'Bersaglio Italia', *L'Europeo*, 29 April 1988, pp. 34–9.

ROTELLA, MARIO (1986) 'Memoria di Piazza della Loggia (Brescia, 18 Maggio 1974)', in Vittorio Borraccetti (ed.) (1986b), pp. 120–53.

RUBENSTEIN, RICHARD E. (1987) *Alchemists of Revolution – Terrorism in the Modern World* (New York: Basic Books).

SALVANI, GUIDO (1982) 'La sentenza n. 15 del 1982 della Corte Costituzionale: prolungamento dei termini massimi di custodia preventiva ed immediata applicazione nei processi pendenti di norme processuali più sfavorevoli', *Rivista italiana di diritto e procedura penale*, no. 3, July–September 1982, pp. 1214–39.

SALVINI, GUIDO (1983) *La legge sui terroristi pentiti – Un primo bilancio* (Milan: Unicopli).

SALVIONI, DANIELA and ANDERS STEPHANSON (1985) 'Reflections on the Red Brigades', *Orbis*, Fall 1985, pp. 489–506.

SANTOSUOSSO, AMEDEO (1984) 'Contro l'emergenza', *Critica del diritto*, no. 33, June, pp. 11–26.

SAVASTA, ANTONIO (1988) Interview (Written) by Sandro Acciari, 'Caso Moro – Parla Savasta: A domanda rispondo', *L'Espresso*, 26 June 1988, pp. 36–8.

SAVILLE, LLOYD B. (1967) *Regional Economic Development in Italy* (Durham, N.C.: Duke University Press).

SBROGIÒ, ITALO (1979) Interview by Gianni Moriani, *Lotta Continua*, 20 July 1979, pp. 10–11.

SCALFARI, EUGENIO (1984) *L'anno di Craxi (o di Berlinguer?)* (Milan: Mondadori).

SCALZONE, ORESTE (1987) 'Io, Feltrinelli e le BR', Interview by Mario Scialoja, *L'Espresso*, 22 February 1987, pp. 25–6.

SCARANO, MIMMO and MAURIZIO DELUCA (1985) *Il manderino è marcio – Terrorismo e cospirazione nel caso Moro* (Rome: Riuniti).

SCARPARI, GIANCARLO (1986) 'Il 1974, l'anno della svolta', in Vittorio Borraccetti (ed.) (1986b), pp. 97–119.

SCIALOJA, MARIO (1978) 'Libro bianco sul caso Moro', *L'Espresso*, 15 October 1978, pp. 6–19.

SCIALOJA, MARIO (1985) 'Post-terrorismo: Sconti per dissociati', *L'Espresso*, 31 March 1985, pp. 18–20.

SCIALOJA, MARIO (1987) 'Il silenzio è di piombo', *L'Espresso*, 25 January 1987, pp. 20–2.

SCIASCIA, LEONARDO (1974) *Todo Modo* (Turin: Einaudi).

SCIASCIA, LEONARDO (1978a) *L'affaire Moro* (Palermo: Sellerio).

SCIASCIA, LEONARDO (1978b) 'Libertà è il diritto di contraddire tutto e tutti, anche me stesso', *Epoca*, 12 April 1978, pp. 28–9.

SCOPPOLA, PIETRO *et al.* (1979) *Moro, la Democrazia cristiana e la cultura cattolica* (Rome: Cinque Lune).

SCORTI, PIERO V. (1985) *Il delitto paga?* (Milan: Sugarco).

SEGRE, SERGIO (1976) 'The "Communist Question" in Italy', *Foreign Affairs*, 54(4) July.

SEGRE, SERGIO (1978) 'La questione dell'eurocomunismo', in Antonio Lombardo (ed.) (1978).

SELVA, GUSTAVO and EUGENIO MARCUCCI (1978) *Il martirio di Aldo Moro – Cronaca e commenti sui 55 giorni più difficili della Repubblica* (Bologna: Cappelli).

'Seminario di Rebibbia – Dal terrorismo al riformismo', *MicroMega*, no. 1, 1987, pp. 83–114.

SENATO DELLA REPUBBLICA – CAMERA DEI DEPUTATI (1983) Commissione parlamentare d'inchiesta sulla strage di Via Fani, sul sequestro e l'assassinio di Aldo Moro e sul terrorismo in Italia, VIII Leg., Doc. XXIII, no. 5, Relazione, vol. 1 (1983).

Relazione di minoranza di Luigi Covatta *et al.* (PSI).
Relazione di minoranza di Franco Franchi *et al.* (MSI).
Relazione di minoranza di Leonardo Sciascia (Radical Party).
Relazione di minoranza di Egidio Sterpa (Liberal Party).

Relazione di minoranza di Raniero LaValle (Independent Left).

vol. 2 (1983)

Atti allegati, vols 3–10.

SENATO DELLA REPUBBLICA – CAMERA DEI DEPUTÀTI (1984) Commissione parlamentare d'inchiesta sulla loggia massonica P2, IX Leg., Doc. XXIII, no. 2, Relazione (1984).

SENZANI, GIOVANNI (1979) 'Introduzione', pp. 9–40, and 'Il fenomeno criminale negli anni settanta: "La criminalità di massa"', pp. 149–72, in Giovanni Senzani (ed.) *Economia politica della criminalità* (Florence: Uniedit).

SERVAN-SCHREIBER, JEAN-JACQUES (1969) *The Spirit of May* (New York: McGraw-Hill).

'Il sessantotto quindici anni dopo', *Gazzetta di Reggio*, 27–8 January 1983.

SHEEHAN, THOMAS (1979) 'Italy: Behind the Ski Mask', *New York Review of Books*, 16 August 1979, pp. 20–7.

SHEEHAN, THOMAS (1980) 'Terror in Italy: An Exchange', *New York Review of Books*, 17 April 1980, pp. 46–7.

SHEEHAN, THOMAS (1981) 'Italy: Terror on the Right', *New York Review of Books*, 22 January 1981, pp. 23–6.

SIGNORILE, CLAUDIO (1988) 'Così non ho salvato Moro', Interview by Enrico Deaglio, *Epoca*, 27 March 1988, pp. 20–3.

SILJ, ALESSANDRO (1977) *Mai più senza fucile!* (Florence: Vallecchi).

SILJ, ALESSANDRO (1978) *Brigate Rosse – Stato* (Florence: Vallecchi).

SILVESTRI, STEFANO (1988) Interview by Barbara Palombelli, 'Cossiga e il canale', *Panorama*, 26 June 1988, pp. 58–60.

SIMIONI, CORRADO (1985) Interview by Sandro Acciari, 'Parla Corrado Simioni – Eravamo io, Curcio, Moretti . . .', *L'Espresso*, 13 January 1985, pp. 22–5.

SIMON, JEFFREY D. (1987) 'Misunderstanding Terrorism', *Foreign Policy*, no. 67, Summer, pp. 104–20.

SMITH, DENIS MACK (1969) *Italy – A Modern History* (Ann Arbor: University of Michigan Press).

SMITH, DENIS MACK (1982) *Mussolini – A Biography* (New York: Knopf).

SOCCORSO ROSSO NAPOLETANO (1976) *Brigate Rosse* (Milan: Feltrinelli).

SOCCORSO ROSSO NAPOLETANO (ed.) (1976) *I NAP – Storia politica dei Nuclei Armati Proletari e requisitoria del Tribunale di Napoli* (Cologno Monzese: Collettivo Editoriale Librirossi).

SOFAER, ABRAHAM D. (1986) 'Terrorism and the Law', *Foreign Affairs*, 64(5), Summer, pp. 901–22.

SOSSI, MARIO (1979) *Nella prigione delle BR* (Milan: Editoriale Nuova).

SPADOLINI, GIOVANNI (1978) *Diario del dramma Moro (Marzo-maggio 1978)* (Florence: LeMonnier).

SPENDER, STEPHEN (1968) *The Year of the Young Rebels* (New York: Random House).

STAJANO, CORRADO (1982) *L'Italia nichilista – Il caso di Marco Donat Cattin, la rivolta, il potere* (Milan: Mondadori).

STAJANO, CORRADO (1985) 'Quelle orme di Negri & c.', *Panorama*, 14 April 1985, pp. 254–65.

STAJANO, CORRADO and MARCO FINI (1977) *La forza della democrazia –
La strategia della tensione in Italia, 1969–1976* (Turin: Einaudi).

STATERA, GIANNI (1975) *Death of a Utopia – The Development and Decline of
Student Movements in Europe* (New York: Oxford University Press).

STERLING, CLAIRE (1982) *The Terror Network* (New York: Berkeley).

SZUMSKI, BONNIE (ed.) (1986) *Terrorism: Opposing Viewpoints* (St. Paul,
Minn.: Greenhaven Press).

TANNENBAUM, EDWARD R. and EMILIANA P. NOETHER (eds) (1974)
Modern Italy – A Topical History Since 1861 (New York: New York
University Press).

TARANTELLI, CAROLE (1985) Interview by Ida Dominijanni and Nadia
Fusini, 'Io, Ezio e i terroristi', *Antigone*, no. 3–4, Summer–Autumn, pp.
3–5.

TEMPLEMAN, DONALD C. (1981) *The Italian Economy* (New York:
Praeger).

'Terrorism in Italy', *Terrorism*, 2(3–4), 1979, special issue.

TESSANDORI, VINCENZO (1977) *BR – Imputazione: Banda armata* (Milan:
Garzanti).

TITO, MICHELE (1978) 'Uno scettico che crede nella ragione', *Epoca*, 15
March 1978, pp. 26–8.

TOBAGI, WALTER (1970) *Storia del movimento studentesco e dei marxisti-
leninisti in Italia* (Milan: Sugarco).

TOKES, RUDOLF L. (ed.) (1978) *Eurocommunism and Detente* (New York:
New York University Press).

TORTORELLA, ALDO (1978) 'Le responsabilità', *L'Unità*, 2 April 1978, p.
1.

TRIBUNALE DI MILANO (1981) Sentenza of GI Antonio Lombardi in
penal proceedings against Azzolini Lauro & 26, no. 1094/78F etc., 28 May
1981.

TRIBUNALE DI MILANO (1983) Ordinanza-Sentenza of GI Antonio
Lombardi in penal proceedings against Bellosi Francesco & 37, no.
624/83F etc., 19 July 1983.

TRIBUNALE DI ROMA (1983) Ordinanza-Sentenza of GI Claudio D'Angelo in penal proceedings against Morucci Valerio & 19, no. 5438/83A, 18
October 1983.

TRIBUNALE DI TORINO (1982) Ordinanza di rinvio a giudizio e sentenza
of GI Antonino Palaja in penal proceedings against Acella Vincenzo &
76, no. 6448/75 etc., 9 December 1982.

TRIBUNALE DI VENEZIA (1982) Sentenza of GI Carlo Nordio in penal
proceedings against Fasoli Marco & 8, no. 274/80, 3 February 1982.

TURONE, SERGIO (1981) *Storia del sindacato in Italia, 1943–1980* (Rome:
Laterza).

UBOLDI, RAFFAELO (1978) 'Carte in tavola, professore', *Epoca*, 11 January
1978, pp. 12–15.

URBINI, REMO (1988) 'Il prelato del Caso Moro', *Epoca*, 19 May 1988, pp.
16–18.

VALENTINI, CHIARA (1984) 'Terrorismo: Renato Curcio rompe il silen-
zio-La chiave della verità', *Panorama*, 3 December 1984, pp. 162–83.

VALIANI, LEO (1984) 'La legge sui pentiti e le esigenze di giustizia',
Corriere della Sera, 5 December 1984, p. 4.

VALIANI, LEO (1986) 'Discussioni: Ancora sulla "Storia del partito armato" del politologo Giorgio Galli', *Corriere della Sera*, 18 May 1986, p. 3.

Le vere ragioni – 1968–1976, Convention organized by Democrazia Proletaria, 12 October 1985 (Milan: Mazzotta).

'Il vero e il falso Moro' (1978) *L'Espresso*, 22 October 1978, pp. 11–20.

VETTORI, GIUSEPPE (1973) *La sinistra extraparlamentare in Italia – Storia, documenti, analisi politica* (Rome: Newton Compton).

VICINI, VITTORIO (1982) *Processo e giustizia penale – Alla ricerca di una riforma* (Bologna: Il Mulino).

VIDAL, GORE (1979) 'On the Assassins' Trail', *New York Review of Books*, 25 October 1979.

VIGLIETTA, GIANFRANCO (1986) 'Golpismo e servizi segreti nei primi anni '70', in Vittorio Borraccetti (ed.) (1986b), pp. 42–70.

VIOLANTE, LUCIANO (1979) 'Magistrati nel mirino', *Rinascita*, 2 February 1979, pp. 3–4.

VIOLANTE, LUCIANO (1984) 'Pentiti e dissociati', in Carlo Ceolin (ed.) (1984).

VIVIANI, AMBROGIO (1986) Interview by Romano Cantore and Carlo Rossella, 'Misteri d'Italia – Un generale del controspionaggio vuota il sacco', *Panorama*, 18 May 1986, pp. 40–5.

WAGNER-PACIFICI, ROBIN E. (1986) *The Moro Morality Play: Terrorism as Social Drama* (Chicago: University of Chicago Press).

WEINBERG, LEONARD (1986) 'The Violent Life: An Analysis of Left- and Right-Wing Terrorism in Italy', in Peter H. Merkl (ed.) (1986), pp. 145–67.

WEINBERG, LEONARD and WILLIAM LEE EUBANK (1987) *The Rise and Fall of Italian Terrorism* (Boulder, Col.: Westview Press).

WHETTEN, LAWRENCE L. (1978) 'Italian Terrorism: Record Figures and Political Dilemmas', *Terrorism*, 1(3–4), pp. 377–95.

WILKINSON, PAUL (1977) *Terrorism and the Liberal State* (New York: John Wiley).

WISKEMANN, ELIZABETH (1971) *Italy Since 1945* (London: Macmillan).

ZAMPA, RENATO (1976) Interview, *Gente*, 2 February 1976, pp. 4–8.

ZINCANI, VITO and SERGIO CASTALDO (1986) Giudici Istruttori, 'Sentenza-Ordinanza, June 1986, Strage di Bologna', in Giuseppe DeLutiis (ed.) (1986a), pp. 3–301.

ZUCKERMAN, ALAN S. (1979) *The Politics of Faction: Christian Democratic Rule in Italy* (New Haven, Conn.: Yale University Press).

ZUPO, GIUSEPPE and VINCENZO MARINI RECCHIA (1984) *Operazione Moro* (Milan: Angeli).

Journals and newspapers consulted

Antigone
L'Avanti
Il Borghese
Cattaneo
Controinformazione
Corriere della Sera
Corrispondenza Internazionale
Critica del Diritto
Democrazia e Diritto
The Economist
Encounter
Epoca
L'Espresso
L'Europeo
Foreign Affairs
Foreign Policy
Gazzetta di Reggio
Gente
Harper's
La Legislazione Penale
Lotta Continua
Il Manifesto

Il Messaggero
MicroMega
Il Mulino
La Nazione
The New Criterion
The New Yorker
The New York Review of Books
Oggi
Orbis
Paese Sera
Panorama
Potere Operaio
Questione Giustizia
La Repubblica
Rinascita
Rivista Italiana di Diritto e Procedura
    Penale
Spectator
La Stampa
Tempo
Terrorism
L'Unità

Index